Creator's Economy in Metaverse Platforms:

Empowering Stakeholders Through Omnichannel Approach

Babita Singla
Chitkara Business School, Chitkara University, India

Kumar Shalender
Chitkara Business School, Chitkara University, India

Nripendra Singh
Pennsylvania Western University, USA

A volume in the Advances in
Social Networking and Online
Communities (ASNOC) Book Series

Published in the United States of America by
    IGI Global
    Engineering Science Reference (an imprint of IGI Global)
    701 E. Chocolate Avenue
    Hershey PA, USA 17033
    Tel: 717-533-8845
    Fax: 717-533-8661
    E-mail: cust@igi-global.com
    Web site: http://www.igi-global.com

Library of Congress Cataloging-in-Publication Data

Names: Singla, Babita, 1988- editor. | Shalender, Kumar, 1984- editor. |
  Singh, Nripendra, 1975- editor.
Title: Creator's economy in metaverse platforms : empowering stakeholders
  through omnichannel approach / edited by Babita Singla, Kumar Shalender,
  Nripendra Singh.
Description: Hershey, PA : Engineering Science Reference, [2024] | Includes
  bibliographical references and index. | Summary: "The book discusses how
  to interconnect the creators' economies on different platforms, and by
  suggesting ways to facilitate interoperability, the title will prove a
  step in the direction of leveraging the metaverse for holistic financial
  and social gains"-- Provided by publisher.
Identifiers: LCCN 2024002046 (print) | LCCN 2024002047 (ebook) | ISBN
  9798369333587 (hardcover) | ISBN 9798369333594 (ebook)
Subjects: LCSH: Technological innovations--Economic aspects. |
  Metaverse--Economic aspects.
Classification: LCC HC79.T4 C745 2024 (print) | LCC HC79.T4 (ebook) | DDC
  338/.064--dc23/eng/20240118
LC record available at https://lccn.loc.gov/2024002046
LC ebook record available at https://lccn.loc.gov/2024002047

This book is published in the IGI Global book series Advances in Social Networking and Online
Communities (ASNOC) (ISSN: 2328-1405; eISSN: 2328-1413)

British Cataloguing in Publication Data
A Cataloguing in Publication record for this book is available from the British Library.

All work contributed to this book is new, previously-unpublished material.
The views expressed in this book are those of the authors, but not necessarily of the publisher.

For electronic access to this publication, please contact: eresources@igi-global.com.

Advances in Social Networking and Online Communities (ASNOC) Book Series

ISSN:2328-1405
EISSN:2328-1413

Editor-in-Chief: Hakikur Rahman, Ansted University Sustainability Research Institute, Malaysia

MISSION

The advancements of internet technologies and the creation of various social networks provide a new channel of knowledge development processes that's dependent on social networking and online communities. This emerging concept of social innovation is comprised of ideas and strategies designed to improve society.

The **Advances in Social Networking and Online Communities** book series serves as a forum for scholars and practitioners to present comprehensive research on the social, cultural, organizational, and human issues related to the use of virtual communities and social networking. This series will provide an analytical approach to the holistic and newly emerging concepts of online knowledge communities and social networks.

COVERAGE

- Importance and Role of Knowledge Communities in R&D and Innovative Knowledge Creation
- Information Policy Overview
- Organizational Knowledge Communication
- Knowledge Management and Business Improvement
- Knowledge as a Competitive Force
- Methods, Measures and Instruments of Knowledge Management
- Strategic Management and Business Process Analysis
- Communication and Agent Technology
- Knowledge Management Practices and Future Perspectives
- Application of Social Network Analysis as a Knowledge Management Tool

IGI Global is currently accepting manuscripts for publication within this series. To submit a proposal for a volume in this series, please contact our Acquisition Editors at Acquisitions@igi-global.com or visit: http://www.igi-global.com/publish/.

Titles in this Series

For a list of additional titles in this series, please visit:
http://www.igi-global.com/book-series/advances-social-networking-online-communities/37168

Spectral Media and Social Justice in the 21st Century
Raymond Aaron Younis (University of Sydney, Australia)
Information Science Reference • copyright 2024 • 320pp • H/C (ISBN: 9781668493052) • US $250.00 (our price)

Critical Roles of Digital Citizenship and Digital Ethics
Jason D. DeHart (University of Tennessee, Knoxville, USA)
Information Science Reference • copyright 2023 • 296pp • H/C (ISBN: 9781668489345) • US $235.00 (our price)

Global Perspectives on Social Media Usage Within Governments
Chandan Chavadi (Presidency Business School, Presidency College, Bengaluru, India) and Dhanabalan Thangam (Presidency Business School, Presidency College, Bengaluru, India)
Information Science Reference • copyright 2023 • 353pp • H/C (ISBN: 9781668474501) • US $215.00 (our price)

Social Capital in the Age of Online Networking Genesis, Manifestations, and Implications
Najmul Hoda (Umm Al-Qura University) and Arshi Naim (King Kalid University, Saudi Arabia)
Information Science Reference • copyright 2023 • 301pp • H/C (ISBN: 9781668489536) • US $215.00 (our price)

Advanced Applications of NLP and Deep Learning in Social Media Data
Ahmed A. Abd El-Latif (Menoufia University, Egypt & Prince Sultan University, Saudi Arabia) Mudasir Ahmad Wani (Prince Sultan University, Saudi Arabia) and Mohammed A. El-Affendi (Prince Sultan University, Saudi Arabia)
Engineering Science Reference • copyright 2023 • 303pp • H/C (ISBN: 9781668469095) • US $270.00 (our price)

For an entire list of titles in this series, please visit:
http://www.igi-global.com/book-series/advances-social-networking-online-communities/37168

701 East Chocolate Avenue, Hershey, PA 17033, USA
Tel: 717-533-8845 x100 • Fax: 717-533-8661
E-Mail: cust@igi-global.com • www.igi-global.com

Table of Contents

Detailed Table of Contents

Chapter 1
    Kumar Shalender, Chitkara Business School, Chitkara University,
        Punjab, India
    Babita Singla, Chitkara Business School, Chitkara University, Punjab,
        India

The creator economy is quickly spreading its influence across the industrial sectors thanks to the evolution of the metaverse platforms. This research specifically investigates the use cases of the creator economy and how stakeholders can potentially widen its scope and application areas. The chapter also delves into the details of the challenges the creator economy faces across the spectrum. It offers an adoption framework to help integrate the concept of creator economy in the right spirit and manner. The conclusion section of the research offers important implications for the adoption of the creator economy and how going forward the concept will lead to generate more avenues of growth and profitability across the ecosystems in different industries. The research is significant in the sense that it offers profound insights into the future of the creator economy and how its adoption will boost the overall economic progress of countries across the globe.

Chapter 2
    R. Akash, SRM Institute of Science and Technology, Chennai, India
    V. Suganya, SRM Institute of Science and Technology, Chennai, India

As the Metaverse continues to surge in prominence, this chapter delves into the often-overlooked realm of customer retention within this digital landscape. Recognizing the pivotal role that customer retention plays in ensuring the long-term sustainability and profitability of virtual economies, this study endeavors to uncover the intricate secrets that drive lasting customer engagement within the Metaverse. At the heart of this chapter lies the development of a comprehensive conceptual framework designed for adoption by industry stakeholders. This framework acts as a bridge between theory and practical implementation, offering a multifaceted perspective on the factors that influence customer retention. Through literature research with a rigorous analytical lens, this study aims to equip businesses, creators, and investors with the knowledge necessary to thrive in the ever-evolving Metaverse. By applying this framework, stakeholders can cultivate enduring customer relationships, thereby transforming the Metaverse into a hub of sustainable profitability within the virtual economy.

Chapter 3

    Prathmesh Singh, Pennsylvania Western University, USA
    Arnav Upadhyaya, Monta Vista High School, USA
    Nripendra Singh, Pennsylvania Western University, USA

Metaverse uses artificial intelligence and machine learning along with augmented reality to create immersive digital experiences where users can interact with other users and computer-generated environments. This creates new ways for people to connect, collaborate, experience digital content, and opens up exciting new possibilities. It also creates interesting questions on the responsible use of AI. This chapter will explore what mechanisms and frameworks should be evaluated for responsible AI- which allows humanity to enjoy the benefits of AI on augmented reality platforms like metaverse.

Chapter 4

    Arpan Anand, Jaipuria Institute of Management, Noida, India
    Priya Jindal, Chitkara Business School, Chitkara University, Punjab,
        India

The metaverse is a shared, virtual space where people can meet and interact with each other. It is a digital world that is built on top of the existing Internet. The Metaverse is still in its early stages of development, but it has the potential to revolutionize the way we communicate, work, and even live. A Metaverse is a place where people can assume any identity they desire. People can create a completely new identity for themselves, or they can use their real name and look just like they do in the real world. Metaverse can be used for a wide range of business applications, including building brands, managing supply chain management, loyalty programs, and developing new online marketplaces. In the meantime, we all have to adjust to living in a world that is gradually becoming more virtual. To understand how the metaverse will change us, it is necessary for us to first comprehend our origins and how they will direct the development of the immersive internet. The metaverse is a space that is created by the combination of virtual reality and augmented reality.

Chapter 5

Surjit Singha, Kristu Jayanti College (Autonomous), India
K. P. Jaheer Mukthar, Kristu Jayanti College (Autonomous), India

This chapter examines the dynamic fusion of the Metaverse and the retail industry, highlighting the fundamental shift toward digital goods and immersive purchasing experiences. It investigates the Metaverse's fundamental concepts, historical development, and current impact on retail. Digital products, such as non-fungible tokens (NFTs), virtual goods, and augmented reality products, assume centre stage and potentially transform shopping experiences. However, it also faces obstacles during this metaverse transition, including technological hurdles, security concerns, and challenges related to customer adoption. Future trends and practical strategies for seamless integration, customer engagement, and marketing are discussed—the metaverse ushers in a revolutionary era for retail, presenting boundless opportunities for those who embrace it. Retailers are urged to embark on this journey to satisfy evolving customer expectations and remain competitive in the future retail landscape.

Chapter 6

M. Vaishali, SRM Institute of Science and Technology, Chennai, India
V. Kiruthiga, SRM Institute of Science and Technology, Chennai, India

In the ever-evolving retail industry landscape of digital transformation and virtualization, practical leadership training has emerged as a pivotal factor in enhancing employee retention. This study delves into the role of metaverse in retail leadership training for enhanced employee retention to illuminate the symbiotic relationship between metaverse technologies and the cultivation of solid retail leaders. The research seeks to understand how metaverse-based leadership training programs shape leadership competencies within the retail sector and, in turn, influence employee satisfaction and loyalty. This study uncovers a dynamic shift in leadership development by exploring the methods, technologies, and strategies employed in these innovative programs. The findings suggest that metaverse-based training holds the potential to redefine leadership excellence in the retail metaverse, where employees are increasingly operating in virtual spaces. As the digital sphere and physical reality continue to converge, organizations harness the metaverse's power for leadership development.

The metaverse, a breakthrough virtual reality environment, offers boundless retail potential. Metaverse-driven retail needs a good strategy to succeed in a time of changing consumer expectations and the digital revolution. This chapter covers metaverse-driven retail preparation tactics. The metaverse allows retail innovation and adaptation during e-commerce and COVID-19 pandemic upheavals. Understanding metaverse dynamics and developing the abilities is crucial. Determine metaverse applicability to retail, define requisite capabilities, analyze staff competencies, and establish practical training and development programs. Examples include understanding metaverse technology, immersive shopping, data-driven personalization, and strong cybersecurity. Digital fluency, collaboration, design, and cybersecurity awareness are workforce competencies. This chapter stresses metaverse readiness through training, growth, and strategic alignment. It emphasizes that the metaverse transforms reality and opens up new possibilities.

Metaverse is a 21st-century, cutting edge technology that evolved as a science fiction in the early 90's in the western world, which captured the imagination of people across the globe. India, with its 1.4 billion population, the fifth largest economy in the world, and exalted position in software and information technology augurs well for embracing metaverse in future businesses. The present chapter aims to find the acceptance and readiness of Indian retail industry for the use of metaverse in its operation. Authors tried to do qualitative analysis of industry experts' and business consultants' opinion on metaverse in retail sector to find the opportunities and likely trends. This chapter also takes Google trend on metaverse searches into account. A systematic general review of published articles and cases from secondary sources forms the basis of this chapter. Findings suggest that the changing dynamics of social interactions in the Metaverse are on the brink of a revolution, promising transformative impacts on the retail industry and consumer behaviors.

Chapter 9

  Manish Bansal, Malout Institute of Management and Information
    Technology, India
  Sukhbir Kaur, Malout Institute of Management and Information
    Technology, India

Customer expectations are a set of ideas about a product, service, or brand that a customer holds in their mind. Customer expectations can be influenced by a customers' perception of the product or service and can be created or modified by previous experience, advertising, word of mouth, awareness of competitors, and brand image. Rising expectations and changing customers' needs are shaping the face of modern retail. Whenever customers visit an organized retail store, they expect convenience and a better experience. Omnichannel approach encompasses a business strategy that is intended to offer a magnificent shopping experience across all channels i.e. in-store, mobile, and online. An effective omnichannel retail strategy covers the major areas of contact across all possible communication channels to facilitate seamless, customized customer interaction. An omnichannel experience assures a better customer experience and helps in sustaining customer loyalty in the long run.

Chapter 10

  Ravishankar Krishnan, Vel Tech Rangarajan Dr. Sagunthala R&D
    Institute of Science and Technology, India
  Elantheraiyan Perumal, VelTech Rangarajan Dr. Sagunthala R&D
    Institute of Science and Technology, India
  Logasakthi Kandasamy, Universal Business School, Universal AI
    University, India
  G. Manoj, Vel Tech Rangarajan Dr. Sagunthala R&D Institute of
    Science and Technology, India

Companies selling electronic items face the challenge of adapting to the rapidly shifting landscape of customer expectations in the digital era. This chapter, presented by the authors, delves deeply into the integration of pioneering metaverse concepts within omnichannel strategies specific to the electronics domain. As a transformative force, the metaverse redefines the traditional paradigms of promotion, sale, and customer experience, answering the burgeoning demand for immersive and personalized shopping journeys. The authors extensively explore the potential and application of groundbreaking technologies such as virtual reality (VR) and augmented reality (AR). Emphasis is given to how the metaverse can seamlessly enhance online shopping platforms, in-store interactions, and proactive customer service initiatives. Furthermore, the chapter illuminates the broad-ranging impact of the metaverse on the retail sector, shedding light on intricate facets such as data-driven insights, requisite infrastructure evolution, and paramount privacy considerations.

The industrial revolution is facilitated by metaverse platforms, which encompass and integrates artificial intelligence (AI), machine learning methodologies (ML), augmented and virtual reality (AVR), industrial internet of things (IIoT), digital business transformation, and cloud computing services in the oil and gas service industries. The researchers conducted a literature analysis, analyzing case studies and concept studies from original equipment manufacturers (OEMs) and oil and gas operational service businesses. This research investigates the correlation between metaverse platforms, emotional intelligence, co-creation, and autonomous systems in relation to project quality and delivery throughout the Industrial Revolution. Scientists undertook an empirical investigation to comprehend the effects of metaverse platforms and entrepreneurs' emotional intelligence in the oil and gas industry during the Industrial Revolution.

The Metaverse economy represents a paradigm shift in the realm of finance, poised to redefine the concept of money through the utilization of digital currency within virtual environments. Within the metaverse, digital currency facilitates transactions for shopping, gaming, and a diverse array of goods and services. To traverse the virtual realm using a virtual reality headset and controllers purely for recreational purposes, without any predefined objectives. The Metaverse offers unprecedented opportunities for businesses and individuals to engage the exchange, and accumulation. Through immersive experiences, luxury brands and retailers are already capitalizing to cater to evolving consumer preferences, with cutting-edge technologies such as augmented reality and artificial intelligence. The brand Gucci has initiated the sale of their products within the Metaverse, utilizing digital currency for transactions. As the metaverse continues to evolve through advancements in digital currency and technology, it promises to revolutionize the future of money and commerce.

Big data is a rapidly expanding and applied field that offers the potential to transform the healthcare industry. It enables efficient data modification for patient physiological analysis in bioinformatics. This assessment highlights the current status of big data and analytical techniques in all five healthcare subdisciplines. Stakeholders, including government agencies, healthcare professionals, hardware manufacturers, pharmaceutical companies, individuals, data scientists, scholars, and vendors, are responsible for developing and evaluating big data policies to improve patient outcomes.

The metaverse, a burgeoning digital universe of immersive experiences and interactions, has captured the imagination of individuals and industries alike. As people increasingly gravitate towards extended engagement within these virtual realms, questions arise about the potential consequences for mental and physical health. This analysis provides an in-depth examination of the multifaceted health implications stemming from prolonged immersion in the metaverse. In this exploration, we investigate the psychological effects of extended metaverse use, including issues related to social isolation, addiction, and the potential for disconnection from the physical world. We delve into the emotional aspects, exploring how interactions within the metaverse may impact users' self-esteem, emotional well-being, and social relationships. This research seeks to contribute to the growing body of knowledge surrounding the metaverse by offering insights into the intricate relationship between immersive digital experiences and human health.

This study aims to explore the awareness and perceptions of green banking among bankers and customers in rural and semi-urban areas of India. A structured questionnaire was employed to gather information from 807 customers and 200 officials of selected commercial banks, utilizing the snowball sampling method. The study utilized chi-square and factor analysis techniques. The chi-square test results revealed an association between educational status and the customer's opinion regarding green banks. Factor analysis derived three key factors influencing the adoption of green banking: convenience and environmental sustainability, financial and technological advantages, and customer retention and prestige. The findings indicate that green banking services provide more benefits to its customers than traditional banking.

Preface

We are delighted to present an edited reference book titled *Creator's Economy in Metaverse Platforms: Empowering Stakeholders Through Omnichannel Approach.* The title is extremely relevant in today's contemporary business scenario and thanks to its holistic approach, it is expected to offer profoundly important insights to all the stakeholders of the creator economy in digitally connected universes. The comprehensive coverage, in-depth details, and thorough viewpoints of the contributors are some of the striking features of the edited title.

The book explores and investigates concepts of creator economy across different industrial sectors and offers useful insights, guidelines, and recommendations for integrating the concept into business models. The frameworks discussed in the book can easily serve as a roadmap for professionals, policymakers, and administrators and help in evolution of the sector in a manner that will accelerate the adoption of the creator economy in the metaverse space.

ORGANISATION OF BOOK

Chapter 1 introduces the concept of creator economy and how it has gained prominence in digitally connected universes. Citing the different use cases of the creator economy, the chapter also investigates the challenges that continue to dampen the growth prospects of the segment besides throwing light on the adoption roadmap that can help in integration of the creator economy in metaverse platform with desired efficiency and effectiveness.

Chapter 2 is specifically concerned with aspect of retaining the profitability in virtual spaces. The authors have gone into detail about how to retain customers in metaverse platforms and what retention strategies must be employed by the organisations to ensure that customers continue to stick with their brand portfolios for an extended period. The focus is on the profitability and retention strategies that will help firms integrate the concept of metaverse into their business models.

Touching upon the important aspect of ethics and governance in metaverse platforms, chapter 3 delves into the details of what an ideal and responsible AI governance framework looks like in digitally connected universes. The insights offered by the authors are very relevant in the wake of increasing instances of cybercrimes which pose a great threat for all stakeholders in the creator economy space.

Brand-building exercises have always been one of the most significant aspects of profitability and chapter 4 specifically focuses on this aspect in the metaverse space. The chapter offers details on how organisation should connect their branding elements in a manner that will help them project a positive and sustainable image in the minds of customers. The chapter offers significant measures for brand building and concludes that revisiting basics is key to building a sustainable brand in the metaverse space.

Chapter 5 is focused on digital merchandising with specific reference to building the metaverse platforms into retail formats. Authors have discussed the enormous potential of digital merchandising while reflecting on the various issues and challenges that retail organisations face while integrating digitally connected universes into their offerings. The importance of unifying metaverse platforms and retail formats has also been discussed in detail in the chapter.

The authors of Chapter 6 have contributed by highlighting the role of metaverse platforms in retaining employees in the retail sector. Here the significance of virtual platforms in delivering effective and efficient training to employees has been highlighted in detail. The authors have also given information related to leadership programs that can be delivered efficiently with the use of metaverse platforms and how these can prove instrumental in driving the growth and profitability of organisations.

Chapter 7 specifically investigates strategies that can help in building capabilities related to the workforce in the metaverse-driven formats of retail organisations. The analysis takes a comprehensive approach and uses the encompassing perspective of analysing, reviewing, and recommending the best strategies for building strategic capabilities in the retail space. The chapter also offers insights into how the use of metaverse platforms can help the retail economy to grow at a renewed pace.

Looking into the retail space from the perspectives of experts and specialists, chapter 8 offers a comprehensive view of the readiness of the Indian retail sector to adopt and integrate metaverse platforms. The chapter investigates how receptive Indian retailers are to the concept of virtual space and finds that the overall retail scenario in India is changing with both customers as well as retailers willing to embrace the concept of metaverse with open arms.

The concept of Omni channel retail and its implications for meeting the Expectations of retail consumers have been discussed in Chapter 9. It is significant in the backdrop of changing consumer dynamics in the retail sector with most of the retail players becoming concerned about decreasing levels of loyalty among the target consumers. The application of the effective Omni channel strategy can help retailers regain the confidence of customers and achieve desired levels of profitability in their business.

The focus of Chapter 10 is on the electronic goods industry with authors specifically investigating the strategies to optimise omnichannel retail in the segment. Especially the integration of the metaverse in the electronic goods industry and the use of new-age technologies including AR and VR have been discussed by the authors. The insights from the chapter will prove beneficial for all the stakeholders in the electronic goods segment.

The role of the metaverse in the service industry with specific reference to the emotional intelligence of entrepreneurs has been discussed in Chapter 11. The authors have also focused on the co-creation concept and discussed how this can greatly enhance the quality of the Service Delivery for end consumers. The chapter offers significant implications for service providers, consumers, and policymakers besides encouraging scholars to further research in the domain.

The role of digital currency in expanding the metaverse economy is a matter of discussion in Chapter 12. The multifaceted approach of the chapter discusses both the use cases of digital currencies and how brands are using the new technology to drive loyalty among their target consumers. The use cases discussed in the chapter offer a profound understanding to readers of how to incorporate digital currency to boost their business and acquire new customer segments.

The game-changing potential of bioinformatics in the Healthcare sector along with the complimentary role of Data Analytics have been discussed in chapter 13. The authors have gone into great detail and discussed the complementary role of these technologies in enhancing effectiveness and efficiency of procedures in all subdisciplines of the healthcare sector. The chapter is significant from the perspective of healthcare practitioners as well as policymakers.

The health implications related to spending time in the virtual space have been discussed in detail in chapter 14. Authors have gone into investigations related to the potentially ill aspects of metaverse platforms and how spending time beyond the desired limit can adversely impact the health parameters of the users, thereby leaving them to depression, anxiety, and other kinds of mental disorders.

Chapter 15 explores the possibility of integrating metaverse platforms to kickstart the green Banking revolution. The study is significant in the sense that it can pave the way for the adoption of environment-friendly policies in the banking sector and help the sector reduce its carbon footprint. The concept of green banking has immense potential and by implementing the practices associated with it, the banking sector can contribute significantly in fighting climate change and reversing the adverse impact of global warming.

Editors:

Preface

Babita Singla
Chitkara Business School, Chitkara University, India

Kumar Shalender
Chitkara Business School, Chitkara University, India

Nripendra Singh
Pennsylvania Western University, Clarion, USA

Chapter 1
Creator Economy in Metaverse Space:
Use Cases, Adoption Challenges, and Integration Roadmap

Kumar Shalender
(iD) https://orcid.org/0000-0002-7269-7025
Chitkara Business School, Chitkara University, Punjab, India

Babita Singla
(iD) https://orcid.org/0000-0002-8861-6859
Chitkara Business School, Chitkara University, Punjab, India

ABSTRACT

The creator economy is quickly spreading its influence across the industrial sectors thanks to the evolution of the metaverse platforms. This research specifically investigates the use cases of the creator economy and how stakeholders can potentially widen its scope and application areas. The chapter also delves into the details of the challenges the creator economy faces across the spectrum. It offers an adoption framework to help integrate the concept of creator economy in the right spirit and manner. The conclusion section of the research offers important implications for the adoption of the creator economy and how going forward the concept will lead to generate more avenues of growth and profitability across the ecosystems in different industries. The research is significant in the sense that it offers profound insights into the future of the creator economy and how its adoption will boost the overall economic progress of countries across the globe.

DOI: 10.4018/979-8-3693-3358-7.ch001

INTRODUCTION

The concept of metaverse can be easily considered one of the most talked about business models of our contemporary times. It has already started sweeping the industries and by bringing the reality of digital connected universes into the limelight, the metaverse is expected to become instrumental in taking the growth of global commerce to a whole new level. Metaverse popularity has been fuelled by several dimensions primarily among which are enhanced digitalisation, widening use of digital currencies, and fast-changing tastes and preferences of new-age customers. The concept has also gained traction amidst the rise of Generation Z and Alpha, both of which are coming together to ask for immersive products and services that can be co-created with the help of digital mediums. No wonder, a study recently conducted by PwC found that around 70% of the executives working in the Indian corporate sector expressed their intent to incorporate metaverse into their business models. The same report went on to highlight that 25% of Indian businesses are fully ready to use the concept of a metaverse by the next year while close to 50% are hopeful that the integration of the creator economy will complete in three to four years. Not only in India, the affinity of the global corporate sector towards the metaverse is also on the rise. The primary segment that stands to benefit most from the revolution of digitally connected universes is of creator community. Artists, composers, lyricists, and other creators working in the different spheres of life are embracing the metaverse revolution and by offering immersive platforms, these are becoming the flag bearers of the metaverse economy across the globe (Autio & Fu 2015). In the context of this fast-emerging metaverse economy, this research specifically looks into use cases of the creator economy across business segments and challenges that the creator economy is facing while offering an adoption roadmap to help the creator economy lead economic development across the globe. The chapter also offers important implications for stakeholders so that the desired growth can be achieved in developing a holistic creator economy ecosystem in the metaverse. Especially when it comes to the adoption of the creator economy in the different industrial segments, the use of the integration framework suggested by the study can prove to be of immense benefit. The guidelines suggested by the researchers can also help regulators and policymakers envisage the ideal regulations for the growth of the creator economy in digital spaces (Aggarwal et al. 2020).

CREATOR ECONOMY: SIGNIFICANT USE CASES

As mentioned above in the introduction section, the metaverse can be described as a network of digitally connected universes that are shared among the participants and community members. These spaces offer immersive digital experiences and thanks to their connected nature, these are becoming ideal platforms for creators to directly strike relationships with their target audiences. Here are the details of some most promising use cases of metaverse and how these can become game changers for the economy:

Music Labels

Arguably the most promising application of the creator economy is in the space of music and entertainment. Many creators in the past heavily relied upon big labels and music companies to create the music and take it to their target markets. While these companies help in the creation and distribution of the music, they also take away a big chunk of the revenue and the profit margins associated with the music, leaving only sparse money with creators. However, thanks to the emergence of metaverse platforms, artists, composers, lyricists, and associated performers can directly connect with their audiences without the help of any intermediary. This disintermediation is not only helpful for bringing more money to the class of creators but also encourages a lot of potential artists to come forward and display their talent to the world (Calvo 2023). The growth in metaverse platforms specifically designated to the music and entertainment category is a testimony that the concept has struck a chord with all relevant stakeholders and will emerge as one of the most promising segments to take the growth story of metaverse expansion forward in the future. The monopoly of the big names in the music industry has almost gone now and by offering a level playing field to all the talented artists, the concept of creator economy is democratizing the way music is being created, produced, and distributed in the industry.

Gaming Sector

Along with music and entertainment, the gaming sector has also witnessed tremendous growth thanks to the inception of the creator economy. Metaverse platforms are today being utilised as the major gaming avenues as they can offer an enthralling, immersive, and connected experience to users (Shalender 2022). The creator economy is flourishing in the sector thanks to the extra element of multiplayer gaming and the connected experience that it brings to the table. Unlike ordinary gaming platforms, metaverse offers immense opportunities for creators to offer multiplayer games that are fully connected, thereby allowing communities to play and compete in a multiplayer contest. Before the evolution of the metaverse platforms, these kinds of gaming capabilities were very rare (Davenport & Kalakota 2019). The concept of in-game rewards has also picked the pace thanks to the increasing interest of users in multiplayer gaming. Another important aspect of the metaverse that is helping prospects of the in-gaming economy is its immersive and connected characteristics. The use of cryptocurrency, non-fungible tokens, and other associated rewards are now being fully utilised in the gaming industry, thereby opening a new stream of revenue for creators, developers, gaming organisations, and players among others. This particular aspect can also be used by governments and policymakers to draft policies so that a handsome amount of revenue can be generated from the gaming sector in the form of taxes and duties associated with them. It's noteworthy that the gaming sector has immense potential and by utilising the creator economy in the right spirit with the right set of implementation measures, the overall growth prospects of the creator economy can be multiplied, leading to holistic benefits for every stakeholder in the gaming sector.

Digital Land

Purchasing land in the digital space might seem a farfetched reality for many although virtual realty is increasingly becoming part of the creator economy in the metaverse space. Platforms such as Decentraland and Sandbox are responsible for this revolution and there has been a great deal of interest in buying and trading digital land among individual buyers, big corporates, large MNCs, and consumer goods firms among others. In addition to buying the land, these digital platforms also offer the facility to rent, lease, and other allied models of revenue generation. These digital spaces can also be used for promotion and advertisement purposes, thereby helping brands make a lasting connection with audiences in digital space (Dhiman et al. 2018). Just consider the example of the Nike sportswear brand which is currently relishing in the success of Metaverse. Buoyed by the strong initial response. Nike pursued the metaverse space that led to the creation of Nikeland, the digital Nike space which not only offers an attractive avenue for its customers to connect, communicate, and hang out but also helps the organisation strengthen its brand equity while reinforcing loyalty among the existing customers. A similar strategy has been adopted by the world's leading beverage producer, Coca-Cola which has specifically launched Sugar Byte beverage to celebrate its investment in the digital space. The new beverage has been completely inspired by the metaverse concept and along with this new beverage, Coca-Cola has also gone ahead with the launch of a slew of its new products including digital collectables, virtual promotions, and advertising in the metaverse platforms. All these activities, in turn, are boosting the prospects of the creator economy. The appeal of buying, selling, and renting digital lands (often referred to as land parcels) is also being augmented by the fact that there is limited space in the metaverse platforms and once all these land parcels are sold out, the demand for the digital land will go north. This anticipation is also helping to enhance the demand for digital land.

Retail Space

Creator economy and metaverse platforms hold special significance for the retail industry. These platforms have specifically been useful for retailers and by allowing customers to try, alter, and customise their shopping experiences, digitally connected universes are proving a significant booster for the growth in the retail space. The interactive and immersive nature of the metaverse combined with the AR/VR capabilities of the retail platforms are proving specifically beneficial for customers. The different kinds of avatars created in metaverse platforms and their accessories command a high appeal among target audiences and by stocking, promoting, and selling these items, retailers can augment their revenue and business profitability in the long run. Over and above the normal items, metaverse platforms are also opening new revenue streams for retail organisations. Another important advantage that Metaverse offers to retailers is the emotional connection between customers and brands (Kolo 2021). This facet is especially relevant to establishing brand loyalty and by offering customers products and services that are aligned with their needs and preferences, retailers can convert their present customers into loyal ones. Also, by replicating the physical, in-store experience, the creator economy helps retailers present an omnichannel perspective for multiplying business opportunities and growth prospects (Singh et al. 2022). The ongoing evolution in technology is also making digital spaces more capable so much so that they are increasingly becoming capable of offering smell, touch, and other responses to prospective audiences in the digital space.

CREATOR ECONOMY: CHALLENGES AND ISSUES

Incomplete Knowledge

To achieve success in the metaverse space, all the stakeholders need to have complete knowledge of the operating mechanism that powers the concept of creator economy. Importantly, knowing the use cases of the segment wherein creators want to start the business is of paramount importance. Like all other decisions of strategic interest, the foray into the creator economy also requires a clear-cut vision, well-defined objectives, and implementation strategies. Leaving anything to chance can prove detrimental to the metaverse strategy of the organisation and can restrict the benefits associated with the metaverse foray strategy. Taking the help of an external consultant who has experience working in creator economy and metaverse platforms can be a preferred path for organisations who are still to foray into the segment. Case studies of various organisations that have successfully marked their presence in digitally connected spaces can also act as a guiding light for the companies who are preparing to start their metaverse innings. Remember, the most important thing is to align the demographics of the target consumers with the activities that an organisation plans to boost the creator economy as this alignment will be crucial for offering desirable results to the metaverse strategy (Kulshrestha et al. 2022). Therefore, just like companies follow the segmentation, targeting, and positioning model in other aspects of business, a similar STP model has to be considered for the entry of organisations into the digital space.

Lack of Tangible Solutions

Owing to the very basic digital nature of the metaverse, most organisations fail to deliver tangible solutions that have a lasting impact on the psyche of customers. To widen the adoption of the creator economy among the target consumers, solutions in the metaverse spaces must assume a higher degree of tangibility containing lots of physical cues and elements. This characteristic can be achieved using AI, Graphics, and other smart elements related to the technology. Further, the emergence of low-code and no-code development has made this process even simpler and by offering developers an opportunity to curate elements of their choice without getting into the complication of coding, these new techniques are proving instrumental in the growth of tangible solutions in digital spaces. This approach of offering something tangible has already been adopted by the gaming industry and this factor has proved extremely beneficial for the growth and profitability of the segment. Replicating the same approach in the different spheres of business will result in impressive economic results which, in turn, will help to widespread the use of metaverse and associated technologies in the digital space (Ledro et al. 2022). Increasing the tangible touch points will help digital platforms reassure prospective buyers about their value propositions and emerge victorious in terms of acquiring more customers, enhancing their profitability, and emerging as leading players in their operation segments.

Unrealistic expectations

Like other business realities, setting unrealistic expectations is also a problem in the metaverse space. Replicating the success of Nike, Coca-Cola, and Rolex is not a mean feat and mandates a proper planning and implementation framework along with the support of the top management. While many firms envy the success of big brands in the metaverse and plan their foray along the same lines, they lack the business plan to appropriately target their prospective buyers in the digital space. Setting expectations too high in the beginning is also a major problem and given the pressure from the shareholders on ROI, sometimes top management also caves in and starts asking the quick results from the execution teams (Saxena 2023). Just like any other business strategy, deriving results from digital spaces is a long-term process. Organisations need to put in effort for years in engaging with prospective buyers, establishing communication channels with them, curating the right products and experiences, and finally achieving desired results. All these processes take time and within the broader framework of strategic planning and execution, one has to exercise patience while deciding to foray into the digital spaces. Hence, in the backdrop of all these observations, companies need to take a long-term perspective of their creator economy approach and stay put with their investment in both the human and monetary fronts to achieve significant results on the business front.

Lack of Implementation

A couple of years back, the primary question for most social media strategists was how to have their presence felt on social media platforms and now this moot question has changed to what we need to do on social media and what to accomplish there. The focus of the approach has now shifted to a meaningful presence on social media and the same is going to be true for the metaverse platforms (Shaheen 2021). While most debates and deliberations today concerning metaverse platforms are regarding the presence of organisations, the need of the hour is to deliberate on what needs to be done to engage with customers and how to make that engagement more lasting and social-issue oriented. Taking a socially constructive and all-encompassing approach will help organisations build lasting relationships with customers and help firm strengthen their brand equity in the process. Proactively shifting focus from what, why, and how is a sure-shot strategy for building a meaningful presence in the digital universe. Undoubtedly, there is a first-mover advantage associated with some organisations but the fast-evolving democratization of the segment will soon make the field level-playing for everyone. The real issue organisations have to ponder upon is to strive to present a holistic and complete picture related to their presence in the metaverse world and by associating with the social cause, firms can take their level of engagement to a new level.

ENCOURAGING CREATOR ECONOMY: DEVELOPMENT OF ADOPTION ROADMAP

The adoption framework that is desired to push the adoption of the creator economy is multidimensional. Given the influence of many factors that go into the development of the creator economy, it's necessary to consider a Holistic approach to developing an adoption framework. As shown in Figure 1, the three primary stakeholders that can play a crucial role in enhancing the prospects of the economy are a) customers, b) companies, and c) policymakers. Customers, as with any other industry, are the building block of the framework. These are essential for vitalising the growth of the creator economy as all products and services conceptualised by the creators are primarily for the end-use of the customers. The good thing about customers is their higher level of awareness about digital technologies and metaverse platforms. (Siririka 2023). Unlike many other business segments, the influence of Gen Alpha and Gen Z is quite dominating in the metaverse segment which hands over an added advantage to both corporates and policymakers. While the enhanced level of awareness will save organisations a lot of advertisement costs, policymakers won't need to spend heavily on promotional costs. The second stakeholder of the framework is the corporate sector and as mentioned above in the use cases and challenges faced by the creator economy, the need to take a holistic, complete, and encompassing approach should be the priority of the businesses (insert figure 1 here)

Organisations also need to take a long-term perspective towards adoption of the digital spaces and it is best not to get swayed by pressures from shareholders to mint the quick money. Comprehensive planning and implementation of strategies adopted for the adoption and implementation of metaverse spaces also need to be the focus of metaverse teams which are tasked with the responsibility of making the organisation's presence felt in the digital spaces. Perhaps the most important role that has to be played in the creative economy is of policymakers. Legislators, regulators, and administrators have to play a constructive role in a manner that will help the creator economy flourish from a multidimensional perspective. On the one hand, rules and regulations must be framed to preserve the sanctity of the customers' data and privacy, regulations must also not impede the growth potential of the creator economy in the long term (Williams & Vorley 2015). Balancing both these aspects is not an easy task and requires comprehensive deliberations between different stakeholders of the creator economy. Both customers and corporates need to be consulted before finalizing any such policy framework. Furthermore, it is important to take suggestions from technology developers, IT organisations, digital marketing firms, and metaverse platforms so that a win-win situation can be created for all stakeholders in the metaverse ecosystem.

CONCLUSION AND DISCUSSION

The creator economy has the potential to change the fortunes of many industries across the globe. The revolution in the digital spaces, especially among the metaverse platforms has led to the evolution of the creator economy. The game-changing potential of the concept is very much evident from the fact that its use in the customer and business space is changing the way brands interact, communicate, and strike relationships with the target audiences. The increasing purchasing power of the young generation around the globe is also helping the creator economy to become a preferred medium of transaction among the stakeholders. Various research reports have suggested that around 75-80% of customers are likely to engage with the concept of digitally connected universes positively. The specific characteristic of disintermediation is specifically proven beneficial as it allows creators to retain the maximum share of their profit rather than forfeiting it to big companies, firms, and organisations. The freedom of creation that the creator economy has bestowed is truly amazing and can set the tone for a paradigm shift in how the relationship between creators and target audiences will be defined in the future. The significant role of social media platforms which are now increasingly replaced by the digitally connected universes cannot be underestimated in the evolution of the creator economy. To bring a new impetus to the entire process, it's quite important to understand the role of government and policymakers in furthering the prospects of the creator economy. Especially about the data preservation policies and the possible threat of cyber-attacks need to be taken into serious consideration. Regulators also need to be cognizant of the interests of all stakeholders involved in a business ecosystem as it will help in maintaining the sustainability of the economy for the long term. Going forward, the key characteristic that creators need to keep in mind to become part of the successful creator economy is the relevance of their content for the target audiences. The creation of reliable content is a must and this coupled with the authenticity and trustworthiness of the creator will help in the overall sustainability of the economy in the future. The onus of responsible creation is also on developers as these people are likely to set the stage for creating a more engaging, immersive, and attractive experience for prospective buyers. The developers also need to ensure that the overall process of metaverse adoption reaches a large number of people across the globe as this fact remains the prerequisite for wider adoption of the creator economy. Issue of the generative AI and its impact on the content creation is also making waves in the creator economy and although the full impact of the generative technologies is yet to be materialised, the fast-growing AI landscape will likely impact the content creation process in a significant manner.

REFERENCES

Aggarwal, A., Chand, P. K., Jhamb, D., & Mittal, A. (2020). Leader–Member Exchange, Work Engagement, and Psychological Withdrawal Behavior: The Mediating Role of Psychological Empowerment. *Frontiers in Psychology*, *11*(423), 423. doi:10.3389/fpsyg.2020.00423 PMID:32296361

Autio, E., & Fu, K. (2015). Economic and political institutions and entry into formal and informal entrepreneurship. *Asia Pacific Journal of Management*, *32*(1), 67–94. doi:10.1007/s10490-014-9381-0

Calvo, A. V., Franco, A. D., & Frasquet, M. (2023). The role of artificial intelligence in improving the omnichannel customer experience. *International Journal of Retail & Distribution Management*, *51*(9/10), 1174–1194. doi:10.1108/IJRDM-12-2022-0493

Davenport, T., & Kalakota, R. (2019). The potential for artificial intelligence in healthcare. *Future Healthcare Journal*, *6*(2), 94–98. doi:10.7861/futurehosp.6-2-94 PMID:31363513

Dhiman, R., Chand, P. K., & Gupta, S. (2018). Behavioural Aspects Influencing Decision to Purchase Apparels amongst Young Indian Consumers. *FIIB Business Review*, *7*(3), 188–200. doi:10.1177/2319714518790308

Kolo, K. (2021). *9 AR Platforms Bring Augmented Reality Content in the Classroom*. The VRARA. https://www.thevrara.com/blog2/2021/10/26/9-desktop-ar-platforms-to-bring-ar-content-in-the-classroom

Kulshrestha, D., Tiwari, M. K., Shalender, K., & Sharma, S. (2022). Consumer Acatalepsy Towards Buying Behaviour for Need-Based Goods for Sustainability During the COVID-19 Pandemic. *Indian Journal of Marketing*, *52*(10), 50–63. doi:10.17010/ijom/2022/v52/i10/172347

Ledro, C., Nosella, A., & Vinelli, A. (2022). Artificial intelligence in customer relationship management: Literature review and future research directions. *Journal of Business and Industrial Marketing*, *37*(13), 48–63. doi:10.1108/JBIM-07-2021-0332

Saxena, K. (2023). *Future Prospects of Augmented Reality in the Education Industry*. Coding Ninjas. https://www.codingninjas.com/studio/library/augmented-reality-in-education-industry

Shaheen, M. Y. (2021). Applications of Artificial Intelligence (AI) in healthcare. *RE:view*. doi:10.14293/S2199-1006.1.SOR-.PPVRY8K.v1

Shalender, K. (2022). Key variables in team dynamics in small businesses and start-ups. In New teaching resources for management in a globalised world (pp. 141–153). World Scientific. doi:10.1142/9789811239212_0007

Singh, J. P., Chand, P. K., Mittal, A., & Aggarwal, A. (2020). High-performance work system and organizational citizenship behaviour at the shop floor. *Benchmarking*, *27*(4), 1369–1398. doi:10.1108/BIJ-07-2019-0339

Siririka, P. (2023). *Integrating informal sector can propel financial reach.* Newer Alive. https://neweralive.na/posts/integrating-informal-sector-can-propel-financial-reach

Williams, N., & Vorley, T. (2015). Institutional asymmetry: How formal and informal institutions affect entrepreneurship in Bulgaria. *International Small Business Journal*, *33*(8), 840–861. doi:10.1177/0266242614534280

Chapter 2
Unraveling Metaverse's Retention Secrets:
The Key to Profitability in a Virtual Economy

R. Akash

ⓘ https://orcid.org/0009-0002-3777-0781

SRM Institute of Science and Technology, Chennai, India

V. Suganya

ⓘ https://orcid.org/0000-0001-5301-8317

SRM Institute of Science and Technology, Chennai, India

ABSTRACT

As the Metaverse continues to surge in prominence, this chapter delves into the often-overlooked realm of customer retention within this digital landscape. Recognizing the pivotal role that customer retention plays in ensuring the long-term sustainability and profitability of virtual economies, this study endeavors to uncover the intricate secrets that drive lasting customer engagement within the Metaverse. At the heart of this chapter lies the development of a comprehensive conceptual framework designed for adoption by industry stakeholders. This framework acts as a bridge between theory and practical implementation, offering a multifaceted perspective on the factors that influence customer retention. Through literature research with a rigorous analytical lens, this study aims to equip businesses, creators, and investors with the knowledge necessary to thrive in the ever-evolving Metaverse. By applying this framework, stakeholders can cultivate enduring customer relationships, thereby transforming the Metaverse into a hub of sustainable profitability within the virtual economy.

DOI: 10.4018/979-8-3693-3358-7.ch002

INTRODUCTION

The dawn of the Metaverse era marks a paradigm shift in our digital landscape, challenging conventional perceptions of cyberspace and reshaping the very fabric of reality as we know it. This chapter navigates through the uncharted territories of the Metaverse, a vast digital expanse where immersive experiences (Bandyopadhyay et al., 2023), decentralized economies (Aydoğan, 2023), and interconnected digital ecosystems converge (Jung, 2022). Amidst this transformative landscape, the chapter recognizes the pivotal role of customer engagement and how it leads to customer retention as the anchor for sustainability and profitability in the burgeoning virtual economy (Grewal et al., 2009).

As the Metaverse captivates our collective imagination with its boundless possibilities (Papa, 2022), it grapples with a fundamental challenge – the sustainability of customer interest over time (Lee, 2021). The allure of novel experiences in the Metaverse inevitably diminishes (Golf-Papez et al., 2022), emphasizing the critical need to understand and master the intricacies of customer retention within this digital frontier (Dwivedi et al., 2023). This chapter addresses a notable gap in the existing literature, venturing into the cryptic realm of Metaverse customer retention to unravel the elusive secrets that underpin sustained customer engagement.

Recognizing the Metaverse as a complex ecosystem with diverse participants – from individuals seeking immersive experiences (Golf-Papez et al., 2022) to entrepreneurs and investors aiming to unlock new frontiers (Ante et al., 2023) – this chapter positions customer relationships as central to the longevity and profitability of this digital realm. The chapter's primary objective is to develop a comprehensive conceptual framework grounded in the expectancy-value theory (Wigfield, 1994), transcending theoretical insights and serving as a bridge between academia and practical implementation. This framework, to be embraced by all Metaverse stakeholders, offers a multifaceted perspective on the myriad factors influencing customer retention.

We adopted expectancy-value theory based on social interaction and technological accessibility to explore customer retention and therefore narrowed it down to customer loyalty. Expectancy-value theory provides insights into individuals' decision-making processes, behaviors, and attitudes based on their expectations and perceived values associated with an action or outcome (Wigfield, 1994). The conceptual framework explains that engaging and interacting with customers in social gathering and getting their feedback gives a self of satisfaction and a sense of encouragement (Patel, 2018) which leads to customer loyalty and ultimately to sustainable growth and profitability (Innis and Londe, 1994). On a similar vein the customer experience towards accessing proper technology to actually use the service (Ertemel, 2021) leads the customers to comeback again and again and make use of the platform makes them loyal to the platform thus as said before leads to sustainable growth and profitability.

Equipped with rigorous empirical literatures and a discerning analytical lens, this chapter endeavors to demystify the enigmatic forces that shape Metaverse consumer behavior. By providing a deeper understanding of the drivers behind lasting customer engagement (Mittal et al., 2023), the aim is to empower businesses, creators, and investors (Yawised et al., 2022) to navigate the ever-evolving Metaverse landscape with confidence and foresight. The practical application of this framework holds the promise of transforming the Metaverse from a realm of fleeting fascination into a hub of sustainable profitability within the virtual economy (Anshari et al., 2022).

Structured to unfold the layers of this exploration, the chapter progresses to a review of literature on customer loyalty in relation to sustainable profitability (Arslan, 2020) and its independent constructs, grounding the discussion in the theoretical foundations of the Expectancy-Value Theory (Wigfield, 1994). Subsequently, the conceptual framework, accompanied by propositions, takes center stage. The next parts thoroughly explore topics, practical ramifications, and the future research potential, providing a complete guide for understanding and optimizing customer relationships within the Metaverse (Han, 2022). Ultimately, by unraveling the secrets of customer retention grounded in the Expectancy-Value Theory (Wigfield, 1994), this chapter aims not only to unlock the full potential of the virtual frontier but also to usher in a new era of innovation, economic prosperity, and enduring digital relationships.

BACKGROUND AND SIGNIFICANCE OF THE METAVERSE IN THE VIRTUAL ECONOMY

The Metaverse, first proposed by Neal Stephenson in his 1992 science fiction book "Snow Crash", has evolved from a theoretical notion to a concrete digital environment with significant ramifications for the virtual economy. The portrayal of a virtual world known as the Metaverse, as described in Stephenson's work, laid the foundation for subsequent explorations of the Metaverse as a convergence of augmented reality, virtual reality, and digital spaces, creating a multidimensional and interconnected digital realm (Visconti, R 2022).

The metaverse has emerged as a transformative force in the virtual economy, ushering in a new era of digital interaction, commerce, and socialization. Rooted in the convergence of virtual reality, augmented reality, and immersive technologies, the metaverse represents a dynamic and interconnected digital universe where users can engage, create, and transact. The significance of the metaverse lies in its ability to transcend traditional online experiences, offering users a multi-dimensional space that blurs the boundaries between the physical and virtual worlds (Ning et al., 2023).

The emergence of the Metaverse raises profound ethical and societal questions. (Wang, Y., 2022) explores the implications of privacy, security, and digital ethics within the Metaverse, shedding light on the broader societal impacts of this digital shift.

One key aspect emphasizing the background and significance of the metaverse is its role as a thriving virtual economy (Filipova, 2023). The metaverse has evolved into a complex ecosystem where users actively participate in economic activities, ranging from virtual goods and services to digital asset ownership (Allam et al., 2022). The virtual economy within the metaverse is characterized by a dynamic marketplace, driven by user interactions (Njoku et al., 2023), transactions (Chen and Cheng, 2022), and the creation of value (Kraus et al., 2022). Thus, understanding the metaverse's economic dynamics is crucial for businesses and creators seeking sustainable profitability within this digital frontier.

Moreover, the metaverse serves as a catalyst for redefining consumer behavior and engagement (Jo, 2023). Customers within the metaverse extend their identities and activities beyond the constraints of the physical world, forming a digital extension of self (Chen et al., 2022). This transformation in consumer behavior is integral to the conceptual framework discussed earlier, where metaverse engagement becomes a key driver for customer loyalty and, consequently, sustainable profitability. The metaverse's unique ability to shape user behavior and foster extended connections holds profound implications for businesses seeking to navigate the virtual economy.

Technological advancements have been instrumental in transforming the Metaverse from a conceptual idea into a tangible digital ecosystem. Notable developments include augmented and virtual reality technologies, blockchain, and the Internet of Things (IoT), which provide the essential infrastructure for immersive experiences, decentralized digital economies, and secure digital asset ownership within the Metaverse (Gadekallu, 2022).

The emergence of the Metaverse holds profound significance for the virtual economy, with a transformative impact on various aspects of economic activities, consumer behavior, and innovation. This significance is well-documented in academic literature and recognized by experts in the field. The Metaverse introduces new economic models and opportunities. (Kop M, 2019) highlights how digital transactions within the Metaverse are creating novel revenue streams and transforming traditional business practices, leading to an era of "post-scarcity" economics.

Additionally, the metaverse stands as a testament to the evolving landscape of social interaction. The interconnectedness of users within the virtual environment fosters a sense of community and shared experiences (Oh et al., 2023). This communal aspect is a fundamental element in the framework, where social interaction within the metaverse is identified as a key antecedent influencing customer loyalty. Businesses that recognize and leverage the social dynamics of the metaverse can strategically enhance customer retention and, in turn, contribute to sustainable profitability.

The Concept of Metaverse and its Relevance Towards Customer Retention

The Metaverse, as previously established, represents a convergence of digital spaces, augmented reality, and virtual reality, offering a complex and interconnected environment for users to engage and interact in ways previously unimaginable (Koohang, A., 2023). Understanding the concept of the Metaverse is integral to comprehending its relevance in the context of customer retention within this digital landscape.

Customer retention within the Metaverse is a dynamic and multifaceted challenge, influenced by various factors, both unique to this digital realm and reflective of broader trends in consumer behavior. As users navigate the Metaverse, they engage in a wide array of experiences, transactions, and interactions, making the retention of their engagement a pivotal concern for businesses, creators, and investors operating within this space (Chen and Cheng, 2022) (Njoku et al., 2023).

The concept of the Metaverse introduces novel dimensions to customer retention. Customers within the Metaverse are driven by a desire for immersive experiences (Njoku et al., 2023) and a sense of belonging in digital environments (Zallio and Clarkson, 2022). This introduces distinct patterns of engagement that may differ significantly from traditional consumer behaviors (Mogaji, E., 2023). Understanding and catering to these unique motivations are central to retaining users within the Metaverse.

Moreover, digital ownership and the notion of scarcity versus abundance take on new meanings within the Metaverse. The use of blockchain technology, as highlighted by (Gadekallu, T. R 2022), empowers users with control over their digital assets, creating a sense of ownership that transcends the virtual realm. The management of digital assets and their potential scarcity or abundance can directly impact customer retention, as users seek to protect and grow their digital possessions within the Metaverse.

In essence, the Metaverse presents a paradigm shift in consumer behavior, where the lines between physical and digital worlds blur. Businesses and content creators must navigate this complex landscape to retain users effectively. Recognizing the profound implications of the Metaverse for customer retention is pivotal in the pursuit of long-term success in this evolving digital economy.

LITERATURE REVIEW

The extensive review of the existing literature emphasizes a notable gap in research pertaining to customer engagement and customer loyalty within the dynamic realm of the metaverse. Despite the meteoric rise of virtual environments, augmented reality, and interconnected digital ecosystems (Jung, 2022), the current body of knowledge is characterized by a dearth of comprehensive investigations into the factors influencing sustained consumer engagement and loyalty within these virtual landscapes. As the metaverse becomes an increasingly integral part of our daily lives, there is a pressing need for exploring and delving into the intricacies of consumer behavior, the dynamics of customer engagement, and the pathways leading to enduring customer loyalty (Gunawan, 2022).

While traditional studies on consumer behavior and loyalty abound, the metaverse presents a novel and evolving landscape that demands specialized attention. The scarcity of research in this domain inhibits our understanding of the unique challenges and opportunities posed by virtual environments, hindering the development of effective strategies for fostering consumer loyalty. The literature gap becomes particularly pronounced as the metaverse encompasses diverse participants, from individual users seeking immersive experiences (Bandyopadhyay et al., 2023) to entrepreneurs and investors navigating the potential of this burgeoning digital frontier (Knox, 2022) and (Belk, 2023). Bridging this gap is imperative for advancing both theoretical perspectives and practical insights that can inform stakeholders across various sectors.

Several foundational elements within the metaverse, such as metaverse engagement, social interaction, and technological accessibility, remain underexplored in the existing literature. Understanding the interconnectedness of these variables and their impact on customer loyalty is crucial for businesses and creators seeking sustained success in the metaverse. A comprehensive review of literature is essential to identify the existing gaps, synthesize relevant theories, and lay the groundwork for the development of a robust conceptual framework. By addressing this research void, further researches can contribute to the evolution of metaverse studies and provide actionable insights for businesses and stakeholders navigating this uncharted digital landscape (Schmitt, 2023).

In light of the current state of the literature, this chapter aims to enrich and understand on metaverse consumer behavior, engagement, and loyalty. Through an exhaustive review of existing studies, coupled with a critical analysis of the theoretical frameworks employed, this chapter seeks to unearth patterns, identify gaps, and propose a comprehensive conceptual framework grounded in the Expectancy-Value Theory. By doing so, this literature review sets the stage for a deeper exploration into the metaverse's enigmatic forces that shape consumer retention and contribute to the sustainability and profitability of this digital frontier.

Metaverse Engagement

In recent years, the Metaverse has experienced an unprecedented boom, capturing widespread academic interest, particularly in the exploration of customer engagement. Various researchers have contributed to the conceptualization of customer engagement within the Metaverse, drawing inspiration from foundational works such as Van Doorn's seminal contribution in 2010. Van Doorn et al. (2010) defined customer engagement as a "developmental relationship characterized by a customer's behavioral manifestations, focusing on a brand or firm beyond the point of purchase and stemming from intrinsic motivational drivers". This definition underscores the multidimensional nature of customer engagement, emphasizing "digital technologies allow consumers to co-create value by designing and customizing products, perform last-mile distribution activities, and help other customers by sharing product reviews" (Verhoef et al., 2021).

Building upon Van Doorn's framework, Harmeling (2017) further enriched the understanding of customer engagement. Harmeling conceptualized customer engagement as a "customer's voluntary resource contribution to a firm's marketing function, surpassing mere financial patronage". This broader perspective acknowledges that customer engagement extends beyond the economic transaction and involves active participation and resource contributions from customers. Such contributions can take various forms, including sharing user-generated content, providing feedback, and participating in brand-related activities within the Metaverse. By incorporating voluntary resource contributions, with interconnected digital ecosystems (Jung, 2022), where customer involvement goes beyond traditional consumer behaviors (Jansson et al., 2011).

While these foundational definitions provide a robust starting point, the evolving nature of the Metaverse necessitates a continuous exploration of the dimensions and drivers of customer engagement. Recent scholarship has delved into the role of immersive experiences (Han, 2022), gamification elements (Agustini et al., 2023), and virtual interactions (Strutt, 2022) in shaping customer engagement within the Metaverse. Understanding the intricacies of these factors is essential for businesses and creators aiming to cultivate and leverage customer engagement as a cornerstone for sustained success in this dynamic digital landscape. As we embark on a deeper review of the literature surrounding Metaverse engagement, it becomes evident that synthesizing these diverse perspectives is crucial for constructing a comprehensive understanding of customer engagement in this virtual frontier (Valaskova et al., 2020).

Social Interaction

Over the recent years, there has been a significant increase in focus on social interaction, particularly in relation to the changing Metaverse. Scholars and researchers, recognizing the transformative impact of digital environments, have increasingly turned their focus toward understanding the nuances of social interaction within virtual spaces. This burgeoning interest is underpinned by the recognition that the Metaverse, with its immersive experiences (Bandyopadhyay et al., 2023) and interconnected digital ecosystems (Jung, 2022), serves as a unique arena for social interactions that transcend traditional boundaries (Glimmerveen et al., 2020).

One prominent dimension of social interaction within the Metaverse is the creation and cultivation of virtual communities. The establishment of these digital communities is a focal point in recent literature (Oh et al., 2023), exploring how users engage, communicate, and form connections within these novel social spaces. Researchers such as Wang et al. (2019) emphasize the role of shared experiences and collaborative activities as essential drivers of social interaction. The formation of virtual communities is not only a testament to the human need for social connection but also a reflection of the Metaverse's capacity to facilitate meaningful interactions, fostering a sense of belonging and shared identity among participants (Arntsen et al., 2023).

Moreover, the exploration of social interaction within the Metaverse extends beyond the confines of virtual communities. Researchers have delved into the dynamics of interpersonal relationships, examining how users engage with one another through avatars, virtual communication tools, and collaborative activities (Nagendran et al., 2022). The concept of social presence, as articulated by Biocca and Harms (2003), plays a pivotal role in understanding the extent to which users feel connected and socially present in the virtual environment. As the Metaverse continues to evolve, the study of social interaction remains a dynamic and evolving field, necessitating ongoing research to uncover the intricacies of human connections within these digital realms (George et al., 2021).

In addition to interpersonal interactions, the exploration of social interaction within the Metaverse encompasses the intersection of real and virtual worlds. The concept of augmented reality (AR) and mixed reality (MR) has introduced new dimensions to social interaction, allowing users to overlay digital information onto their physical environment (Mystakidis, 2022). This amalgamation of physical and virtual spaces further underscores the need for a comprehensive literature review to elucidate the evolving landscape of social interaction within the Metaverse. By synthesizing these diverse perspectives, researchers such as (Hespanhol, 2015) contribute to a nuanced understanding of how social interactions unfold in these digital domains, shaping the user experience and influencing the broader social fabric of the Metaverse (Hennig-Thurau et al., 2023).

Technological Accessibility

Technological accessibility stands as a cornerstone in the Metaverse context, garnering widespread recognition for its profound influence on user experiences and engagements. Acknowledging the pivotal role of technology in shaping interactions within virtual environments, researchers have dug into various facets of technological accessibility to discern its multifaceted impact. A seminal work by Biocca and Levy (1995) underscores the significance of technological accessibility, emphasizing its role in mediating the user's perception and engagement within virtual spaces. As technology continues to evolve, exploring the implications of accessibility on user navigation, ease of use, and overall experience becomes imperative to unravel the complexities of user interactions in the Metaverse (Aburbeian et al., 2022).

A central aspect of technological accessibility within the Metaverse revolves around user interface design and usability. Researchers, such as Tractinsky et al. (2000), have investigated how the design of interfaces influences user perceptions of accessibility and usability. User-friendly interfaces that prioritize simplicity and efficiency play a crucial role in facilitating technological accessibility, ensuring that users can navigate the Metaverse seamlessly. This strand of literature delves into the principles of human-computer interaction, shedding light on how design choices impact user perceptions of accessibility, ultimately shaping their engagement and experience within virtual environments (Tractinsky et al., 2000).

Furthermore, the exploration of technological accessibility extends to considerations of device compatibility and connectivity. Scholars have examined how the diversity of devices and the robustness of connectivity infrastructure contribute to or hinder technological accessibility in the Metaverse. Particularly noteworthy are the ways in which technological accessibility has been expanded by developments in AR and VR. Studies by Lee and Lee (2019) dove into the implications of these technological advancements, emphasizing the need for seamless integration across devices and reliable connectivity to enhance accessibility within the Metaverse. As technology continues to advance, the literature on technological accessibility provides valuable insights into optimizing the user experience and ensuring that virtual environments are accessible to a diverse user base (Hartson and Pyla, 2012).

Further exploration of technological accessibility within the Metaverse context is a dynamic and evolving field of study. Researchers have laid the groundwork for understanding the nuanced relationship between technological accessibility and user engagement (Suh, 2019), diving into interface design, device compatibility, and connectivity considerations. This literature review highlights the importance of synthesizing these diverse perspectives to gain a comprehensive understanding of the role technological accessibility plays in shaping user experiences within the Metaverse.

Economic Incentives

In navigating the intricate landscape of the Metaverse, a compelling argument emerges, asserting that a decentralized Metaverse not only fosters greater privacy, security, equity, and inclusion but is also intrinsically tied to the notion of economic incentives. Researchers such as (Maksymyuk et al., 2022), (Valaskova et al., 2022), (Beckett, 2022) have explored the dichotomy of a decentralized Metaverse, emphasizing its potential to provide a more secure and inclusive digital environment. Notably, as postulated by Nakamoto (2008) in the foundational paper on blockchain technology, decentralization has been lauded for its ability to mitigate centralized control, offering users greater autonomy over their digital experiences. This decentralization aligns with the ideals of privacy and security, creating an environment that champions equity and inclusion within the Metaverse (Almusaed et al., 2020).

However, the crux of the matter lies in the intersection of decentralization and economic incentives. While a decentralized Metaverse lays the groundwork for a more secure and equitable digital space, the absence of economic incentives poses a critical challenge. This nexus becomes particularly pronounced when considering customer engagement and retention. As posited by Gamma et al. (2021), the allure of economic incentives acts as a catalyst for sustained customer engagement within the Metaverse. Without the driving force of economic rewards, users may lack the motivation to actively participate and contribute, ultimately hindering customer retention in the longer run (Gamma et al., 2021).

This intricate balance between decentralization and economic incentives unfolds in the context of sustainable profitability. The absence of economic incentives not only impacts customer engagement but also reverberates through the economic sustainability of the Metaverse. Economic incentives serve as a linchpin, influencing users to invest time, resources, and creativity, thereby contributing to the overall vibrancy in terms with metaverse. In the absence of these incentives, the Metaverse risks stagnation, hindering its potential for sustainable profitability. Researchers such as (Salvioni et al., 2020) and (Martínez-Peláez et al., 2023) argue that understanding this delicate equilibrium is crucial for stakeholders aiming to cultivate enduring customer relationships and fortify the economic foundations for a sustainable growth.

Moreover, the impact of economic incentives as a moderator (Wang et al., 2019) extends beyond customer retention to shape the broader landscape of sustainable profitability. Few literatures such as (Vadakkepatt et al., 2021) emphasizes the need for empirical investigations that explore how economic incentives, or their absence, influence consumer behaviors, contribute to customer loyalty, and ultimately shape the sustainable profitability. Thus, the moderator role of economic incentives stands as a critical dimension in understanding the intricate dynamics how incentives could affect customer loyalty with or without it, thus how it affects sustainable growth and profitability.

THEORETICAL PERSPECTIVES AND MODELS RELATED TO METAVERSE AND CUSTOMER RETENTION

In the immersive realm of the Metaverse, where virtual landscapes unfold as dynamic digital canvases, understanding the factors that drive user engagement and retention is paramount. Amidst the myriad theoretical frameworks, the Expectancy-Value Theory, as expounded by Wigfield (1994), emerges as a compelling lens through which we can unravel the intricate dynamics of user expectations and perceived values within this ever-evolving digital frontier.

The Expectancy-Value Theory, deeply rooted in cognitive psychology, provides a nuanced understanding of how individuals form expectations and evaluate the perceived value associated with their experiences. In the context of the Metaverse, users embark on virtual journeys with preconceived notions about the digital environment, social interactions, and the potential benefits they may glean. Wigfield's theory posits that these expectations are intricately interwoven with the perceived value users attribute to their engagements, encompassing elements such as entertainment, social connection, and economic incentives (Wigfield, 1994).

Central to this idea is the concept of expectancy—an individual's anticipation of success or failure in a given task or activity. In the Metaverse, this translates into users' anticipations regarding the fulfillment of their goals, be they social, recreational, or economic. Simultaneously, the theory underscores the importance of perceived value, encapsulating the subjective assessment of the rewards and benefits derived from engagement. Within the Metaverse, this spans the emotional satisfaction derived from immersive experiences, the sense of community fostered through social interactions, and the economic incentives contributing to sustained engagement (Wigfield, 1994).

Users within the Metaverse continually engage in a delicate dance between expectancy and value, evaluating whether their experiences align with expectations and whether the perceived value justifies sustained involvement. This ongoing assessment influences the level of satisfaction, enjoyment, and fulfillment derived from Metaverse interactions, ultimately shaping decisions to remain active participants. Recent scholarly endeavors have extended the Expectancy-Value Theory to incorporate the unique features of virtual environments, encompassing factors such as technological reliability (Ma, 2023), interface intuitiveness (Pacifico, 2023), and the novelty of interactions (Zhao et al., 2022).

In essence, the Expectancy-Value Theory offers a robust and insightful theoretical framework to fathom the cognitive intricacies of customer retention within the Metaverse. As this digital realm continues to evolve, understanding the psychological underpinnings that drive user engagement and retention remains pivotal. The Expectancy-Value Theory stands as an invaluable tool for researchers and practitioners seeking to navigate the complex terrain of user experiences and decision-making in the immersive landscapes of the Metaverse (Hudson 2022).

METHODOLOGY

This chapter attempts to understand the antecedent of sustainable profitability among the metaverse's virtual economy and retaining them in a longer run. This chapter proposes a comprehensive framework to sustainable profitability in a virtual economy. This chapter also introduces a moderating role of economic incentives and state the key ideas to sustainable profitability. This conceptual study employs a qualitative approach to clarify the fundamental components supporting long-term user retention and sustained profitability in the metaverse's virtual economy. By means of an extensive analysis of the literature, the technique aims to include pre-existing theoretical frameworks and insights from other fields, including virtual economics, marketing, and user experience design. The combination of different viewpoints aids in the creation of a conceptual framework that clarifies the complex aspects of metaverse involvement and how it affects long-term profitability. The research entails a detailed investigation of the conceptual interactions between social interaction and technological accessibility on customer loyalty, clarifying the complex processes from metaverse engagement to long-term user commitment which leads to sustainable profitability. With a focus on theoretical coherence and conceptual clarity this methodological approach seeks to provide a comprehensive theoretical framework for comprehending the virtual economy of the metaverse. With future empirical evidences, this chapter will solidify the key to profitability in a virtual economy.

The chapters provide a comprehensive examination of both theoretical and empirical literature, including a range of formats including research papers, book chapters, governmental reports, professional surveys, and dissertations. As the primary focus is to explore key aspects to retain customers in a virtual economy of metaverse, articles that studies customer retention related to virtual economy with reference to metaverse's preferences, needs and traits were selected. In the related vein, articles related to customer loyalty and customer engagement were selected

Figure 1. Conceptual framework

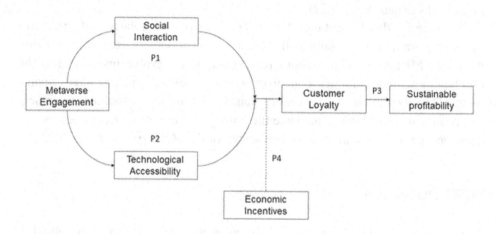

to understand the pattern of how engaging customers leads to customer loyalty and therefore a sustainable profitability and growth. The guidelines for conducting a literature examination include the use of both individual and combined keywords, such as "metaverse", "meta", "customer retention", "sustainable profitability", "virtual reality" and "economic regulations, incentives".

The criteria for choosing content for our comprehensive review were determined by specific inclusion and exclusion guidelines. We considered studies concentrating on customer retention and loyalty within the metaverse environment, emphasizing their relevance to the virtual economy. Inclusion criteria encompassed research articles and papers in the English language that delved into the dynamics of customer loyalty and metaverse engagement. On the flip side, we excluded materials in languages other than English, those focusing solely on marketing aspects related to metaverse users, studies where customer loyalty wasn't a primary focus, and investigations centered on populations unrelated to metaverse users and excluding studies involving multiple generations exploring metaverse engagement.

CONCEPTUAL FRAMEWORK AND PROPOSITIONS

Metaverse Engagement, Social Interaction and Customer Loyalty

Engaging customers within the metaverse is a pivotal step in establishing a pathway to customer loyalty, and existing literature provides valuable insights into this dynamic (Adams, 2022). Customer engagement in the metaverse goes beyond mere participation; it involves a rich interplay of social interactions that significantly influence the development of customer loyalty. A foundational aspect highlighted in the literature is the role of social interactions within virtual environments. As users engage with the metaverse, their interactions with others contribute to a sense of community and shared experiences. Numerous studies emphasize the positive impact of social interactions on customer loyalty, suggesting that a vibrant and supportive community within the metaverse fosters a sense of belonging and attachment among users (Upadhyay et al., 2023). These social connections play a crucial role in shaping sustained customer engagement and, consequently, loyalty.

Furthermore, the literature underscores the psychological dimensions of customer engagement within the metaverse. Beyond the functional aspects of virtual interactions, users often seek emotional fulfillment and a sense of identity within these digital spaces. Studies have identified that metaverse engagement, when coupled with meaningful social interactions, satisfies psychological needs, reinforcing a positive emotional connection with the virtual environment (Tayal et al., 2022). This emotional connection forms a basis for customer loyalty, as users are more likely to remain committed to a platform that addresses not only their functional needs but also their emotional and social desires.

Building on the psychological aspect, the literature also explores the cognitive impact of metaverse engagement on customer loyalty (Zhang et al., 2022). Engaging users in virtual environments often involves cognitive stimulation, such as problem-solving, creativity, and skill development. Studies suggest that customers who actively participate in intellectually stimulating activities within the metaverse are more likely to develop a cognitive attachment to the platform, leading to increased loyalty (Allal-Chérif et al., 2022). In summary, the literature paints a comprehensive picture of how metaverse engagement, fueled by social interactions and addressing psychological and cognitive needs, contributes to the development of customer loyalty. Active metaverse engagement not only satisfies users' social, psychological, and cognitive needs but also fosters a positive impact on customer loyalty. Thus, we propose:

P1: Metaverse engagement enriched by social interactions catering to psychological and cognitive needs, is positively associated with the development of customer loyalty.

Metaverse Engagement, Technological Accessibility and Customer Loyalty

Ensuring technological accessibility within the metaverse is a critical factor in understanding its impact on customer loyalty, and review of existing literature sheds light on the intricate relationship between metaverse engagement, technological accessibility, and customer loyalty. Technological accessibility, in the context of the metaverse, involves the ease with which users can access and navigate the virtual environment (Aburbeian et al., 2022). Studies highlight that a seamless and user-friendly technological interface contributes significantly to metaverse engagement, as users are more likely to actively participate when technology facilitates a smooth and intuitive experience (Lee and Gu, 2022). Technological accessibility is pivotal in shaping the user experience within the metaverse, influencing the extent to which customers can effectively engage with the platform and its offerings.

Furthermore, the past literature emphasizes the role of technological accessibility in fostering customer loyalty within the metaverse (Rane et al., 2023). Users who perceive the metaverse as easily accessible and responsive are more likely to develop a positive perception of the platform, leading to sustained engagement and loyalty. Studies suggest that a lack of technological barriers contributes to a positive customer experience, fostering a sense of trust and reliability in the metaverse (Dinh, 2023). This trust, cultivated through technological accessibility, forms a foundational element in the development of customer loyalty.

Building on these insights, some literatures also explore the impact of technological advancements on the overall metaverse experience and its subsequent influence on customer loyalty. However, according to (Rathore, 2019), technological enhancements, such as virtual reality innovations and improved connectivity, have been linked to heightened customer satisfaction and increased loyalty. The ability of users to seamlessly navigate and access diverse features within the metaverse contributes to a positive overall perception, reinforcing their commitment to the platform. Therefore, technological accessibility not only facilitates metaverse engagement but also plays a pivotal role in shaping customer loyalty. Thus, we propose

P2: Technological accessibility, characterized by a user-friendly interface and seamless navigation, is positively associated with the development of customer loyalty within the metaverse.

Customer Loyalty and Sustainable Profitability

Understanding the link between customer loyalty and sustainable profitability within the metaverse entails a thorough examination of the interconnected paths leading up to this crucial nexus. The literature highlights that metaverse engagement, driven by social interaction and technological accessibility, plays a pivotal role in shaping customer loyalty. According to (Maloney, 2021) users who actively engage within the metaverse, forming meaningful social connections and benefiting from seamless technological accessibility, are more likely to develop a sense of commitment to the platform. This loyalty is further enhanced by the metaverse's ability to cater to users' psychological, emotional, and cognitive needs, as discussed in previous sections.

Furthermore, existing research suggests that customer loyalty, as an outcome of metaverse engagement, is a key driver of sustained profitability (Yawised et al., 2022). Loyal customers tend to exhibit repeated engagement and are more likely to explore and utilize premium features, virtual goods, and other monetization opportunities within the metaverse. This ongoing commitment translates into increased revenue streams, forming a foundational aspect of sustainable profitability. Studies also underscore the role of psychological and emotional connections in fostering customer loyalty, emphasizing that users who feel a sense of identity and belonging within the metaverse are more likely to contribute positively to its financial sustainability (Tayal et al., 2022).

In addition to the direct impact of customer loyalty on sustainable profitability, the literature explores the moderating role of economic incentives in this relationship (Vadakkepatt et al., 2021). Economic incentives, such as virtual currency, rewards, and premium offerings, have been identified as influential factors that shape user behavior within the metaverse. These incentives not only contribute to enhanced customer loyalty but also act as catalysts in driving sustained profitability. Users motivated by economic incentives are more likely to engage in revenue-generating activities, such as virtual transactions and in-app purchases, thus directly influencing the financial sustainability of the metaverse.

Moreover, studies suggest that the pathways leading to customer loyalty and, consequently, sustainable profitability, are contingent on effective metaverse governance and community dynamics (Sia, 2023). A well-governed metaverse, characterized by transparent rules, community participation, and responsive management, fosters an environment conducive to sustained customer loyalty. Users are more likely to commit to a platform that values their input and ensures a fair and enjoyable experience. This governance dynamic contributes to the overall profitability of the metaverse by creating a positive user ecosystem.

Inspired by the insights from literature exploring customer retention, we propose a parallel notion within the metaverse context. Hence, the interplay between, loyalty and profitability, not only defines the financial sustainability of the virtual environment but also reinforces the importance of effective metaverse governance in achieving this sustainability. Thus, we propose

P3: The interplay between metaverse engagement, customer loyalty, guided by effective metaverse governance, is positively associated with sustainable profitability.

Economic Incentives, Customer Loyalty, and Sustainable Profitability

Economic incentives play a crucial role in shaping user behavior within the metaverse, influencing customer loyalty and, subsequently, the sustainable profitability of the virtual environment. Existing literature suggests that economic incentives, ranging from virtual currency to rewards and premium offerings, serve as motivators that directly impact customer engagement and loyalty (Gamma et al., 2021). Studies indicate that users enticed by economic incentives are more likely to participate in revenue-generating activities, such as virtual transactions and in-app purchases, contributing to increased customer loyalty. These economic motivators act as powerful tools in shaping user behavior and fostering a positive perception of the metaverse.

Furthermore, the chapter tries the moderating role of economic incentives in the relationship between customer loyalty and sustainable profitability. While economic incentives positively contribute to customer loyalty, their effectiveness as moderators is contingent on the overall metaverse environment. In instances where the metaverse lacks effective governance, clear rules, or a responsive community, the impact of economic incentives on sustaining customer loyalty may be hindered. Studies suggest that economic incentives alone are not sufficient; they need a supportive metaverse ecosystem to maximize their potential in fostering long-term customer commitment and, consequently, sustainable profitability.

Moreover, research delves into the potential drawbacks of overreliance on economic incentives within the metaverse (Hahn and Stavins, 1992). While these incentives can drive short-term engagement, an excessive focus on monetary rewards may lead to a transactional relationship between users and the virtual environment. This transactional nature, devoid of deeper emotional and social connections, may hinder the development of genuine customer loyalty. Therefore, the literature suggests a need for a balanced approach, wherein economic incentives complement a well-governed metaverse environment rather than acting as sole determinants of sustained customer commitment.

Inspired by these insights, we propose a parallel notion within the metaverse context. The effectiveness of economic incentives in shaping customer loyalty and, consequently, sustainable profitability is contingent on the metaverse's overall governance and community dynamics. Thus, we propose

P4: The relationship between customer loyalty, and sustainable profitability is moderated by the effectiveness of economic incentives, with a well-governed environment maximizing the impact of economic incentives on long-term user commitment and financial sustainability.

DISCUSSIONS AND INTERVENTIONS

Discussion of the Identified Antecedents Influencing Customer Retention in the Virtual Economy of Metaverse

Understanding the dynamics of customer retention within the Metaverse necessitates an in-depth examination of the antecedents and underlying factors that influence user engagement in this digital realm. These antecedents, informed by a range of scholarly perspectives, play a pivotal role in shaping the strategies and interventions designed to enhance customer retention in the Metaverse.

One of the central antecedents influencing customer retention is the concept of metaverse engagement. As elucidated by (Chen et al., 2022), active participation and engagement within the metaverse are essential drivers of customer retention. Metaverse engagement involves various dimensions such as social interaction, technological accessibility, and economic incentives, which collectively contribute to the perceived value of the virtual environment. Recognizing the importance of metaverse engagement underscores the need for interventions that stimulate user activity, foster social connections, ensure technological ease, and strategically employ economic incentives to enhance customer retention within the Metaverse.

Moreover, the Extended Self theory, as advanced by (Belk, 2013), remains relevant in understanding customer retention within the metaverse. Users extend their identities into the digital spaces of the Metaverse, and the preservation and enhancement of digital possessions and experiences become crucial aspects of customer retention strategies. Building upon this, interventions should focus on personalized customization, content creation, and collaborative experiences to resonate with users' extended selves, fostering a deeper sense of belonging and engagement in the metaverse.

Furthermore, the Network Effects Model, as articulated by (Shapiro and Varian, 1999), continues to play a significant role in customer retention strategies. Fostering a thriving user community within the Metaverse is crucial, as the value of the virtual environment is intrinsically linked to the number and engagement of its users. Interventions should prioritize the creation of an environment that encourages social interactions, collaborative activities, and network growth. By nurturing a vibrant user community, businesses and creators can exponentially increase the perceived value of the Metaverse, thereby enhancing customer retention.

Additionally, Behavioral Economics, as expounded by (Thaler and Sunstein, 2009), provides valuable insights into cognitive biases and irrational behaviors within the metaverse context. Understanding these biases informs interventions that leverage behavioral insights to nudge users toward choices that benefit both their extended selves and the digital economy. Aligning interventions with the psychological tendencies of metaverse users, businesses and creators can enhance customer retention through more effective design and communication strategies, ultimately contributing to the sustainability of the virtual economy.

In summation, the discussions and interventions related to customer retention in the Metaverse are deeply rooted in a comprehension of the antecedents that influence user behavior. The concepts of metaverse engagement, the extended self, network effects, and behavioral economics serve as foundational pillars upon which effective retention strategies are constructed. By embracing these antecedents and developing interventions that cater to the unique dynamics of the Metaverse, businesses and creators can cultivate enduring relationships with users, thus fortifying the virtual economy of this digital frontier.

Strategies for Enhancing Customer Retention in the Virtual Economy of Metaverse

Customer retention within the Metaverse is more than just a matter of keeping users engaged; it is the foundation upon which customer loyalty is built. In the ever-evolving digital landscape of the Metaverse, where users have a multitude of options at their fingertips, establishing and maintaining loyalty is the cornerstone of profitability (Visconti, R 2022). This section delves into strategies for enhancing customer retention in the Metaverse and underscores the vital connection between retention and loyalty, a linchpin for sustained profitability.

Another emerging strategy involves the gamification of metaverse platforms. By incorporating game-like elements, challenges, and rewards within the virtual environment, businesses can tap into users' intrinsic motivation for competition and achievement. Gamification not only adds an element of fun to the metaverse but also provides users with tangible goals and incentives, encouraging continued participation and loyalty.

Moreover, the strategic implementation of user-generated content (UGC) features can significantly enhance customer loyalty. Empowering users to contribute to the metaverse's content creation process fosters a sense of ownership and co-creation. Platforms that facilitate UGC not only diversify the content available but also strengthen the community aspect of the metaverse, encouraging users to remain actively involved and loyal to the platform.

This section delves into strategies for enhancing customer retention in the Metaverse and underscores the vital connection between retention and loyalty, a linchpin for sustained profitability.

Additionally, the introduction of real-time events and experiences within the metaverse can be a powerful strategy (Simpson, 2023). Hosting live events, virtual concerts, or exclusive product launches creates a sense of immediacy and exclusivity, driving user engagement and loyalty. By consistently offering time-sensitive and unique experiences, businesses can keep users excited and invested in the metaverse, thereby ensuring sustained customer loyalty. And following is a list of suggestions and things that can be done to enhance customer loyalty and retention.

Personalized Experiences: Tailoring experiences to individual preferences is a potent strategy for enhancing customer retention. By harnessing user data and insights, businesses and content creators can craft experiences that resonate with each user's unique tastes. When users feel that their needs and preferences are understood and catered to, they are more likely to remain engaged and return to the Metaverse, laying the foundation for long-term loyalty.

Community Building: Fostering a sense of community within the Metaverse is a powerful means of retaining customers. Encouraging users to connect, collaborate, and share their experiences with others creates a sense of belonging. Businesses and creators can facilitate this by organizing virtual events, forums, and social spaces, nurturing a loyal user base that values the connections they've made (Belk, 2013).

Incentivized Rewards and Benefits: Offering incentives and rewards for continued engagement is a powerful tool for customer retention. Incorporating gamification elements, loyalty programs, and digital currency rewards not only keeps users engaged but also motivates them to stay active and committed to the Metaverse, ultimately fostering long-term loyalty.

Content Quality and Innovation: Consistently delivering high-quality and innovative content is vital for retaining users. Keeping experiences fresh, exciting, and aligned with emerging trends in the Metaverse prevents user boredom and attrition. Users who find value in the content and see regular innovations are more likely to stay loyal to the platform.

User Education and Support: Providing user education and support resources can significantly enhance retention. Guiding users in navigating the intricacies of the Metaverse and offering responsive customer support helps address issues promptly. Users who feel well-informed and supported are more likely to stay engaged and develop loyalty (Gadekallu, T. R 2022).

Communication and Feedback Loop: Maintaining open channels of communication with users and actively seeking feedback is essential. User insights can guide improvements and adjustments, demonstrating a commitment to meeting user needs. When people feel that their opinions are acknowledged, they are more inclined to stay committed and loyal. (Thaler and Sunstein, 2009).

The intrinsic link between customer retention and loyalty in the Metaverse is a key driver of profitability. Retained users who continue to engage, transact, and collaborate within the virtual economy are more likely to develop a sense of loyalty. This loyalty, characterized by repeated interactions, trust, and a sense of belonging, becomes the cornerstone of profitability. Loyal users are not only more inclined to make regular transactions but also to advocate for and defend the Metaverse, driving its growth and success.

In addition to the established strategies discussed earlier, new and innovative approaches can further bolster customer loyalty, contributing to sustainable profitability within the metaverse. One key strategy involves the implementation of dynamic and immersive storytelling within the metaverse environment (Karapakdee and Wannapiroon, 2021). By crafting compelling narratives that unfold seamlessly within the virtual realm, businesses can create a more engaging and memorable user experience. Storytelling not only enhances the entertainment value but also forms an emotional connection with users, fostering a sense of attachment and loyalty.

LIMITATIONS AND FUTURE RESEARCH PERSPECTIVE

While this conceptual chapter provides valuable insights into the interplay between metaverse engagement, economic incentives, customer loyalty, and sustainable profitability, it is crucial to acknowledge certain limitations in the current framework. Firstly, the proposed model is based on existing literature and conceptual reasoning, lacking empirical validation. The absence of empirical data restricts the ability to make definitive claims about the causal relationships and moderating effects outlined in the framework. Future research endeavors should focus on empirical investigations to test and refine the proposed relationships, providing a more robust foundation for understanding the dynamics within the metaverse's virtual economy.

Secondly, the conceptual framework assumes a certain level of homogeneity in user behaviors and preferences within the metaverse. However, the metaverse user base is diverse, comprising individuals with varied backgrounds, motivations, and expectations. Future research should delve into segmenting and understanding these diverse user groups to uncover nuanced patterns of metaverse engagement, economic incentive responsiveness, and loyalty. Empirical studies exploring user demographics, psychographics, and behavioral patterns can contribute to a more nuanced understanding of the proposed relationships.

Furthermore, the proposed model primarily focuses on economic incentives as a moderating variable, acknowledging its impact on customer loyalty within the metaverse. However, future research could explore additional moderating variables that may influence the pathways between metaverse engagement, customer loyalty, and sustainable profitability. Factors such as technological advancements, evolving user preferences, and changes in the competitive landscape could serve as dynamic moderators shaping the metaverse's economic dynamics. Empirical studies that consider these factors can enhance the model's applicability and relevance in dynamic virtual environments.

Finally, the conceptual framework presented here is based on the current state of knowledge and technological advancements to the time of publication. The metaverse is a rapidly evolving concept, and its landscape may undergo substantial changes in the future. Future research should thus remain attentive to emerging technologies, evolving user behaviors, and shifts in the metaverse ecosystem to ensure the continued relevance and applicability of the proposed framework. Empirical studies tracking the metaverse's evolution over time can provide valuable insights into the sustainability of profitability in virtual economies.

Whether or not the framework is effective in the context of other online platforms is debatable. Future research may assess this by conducting a comparative analysis utilizing a heterogeneous sample comprising individuals from various generations. In our study, economic incentives were employed as a moderator; however, it is important to note that additional factors, including gender, age groups, expertise, and willingness of use, also influenced the results (Teng et al., 2022). And rewards, trust, cultural differences, privacy concerns and psychological traits, may have moderating effect on outcome variables would be suggestions from our perspective. Empirical evidence regarding metaverse profiling in terms of customer loyalty is still scarce as a lot of studies are based on marketing the platform and few on retaining them. Hence, there is a need to study for customer retention for sustainable growth and profitability.

CONCLUSION

In conclusion, strategies for enhancing customer retention in the Metaverse must be designed with a long-term perspective, emphasizing the cultivation of customer loyalty. By providing personalized experiences, fostering a sense of community, offering incentives, consistently delivering quality content, providing support, preserving digital value, and maintaining open communication, businesses and creators can establish enduring relationships with users, thereby ensuring the sustainability and profitability of the virtual economy in the Metaverse.

In this exploration of the Metaverse and customer retention, we've embarked on a journey to understand the intricate dynamics of this digital realm. From the inception, where This chapter uncovered the emergence of the Metaverse as a transformative force, to the significance it holds within the virtual economy, the groundwork was laid. It became evident that the Metaverse is not merely a technological construct but a complex landscape that touches upon economic transformation, digital ownership, innovation, and societal ethics.

At the heart of it all, this chapter uncovers the critical link between customer retention and loyalty. As retained users continue to engage and interact within the

Metaverse, they are more likely to develop a profound sense of loyalty. This loyalty, marked by trust, commitment, and a sense of belonging, emerges as the linchpin of profitability within the Metaverse's virtual economy. Loyal users are not only valuable in terms of their regular transactions, but they also act as advocates and defenders of the Metaverse, driving its growth and success. As the Metaverse continues to evolve, it offers boundless potential, but also raises significant questions. The journey of unraveling its retention secrets is an ongoing one, reflecting the dynamic nature of the digital frontier. With the knowledge and insights gained here, stakeholders are well-equipped to navigate this ever-evolving terrain, building a sustainable and profitable future within the Metaverse.

Competing Interests

The authors of this publication declare there are no competing interests.

Funding

This research received no specific grant from any funding agency in the public, commercial, or not-for-profit sectors. Funding for this research was covered by the authors of the article.

REFERENCES

Aburbeian, A. M., Owda, A. Y., & Owda, M. (2022). A technology acceptance model survey of the metaverse prospects. *AI, 3*(2), 285–302. doi:10.3390/ai3020018

Adams, D. (2022). Virtual retail in the metaverse: Customer behavior analytics, extended reality technologies, and immersive visualization systems. *Linguistic and Philosophical Investigations*, (21), 73–88.

Agustini, K., Putrama, I. M., Wahyuni, D. S., & Mertayasa, I. N. E. (2023). Applying gamification technique and virtual reality for prehistoric learning toward the metaverse. *International Journal of Information and Education Technology (IJIET), 13*(2), 247–256. doi:10.18178/ijiet.2023.13.2.1802

Allal-Chérif, O. (2022). Intelligent cathedrals: Using augmented reality, virtual reality, and artificial intelligence to provide an intense cultural, historical, and religious visitor experience. *Technological Forecasting and Social Change, 178*, 121604. doi:10.1016/j.techfore.2022.121604

Allam, Z., Sharifi, A., Bibri, S. E., Jones, D. S., & Krogstie, J. (2022). The metaverse as a virtual form of smart cities: Opportunities and challenges for environmental, economic, and social sustainability in urban futures. *Smart Cities*, *5*(3), 771–801. doi:10.3390/smartcities5030040

Almusaed, A., Yitmen, I., & Almssad, A. (2023). Reviewing and integrating aec practices into industry 6.0: Strategies for smart and sustainable future-built environments. *Sustainability (Basel)*, *15*(18), 13464. doi:10.3390/su151813464

Anshari, M., Syafrudin, M., Fitriyani, N. L., & Razzaq, A. (2022). Ethical Responsibility and Sustainability (ERS) Development in a Metaverse Business Model. *Sustainability (Basel)*, *14*(23), 15805. doi:10.3390/su142315805

Ante, L., Wazinski, F. P., & Saggu, A. (2023). Digital real estate in the metaverse: An empirical analysis of retail investor motivations. *Finance Research Letters*, *58*, 104299. doi:10.1016/j.frl.2023.104299

Arntsen, R. (2023). *The Future People's Sense of Belonging in The City* (Doctoral dissertation, The Savannah College of Art and Design).

Arslan, I. K. (2020). The importance of creating customer loyalty in achieving sustainable competitive advantage. *Eurasian Journal of Business and Management*, *8*(1), 11–20. doi:10.15604/ejbm.2020.08.01.002

Aydoğan, S. (2023). Connecting Sustainable Development Goals To Airport Sustainability Practices. *The Sdgs And Entrepreneurship*, 282.

Bandyopadhyay, A., Sarkar, A., Swain, S., Banik, D., Hassanien, A. E., Mallik, S., Li, A., & Qin, H. (2023). A Game-Theoretic Approach for Rendering Immersive Experiences in the Metaverse. *Mathematics*, *11*(6), 1286. doi:10.3390/math11061286

Belk, R. (2023). The digital frontier as a liminal space. *Journal of Consumer Psychology*.

Belk, R. W. (2013). Extended self in a digital world. *The Journal of Consumer Research*, *40*(3), 477–500. doi:10.1086/671052

Biocca, F., Harms, C., & Burgoon, J. K. (2003). Toward a more robust theory and measure of social presence: Review and suggested criteria. *Presence (Cambridge, Mass.)*, *12*(5), 456–480. doi:10.1162/105474603322761270

Biocca, F., & Levy, M. R. (1995). Virtual reality as a communication system. *Communication in the age of virtual reality*, 15-31.

Chen, Y., & Cheng, H. (2022). The economics of the metaverse: A comparison with the real economy. *Metaverse*, *3*(1), 19. doi:10.54517/met.v3i1.1802

ChenY.LinW.ZhengY.XueT.ChenC.ChenG. (2022). Application of active learning strategies in metaverse to improve student engagement: An immersive blended pedagogy bridging patient care and scientific inquiry in pandemic. Available at SSRN 4098179. doi:10.2139/ssrn.4098179

Chen, Z., Wu, J., Gan, W., & Qi, Z. (2022, December). Metaverse security and privacy: An overview. In *2022 IEEE International Conference on Big Data (Big Data)* (pp. 2950-2959). IEEE.

Csikszentmihalyi, M., and Csikszentmihalyi, M. (2014). Toward a psychology of optimal experience. *Flow and the foundations of positive psychology: The collected works of Mihaly Csikszentmihalyi*, 209-226.

Dinh, T. L. H. (2023). *Customer behaviors toward Metaverse/Metaverse as a stimulus for customer experience: implications for Marketing*. Research Gate.

Dionisio, J. D. N., Iii, W. G. B., & Gilbert, R. (2013). 3D virtual worlds and the metaverse: Current status and future possibilities. *ACM Computing Surveys*, *45*(3), 1–38. doi:10.1145/2480741.2480751

Dwivedi, Y. K., Hughes, L., Wang, Y., Alalwan, A. A., Ahn, S. J., Balakrishnan, J., Barta, S., Belk, R., Buhalis, D., Dutot, V., Felix, R., Filieri, R., Flavián, C., Gustafsson, A., Hinsch, C., Hollensen, S., Jain, V., Kim, J., Krishen, A. S., & Wirtz, J. (2023). Metaverse marketing: How the metaverse will shape the future of consumer research and practice. *Psychology and Marketing*, *40*(4), 750–776. doi:10.1002/mar.21767

Dwivedi, Y. K., Hughes, L., Wang, Y., Alalwan, A. A., Ahn, S. J., Balakrishnan, J., Barta, S., Belk, R., Buhalis, D., Dutot, V., Felix, R., Filieri, R., Flavián, C., Gustafsson, A., Hinsch, C., Hollensen, S., Jain, V., Kim, J., Krishen, A. S., & Wirtz, J. (2023). Metaverse marketing: How the metaverse will shape the future of consumer research and practice. *Psychology and Marketing*, *40*(4), 750–776. doi:10.1002/mar.21767

Ertemel, A. V., Civelek, M. E., Eroğlu Pektaş, G. Ö., & Çemberci, M. (2021). The role of customer experience in the effect of online flow state on customer loyalty. *PLoS One*, *16*(7), e0254685. doi:10.1371/journal.pone.0254685 PMID:34264997

Filipova, I. A. (2023). Creating the Metaverse: Consequences for Economy, Society, and Law. *Journal of Digital Technologies and Law*, *1*(1), 7–32. doi:10.21202/jdtl.2023.1

Gadekallu, T. R., Huynh-The, T., Wang, W., Yenduri, G., Ranaweera, P., Pham, Q. V., & Liyanage, M. (2022). Blockchain for the metaverse: A review. arXiv preprint arXiv:2203.09738.

Gamma, K., Mai, R., Cometta, C., & Loock, M. (2021). Engaging customers in demand response programs: The role of reward and punishment in customer adoption in Switzerland. *Energy Research & Social Science, 74,* 101927. doi:10.1016/j.erss.2021.101927

George, A. H., Fernando, M., George, A. S., Baskar, T., & Pandey, D. (2021). Metaverse: The next stage of human culture and the internet. [IJARTET]. *International Journal of Advanced Research Trends in Engineering and Technology, 8*(12), 1–10.

Glimmerveen, L., Ybema, S., & Nies, H. (2020). Engaged yet excluded: The processual, dispersed, and political dynamics of boundary work. *Human Relations, 73*(11), 1504-1536.

Golf-Papez, M., Heller, J., Hilken, T., Chylinski, M., de Ruyter, K., Keeling, D. I., & Mahr, D. (2022). Embracing falsity through the metaverse: The case of synthetic customer experiences. *Business Horizons, 65*(6), 739–749. doi:10.1016/j.bushor.2022.07.007

Grewal, D., Levy, M., & Kumar, V. (2009). Customer experience management in retailing: An organizing framework. *Journal of Retailing, 85*(1), 1–14. doi:10.1016/j.jretai.2009.01.001

Gunawan, I. (2022). CUSTOMER LOYALTY: The Effect Customer Satisfaction, Experiential Marketing and Product Quality. *KINERJA: Jurnal Manajemen Organisasi dan Industri, 1*(1), 35-50.

Hahn, R. W., & Stavins, R. N. (1992). Economic incentives for environmental protection: Integrating theory and practice. *The American Economic Review, 82*(2), 464–468.

Han, D. I. D., Bergs, Y., & Moorhouse, N. (2022). Virtual reality consumer experience escapes: Preparing for the metaverse. *Virtual Reality (Waltham Cross), 26*(4), 1443–1458. doi:10.1007/s10055-022-00641-7

Harmeling, C. M., Moffett, J. W., Arnold, M. J., & Carlson, B. D. (2017). Toward a theory of customer engagement marketing. *Journal of the Academy of Marketing Science, 45*(3), 312–335. doi:10.1007/s11747-016-0509-2

Hartson, R., & Pyla, P. S. (2012). *The UX Book: Process and guidelines for ensuring a quality user experience.* Elsevier.

Hennig-Thurau, T., Aliman, D. N., Herting, A. M., Cziehso, G. P., Linder, M., & Kübler, R. V. (2023). Social interactions in the metaverse: Framework, initial evidence, and research roadmap. *Journal of the Academy of Marketing Science, 51*(4), 889–913. doi:10.1007/s11747-022-00908-0

Hespanhol, L., & Dalsgaard, P. (2015). Social interaction design patterns for urban media architecture. In Human-Computer Interaction. Springer.

Hudson, J. (2022). Virtual immersive shopping experiences in metaverse environments: Predictive customer analytics, data visualization algorithms, and smart retailing technologies. *Linguistic and Philosophical Investigations*, (21), 236–251.

Innis, D. E., & La Londe, B. J. (1994). Customer service: The key to customer satisfaction, customer loyalty, and market share. *Journal of Business Logistics, 15*(1), 1.

Jansson, J., Marell, A., & Nordlund, A. (2011). Exploring consumer adoption of a high involvement eco-innovation using value-belief-norm theory. *Journal of Consumer Behaviour, 10*(1), 51–60. doi:10.1002/cb.346

Jo, H. (2023). Tourism in the digital frontier: A study on user continuance intention in the metaverse. *Information Technology & Tourism, 25*(3), 307–330. doi:10.1007/s40558-023-00257-w

Jung, S. H., & Jeon, I. O. (2022). A study on the components of the Metaverse ecosystem. *Journal of Digital Convergence, 20*(2).

Knox, J. (2022). The metaverse, or the serious business of tech frontiers. *Postdigital Science and Education, 4*(2), 207–215. doi:10.1007/s42438-022-00300-9

Koohang, A., Nord, J., Ooi, K., Tan, G., Al-Emran, M., Aw, E., & Wong, L. (2023). Shaping the metaverse into reality: Multidisciplinary perspectives on opportunities, challenges, and future research. *Journal of Computer Information Systems*. doi:10.1080/08874417.2023.2165197

Kop, M. (2022). Abundance and Equality. *Frontiers in Research Metrics and Analytics, 7*, 977684. doi:10.3389/frma.2022.977684 PMID:36531753

Kraus, S., Kanbach, D. K., Krysta, P. M., Steinhoff, M. M., & Tomini, N. (2022). Facebook and the creation of the metaverse: Radical business model innovation or incremental transformation? *International Journal of Entrepreneurial Behaviour & Research, 28*(9), 52–77. doi:10.1108/IJEBR-12-2021-0984

Lacity, M., Mullins, J. K., & Kuai, L. (2022). What type of metaverse will we create. (BCoE Whitepaper) University of Arkansas.

Lee, C., Kogler, D. F., & Lee, D. (2019). Capturing information on technology convergence, international collaboration, and knowledge flow from patent documents: A case of information and communication technology. *Information Processing & Management, 56*(4), 1576–1591. doi:10.1016/j.ipm.2018.09.007

Lee, H. J., & Gu, H. H. (2022). Empirical Research on the Metaverse User Experience of Digital Natives. *Sustainability (Basel), 14*(22), 14747. doi:10.3390/su142214747

Lee, J. Y. (2021). A study on metaverse hype for sustainable growth. *International journal of advanced smart convergence, 10*(3), 72-80.

Ma, Z. (2023). Energy metaverse: The conceptual framework with a review of the state-of-the-art methods and technologies. *Energy Informatics, 6*(1), 42. doi:10.1186/s42162-023-00297-w

Maksymyuk, T., Gazda, J., Bugár, G., Gazda, V., Liyanage, M., & Dohler, M. (2022). Blockchain-empowered service management for the decentralized metaverse of things. *IEEE Access : Practical Innovations, Open Solutions, 10*, 99025–99037. doi:10.1109/ACCESS.2022.3205739

Maloney, D. (2021). *A youthful metaverse: Towards designing safe, equitable, and emotionally fulfilling social virtual reality spaces for younger users.*

Martínez-Peláez, R., Ochoa-Brust, A., Rivera, S., Félix, V. G., Ostos, R., Brito, H., Félix, R. A., & Mena, L. J. (2023). Role of digital transformation for achieving sustainability: Mediated role of stakeholders, key capabilities, and technology. *Sustainability (Basel), 15*(14), 11221. doi:10.3390/su151411221

Mittal, G., & Bansal, R. (2023). Driving Force Behind Consumer Brand Engagement: The Metaverse. In Cultural Marketing and Metaverse for Consumer Engagement (pp. 164-181). IGI Global.

Mogaji, E., Wirtz, J., Belk, R. W., & Dwivedi, Y. K. (2023). Immersive time (ImT): Conceptualizing time spent in the metaverse. *International Journal of Information Management, 72*, 102659. doi:10.1016/j.ijinfomgt.2023.102659

Nagendran, A., Compton, S., Follette, W. C., Golenchenko, A., Compton, A., & Grizou, J. (2022). Avatar led interventions in the Metaverse reveal that interpersonal effectiveness can be measured, predicted, and improved. *Scientific Reports, 12*(1), 21892. doi:10.1038/s41598-022-26326-4 PMID:36535981

Nakamoto, S. (2008). Bitcoin: A peer-to-peer electronic cash system.

Ning, H., Wang, H., Lin, Y., Wang, W., Dhelim, S., Farha, F., & Daneshmand, M. (2023). A Survey on the Metaverse: The State-of-the-Art, Technologies, Applications, and Challenges. *IEEE Internet of Things Journal.*

Njoku, J. N., Nwakanma, C. I., Amaizu, G. C., & Kim, D. S. (2023). Prospects and challenges of Metaverse application in data-driven intelligent transportation systems. *IET Intelligent Transport Systems, 17*(1), 1–21. doi:10.1049/itr2.12252

Pacifico, A., Giraldi, L., & Cedrola, E. (2023). Student Performance in E-learning Systems: An Empirical Study.

Papa, A. M. (2022). The Metaverse, at the crossroads of creating a new world and ambiguous predictions-analysis of trends, features and impacts on consumers and businesses. [JRISS]. *Journal of Research & Innovation for Sustainable Society, 4*(2).

Patel, N. (2018). *The benefits and importance of customer satisfaction.* neilpatel.com.

Rane, N., Choudhary, S., & Rane, J. (2023). Metaverse for Enhancing Customer Loyalty: Effective Strategies to Improve Customer Relationship, Service, Engagement, Satisfaction, and Experience. *Service, Engagement, Satisfaction, and Experience.*

Rathore, B. (2019). From Trendy to Green: Exploring AI's Role in Sustainable Fashion Marketing. *International Journal of New Media Studies: International Peer Reviewed Scholarly Indexed Journal, 6*(2), 12–22. doi:10.58972/eiprmj.v6i2y19.120

Salvioni, D. M., & Almici, A. (2020). Transitioning toward a circular economy: The impact of stakeholder engagement on sustainability culture. *Sustainability (Basel), 12*(20), 8641. doi:10.3390/su12208641

SchmittM. (2023). Big Data Analytics in the Metaverse: Business Value Creation with Artificial Intelligence and Data-Driven Decision Making. Available at SSRN 4385347. doi:10.2139/ssrn.4385347

Shapiro, C., & Varian, H. R. (1999). *Information rules: A strategic guide to the network economy.* Harvard Business Press.

Sia, C. C. (2023). The Role of Legal Governance Framework in the Metaverse World. In *Strategies and Opportunities for Technology in the Metaverse World* (pp. 321–330). IGI Global. doi:10.4018/978-1-6684-5732-0.ch017

Strutt, D. (2022). A Simple Tool for Remote Real-Time Dance Interaction in Virtual Spaces, Or "Dancing in the Metaverse". *Critical Stages/Scènes critiques, 25.*

Suh, A., Cheung, C. M., & Lin, Y. Q. (2019, July). Revisiting User Engagement: Concepts, Themes, and Opportunities. In PACIS (p. 150).

Tayal, S., Rajagopal, K., & Mahajan, V. (2022, March). Virtual reality based metaverse of gamification. In *2022 6th International Conference on Computing Methodologies and Communication (ICCMC)* (pp. 1597-1604). IEEE. 10.1109/ICCMC53470.2022.9753727

Teng, Z., Cai, Y., Gao, Y., Zhang, X., & Li, X. (2022). Factors affecting learners' adoption of an educational metaverse platform: An empirical study based on an extended UTAUT model. *Mobile Information Systems*, *2022*, 2022. doi:10.1155/2022/5479215

Thaler, R. H., & Sunstein, C. R. (2009). *Nudge: Improving decisions about health, wealth, and happiness.* Penguin.

Tractinsky, N., Katz, A. S., & Ikar, D. (2000). What is beautiful is usable. *Interacting with Computers*, *13*(2), 127–145. doi:10.1016/S0953-5438(00)00031-X

Upadhyay, U., Kumar, A., Sharma, G., Gupta, B. B., Alhalabi, W. A., Arya, V., & Chui, K. T. (2023). Cyberbullying in the Metaverse: A Prescriptive Perception on Global Information Systems for User Protection. [JGIM]. *Journal of Global Information Management*, *31*(1), 1–25. doi:10.4018/JGIM.325793

Vadakkepatt, G. G., Winterich, K. P., Mittal, V., Zinn, W., Beitelspacher, L., Aloysius, J., Ginger, J., & Reilman, J. (2021). Sustainable retailing. *Journal of Retailing*, *97*(1), 62–80. doi:10.1016/j.jretai.2020.10.008

Valaskova, K., Machova, V., & Lewis, E. (2022). Virtual Marketplace Dynamics Data, Spatial Analytics, and Customer Engagement Tools in a Real-Time Interoperable Decentralized Metaverse. *Linguistic and Philosophical Investigations*, *21*(0), 105–120. doi:10.22381/lpi2120227

Van Doorn, J., Lemon, K. N., Mittal, V., Nass, S., Pick, D., Pirner, P., & Verhoef, P. C. (2010). Customer engagement behavior: Theoretical foundations and research directions. *Journal of Service Research*, *13*(3), 253–266. doi:10.1177/1094670510375599

Verhoef, P. C., Broekhuizen, T., Bart, Y., Bhattacharya, A., Dong, J. Q., Fabian, N., & Haenlein, M. (2021). Digital transformation: A multidisciplinary reflection and research agenda. *Journal of Business Research*, *122*, 889–901. doi:10.1016/j.jbusres.2019.09.022

Visconti, R. M. (2022). From physical reality to the Metaverse: A Multilayer Network Valuation. *Journal of Metaverse*, *2*(1), 16–22.

Wang, D., Fu, H., & Fang, S. (2019). The relationship between relational quality and megaproject success: The moderating role of incentives. *Engineering Management Journal*, *31*(4), 257–269. doi:10.1080/10429247.2019.1624099

Wang, Y., Su, Z., Zhang, N., Xing, R., Liu, D., Luan, T. H., & Shen, X. (2022). A survey on metaverse: Fundamentals, security, and privacy. *IEEE Communications Surveys and Tutorials*.

Wigfield, A. (1994). Expectancy-value theory of achievement motivation: A developmental perspective. *Educational Psychology Review*, *6*(1), 49–78. doi:10.1007/BF02209024

Yawised, K., Apasrawirote, D., & Boonparn, C. (2022). From traditional business shifted towards transformation: The emerging business opportunities and challenges in 'Metaverse' era. *Incbaa*, *2022*, 162–175.

Zallio, M., & Clarkson, P. J. (2022). Designing the metaverse: A study on inclusion, diversity, equity, accessibility and safety for digital immersive environments. *Telematics and Informatics*, *75*, 101909. doi:10.1016/j.tele.2022.101909

Zhang, X., Chen, Y., Hu, L., & Wang, Y. (2022). The metaverse in education: Definition, framework, features, potential applications, challenges, and future research topics. *Frontiers in Psychology*, *13*, 6063. doi:10.3389/fpsyg.2022.1016300 PMID:36304866

Zhao, Y., Jiang, J., Chen, Y., Liu, R., Yang, Y., Xue, X., & Chen, S. (2022). Metaverse: Perspectives from graphics, interactions and visualization. *Visual Informatics*, *6*(1), 56–67. doi:10.1016/j.visinf.2022.03.002

ADDITIONAL READING

Bokadia, H., Rai, R., & Torres, E. B. (2020). Digitized ADOS: Social interactions beyond the limits of the naked eye. *Journal of Personalized Medicine*, *10*(4), 159. doi:10.3390/jpm10040159 PMID:33050080

Karapakdee, J., & Wannapiroon, P. (2021). Immersive Digital Storytelling Learning Experience with a Metaverse Gamification Game Platform to Enhance Game Developer Competency. *Environment*, *5*, 10.

Mystakidis, S. (2022). Metaverse. *Metaverse. Encyclopedia*, *2*(1), 486–497. doi:10.3390/encyclopedia2010031

Oh, H. J., Kim, J., Chang, J. J., Park, N., & Lee, S. (2023). Social benefits of living in the metaverse: The relationships among social presence, supportive interaction, social self-efficacy, and feelings of loneliness. *Computers in Human Behavior, 139*, 107498. doi:10.1016/j.chb.2022.107498

Simpson, J. (2023). Hello World: Liveness in Virtual Theatre for the Metaverse. In *XR-Metaverse Cases: Business Application of AR, VR, XR and Metaverse* (pp. 55–65). Springer International Publishing. doi:10.1007/978-3-031-30566-5_6

Verma, J. K., & Paul, S. (Eds.). (2022). *Advances in Augmented Reality and Virtual Reality*. Springer. doi:10.1007/978-981-16-7220-0

Chapter 3
Responsible AI:
Governance and Ethics in Metaverse

Prathmesh Singh
Pennsylvania Western University, USA

Arnav Upadhyaya
Monta Vista High School, USA

Nripendra Singh
ⓘ https://orcid.org/0000-0001-5775-8013
Pennsylvania Western University, USA

ABSTRACT

Metaverse uses artificial intelligence and machine learning along with augmented reality to create immersive digital experiences where users can interact with other users and computer-generated environments. This creates new ways for people to connect, collaborate, experience digital content, and opens up exciting new possibilities. It also creates interesting questions on the responsible use of AI. This chapter will explore what mechanisms and frameworks should be evaluated for responsible AI- which allows humanity to enjoy the benefits of AI on augmented reality platforms like metaverse.

INTRODUCTION

ChatGPT from OpenAI, an artificial intelligence firm bought AI and ML to limelight in 2023, but AI/ML has been with us for some time and has led to innovations like autonomous driving, robots which can do specific specialized tasks and has also benefited industries like healthcare where AI is used for better patient diagnosis.

DOI: 10.4018/979-8-3693-3358-7.ch003

At the same time the misuse of AI is also on the rise: use of deepfake technology to create false audio/video recordings for celebrities and use of AI to automate creation of malicious security threats to organizations for stealing sensitive data or for cyberterrorism.

Metaverse uses Augmented reality and machine learning to create immersive digital experiences where users can interact with other users and computer-generated environments. While this creates new ways for people to connect, collaborate, and experience digital content it also creates interesting questions on responsible use of AI. This chapter will explore what mechanisms should be evaluated for responsible AI- which allows humanity to enjoy the benefits of AI responsibly.

The Limitless Possibilities With Metaverse

Metaverse has the potential to redefine the fields of education, gaming, office experiences and health. Virtual classrooms with augmented reality can provide real class-like experiences while allowing teachers and students across the globe to connect. This can alleviate shortage of teachers and provide wider reach to economically disadvantaged students. Metaverse will redefine the gaming experience by augmenting it with virtual and augmented reality. The impact of Metaverse on health care can be transformational. Virtual medical consultations could redefine how doctors interact with patients and make healthcare more affordable. Remote Monitoring and Telemedicine will allow healthcare providers to track vital signs and provide timely interventions. Virtual metaverse environments can help facilitate remote clinical research with a diverse set of participants at a fraction of today's cost. Let us not forget the positive environmental impact that Metaverse can have on the planet. Visual and immersive interactions can drastically reduce the need for physical travel and resources. This will result in reduced carbon emission and a greener planet. These possibilities allow new economic and job opportunities in Metaverse. However, if there are no safeguards around the digital interactions it can result in unfavorable consequences such as discrimination, theft of intellectual property, misinformation and misuse of private data.

Dangers of Metaverse

As noted above Metaverse can have huge benefits to society but also brings its own set of challenges with its widespread adoption and use of customer data. Some of the dangers of metaverse include the following:

- **Data Privacy issues**: Metaverse has access to user profiles, their interactions in form of text, calls and other interactive conversations. Some metaverse experiences also use biometric data such as facial recognition or fingerprints. Also, Metaverse applications can build a deep understanding of user behavior and interaction to offer targeted services to the user. This information is presented in the wrong hands can have disastrous consequences.

- **Misinformation and social engineering**: Just like in the real world, Metaverse can be used by malicious individuals to spread misinformation for their advantage or further causes that they believe in. Fake avatars and identities created in metaverse can make it harder to verify authenticity of information shared. A combination of manipulated content delivered by a fake identity makes it harder to resist misinformation. Malicious content creators can leverage the deep user insights that they have to create information bubbles for users that align with their existing beliefs but promote misinformation. All the deep insights about the user can also be used to trick users into disclosing confidential information that can be used against them, gain access to confidential data or perform harmful actions against an individual or a group.
- **Addiction:** Immersive life experiences can lead to a user spending most of their time in the metaverse and participating in experiences that meet their approval. This over the long term can result in shunning real world experiences and having a diminished ability to deal with conflict. This can also result in diminished attention span with a reduced ability to learn and process new information.
- **Social Isolation:** Spending excessive time in the digital world can result in feeling of being disconnected from the real world. Real world interactions can suffer which can result in feelings of isolation and depressions.
- **Digital inequality:** There is inequality in access, skillset and participation in the metaverse which can further broaden the digital divide and deepen social inequality. Not everyone has access to the latest and greatest technology such as Augmented reality headsets, the latest in computers which can have an impact on their ability to participate in the metaverse ecosystem. This can over the long run have an impact on literacy and economic opportunities.
- **Harassment:** If unchecked or without any oversight mechanisms, Metaverse can become a breeding ground for activities like cyberbullying, sexual harassment in the form of explicit content and unwelcome advances. Discriminatory and hate speech can also be used to harass specific individuals or groups.

Some real-life examples to showcase the negative issues with Metaverse are necessary to be discussed in this section.

- **Sexual Harassment:** MIT technology review in December 2021 edition (Basu, 2022) published an article which details an unfortunate incident of sexual harassment with a female who was participating in Horizon worlds, a social media platform in Metaverse. A beta tester reported that her avatar was groped by some strangers. Although the platform has safeguards, they could not be used to safeguard against this incident. Per a Forbes article (Marr, 2024) a young girl under the age of 16 was sexually attacked by adult men in the metaverse. The UK police are investigating it now. The article goes on to suggest that the integration of wearable technology and haptic suits can further blur the line of virtual vs reality by allowing the user to mimic and experience real life sensations.

- **Exposure to bigotry and harassment:** Parents worry about the negative exposure that their kids can get from social media platforms like Horizon world in Metaverse. Per an article in Washington Post "Zach Mathison, 28, sometimes worries about the hostility in Meta's virtual reality-powered social media game Horizon Worlds. When his 7-year-old son, Mason, explores the app he encounters users, often other children, screaming obscenities or racist slurs."

The above examples illustrate that AI powered tools, if used by the wrong people can have negative impact on society and individuals.

Next, we would like to present some newer and more recent issues related to AI and Metaverse to help readers and policy makers to understand the urgency needed to promote and implement responsible use of AI.

Deepfakes: Per arXiv:2303.14612v2 (Tariq, Abuadbba & Moore, 2023) "Deepfakes are computer-generated images or videos that can be manipulated to look like real people or events. The ability to generate such content has significantly increased with advances in machine learning and artificial intelligence". Deepfakes started way back in the 1990s with technologies like face swapping. Now with AI tools readily available, adversaries can use Encoder or Deep Neural Network (DNN) technology to create a face swap, which is real and convincing. Per an article published by dhs.gov, harmful uses of deepfakes can vary from

- Deep fake pornography, where Face swap technology was used to put actors Kristin Bell and Scarlett Johansson in several pornographic videos.
- Lip Syncing which involves "mapping voice recording from one or multiple contexts to a video recording in another, to make the subject of the video appear to say something authentic.

A new tool, AI Dungeon that rely on OpenAI's GPT-3 (an auto-regressive language model) has a number of different capabilities such as natural language generation, text-to image generation, translation, and other text-based tools. As per Simonite (2021), AI Dungeon generated text that depicted sexual exploitation of children. Though, the synthetically generated text used in AI Dungeon was based on user input and vast training data, this example demonstrates that there are very limited constraints on the unintended consequences of AI-based content generation. Deepfakes, if left unchecked, can become powerful adversarial tools in the Metaverse to harass people and create fake identities for the purpose of espionage and stealing of information, intellectual property etc.

Regulation: There is an increasing risk of technological advances in AI/ML outpacing regulatory frameworks. This will present complex challenges for jurisdiction, property rights and legal rights in a virtual world. Data from Deloitte's 2023 Digital Media Trends survey shows that digital "places" are a very real part of users' lives. Around one-third of US respondents consider online experiences to be meaningful replacements for in-person experiences, and half of all Gen Zs and millennials surveyed agree. Among these younger generations, 48% agree that they spend more time interacting with others on social media than in the physical world, and 40% say they socialize more in video games.

In the metaverse, millions of users interact virtually which amplifies the challenges of moderation, behavior, harassment, and misinformation. It raises some interesting questions: Is speech from a virtual character in metaverse the same as posting content? Who is the owner of the content and who is responsible? Does the avatar enjoy the same freedom of speech as an individual in the physical world? Who defines the rules? Is it defined by the authorities of the location of the user, application or location of the creator of the game?

These are not easy problems to solve and require a thoughtful and nimble approach which can be adapted as technologies evolve and we learn and adapt. These rules will have to be universally accepted and enforceable which makes this a much harder problem. In absence of clear regulations, bad actors can use powerful AI/ML tools in metaverse and not be accountable for their bad deeds.

Identity: Metaverse allows one to create an identity which is very different from who they are in real life and explore interests that might be hard to do in real life. This can be very liberating and allow one to experiment and experience events which can enrich the soul and the mind, but this also creates interesting identity challenges. The risk of identity theft, unauthorized access, and impersonation is a real threat.

We all know about the dark web, which is an underground online realm not discoverable through traditional search engines, known for its anonymity and often associated with criminal activities, such as the sale of stolen data and illegal goods. Now imagine the dark verse, where cyber criminals use automated bots and AI tools to lure unsuspecting victims to steal information or credit card information. There is a well-established network to steal data, value data and auction data. Per SEAD FADILPAŠIĆ in an article published at makeuseof.com Cybercriminals have adapted to metaverse to sell all types of stolen data to the highest bidders in bustling data marketplaces. First on the list is personal data, which can include your name, address, phone number, and much more. Identity theft is popular in the metaverse, as bad actors can assume your online persona for profits or other reasons.

Financial data is another popular commodity. Credit card details, bank account information, and digital wallets are highly sought after: cybercriminals can use this data for unauthorized transactions, draining victims' accounts in the blink of an eye. Access credentials are another staple in the black market. If hackers get their hands on your usernames and passwords, they'll enter your digital life. In virtual worlds and blockchain-based games, rare skins, powerful weapons, and unique collectibles are stolen and sold for real-world profits. Even private conversations containing sensitive information can be sold in a bid to collect confidential and compromising information that can be used against the user.

Without strong measures to safeguard identity, Meta verse can become a breeding ground for cyber criminals to operate at scale and effectively, ironically- using the latest and greatest AI technology.

Content Moderation

We have covered some of this in the previous sections but lack of content moderation on a continual basis can result in many issues. We all have heard about fake news and how social media platforms have become the go to place for fake news perpetrators. Metaverse with tools such as AI, immersive media and deepfakes can take "fake news" to the next level of believability. Imagine someone using deep fake technology to pose as a famous person and use their voice and mannerism to deliver fake news in a very convincing and authoritative fashion. If not moderated, Metaverse can easily blur boundaries between real and fake, genuine and fiction and what's real. Per an article in medium from Joshua "The misuse of deepfakes poses significant risks, particularly in the context of the metaverse. One of the most pressing concerns is the spread of misinformation or 'deepfake news'. With the ability to create convincing fake videos of public figures, malicious actors could spread false information, stir up controversy, or manipulate public opinion."

Blurring of Virtual and Physical Boundaries

With teenagers and youth spending a lot of time in the metaverse using advanced technologies such as AR/VR headsets, it is very easy to lose touch with reality and start believing that the world of the metaverse is the real world. This, while in the short term might give users a sense of empowerment and ability to partake in new experiences, can have lasting long term consequences. This can lead to users having weaker family and friend connections and with reduced ability to deal with real world situations, where everything can be solved with a click of a few buttons as it is done in the metaverse.

The long-term impact of spending prolonged time in metaverse needs to be understood and right mechanisms need to be in place so as users can benefit from metaverse while keeping their mental and physical wellbeing intact.

Safeguards in a Virtual World With Metaverse

The first step towards safeguards is *transparency*. Customers, Content creators should have a good understanding of how AI makes decisions when it recommends contents, products etc. Transparency allows Customers and creators to understand AI bias and adjust for it. To illustrate - if an AI algorithm is written and trained by a programmer with bias towards a certain race or product - the recommendations can also be biased. This can be corrected by understanding the bias and training the algorithm with a more diverse and representative data.

The second step is to have *strong privacy and data protection controls*. User data should be stored in a reliable and secure manner with strong encryption measures. There should be clear and concise explanation to the user about how data is stored and safeguarded. This allows for two things to happen - create strong privacy measures that can't be easily hacked and give end users confidence that their data is protected.

The third and probably the most important step is *fairness and inclusivity* in how AI is trained. If there is inherent bias in how AI algorithms are trained, it will result in spread of misinformation which can have undesired consequences. There should be guidelines on how AI is trained and there should be standards on diversity, inclusivity and fairness that should be met before the AI tool/algorithm is adopted in the metaverse.

Last but not the least there should be a *regulatory oversight* committee which does regular audits of AI/ML systems to identify and correct biases. There should be diverse representation of thoughts, backgrounds in the committee to minimize biases. These measures by themselves might not be sufficient as we will lean in the next section.

How to Protect Against Bad Actors: Real and Virtual

Despite all the measures above - there is one more threat that we need to be cognizant about. AI/ML evolving in a bad direction, learning bad things and working against the best interest of humans. The second threat is bad actors using ever evolving AI/ML tools with more and more intelligence to circumvent all regulation, transparency and data controls to commit crimes.

Let's first dive deeper into AI/ML evolving in a bad way. AI is very much like human beings. When we are born as babies a lot of our thinking is shaped by our surroundings, our interactions with our parents, family and friends. This helps refine our sense of right and wrong and provides reinforcement for what we should do and what we should not do. In the same way AI/ML are learning algorithms that learn and adapt from data provided to them. For an AI/ML to have unbiased learning the data must be representative of real world thinking and not be biased in any way. To understand this further let us try to understand how AI/Ml uses data to learn?

Data Training for AI/ML

The neural network algorithms powering AI/ML tools can learn in three ways.

Supervised learning: This is very well explained by Google cloud. (Google, 2023)"The data used in supervised learning is labeled — meaning that it contains examples of both inputs (called features) and correct outputs (labels). The algorithms analyze a large dataset of these training pairs to infer what a desired output value would be when asked to make a prediction on new data. An example of this from Google is if you want to teach a model to identify trees you can provide a dataset that contains many examples and then the algorithm can try to define characteristics for every tree, after that you can test the model by showing it a picture of a tree. You can keep training the algorithm to minimize errors. "Once the model has been trained and tested, you can use it to make predictions on unknown data based on the previous knowledge it has learned" (Google, 2023). It is very easy to bias the learning by providing outputs for certain inputs that are biased in a way. Let us say the only output we give for the color of an apple are shades of green, the ML language will infer that all apples are green. In the same way we can teach the AI model to provide bad or harmful outputs for a certain response. This can be used to deceive people or harm them financially.

Unsupervised Learning

Per Google cloud (Google, 2023) unsupervised learning within the realm of artificial intelligence is a category of machine learning wherein the system learns from data without direct human administration. In contrast to supervised learning, unsupervised machine learning models are presented with unlabeled data and are empowered to unveil patterns and glean insights autonomously, devoid of explicit guidance or instructions. Even unsupervised learning can be biased. Bias can be in the machine model itself where incorrect assumptions are made. It can also be in the quality of data used to train which might have user selection bias. Bias can also be injected by providing incomplete data sets which might force the algorithm to make incorrect assumptions.

Here are some examples of bias in unsupervised learning:

Facial recognition: A facial recognition system that is trained mainly on images of lighter-skinned people may have difficulty identifying darker-skinned faces. An algorithm may also be trained to recognize a white person more easily than a black person because of the type of data used in training.

Evaluation bias: Evaluation bias can occur during model evaluation. For example, facial recognition systems may use biased benchmarks that are skin color or gender biased.

Historical bias: Google Translate learns from existing web translations that are often biased in terms of gender. For example, "doctor" is usually assumed male, while "nurse" is assumed female.

Reinforcement learning: Per an article from University of York (Brooks, 2023) "Reinforcement learning is a subset of machine learning that allows an AI-driven system to learn through trial and error using feedback from its actions. This feedback is either negative or positive, signaled as punishment or reward with, of course, the aim of maximizing the reward function". This is where bias can be introduced by skewing the rewards to bias the learning of the algorithm. The same examples that we looked at for unsupervised learning will apply here as well.

An article from MIT Sloan summarizes (DeBrusk, 2020) the pitfall well "But while machine-learning algorithms enable companies to realize new efficiencies, they are as susceptible as any system to the "garbage in, garbage out" syndrome. In the case of self-learning systems, the type of "garbage" is biased data. Left unchecked, feeding biased data to self-learning systems can lead to unintended and sometimes dangerous outcomes."

How to Responsibly Train AI

So now we have discovered the pitfalls of a bad algorithm but more importantly the repercussions of training and rewarding the algorithm with bad data. Let us look at both the aspects in a bit more detail.

Responsible Training of AI Algorithms

There are multiple techniques that can be applied to provide unbiased data and responsibly train AI algorithms. Let us build a better understanding of some of these techniques.

Using diverse and representative data: Data collection and curation should be done by a diverse team which has diversity across age, race, ethnicity, gender and point of views. One should also strive for intellectual diversity in the form of education background, political views and teamwork style. For multinational companies, diversity can be further enhanced by collecting data across geographies and functions. Such diversity in data collection not only allows for elimination of bias but also allows for superior training.

Conducting subpopulation analysis: According to an article on Dataiku, one can use subpopulation analysis to investigate whether the model performs identically across different subpopulations. If the model is found to be better at predicting outcomes for one group over another, it can lead to biased outcomes and unintended consequences when it is put into production. This is another great way to debias data for Machine learning training.

Monitoring for outliers in a data set and adjusting for them: Outliers in a dataset can affect the representation of the data set. Statistical methods like scaling and Winsorization should be applied to adjust and reduce the influence of outlines. Scaling allows for standardizing or normalizing the data to have a mean of zero and a standard deviation of one. Winsorization replaces outlier values with the nearest non-outlier value.

Adjusting for Societal prejudices embedded in datasets: Even with all the measures above, biases common in society can make it to the data sets. The best way to counter this bias is to be open about how data is collected and be transparent on how the AI algorithms are trained and how the data is used for training. The transparency should help recognize and adjust for society bias.

Monitoring and adjusting the model over time for biases: By setting a predictive metrics threshold, one can confirm if the machine learning model consistently returns unreliable results and then analyze the prediction drift (changes in prediction results over time) from there. Monitoring such drifts allows to catch biases early and fix them ahead of time. For more details refer to the Neptune AI blog in the citations.

Establishing corporate governance for responsible AI and end-to-end internal policies to mitigate bias: Although this point might seem repetitive but having a robust governance policy is an absolute must for responsible AI. Genevieve Smith and Ishita Rustagi (2023) (in the article "Mitigating Bias in Artificial Intelligence") biases in AI have high stakes for business leaders . Biased AI systems can unfairly allocate opportunities, resources or information; infringe on civil liberties; pose a detriment to the safety of individuals; fail to provide the same quality of service to some people as others; and negatively impact a person's wellbeing such as by being derogatory or offensive.

They suggest a 7-step model for complete AI corporate governance.

1. Enable diverse and multi-disciplinary teams working on algorithms and AI systems.
2. Promote a culture of ethics and responsibility related to AI.
3. Practice responsible dataset development.
4. Establish policies and practices that enable responsible algorithm development.
5. Establish corporate governance for responsible AI and end-to-end internal policies to mitigate bias.
6. Engage corporate social responsibility (CSR) to advance responsible / ethical AI and larger systems change.
7. Use your voice and influence to advance industry change and regulations for responsible AI.

Responsible AI Principles

We have talked a lot about data in this chapter. Let's finally talk about how developers should think when they think about developing responsible AI algorithms. Just as we have Corporate Social responsibility principles, Cheng, Varshney, & Liu in their paper "*Socially Responsible AI Algorithms: Issues, Purposes, and Challenges*" outline the following principles.

1. PHILANTHROPIC: Responsibilities: Be a good AI citizen. Build the AI ecosystem to address societal challenges.
2. ETHICAL Responsibilities: Be ethical. Obligation to do what is right, fair, and just. Prevent harm.
3. LEGAL Responsibilities: Obey the law. Act for a certain sort of reason provided by the law. Play by the rules of the game.
4. FUNCTIONAL Responsibilities: Be functional. Create technology that allows computers and machines to function in an intelligent manner.

The role of developers in building responsible AI algorithms is still evolving and does not have clear industry guidelines, but every developer should strive to be a good citizen where they purposefully ensure that their algorithms do not have any conscious or subconscious biases. They should ensure that they have code reviews and unit testing done by a diverse set of testers and developers. Cross group reviews should be encouraged to account for implicit group biases. Corporations should invest and encourage interdisciplinary collaboration, including ethicists and social scientists.

APIs developed by developers should be clearly documented with clear explanation of uses, limitations and tested boundaries. This is especially important in an interconnected world such as metaverse, where developers leverage modules from other developers and if unchecked the biases in each module can create a complex web of AI bias which will be hard to trace back and resolve for. As part of an open and inclusive AI API framework User developers and users of APIs should be allowed control and ability to customize algorithmic interactions. They should also be provided options to understand and modify algorithmic recommendations.

We also need to understand that Metaverse is a platform which impacts developers of services and consumers of services built on the platform. So, it is of utmost importance to encourage and foster Public Engagement of consumers of services on the platform. Seeking input from the public, especially those affected by algorithmic decisions will help developers build empathy from an end user perspective and bake in their perspectives as part of the development and testing framework. Fostering a dialogue on the ethical use of algorithms and incorporating public feedback will further help in building a diverse viewpoint representation.

This must be coupled with adaptability and responsiveness. Developers and creators of applications in the metaverse should be ready to adapt algorithms based on feedback and changing societal values. They should be willing to quickly address any issues that arise and be responsive to user concerns.

CONCLUSION

Metaverse will have a profound impact on how we work, socialize, learn and can extend accessibility of content and media across the world. As discussed in this chapter, the benefits of Metaverse span various domains, offering enhanced collaboration through virtual workspaces, immersive learning experiences in education, and innovative gaming and entertainment possibilities. Businesses can establish a virtual presence, opening new avenues for e-commerce and virtual trade. Healthcare stands to benefit from virtual medical services and training simulations, while virtual social spaces provide a novel way for people to connect and share experiences. Beyond these obvious uses, Metaverse can also help unleash creativity by offering platforms for virtual art galleries and immersive storytelling. Additionally, its potential to redefine remote work by creating virtual office spaces and contributing to environmental sustainability through reduced physical travel further underscores the manifold advantages of this emerging digital frontier. However, it is crucial to navigate ethical considerations to ensure responsible and equitable development in the metaverse. As discussed in the chapter, if left unsupervised Metaverse can expose users to many dangers ranging from data privacy, harassment, addiction, social engineering, misinformation, digital inequality to feeling of social isolation and inadequacy

With the use of responsible AI and a framework to implement, monitor, measure, control and remove the biases and dangers of AI. Metaverse has limitless possibilities for positive social impact on our world.

REFERENCES

Aritonang, J. (2023, July 21). Deepfakes in the metaverse: Challenges, opportunities, and the road ahead. *Medium*. https://medium.com/@aritonangjoshua95/deepfakes-in-the-metaverse-challenges-opportunities-and-the-road-ahead-e012e83473ed

Basu, T. (2022, February 4). The metaverse has a groping problem already. *MIT Technology Review*. https://www.technologyreview.com/2021/12/16/1042516/the-metaverse-has-a-groping-problem/

Brooks, R. (2023, August 17). *What is reinforcement learning?* University of York. https://online.york.ac.uk/what-is-reinforcement-learning/

Brooks, T. (2023). Increasing threat of Deepfake Identities. Homeland Security.

Buana, I. (2023, June 30). *Metaverse: Threat or opportunity for our social world? in understanding metaverse on sociological context*. Journal of Metaverse. https://dergipark.org.tr/en/pub/jmv/issue/72588/1144470

Concept: Subpopulation analysis. (n.d.). Dataiku Knowledge Base. https://knowledge.dataiku.com/latest/ml-analytics/model-results/concept-subpopulation-analysis.html

DeBrusk, C. (2020, September 3). The risk of machine-learning bias (and how to prevent it). *MIT Sloan Management Review*. https://sloanreview.mit.edu/article/the-risk-of-machine-learning-bias-and-how-to-prevent-it/

Fadilpašić, S. (2023, September 10). *How do hackers sell and trade your data in the metaverse?* MUO. https://www.makeuseof.com/how-hackers-sell-trade-data-in-metaverse/

GeeksforGeeks. (2023, December 21). *How to detect outliers in machine learning*. GeeksforGeeks. https://www.geeksforgeeks.org/machine-learning-outlier/

Marr, B. (2024, January 18). The metaverse and its Dark Side: Confronting the reality of virtual rape. *Forbes*. https://www.forbes.com/sites/bernardmarr/2024/01/16/the-metaverse-and-its-dark-side-confronting-the-reality-of-virtual-rape/?sh=77663ef02b66

Nair, V., Garrido, G. M., Song, D., & O'Brien, J. F. (2023, December 13). *Exploring the privacy risks of adversarial VR game design.* arXiv.org. https://arxiv.org/abs/2207.13176

Nix, N. (2023). Meta doesn't want to police the metaverse. kids are paying the price. *Washington Post.* https://www.washingtonpost.com/technology/2023/03/08/metaverse-horizon-worlds-kids-harassment/

Oladele, S. (2023, September 8). *A comprehensive guide on how to monitor your models in production.* neptune.ai. https://neptune.ai/blog/how-to-monitor-your-models-in-production-guide#:~:text=Monitoring%20predictive%20performance%20(with%20evaluation,results%20over%20time)%20from%20there

Petkov, M. (2023). *Metaverse AI: The Definitive Marketing Guide to Navigating a $150 Trillion Opportunity.* Independent publishing.

Simonite, T. (2021, May 5). It began as an AI-fueled dungeon game. it got much darker. *Wired.* https://www.wired.com/story/ai-fueled-dungeon-game-got-much-darker/

Smith, G. (2020). Mitigating Bias in Artificial Intelligence, Berkeley Haas Center for Equity Google. Google Cloud. https://cloud.google.com/discover/what-is-supervised-learning

Tariq, S., Abuadbba, A., & Moore, K. (2023, September 10). *Deepfake in the metaverse: Security implications for virtual gaming, meetings, and offices.* arXiv.org. https://arxiv.org/abs/2303.14612v2 doi:10.1145/3595353.3595880

Westcott, K., Loucks, J., & Arbanas, J. (2023). *2023 Digital media trends: Immersed and connected.* Deloitte Insights.

Chapter 4
Brand Building in the Metaverse

Arpan Anand

ⓘ https://orcid.org/0000-0002-2572-1651
Jaipuria Institute of Management, Noida, India

Priya Jindal
Chitkara Business School, Chitkara University, Punjab, India

ABSTRACT

The metaverse is a shared, virtual space where people can meet and interact with each other. It is a digital world that is built on top of the existing Internet. The Metaverse is still in its early stages of development, but it has the potential to revolutionize the way we communicate, work, and even live. A Metaverse is a place where people can assume any identity they desire. People can create a completely new identity for themselves, or they can use their real name and look just like they do in the real world. Metaverse can be used for a wide range of business applications, including building brands, managing supply chain management, loyalty programs, and developing new online marketplaces. In the meantime, we all have to adjust to living in a world that is gradually becoming more virtual. To understand how the metaverse will change us, it is necessary for us to first comprehend our origins and how they will direct the development of the immersive internet. The metaverse is a space that is created by the combination of virtual reality and augmented reality.

DOI: 10.4018/979-8-3693-3358-7.ch004

INTRODUCTION

Metaverse is the association of two words "meta" and "verse." The verse mentions the world, whereas the meta signifies above or beyond. It will alter the ways in which we communicate with one another as well as with the reality that surrounds us. Additionally, it will alter the ways in which we develop new knowledge and consume and distribute already existing information. The Internet may have taken thirty years to achieve its current condition, but the Metaverse is built for rapid expansion, with humans equipped to traverse into other worlds and with technical knowledge. The Covid-19 pandemic has accelerated developments in a variety of businesses, one of which is the growing dependence of individuals on technology for nearly every facet of their existence, including conducting business and socializing. This concept of the internet's future promises to combine the physical world with new technologies that are only beginning to revolutionize how people communicate with one another, have fun, shop, and participate in other activities that are part of their everyday lives.

The virtual realm in which we will all conduct our activities is referred to as the Metaverse. Currency and an economy are being established for the metaverse, which will pave the way for new opportunities, new products, new services, and even new employment opportunities (Dwivedi et al., 2022). Since the Metaverse is completely digital, information can be tracked on a significantly larger scale than in the present world. This makes it promising to generate substantially more targeted advertisements based on specific measurements of people's habits rather than making educated guesses about those habits. In the near future, we may be able to observe the entire world through augmented reality glasses and use technology to create immersive experiences. Being an avatar in the Metaverse gives you the ability to communicate with other people in a setting that has no physical boundaries. As a result, the advertising industry will enter a new age. People will have access to unheard-of opportunities for socializing, learning, working together, and playing. The companies and brands that are able to recognize the possibilities offered by Metaverse will have the highest rate of return. The goal of advertisers is to maintain Millennial and Gen X users' interest in their products and technology. Metaverse enables advertisers to target Millennials and Gen X users in a more engaging manner, in addition to targeting Gen Z users who are more accustomed to the digital world (Kenney & Zysman, 2019). The world is already witnessing the birth of virtual life in the form of immersive reality, which will soon open the door to a world of new prospects in the field of marketing. We already interact with virtual reality through the use of our home screens, but very soon in the future, we will be able to use a technology called Metaverse, which will add a layer of virtuality to our actual surroundings. Gartner predicts that by the year 2026, approximately one-quarter of the population in the Metaverse for purposes including but not limited to work, retail, education, social networking, and leisure (Lamba & Malik, 2022).

However, in addition to all of its benefits, the Metaverse also poses a substantial number of challenges to the world. One of the most difficult challenges is to provide clients with an experience that is both seamless and realistic. Another challenge to overcome is protecting the users' personal information and privacy. And last but not least, Metaverse needs to figure out how to make money for itself if it is going to continue to expand and flourish. Despite all of these obstacles, the Metaverse has an extremely promising future. With the right team and the right vision, the Metaverse can become a truly transformational technology.

METAVERSE: A HIGHLY IMMERSIVE VIRTUAL WORLD

Metaverse is the seamless integration of our physical and digital lives. It is the creation of a united, digital community in which we can work, play, rest, do business, and interact with one another. One of the most important things to keep in mind is that there is not just one virtual world, but rather several worlds, which are now being developed to give individuals the ability to broaden and intensify their social connections online. The Metaverse has the potential to break down barriers and make it easier for more people to gain access to essential products, services, and experiences without requiring them to leave the comfort of their own homes to do so.

The Metaverse is referred to as "a highly immersive virtual world where people meet to socialize, play, and work". The Metaverse is often mentioned as the "future of the internet". You can play games and engage with others who are represented by avatars in the metaverse. Any computer screen, smartphone, or pair of VR glasses might be used to enter this virtual environment (Meghan, 2022). Shortly, most online experiences will be accessed through the Metaverse, a persistent, unified network of 3D virtual worlds that will also support a large portion of the real world. These concepts, which were previously exclusive to science fiction and video games, are currently being developed to change every sector of society, including finance, healthcare, education, consumer goods, city planning, dating, and many more (Sood et al., 2022). The intention is to provide a world that is drastically different from the one you are presently living.

WHY METAVERSE?

A metaverse is not an entirely new idea. We have reached a tipping point when it seems like hardly a day goes by without a business or renowned person enlightening us that they are trying to build a presence online. This is in stark contrast to the situation just a few years ago. There is a convergence of developing tendencies, even though the noise can be partially due to attention-grabbing headlines. This concept of the metaverse is made possible by the convergence of several different emerging technologies. Both virtual currencies and NFTs are now possible because of blockchain technology. Creators are finding new ways to make money off their work in the form of tokens due to the emergence of new ways to buy and sell digital assets. Token-holders not only have a way of making transactions on the platform but also of influencing its direction and management (e.g. voting on decisions).

From a social perspective, people are able to form communities based on shared values and express themselves in more genuine ways thanks to the evolution of more realistic virtual experiences. At the same time, COVID-19 has standardized more continuous and multi-purpose online engagement and communication, speeding

Figure 1. The evolution of metaverse timeline
Source: Mohanty et al. (2022)

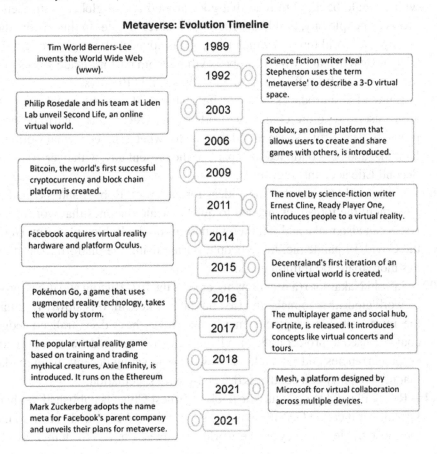

up the process of digitizing our lives. The rapid growth of interest in the Metaverse can be traced to a convergence of technological, social, and economic factors. The evolution of metaverse timeline has been shown in Figure 1.

METAVERSE: EVOLUTION TIMELINE

1989 -- While working at CERN, Tim Berners-Lee, an English computer scientist, laid the foundation for the World Wide Web. This represented a fundamental improvement over already-available text-based sharing services like Gopher and exclusive bulletin board systems. With Berners- Lee's innovation, a client and server for a network of linked web pages with text, pictures, and audio were made publicly available.

1992 -- In his book 'Snow Crash', American science fiction writer Neal Stephenson uses the word "metaverse" to explain a dystopian future world where rich people can escape into a different 3D, connected reality. The alternative reality begins with a single 65,536 km road that goes around a fake globe. From there, it grows as people buy, build, and fix up virtual real estate. In this vision, there is only one world through which everyone is connected. People are in charge of their own avatars, which can be anything from custom-made works of art to cheap items from Walmart called "Clints" and "Brandys."

2003 -- Linden Lab introduces Second Life, a shared 3D virtual environment that allows users to explore, connect with others, construct objects, and trade virtual products. The virtual space paved the way for what a shared virtual world may look like and has continued to expand to the present day, with over 70 million Second Life accounts registered.

2006 -- Users could try out their new ideas for games on Roblox and the platform gave them the tools they needed to quickly scale the ones that worked best. Users can also make and sell their own items on the Roblox platform. During the Covid-19 pandemic, more people started using the platform, and it now has more than 200 million users.

2009 -- Satoshi Nakamoto (a pseudonym), creates the first Bitcoin and uses a proof-of-work algorithm to make the first public blockchain. It is slowly becoming the most valuable cryptocurrency. This shows how decentralized ledgers could be used to protect trade on a large scale. Interest in different alternative cryptocurrencies and research into new ways to set up decentralized markets that no one party can control is driven by wild speculation.

2011 -- Ready Player One, a futuristic book by Ernest Cline, is published. A shared virtual world called OASIS, which is set in the year 2040 and claims to have the most stable currency in the world, becomes a haven for humanity. The

2018 film adaptation, directed by Steven Spielberg, popularised the concept of a shared virtual environment.

2014 -- Facebook purchases Oculus and aids in expanding the 3D infrastructure needed to support it.

2015 -- Gavin Wood, a computer scientist from England, and Vitalik Buterin, a Canadian programmer, introduce Ethereum, a platform for creating decentralized applications on a blockchain. Ethereum presented a realistic take on smart contracts, which is the foundation for services like NFTs and the capacity to "own" assets in a distributed ecosystem.

2016 -- With Pokémon GO, augmented reality games are unleashed upon the world. Players utilize their mobile devices to explore real-world areas in search of, capture, and battle digital monsters.

2018 -- Play-to-earn video game The NFTs linked onto the Ethereum blockchain are made more widely known through the game Axie Infinity, created by the Vietnamese company Sky Mavis. At the height of the epidemic in 2021, it reaches a peak of over 2.7 million users and has the highest overall worth of all play-to-earn games. In 2022, hackers will steal almost $600 million.

2019 -- With over 250 million active players, Epic Games' Fortnite becomes the most well-known shared virtual world ever. The business improves the platform to support additional virtual experiences and games. Rapper Travis Scott headlines a virtual concert in 2020 that draws more than 12 million viewers. Later, Epic incorporates the platform into well-known enterprise applications for infrastructure, design, and geographic information systems.

2021 -- The parent firm of Facebook adopts the name Meta and presents a positive and expanding vision for the metaverse. The renamed business then commits over $10 billion to the creation of new tools, programs, and services to serve this new world. As businesses of all sizes start linking their current offerings to the metaverse, this helps to spark interest in the word "metaverse." Rankings for the phrase skyrocket in Google searches.

2021 -- Microsoft's newest platform, Mesh, is designed to streamline online teamwork. The startup claims that Mesh-enabled metaverse experiences would enhance a meeting, building, and filmmaking processes in businesses.

The seven layers of Metaverse which shows how it works is depicted in Figure 2.

Figure 2. The seven layers of Metaverse
Source: medium.com (2021)

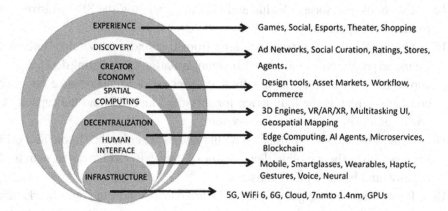

HOW METAVERSE WORKS

- **Experience**

We will be able to enjoy a wide variety of two- and three-dimensional (2D, 3D, and 4D) experiences in the Metaverse that we are currently unable to access.

- **Discovery**

The Metaverse ecosystem supports both inward and outbound discovery methods. Inbound discovery is the process that occurs when people are actively seeking out data. Meanwhile, "outbound" marketing involves reaching out to potential customers whether or not they have specifically asked to be contacted.

- **Creator Economy**

Those who built the early versions of the web needed a basic understanding of computer programming to create the necessary infrastructure. Web application frameworks, however, have made it easy to create web applications without writing any code. As a result, there are an increasing number of people building websites.

- **Spatial Computing**

A technology called spatial computing combines VR and AR. The HoloLens from Microsoft is a great illustration that depicts the capability of this technology. If anyone is incapacitated to acquire a Hololens yet, consider Instagram's facial filters as a form of spatial computing.

- **Decentralization**

Using distributed computing and microservices, developers may take advantage of powerful internet resources in a highly scalable environment. Moreover, blockchain and smart contracts provide authors more control over their work and the use of their data and creations.

- **Human Interface**

Using a combination of spatial computing and human interface, users can look at objects in the real world to create shared augmented reality and get information about their surroundings.

- **Infrastructure**

The foundation of technology is essential for the development of subsequent levels. It incorporates 5G and 6G computing to ease traffic on networks and boost bandwidth.

ROLE OF METAVERSE IN MARKETING

In the context of marketing and advertising, the word "metaverse" refers to the ability of businesses to build their own persistent, 3D virtual worlds where consumers may engage in completely immersive experiences while being exposed to brand-related information and sales enablement techniques. A variety of modern computer-mediated analogues are needed for the metaverse, including social networking sites where users can interact with friends, family, and coworkers while simultaneously getting exposed to brands through sponsored content and promotional advertising. Social media helps businesses grow their brand exposure and customer base through the direct-to-consumer shop and enabling them to sell products and services online and deliver them to their home. Similar to this, the Metaverse is likely to have 3D "stores" users may browse products, try them on, and shop online in addition to seeing adverts. A fully functional Metaverse would combine several technologies, including 3D avatars, augmented reality, virtual reality, mixed reality, and video games even though it is still a few years away.

Users of a metaverse can represent themselves in the virtual space by making use of avatars. Besides serving as a platform for social networking and online gaming, metaverses have the potential to be utilized for advertising. Advertising in a metaverse is indeed a step above the rest because of the interactivity it provides. Some examples of how to advertise in the metaverse are as follows:

1. **Create an interactive product demonstration:** Metaverses are perfect for showcasing products to potential customers. A product showroom or online store can be set up to give customers a feel for a product before they buy it. If you sell cosmetics, for instance, you could offer a virtual makeover station where customers can virtually apply and evaluate a variety of goods.
2. **Offer discounts and coupons.** Promo codes and other discounts are a terrific way to bring in clients in the metaverse. Virtual coupons can be offered and redeemed in your online shop. Incentives like surveys and product demos can earn users discounts on future purchases.
3. **Host special events.** Marketing your business in the virtual world can be a breeze with the help of a well-planned special event. To draw attention to your company, you might throw online parties, fashion shows, and other events. At these gatherings, you can also promote special offers and discounts.
4. **Sponsor a virtual world.** A wonderful method to spread the word about your company is to sponsor a virtual environment. Your company name will be prominently visible in the virtual world if you sponsor a well-known metaverse. This will make a lot of potential clients aware of your brand.
5. **Advertise in a virtual world.** When users enter a virtual world, your advertisement will be displayed on their screens. Your advertisements can be tailored to a specific age range, gender, or interest group.

USE OF METAVERSE IN BRAND BUILDING

To promote goods and services, metaverses provide a novel and engaging platform. Brands can be developed and promoted with the help of the Metaverse, which allows consumers to interact in real-time with digital representations of the brand and each other. Because of this, businesses can give their consumers and followers an engaging and participatory experience (Winter et al., 2021). Additionally, events and advertising campaigns for brands can be held in the Metaverse. Through the creation of a virtual world that embodies the brand and its core values, Metaverse can be utilised for brand development and marketing. This realm can be used to conduct events and attract more customers to the company. Additionally, digital goods that represent the brand and may be sold in the virtual world can be made using Metaverse.

A brand is much more than a name or a logo. It is the sum of all of a company's interactions with its clients, from the things it manufactures to the way it markets and sells them. In today's interconnected world, the brand extends to the digital sphere, where customers increasingly interact with businesses via websites, social media, and mobile apps. The metaverse is a logical extension of the brand's digital presence. It is a three-dimensional virtual world that can be used for everything from marketing and advertising to customer service and support. There are numerous methods to leverage the metaverse for brand development. Companies can design 3D copies of their items to provide a more immersive experience for buyers. They can also design virtual shops and showrooms, giving clients a simple method to browse and buy goods. Additionally, they may use the metaverse for marketing and events to give customers a taste of what it would be like to engage with the brand in person. The metaverse offers businesses a strong platform on which to establish their brands and interact with their customers. The metaverse is positioned to play a crucial role in the marketing mix thanks to its capacity to produce immersive experiences and encourage participation.

The following factors should be taken into account while creating a metaverse brand:

1. **Create a strong and unique identity.** Your product's identity in the metaverse should be distinct and memorable. A unique logo, color scheme, and typeface can all help with this.

2. **Develop a consistent brand experience.** Establishing a unified brand experience across all customer touchpoints and communication channels is crucial. Everything from the visual style of your virtual environment to how your avatar engages with users falls under this category.

3. **Build customer relationships.** The metaverse gives marketers an unprecedented opportunity to connect with their customers. These relationships can be fostered through a range of activities, including customer service, forum moderator, and event planning.

4. **Promote your brand.** Take advantage of the metaverse to spread the word about your company. Advertisements, social media, and content marketing are all effective ways to accomplish this goal.

5. **Analyze and optimize.** Your metaverse brand-building activities should be analyzed and improved just like any other marketing campaign. This can be

accomplished by employing analytics systems that monitor avatar interactions, click-through rates, and other engagement indicators.

METAVERSE: MAJOR CHALLENGES

- The expensive tool is a barrier to the extensive use of metaverse technology, however, it is hoped that this will be solved in the future. There are four types of hazards associated with AR: moral, physical, psychological, ethical, and data privacy dangers.
- Physical mishaps have occurred as a consequence of users' concentration being unfocused by location-based AR applications. Information overload is a psychological problem that needs to be evaded. Moral dilemmas arise from unauthorized augmentation and falsifying information to support biased viewpoints. The risk with the most implications for privacy is the one associated with data gathering and sharing with third parties.
- One of the health problems related to virtual reality is nausea, along with motion sickness and dizziness. Head and neck pain are a drawback for prolonged use sessions of VR headsets due to their weight. Another obstacle to the widespread adoption of the Metaverse is social exclusion and retreat from real-world activities that are accompanied by medical problems.
- In addition to the aforementioned issues, the Metaverse has a serious problem with sexual harassment of women, as shown by a gang rape case where the victim claimed that males had touched her avatar and sexually attacked her. So, who is in charge of protecting the safety of women in virtual worlds? For instance, Meta asserts that it gives users resources to aid in their safety, thereby transferring responsibility to them.

Before entering the Metaverse, users need to know how the risks and benefits of immersive environments compare. They should also be knowledgeable about cyber threats and conduct their own investigation.

THE FUTURE OF METAVERSE

In the next ten years, the metaverse will change almost every part of life and business by making it possible to work together in virtual spaces, augmented real spaces, or a mix of both. It will also open up new business opportunities and change how customers and businesses work together. Some ambitious brands are already working to set the rules and expectations for our new worlds.

There is no doubt that new competitors will join the race, expanding the space for innovation and change. Innovative use cases are already developing throughout the Retail, CPG, Logistics, Manufacturing, and Healthcare industries, although there is countless potential for businesses of all sizes. This will benefit all contexts, not just business-to-consumer ones. Businesses that do business with other businesses will benefit greatly from the metaverse. Think about a manufacturer who is spending money on new parts for its equipment. At the moment, the process requires either a printed brochure or an email with a PDF that contains static 2D pictures. In the metaverse, users might evaluate the products more reasonably in a virtual environment. Imagine being able to construct a complex digital replica of a factory or other industrial facility on a vast scale to assess how robotic technologies might interact with the real world.

REFERENCES

Dwivedi, Y. K., Hughes, L., Baabdullah, A. M., Ribeiro-Navarrete, S., Giannakis, M., Al-Debei, M. M., & Wamba, S. F. (2022). Metaverse beyond the hype: Multidisciplinary perspectives on emerging challenges, opportunities, and agenda for research, practice and policy. *International Journal of Information Management*, *66*(1), 542–555. https://medium.com/building-the-metaverse/the-metaverse-value-chain-afcf9e09e3a7,2021. doi:10.1016/j.ijinfomgt.2022.102542

Kenney, M., & Zysman, J. (2019). Work and value creation in the platform economy. *Work and labor in the digital age, 33*(1), 13-41.

Lamba, S. S., & Malik, R. (2022). Into the metaverse: Marketing to Gen Z consumers. In *Applying Metalytics to Measure Customer Experience in the Metaverse* (pp. 92–98). IGI Global. doi:10.4018/978-1-6684-6133-4.ch008

Meghan, R. (2022). Metaverse Hype to Transition into New Business Models that Extend Digital Business. https://www.gartner.com/en/newsroom/press-releases/gartner-predicts-65--of-b2b-sales-organizations-will-transition.

Mohanty, M. K., Mohapatra, A. K., Samanta, P. K., Agrawal, G., & Agrawal, G. (2022). Exploring metaverse: A virtual ecosystem from management perspective. *Journal of Commerce, 43*(4), 1–11. doi:10.54063/ojc.2022.v43i04.01

Sood, D., Tandon, D., & Sood, P. (2022). Social Influence: Decisions of Online Brand Communities and Millennials. In *Applying Metalytics to Measure Customer Experience in the Metaverse* (pp. 161–172). IGI Global. doi:10.4018/978-1-6684-6133-4.ch014

Winter, C., Kern, F., Gall, D., Latoschik, M. E., Pauli, P., & Käthner, I. (2021). Immersive virtual reality during gait rehabilitation increases walking speed and motivation: A usability evaluation with healthy participants and patients with multiple sclerosis and stroke. *Journal of Neuroengineering and Rehabilitation, 18*(1), 1–14. doi:10.1186/s12984-021-00848-w PMID:33888148

Chapter 5
Transitioning to Digital Merchandise:
Integrating Metaverse Into Retail Offerings

Surjit Singha
https://orcid.org/0000-0002-5730-8677
Kristu Jayanti College (Autonomous), India

K. P. Jaheer Mukthar
https://orcid.org/0000-0002-7888-0242
Kristu Jayanti College (Autonomous), India

ABSTRACT

This chapter examines the dynamic fusion of the Metaverse and the retail industry, highlighting the fundamental shift toward digital goods and immersive purchasing experiences. It investigates the Metaverse's fundamental concepts, historical development, and current impact on retail. Digital products, such as non-fungible tokens (NFTs), virtual goods, and augmented reality products, assume centre stage and potentially transform shopping experiences. However, it also faces obstacles during this metaverse transition, including technological hurdles, security concerns, and challenges related to customer adoption. Future trends and practical strategies for seamless integration, customer engagement, and marketing are discussed—the metaverse ushers in a revolutionary era for retail, presenting boundless opportunities for those who embrace it. Retailers are urged to embark on this journey to satisfy evolving customer expectations and remain competitive in the future retail landscape.

DOI: 10.4018/979-8-3693-3358-7.ch005

INTRODUCTION

This chapter has explored the metaverse, an interconnected digital realm that challenges the distinction between the material and virtual domains. Having established a solid comprehension of the metaverse's fundamental elements and underlying technologies, it examines its significant ramifications on diverse sectors, explicitly focusing on its substantial revolutionary power in the retail industry. The emergence of the metaverse has prompted a profound reconceptualization of conventional retail frameworks, presenting a diverse range of prospects and obstacles. Retailers are increasingly exploring the realm of virtual storefronts, aiming to captivate customers through immersive shopping encounters and conducting trials with inventive sales and marketing approaches. The main characteristics encompass virtual commerce, digital products, and interactive customer experiences, significantly altering consumer-business interaction dynamics (Abumalloh et al., 2023; Shen et al., 2021). The emergence of digital merchandise has become a crucial aspect in the expansion of metaverse retail, effectively meeting consumers' desires for unique and engaging experiences. This transformation has numerous benefits, including eliminating limitations associated with physical inventories, reducing administrative expenses, facilitating extensive personalization, and exploring the possibilities of blockchain and NFTs (Giovanni, 2023; Cheng et al., 2022). One notable advantage is overcoming geographical limitations, enabling businesses to access a worldwide customer base without needing physical expansion.

Furthermore, adopting digital products offers a conducive environment for fostering innovation and conducting experiments, hence granting early adopters a substantial advantage in terms of competition. The importance of this transition towards digital goods inside the metaverse resides in transforming retail into a dynamic and limitless digital realm. The proposition above provides the potential for the collaborative creation of customer experiences that possess distinctiveness and adaptability following the changing demands of consumers (Giovanni, 2023; Cheng et al., 2022).

Blockchain technology is one of the most revolutionary developments of our time. Its transformative effect on numerous industries, especially the financial industry, cannot be exaggerated. In the study by Shalender et al. (2023), the open ledger concept has yielded numerous advantages, such as a decentralized structure, high security, and immutable audit trails. These characteristics have propelled a noteworthy increase in the financial sector's adoption of blockchain technology. The road to widespread blockchain adoption, however, is not without obstacles. This study investigates the obstacles that prevent its complete integration into the financial domain. It identifies cost considerations, regulatory deficits, entrenched corporate cultures, and inadequate infrastructure as primary impediments. In response to these obstacles, the research proposes strategies for overcoming them and nurturing a wider adoption of blockchain technology in the financial sector. In addition, the research increases its influence by introducing a conceptual model. This model incorporates key stakeholders and outlines interaction variables between them, providing a road map for the sector's adoption and implementation of open ledger technology. In doing so, the study emphasizes the significance of blockchain and demonstrates its revolutionary potential beyond the financial sector.

The metaverse, a digital realm that facilitates user engagement with computer-generated surroundings, has the potential for communication and enjoyment. Nevertheless, the growth of this project gives rise to environmental and regulatory apprehensions. To address the energy consumption of data centers in the metaverse, it is imperative to implement energy-efficient technology and utilize renewable energy sources. Reducing carbon footprint by considering energy usage, gear manufacturing, and data transportation is crucial. Adopting responsible recycling practices and implementing eco-friendly design is crucial in addressing the issue of electronic waste. The presence of regulatory obstacles extends across national boundaries, requiring the implementation of uniform policies that tackle environmental and privacy concerns. Establishing a sustainable and ethically controlled Metaverse relies heavily on the collaborative endeavours of governments, tech corporations, and consumers.

The objective of this chapter is to offer a thorough comprehension of the motives, problems, and tactics associated with this transformation. The subject matter encompasses a broad range of subjects, including the fundamental comprehension of the metaverse, its influence on the retail sector, the underlying reasons for adopting digital merchandise, obstacles to overcome, and approaches for achieving smooth integration. This chapter probes into the metaverse's enduring possibilities and evolving directions, offering valuable insights into the ever-changing retail landscape in this virtual domain. The importance of adopting digital merchandise and its pivotal role in creating the future of retail in the current digital landscape is emphasized. The analysis of the impact of the metaverse on the retail industry highlights its extensive revolutionary potential, prompting merchants to adapt, innovate, and thrive in this dynamic and linked digital environment.

UNDERSTANDING THE METAVERSE

The metaverse concept, which refers to a dynamic and interconnected digital cosmos, is now reshaping the modes of interaction inside the digital sphere and among individuals. Consisting of virtual worlds, augmented reality, and virtual reality, this phenomenon surpasses the constraints of the tangible realm, providing a medium for social engagement, commerce, education, entertainment, and creativity. The evolution of this phenomenon possesses a substantial historical background, originating from the realm of science fiction, propelled by advancements in technology, and influenced by cultural factors. Digital environments have evolved from initial text-based platforms to including virtual worlds, extending into augmented and virtual reality domains. In the contemporary period, the metaverse covers various applications, from gaming and social interactions to education, remote employment, healthcare, art, and business. The phenomenon under consideration is distinguished by the possession and exchange of digital assets via blockchain technology and non-fungible tokens (NFTs), thereby bringing the notions of limited availability and distinctiveness within the digital realm (Suh et al., 2023; Cheng et al., 2022). The metaverse has many options and advantages for organizations, particularly those operating in the retail industry. The absence of geographical limitations allows merchants to enter worldwide markets without needing physical growth. Reimagining immersive shopping experiences involves incorporating many elements, such as 3D product research, virtual try-ons, and innovative interactions with AI-driven assistants or fellow shoppers.

The metaverse enables shops to offer an extensive inventory of digital items, unconstrained by physical limits, thereby accommodating a wide range of customer preferences. Another advantage is cost efficiency, as operations in the metaverse typically incur cheaper overhead than physical business maintenance. The amalgamation of blockchain technology and non-fungible tokens (NFTs) offers enhanced trustworthiness and transparency, particularly in the context of collected assets. The metaverse is a dynamic environment for creativity, facilitating swift experimentation and adjustment in response to evolving trends. The implementation of personalization is crucial in the context of AI and data analytics, as it enables the customization of products and recommendations based on the unique preferences of individual customers. Retailers can generate additional sources of income by capitalizing on virtual experiences, events, and digital assets. The metaverse can enhance market presence without the need for physical growth, and being an early adopter of this technology can provide a competitive advantage (Abumalloh et al., 2023; Giovanni, 2023). The metaverse represents more than just a passing technology fad; it is a deliberate reaction to the dynamic changes in the retail industry. Integrating digital merchandise enables businesses to collaboratively build immersive consumer experiences, enhancing their ability to engage and empower customers. This paradigm shift situates the retail industry inside a highly interconnected, ever-evolving, and limitless digital landscape, enabling enterprises to flourish, foster innovation, and deliver customer experiences beyond the physical realm's limitations.

THE CURRENT STATE OF RETAIL IN THE METAVERSE

The retail industry within the metaverse has experienced a notable shift, resulting in a varied and dynamic environment that presents several opportunities for businesses to engage with customers, market digital and physical goods, and establish immersive shopping encounters. Virtual storefronts within metaverse platforms have become increasingly prevalent, emulating the sensory experience of traditional stores and facilitating transactions using virtual currency or digital assets. The emergence of metaverse marketplaces and virtual real estate has facilitated the creation of personalized virtual retail locations by users, encompassing a range of establishments such as art galleries and fashion boutiques. NFT markets have become essential platforms for selling distinctive digital goods, encompassing collectables and artwork. Concurrently, virtual fashion shows let users interact with digital models adorned in virtual garments and accessories. Integrating narrative techniques and gamification in immersive brand experiences allows for the interactive presentation of products.

Additionally, in-game marketplaces inside metaverse components allow users to obtain virtual objects and clothes (Cheng et al., 2022; Shen et al., 2021). The advent of virtual art galleries has provided artists with a platform to showcase and commercialize digital art, frequently using non-fungible tokens (NFTs). This emerging trend is significantly transforming the notion of digital scarcity. Blockchain technology is crucial in assuring transparency and authenticity in selling digital stuff. Additionally, using data analytics and artificial intelligence (AI) facilitates the creation of highly tailored products. The increasing presence of businesses dedicated to metaverse solutions indicates the significant development of the metaverse as a dynamic realm for merchants. This digital environment presents many opportunities, surpassing the physical world's limitations, encompassing various aspects such as digital fashion and virtual real estate. According to Hurst et al. (2023), retailers are actively capitalizing on the potential of the metaverse to effectively engage customers through innovative methods, broaden their range of products, and establish immersive and customized shopping experiences.

The emergence of the metaverse has facilitated the development of a vast array of virtual stores, markets, and experiences, providing a look into the shifting nature of retail and commerce inside this digital domain. Decentraland is a virtual environment that operates on a blockchain infrastructure, allowing participants to engage in activities like purchasing, selling, and constructing virtual properties. Retailers have established virtual platforms and exhibitions, which serve as venues for displaying and promoting digital art, fashion, and collectables. CryptoVoxels is an additional virtual environment constructed upon blockchain technology, allowing users to acquire land parcels and construct edifices. CryptoVoxels frequently feature virtual businesses, galleries, and digital art displays. The Sandbox is an online platform that enables users, both individuals and corporations, to develop and manage virtual environments focused explicitly on gaming experiences. This platform allows users to own their creations and provides monetization opportunities. The Sandbox's virtual shops and marketplaces facilitate the exchange of digital assets, apparel, and in-game objects. VRChat is a virtual reality (VR) platform that facilitates social interaction, enabling users to generate and exchange their virtual environments and digital representations of themselves, known as avatars. The platform facilitates a range of virtual fashion shows, art exhibitions, and interactive retail experiences. AltspaceVR is a virtual reality-based social platform that facilitates hosting various events, encompassing virtual retail encounters among its offerings. The platform facilitates the engagement between companies, producers, and users within the virtual reality (VR) environment.

In May 2021, Gucci formed a collaborative alliance with the online gaming platform Roblox, intending to organize a virtual gathering. Roblox players can engage in virtual experiences related to the fashion industry, such as trying on digital Gucci goods, participating in fashion shows, and acquiring exclusive virtual wearables through purchases. Prada has implemented its proprietary virtual reality store through a collaborative venture with a virtual reality platform. The establishment allowed customers to peruse Prada's assortments, engage in virtual garment trials, and complete transactions. OpenSea is recognized as a prominent platform within non-fungible token (NFT) marketplaces. It facilitates the acquisition, sale, and exchange of an extensive range of digital goods, encompassing artwork, virtual real estate, and collectables. Rarible is an autonomous platform that facilitates the generation, acquisition, and exchange of digital collectables and non-fungible tokens (NFTs) in a decentralized manner. This platform enables artists and creators to convert their work into digital tokens and, after that, offer them for direct purchase by consumers. SuperRare is a Digita platform that facilitates the sale of non-fungible token (NFT) artwork, offering artists a dedicated marketplace to distribute and monetize their digital creations. Individuals can purchase, amass, and exhibit digital artwork within virtual galleries.

The instances mentioned above serve as demonstrations of the vast array of retail encounters present within the metaverse. The metaverse has emerged as a conducive environment for innovative retail enterprises, encompassing virtual real estate, art galleries, user-generated virtual worlds, and blockchain-powered markets. The amalgamation of n-fungible tokens (NFTs), blockchain technology, and customized shopping experiences has fundamentally altered the dynamics of consumer-brand interactions in the digital realm, signifying a paradigm shift in the retail industry within the metaverse. Several retail enterprises operating in virtual settings have demonstrated significant achievements, leading the way in introducing novel methods of conducting business within the metaverse. These case studies provide fascinating illustrations of how businesses have successfully navigated and prospered by embracing and leveraging the opportunities presented by the digital environment. Consider, for example, the case of Gucci, a highly esteemed luxury fashion company which established a strategic alliance with the widely recognized virtual platform Roblox to organize an innovative virtual event. This groundbreaking event provided Roblox users unprecedented opportunities to engage with the Gucci brand, allowing them to experience digital Gucci products and participate in virtual fashion presentations. The reaction was impressive, as Gucci's virtual products quickly sold out in the vast Roblox metaverse. This relationship unequivocally demonstrated the considerable capacity of luxury brands to forge connections with a younger, technologically adept demographic by providing unique virtual fashion encounters and collectable merchandise, thereby exploring novel realms of brand interaction and commercial activity. The Bored Ape Yacht Club is an NFT initiative wherein participants possess distinct and whimsical "ape" souvenirs in the form of non-fungible tokens (NFTs). The project has garnered considerable attention and worth. In addition to its primary functions, the Yacht Club offers a virtual gallery space that enables owners to exhibit their artwork and digital artefacts. The triumph of the Bored Ape Yacht Club exemplifies the capacity of the metaverse to amalgamate collectables, virtual ownership, and a robust community of fans.

Axie Infinity is a decentralized gaming platform that utilizes blockchain technology to include features reminiscent of the popular Pokémon and Tamagotchi franchises. Participants acquire, reproduce, and combat mythical beings called "Axies." These entities are exchanged and transacted inside a digital marketplace, fostering a prosperous virtual economy where participants can generate tangible financial gains. Axie Infinity exemplifies using play-to-earn concepts and blockchain-based virtual economies in the metaverse. Platforms such as SuperRare have garnered significant attention within the art industry, allowing artists to convert their artwork into non-fungible tokens (NFTs). Enthusiasts of art can acquire digital artworks and exhibit them in virtual galleries. Specific digital art creations have been sold for millions of dollars. The proliferation of digital art platforms is evidence of the transformative impact of NFTs and blockchain technology on the art business, as they introduce novel concepts of digital scarcity and individualized ownership. The presented case studies illustrate the varied business possibilities of the metaverse, encompassing a wide array of endeavours, like collaborations between premium fashion brands and digital collectables, the development of blockchain-based games, and the establishment of virtual art galleries. The user emphasizes the potential of the metaverse to bring about a significant transformation in how individuals interact with and assign value to digital commodities. It underscores the importance of digital possession, exclusive content, and immersive virtual encounters in virtual shopping.

The ongoing expansion of the metaverse presents an increasingly diverse range of opportunities for innovation and entrepreneurship inside the digital domain.

DIGITAL MERCHANDISE AND ITS ROLE IN THE METAVERSE

"Digital Merchandise" pertains to intangible products and assets generated, purchased, exchanged, and possessed within virtual realms such as the metaverse and other digital domains. The assortment of digital assets encompasses a broad spectrum of products, including but not limited to digital art, virtual fashion, in-game items, and virtual real estate. Blockchain technology and non-fungible tokens (NFTs) are frequently utilized to represent and authenticate digital assets. These technologies guarantee such assets' distinctiveness, limited availability, and proprietorship (Jauhiainen et al., 2022). Within the metaverse, digital goods are frequently portrayed as non-fungible tokens (NFTs), granting individuals genuine ownership of their digital assets. Every non-fungible token (NFT) possesses distinct characteristics, guaranteeing limited availability and genuineness inside the digital domain. Ownership is essential in the metaverse, as people highly value unique and scarce objects. Individuals within the Metaverse commonly communicate their thoughts and emotions employing their virtual representations, digital avatars, and the virtual goods they possess. Digital merchandise plays a significant role in shaping an individual's digital identity, enabling them to exhibit their preferences, hobbies, and personal aesthetics within the virtual realm. The emergence of digital products has emerged as a prominent catalyst for economic growth within the metaverse. According to Valenti et al. (2021), this phenomenon presents avenues for creators, artists, and marketers to generate revenue from their digital products while offering customers the opportunity to engage in digital collectables and experiences. Customizing digital merchandise enables individualized experiences that cater to individual preferences and tastes. According to Nobile and Kalbaska (2020), individuals can personalize various goods to conform to their distinct preferences, augmenting their level of involvement and contentment.

The acquisition and engagement with digital commodities contribute to the heightened immersion within the metaverse. Individuals can engage with these objects, regardless of whether they take the form of virtual garments, in-game possessions, or digital artwork, thereby cultivating a heightened feeling of immersion within the digital realm. Digital merchandise facilitates the manifestation of artistic expression since individuals are empowered to conceive, alter, and exhibit their digital belongings. This feature enhances the metaverse experience by introducing a creative and personalized element. In general, digital gods inside the metaverse function as a stimulus for distinct digital possession, ingenuity, and customization, augmenting the user's encounter and bolstering the metaverse's development as a vibrant and immersive digital realm. The metaverse contains various virtual and digital commodities, collectively called digital merchandise. The objects mentioned above have acquired considerable importance owing to their distinctiveness, acquisition via non-fungible tokens (NFTs), and the potential they offer users to customize their digital encounters. Non-fungible tokens (NFTs) are frequently linked to digital art. Artisans engage in the production of digital artworks and subsequently convert them into non-fungible tokens (NFTs). Non-fungible tokens (FTs) are digital representations of ownership for distinct artistic creations, frequently exchanged within dedicated NFT marketplaces. Non-fungible tokens (NFTs) serve as the representation for a variety of digital collectables, which span from virtual trading cards to distinct virtual pets. Individuals who engage in collecting can engage in transactions involving the purchase, sale, and exchange of digital things, each possessing its unique non-fungible token (NFT). NFTs are utilized to organize virtual real estate properties within the metaverse. The acquisition and enhancement of virtual land parcels are made possible for users, who can secure ownership of these assets using non-fungible tokens (NFTs) (Alkhudary et al., 2022).

Fashion businesses have recently developed virtual garments and accessories, which users can purchase and utilize within the metaverse. Fashion goods are frequently depicted as non-fungible tokens (NFTs), enabling users to showcase their distinctive style and fashion preferences within the digital realm. In digital commerce, in-game items and skins have emerged as prevalent manifestations of commodities. Individuals who engage in gaming can acquire virtual weaponry, cosmetic alterations, digital representations of themselves, and other in-game assets to augment their overall gaming encounter. The adoption and nurturing ring of virtual pets and creatures have experienced a surge in popularity among users. The digital companion can offer both entertainment and companionship within the metaverse. In addition to NFT-based digital collectables, virtual collectables encompass a range of distinctive and limited-edition things, including toys, accessories, and decorative objects. Virtual art galleries within the metaverse serve as platforms for the exhibition of digital art produced by artists. These galleries facilitate the purchase, sale, and exhibition of digital artworks, cultivating a virtual art ecology. Artistic practitioners can produce digital sculptures and installations, which viewers can actively engage with and navigate throughout the metaverse. These installations offer distinctive creative encounters. Augmented reality technology enables individuals to engage in the virtual experience of trying on digital products, including clothing, accessories, and cosmetics. Augmented reality (AR) technology enables consumers to visually perceive the appearance of various things on their physical selves in real time, augmenting and enriching the overall shopping experience. Artists have explored augmented reality (AR) art and installations, allowing users to experience such artistic expressions through AR applications. These encounters facilitate the integration of art into the tangible realm using digital overlays. Individuals can own and possess virtual land parcels within the metaverse, enabling them to construct, enhance, and generate virtual properties. The properties used in this category may consist of virtual residences, commercial establishments, and recreational facilities (Yang et al., 2023; Cheng et al., 2022).

The metaverse's economy and culture have evolved to rely on various digital products, which let people express themselves, invest in distinctive assets, and engage in individualized digital experiences. Utilizing non-fungible tokens (NFTs) and blockchain technology guarantees the genuineness and proprietorship of these digital assets, hence augmenting their worth and importance within the metaverse. The utilization of digital merchandise within the metaverse presents notable benefits in terms of customization and personalization, augmenting the user experience and fostering more engagement. The utilization of digital products facilitates the provision of extensively customized and individualized experiences. Individuals can personalize many goods, like clothing, virtual properties, avatars, and digital artwork, to conform to their preferences. This degree of customization guarantees that individuals can generate digital assets that align with their distinct preferences and personal aesthetics. The utilization of digital products plays a significant role in shaping an individual's digital persona within the metaverse. Individuals can express their unique characteristics by possessing and exhibiting possessions that mirror their distinctive traits and passions. According to Nobile & Kalbaska (2020), the phenomenon fosters a perception of distinctiveness and proprietorship within the domain of digital platforms.

Individuals can customize and create digital assets, incorporating creative and expressive elements into their interactions. The metaverse allows users to express themselves creatively through constructing virtual homes, personalizing avatars, or curating virtual art collections. Within virtual settings, individuals possess the ability to customize their avatars through the inclusion of virtual garments, accessories, and cosmetic enhancements. Personalizing one's virtual representation enables individuals to manifest their style and personality, fostering a feeling of identity and emotional connection. The availability of digital products provides customers with a diverse selection of options, allowing them to choose from a wide variety of items, designs, and styles. According to Zimmerman et al. (2022), the availability of this diverse range of options enriches the choices and experiences of users, enabling them to discover goods that align with their tastes and preferences. The implementation of customization and personalization strategies has been found to result in increased levels of user engagement. The sense of ownership and attachment experienced by users towards their digital merchandise contributes to an extended duration of engagement within the metaverse and heightened degrees of enjoyment.

Incorporating on-fungible tokens (NFTs) introduces a dimension of scarcity and worth to digital commodities. Individuals are mindful of the distinctiveness of their digital belongings and recognize the potential for their value to appreciate over time, intensifying their emotional connection to these assets. Certain metaverse forms allow users to participate actively in the generation of digital merchandise. The content generated by users promotes a robust feeling of community and engagement since individuals can actively contribute to advancing the metaverse's digital ecology. The integration of personalized digital items within the metaverse serves to increase its immersive qualities. According to Zuo & Hen (2023), individuals can engage with many objects, including virtual apparel, in-game assets, and digital art, contributing to a more profound immersion within the digital realm. Customizing and personalizing digital items within the metaverse provide users with several benefits, including a heightened sense of ownership, enhanced identity formation, and increased opportunities for creative expression. Consequently, this phenomenon increases engagement, enjoyment, and attachment to the digital domain. The attractiveness of the metaverse and the emerging panorama of digital commerce within this digital frontier is enhanced by these individualized and distinctive experiences.

CHALLENGES AND BARRIERS

Retailers exploring the metaverse and adopting digital products encounter many obstacles, encompassing technology, security, and user involvement. To adapt to the evolving digital landscape, individuals and organizations must allocate resources towards establishing metaverse-compatible infrastructure. This infrastructure should contain many components, such as digital storefronts, payment gateways, and seamless interaction with blockchain technology. It is worth noting that the development and maintenance of such infrastructure can require significant resources. The technical problem of ensuring compatibility across multiple metaverse platforms is a significant concern. Implementing scalability measures is crucial to managing a potentially extensive and diverse user population, mitigating system disruption risk. Ensuring the security of high-value digital assets, including non-fungible tokens (NFTs) and virtual products, necessitates implementing protective solid measures against theft and fraud. Retailers must effectively handle and safeguard sensitive user data while protecting data privacy and compliance with relevant regulations. The verification of the legitimacy of digital goods and the mitigation of counterfeit products are of paramount importance in fostering trust (Cho et al., 2023). The metaverse poses a novel and unfamiliar domain for numerous users, requiring educational materials and services. Ensuring equitable access to digital resources and enhancing user interfaces are crucial factors in facilitating widespread acceptance and usage. Retailers face the intricate challenges of intellectual property, licensing, and royalties, especially when collaborating with content creators. Guaranteeing adherence to copyright regulations and resolving conflicts within the decentralized metaverse environment is a complex undertaking. The emerging regulatory landscape contributes to the intricacy, necessitating the ability to adjust to developing legal structures and tax policies. Therefore, adopting a comprehensive and meticulously designed strategy is imperative to address these diverse issues effectively. This strategy should prioritize aspects such as technology infrastructure, data security, user education, and establishing trust within the Metaverse (Li & Yu, 2023; Zhang et al., 2022). In addition, it is crucial to prioritize protecting intellectual property rights, establishing license agreements, and promoting collaboration with content creators to cultivate a societal environment that values and encourages creativity and innovation. Active participation within the metaverse community, advocating for transparency, and embracing technical resources to monitor and uphold intellectual property rights are key factors contributing to the metaverse ecosystem's ethical and prosperous development.

STRATEGIES FOR INTEGRATING THE METAVERSE INTO RETAIL OFFERINGS

Engaging in partnerships with Metaverse platform providers and developers represents a strategic option for merchants seeking to create a presence and harness metaverse's potential. These alliances can facilitate the development of novel features, provide technical assistance, and expand the reach of the product to a broader user base. Establish strategic alliances with metaverse platform providers, such as Decentraland, Roblox, or Fortnite, to develop customized virtual environments within their respective digital realms. These collaborations encompass the creation of digital retail outlets, immersive encounters, and organized activities. Engage in collaboration with experts in metaverse development, focusing on their specialized skills in creating virtual worlds, immersive experiences, and interactive components. It possesses the expertise to assist in conceptualizing and constructing an engaging metaverse representation. This study investigates the feasibility of connecting retail systems with metaverse platforms using Application Programming Interfaces (APIs). It facilitates smooth interactions between one's digital products and the virtual environment. Acquire virtual prope ties within metaverse platforms to develop a digital presence. Specific platforms provide opportunities to acquire parcels of land that can be developed and tailored to embody and promote one's corporate identity effectively. Collaborate with metaverse marketplaces or NFT platforms to list and vend your digital items. According to Shen et al. (2023) and Jauhiainen et al. (2022), these marketplaces might provide functionalities for the creation of non-fungible tokens (NFTs) and the facilitation of digital transactions.

Collaborate with augmented reality developers to design and produce immersive augmented reality experiences that facilitate the integration of the actual and virtual realms. It may encompass augmented reality (AR) applications facilitating virtual try-on experiences for garments or accessories. Engage in collaborative partnerships with game developers to integrate your digital items into widely recognized virtual gaming platforms. The utilization of in-game marketing, skins, and accessories has the potential to enhance the visibility of one's brand. Collaborate with virtual fashion designers and producers to provide distinctive apparel and accessories within the metaverse. Collaborations with fashion influencers within the virtual realm can yield significant value. Engage in or organize virtual events and exhibitions within the metaverse. Partner with event organizers and platform providers to exhibit your digital merchandise. Establishing formal technical support agreements with platform providers is recommended to guarantee the seamless operation of your virtual storefront and facilitate consumer interactions. Engage in collaborative efforts with metaverse communities and user groups. To gain insights into the preferences and needs of these communities, it is essential to engage with them actively. This can be achieved by involving them in the collaborative process of co-creating virtual experiences and goods. To disseminate educational information and resources about the products, it is recommended to establish collaborations with educational institutions and virtual academies operating within the Metaverse (Cheng et al., 2022).

These collaborative efforts have the potential to enhance brand recognition and provide significant benefits to the metaverse community. Engage in partnership with metaverse analytics providers to acquire valuable insights about user behaviour and preferences, enabling the adoption of data-driven decision-making strategies. It is advisable to have legal counsel to guarantee that your agreements about metaverse cooperation follow relevant laws and regulations. Engaging in partnerships with metaverse platform providers and developers can unlock avenues for innovation, growth, and enhanced brand visibility. As the metaverse goes further in development, these collaborations can assist merchants in maintaining a leading position inside this rapidly evolving digital landscape.

CO-CREATING CUSTOMER EXPERIENCES

Cooperatively creating consumer experiences within the metaverse is a dynamic and innovative strategy for effectively engaging customers and fostering a sense of ownership and active participation. The immersive and attractive qualities of the metaverse present a unique opportunity for merchants to collaborate with their customers in designing, customizing, and augmenting digital products and virtual interactions (Buhalis et al., 2022). Individuals assume an active participant role within the metaverse instead of an inert consumer stance. Individuals can actively contribute to creating their own experiences by personalizing digital goods, actively participating in virtual environments, and designing their virtual identities. Active engagement transforms customers from passive buyers to active co-creators and collaborators.

Metaverse platforms frequently provide users with a vast array of customization options. Customers can construct avatars, virtual environments, and digital products that reflect their preferences. Customization fosters a sense of ownership by requiring individuals to invest time and creativity in shaping their virtual representation (Park & Kim, 2022). In the metaverse, the concept of co-creation transcends individual interactions. Customers are incorporated into a larger community where they interact collaboratively with other customers and retailers. The creation of a sense of community and the cultivation of shared experiences have the potential to increase brand loyalty and advocacy. Retailers can use consumer feedback and input to advance and improve their digital products. Organizations can use diverse techniques, such as virtual focus groups, surveys, and real-time consumer interactions, to gain valuable insights that can be used to improve and expand their product or service offerings (HennigThurau et al., 2022; Ylilehto et al., 202).

Co-creation has the potential to facilitate the creation of innovative marketing strategies. Retailers can create marketing campaigns celebrating user-generated content or coordinate online events showcasing user-generated virtual experiences, fostering enthusiasm and engagement. User-generated content plays a crucial role in the metaverse's collaborative creative process. Retailers can incentivize consumers to create and disseminate content pertinent to their digital products. Virtual fashion displays, art exhibitions, and personalized product demonstrations may be included in the content. Co-creation within the Metaverse provides retailers with a unique value proposition. By allowing customers to collaborate on developing their digital experiences, retailers can differentiate themselves in a saturated market and satisfy the growing demand for personalized and engaging digital interactions (Lu & Mintz, 2023; Lee & Gu, 2022). The metaverse offers substantial opportunities for consumer engagement, resulting in the production of voluminous amounts of data. This information can enhance retailers' understanding of consumer behaviour, preferences, and trends. This observation can impact numerous facets of business operations, including product development, marketing strategies, and the consumer experience. Co-creation within the Metaverse frequently involves interpersonal interactions and collective participation in various activities. Customers can extend invitations to friends and family members to join them in virtual spaces or collaborate on design projects. This social element contributes to the enhancement of the overall customer experience. The concept of the me averse blurs the distinction between virtual and physical interactions. Retailers can establish integrated omnichannel experiences that facilitate seamless transitions between physical retail environments and the metaverse, and vice versa, for consumers. Co-creating consumer experiences in the metaverse is a dynamic and influential phenomenon that is in a constant state of evolution. It facilitates the transformation of customers into active participants in the creation process, encourages the customization of products or services to individual preferences, fosters the formation of communities, and provides merchants with a unique strategy to effectively engage and retain customers in an expanding digital and immersive environment. By employing this concept, businesses can develop meaningful and long-lasting relationships with their customers in the Metaverse (Lu & Mintz, 2023; Gerea et al., 2021).

Customer participation in creating digital products is a collaborative effort that fosters a sense of ownership and individualization. Construct immersive virtual storefronts within the metaverse where customers can explore, interact, and customize digital goods. This research seeks to comprehensively analyze the diverse methods and options available to individuals for customizing products, including but not limited to apparel, accessories, and virtual dwellings. Encourage client participation in the content creation process. For instance, retailers can establish platforms that facilitate consumers' creation and submission of virtual product concepts. These can include diverse forms of creative expression, such as apparel designs, accessories, and even virtual real estate concepts. Organize virtual design workshops or events that facilitate collaboration between customers and designers/artists, allowing them to develop digital products collaboratively. The studies mentioned above by Schweidel et al. (2022) and Liu et al. (2021) emphasize the potential for these sessions to provide customers with valuable insights into the design process, allowing them to contribute their opinions actively.

Implement design contests or competitions encouraging customer participation in submitting their ideas for digital product designs. The honorees can see their artistic endeavours materialize and be conspicuously featured within the confines of your digital marketplace. Implementing virtual try-on and customization tools enables customers to visually evaluate the appearance of digital clothing and accessories on their avatars. Before concluding a transaction, this functionality enables users to experiment with numerous appearances. Implementing in-world feedback methods, such as message boards and virtual suggestion boxes, will enable consumers to provide input and suggestions regarding digital products actively. Real-time feedback has the potential to influence and direct the product development process. Invite a carefully selected group of customers to participate in the beta testing portion of novel digital goods. Individuals can offer input regarding usability, design, and technical difficulties, according to Schumacher (2022).

It is recommended to conduct surveys and polls within the metaverse to evaluate consumer preferences, collect feedback, and make informed decisions regarding digital commerce. Organize virtual prod ct launch events that allow consumers to be the first to receive and provide feedback on innovative digital items. This phenomenon generates anticipation and enthusiasm for the products or services you offer. Conduct virtual focus groups to facilitate in-depth conversations with customers about their requirements, preferences, and expectations regarding digital products. These organizations have the potential to offer insightful observations. Promote and incentivize consumers to provide feedback ratings and to share their digital product experiences. Customer evaluations and testimonials can impact the purchasing decisions of other users. Establishing a community encircling one's digital products in the metaverse is essential. (Alfaisal et al., 2022; Shen et al., 2021) The community in question offers a variety of benefits, including support, inspiration, and a platform for members to share their inventions and experiences.

Integrate gamification components that allow customers to engage in digital product-related challenges. Participating in challenges may result in the acquisition of prizes or recognition. Collaborate with influential members of the metaverse community, such as content creators and influencers, to effectively market your digital products. Influencers can provide live demonstrations and valuable insights, captivating and engaging their audience effectively. Recognize and reward customers who actively contribute to developing and promoting digital products. Recognizing their efforts fosters a sense of gratitude and camaraderie. User feedback and input drive perpetually improving and iterating digital products. Hennig-Thurau et al. 2022) and Waqas et al. (2020) demonstrate the significance of demonstrating to consumers that their ideas and preferences are considered.

Actively involving customers in developing digital products has the potential to empower them, allowing them to influence their own experiences actively. This participation fosters brand loyalty and a sense of shared ownership. By utilizing co-creat-on strategies within the metaverse, merchants can offer consumers a diverse selection of digitally rendered products tailored to their interests and desires. This strategy not only improves the level of customization but also creates a more engaging and immersive purchasing experience for consumers.

Roblox is a well-known metaverse platform allowing users to create immersive games. The capacity of the R blox platform to facilitate collaborative development is exemplified by the fact that a significant proportion of the most popular games on the platform were created solely by its users. Through the organization of branded events and the creation of in-game items and accessories, retailers can interact with consumers.

Decentraland is a blockchain-based virtual environment that allows users to acquire and customize virtual real estate. Retailers can collaborate with virtual proprietors to develop branded experiences, pop-up shops, and interactive events within these virtual spaces.

Nike and the video game Fortnite collaborated to create a limited-edition virtual sneaker called the "Nike Air Jordan 1." This partnership is significant due to Fortnite's immense popularity as a virtual gaming platform. The fact that players can acquire and customize these athletic shoes exemplifies the ability of businesses to develop collaboratively appealing virtual merchandise for the gaming community.

Metahero, a metaverse-based platform, facilitates the organization of virtual fashion shows, allowing users to conceptualize and showcase their digital apparel designs. These events allow users to participate in the fashion industry and exhibit their designs in the metaverse.

Decentraland and Atari have partnered to create a virtual casino where users can play classic Atari games, earn rewards, and interact socially in a simulated environment. This highly immersive collaborative environment combines gaming, social interaction, and digital commerce elements.

Using blockchain technology, Cryptovoxels is a digital universe. Individuals with artistic talent can acquire and establish virtual art galleries to exhibit and market their digital artwork. Visitors can erase these galleries and purchase digital artwork using Bitcoin.

Gucci partnered with Arianee, a blockchain technology developer, to create the "Gucci Vault." This initiative enables consumers to register and protect their Gucci products by establishing a blockchain-based certificate of ownership. This implementation adds digital co-creation and authentication to the procedure.

Roblox's Imagination Platform allows users to collaborate on developing virtual products, games, and experiences. The initiative mentioned above assists developers, artists, and creators develop their unique digital products.

Numerous platforms, including OpenSea and Rarible, enable artists to create and trade non-fungible tokens (NFTs) representing their digital artwork. Customers can actively interact with artists, acquire NFT artworks, and partake in the expanding NFT art market.

CryptoKitties is an example of a collectable game that operates on a blockchain infrastructure, allowing players to generate, acquire, and trade digital feline creatures. It demonstrates how purchasers can actively contribute to the collaborative production of unique digital collectables in the metaverse.

Companies and platforms use the metaverse to actively involve individuals in the collaborative creation of digital commerce, virtual experiences, and digital art, as demonstrated by the above examples. The potential for effactive consumer engagement and co-creation in the metaverse transcends specific industries and platforms, presenting many opportunities for brand collaboration and user participation.

MARKETING AND PROMOTION IN THE METAVERSE

By employing a multi-pronged strategy that capitalizes on virtual environments' immersive and interactive nature, retailers can effectively market and promote their digital products within the metaverse. Construct visually engaging and immersive virtual stores within the metaverse where users can interact with digital merchandise. These areas should be actual establishments while utilizing the metaverse's unique capabilities. Utilize augmented reality and virtual reality to improve the purchasing experience. Users can virtually test apparel, accessories, and virtual products within the Metaverse (Cheng et al., 2021).

Permit users to interact with and evaluate your digital products. For example, users should be able to alter virtual apparel and accessories' hues, patterns, or characteristics. Strategically position virtual billboards and displays within the metaverse to promote your digital products. Utilize targeted advertisements to reach specific segments of users based on their interests and behaviours—partner with influential metaverse figures who command a sizeable following. In the virtual environment, these influencers can promote your digital products, conduct reviews, and host events. Encourage consumers to create content associated with your digital products. Exciting and engaging user-generated content can include fashion displays, art exhibitions, and reviews. Create and cultivate virtual communities for your brand and digital products. Engage with users actively, create forums, and promote the sharing of user-generated content. Incorporate feedback mechanisms for users within the metaverse. Permit them to contribute their ideas, thoughts, and suggestions for enhancing your digital products. Virtually host product launches, fashion displays, and art exhibitions. These events must be immersive and engaging to attract a large audience and generate enthusiasm (Zhang et al., 2022).

Integrate your presence in the metaverse with conventional social media platforms. Share content, videos and store updates to bridge the divide between the metaverse and the larger online community. Promote your online store and digital goods on multiple metaverse platforms. This cross-promotion raises awareness and attracts users from various metaverse communities. Incorporate elements of gamification into the purchasing experience. For instance, you can design challenges, missions, and reward systems to encourage user engagement and purchases (HennigThurau et al., 2022).

Create virtual pop-up stores or special events with exclusive or limited-time digital merchandise. These occasions inspire a sense of urgency and exclusivity. Create contests where users can create, modify, or personalize digital merchandise. Provide incentives and acknowledgement for the finest user-generated designs. Utilize data analytics to monitor metaverse user behaviour, preferences, and engagement. Adapt your marketing strategies in light of these observations. Provide customer service within the metaverse in response to user questions and concerns. Positive shopping experiences are fostered by engaging with users and addressing their requirements (Pyae et al., 2023; Bibri & Allam, 2022).

Effective marketing and promotion in the metaverse necessitate a comprehensive comprehension of the virtual environment and user expectations. The distinction between physical and digital purchasing should be blurred by creating engaging, interactive, and user-centred experiences. By incorporating the unique characteristics of the metaverse and actively engaging with users, retailers can effectively market and promote their digital products. Strategically position virtual billboards and displays within the metaverse to promote your digital products. These can be placed in high-traffic areas for optimal exposure (Bibri & Allam, 2022).

Utilize targeted in-game ads to reach specific user segments. For instance, if you promote virtual fashion, you should target users who have previously engaged in fashion-related activities. Develop interactive demonstrations of your digital products for your online store. Permit users to virtually try on items, experiment with features, and visualize how products work in their virtual lives. Collaborate with meta-erase influencers with a significant following on the platform. These influencers can promote your digital products, generating chatter and interest among their respective audiences and inviting influencers to evaluate your digital products in the metaverse. User-generated content can substantially impact other users' purchasing decisions (Abumalloh et al., 2023; Hwang & Lee, 2022).

Partner with influencers to conduct sponsored virtual events, such as fashion shows or product launches, to introduce and promote your digital goods to a larger audience. Create and cultivate virtual communities for your brand and digital products. Engage with users, establish forums, and facilitate sharing of user-generated content in the metaverse. Contests in which users create content related to your digital products should be organized. Provide incentives and acknowledgement for the finest user-generated content (Bibri & Allam, 2022; HennigThurau et al., 2022).

Encourage users to provide feedback and take part in co-creation endeavours. Involving customers in product development or design decisions fosters ownership and loyalty. Retailers can effectively market and promote their digital products within the metaverse by implementing these advertising strategies, forming partnerships with Metaverse influencers, and fostering community engagement. In line with the immersive nature of virtual environments, these methods generate a dynamic and interactive purchasing experience.

Utilize traditional social media platforms such as Facebook, Instagram, Twitter, and LinkedIn to promote your presence in the metaverse. Share content, videos and updates about your online store to engage your social media audience. Launch targeted advertising using campaigns on social media platforms to reach a larger audience and direct them to your Metaverse virtual storefront. Encourage users to share their virtual experiences on social networking sites. Create and promote hashtags related to your digital merchandise or virtual events to attract a larger audience. Participate in metave se-centric social media groups, pages, and forums. To increase brand visibility, participate in discussions, share insights about your digital offerings, and respond to user inquiries (HennigThurau et al., 2022).

Host metaverse product launch events virtually. These events should be comprehensive and captivating to attract a large audience. Utilize interactive e-events, such as virtual fashion shows or art exhibitions, to introduce and market your digital products. In the metaverse, create temporary virtual pop-up stores or special events. These events may feature exclusive or limited-time digital merchandise, fostering a sense of urgency and exclusivity that encourages user participation.

Conduct virtual events featuring contests or giveaways where users can win exclusive digital merchandise or NFTs. These events may increase participation and enthusiasm. Create immersive narratives or stories about your digital products. In storytelling, users can partake in these narratives and interact with your brand, generating engagement and interest. Provide customer service within the metaverse by responding to user questions and concerns. Engaging with users and addressing their requirements in a virtual environment promotes a positive shopping experience (Cheng et al., 2021).

Social media and virtual events are crucial in the metaverse's retail promotion. By integrating social media platforms, engaging in cross-promotion, encouraging the sharing of user-generated content, and hosting interactive virtual events, retailers can effectively reach a larger audience and create immersive, engaging experiences that resonate with the metaverse's distinctive characteristics. Case studies and success tales of retailers who have successfully transitioned to digital merchandise and integrated the metaverse into their retail offerings should be provided.

Numerous successful examples highlight the significance of user-generated content. Users desire to be active participants and co-creators in the metaverse. Encourage and promote user-generated content, whether designs for virtual fashion, digital art, or virtual real estate. This content not only engages users but also expands the scope of your brand. Collaboration with me-averse influencers can substantially increase the exposure of your digital products. Influencers have developed fan bases, and their recommendations convey weight. They can conduct prod ct evaluations, host events, and promote your products to a larger metaverse audience.

Building and engaging virtual communities around your brand and digital products is essential. It promotes a sense of community and motivates users to become brand advocates. Provide opportunities for discussion, user-generated content sharing, and community member interaction. Customer loyalty can be substantially boosted by soliciting user feedback and involving them in co-creation activities. Users value it when their input is considered and incorporated into product design. It fosters a sense of ownership and brand loyalty (Zhang et al., 2022; HennigThurau et al., 2022).

Cross-promotion is an effective method of attracting individuals from various metaverse communities. You can access diverse user bases and expand your reach by promoting your virtual store and digital goods on multiple metaverse platforms. Integrating your presence in the metaverse with traditional social media platforms helps bridge the divide between the virtual and physical worlds. Social media can direct users to your virtual store, share user-generated content, and engage with a larger online audience (HennigThurau et al., 2022).

Interactive virtual events, including product launches, fashion shows, and art exhibitions, can generate enthusiasm and engage a larger audience. These events are memorable and alluring to users due to their immersive nature. Customization and personalization options for digital products substantially impact user engagement. Permit users to alter, experiment with, and customize digital products to their liking. The metaverse thrives on uniqueness and self-expression.

The provision of responsive customer service within the metaverse enhances the purchasing experience. Within the virtual environment, users should have access to assistance, information, and solutions to ensure their satisfaction. Utilize data analytics to monitor metaverse user behaviour, preferences, and engagement. Insights derived from data can assist in refining marketing strategies and product offerings to correlate with user interests (Bibri & Allam, 2022).

These lessons learned and best practices highlight the significance of user engagement, community development, personalization, and interactive experiences in the metaverse. Those retailers who successfully implement these strategies will be able to establish a robust online presence and cultivate brand loyalty.

FUTURE TRENDS AND CONSIDERATIONS

In the retail industry, the future of the metaverse promises significant growth and adoption, making it more accessible to a broader audience of users. As the metaverse grows, there will be an increase in demand for digital goods and immersive purchasing experiences. Advanced immersive technologies such as augmented reality (AR) and virtual reality (VR) will become more refined and cost-effective, allowing users to investigate products and environments virtually before purchasing. The integration of artificial intelligence (AI), augmented reality (AR) and virtual reality (VR) will facilitate highly personalized metaverse experiences, with AI-driven recommendations and virtual assistants boosting user engagement. Moreover, blockchain technology and non-fungible tokens (NFTs) will transform digital goods by introducing authenticity and collectability.

Cross-platform experiences integrating the Metaverse with conventional retail channels will become the norm. Extended Reality (XR), which includes AR, VR, and mixed reality, will offer innovative shopping experiences by further blurring the boundaries between the real and virtual worlds. Virtual fashion and digital devices will experience rapid expansion as users personalize avatars and virtual environments. Social and collaborative purchasing will become more prevalent, attracting users with shared experiences. However, environmental sustainability concerns and the requirement for responsible online business practices will also gain prominence.

As the environment changes, metaverse sustainability will necessitate ongoing innovation and adaptability. Data privacy and security will remain paramount, given the increasing value of user data. Last, developing standardized metaverse ecosystems and interoperable platforms will improve user experience and interactions. By keeping abreast of these emerging trends and factors, retailers can position themselves for success in the ever-changing metaverse environment.

CONCLUSION

This chapter examined the groundbreaking fusion of the metaverse and the retail industry, highlighting the crucial transition to digital goods and immersive shopping experiences. It investigated fundamental metaverse concepts, retracing its historical development and recognizing its immense business potential, particularly in retail. It discovered a prop ring landscape of virtual stores and marketplaces upon examining the current state of metaverse retail. Digital merchandise, such as non-fungible tokens (NFTs), virtual goods, and augmented reality products, seized the spotlight and promised to transform purchasing experiences. It provided practical strategies for seamless integration, customer engagement, and effective marketing within the metaverse while acknowledging the obstacles. Future trends in sustainability, data privacy, and changing regulations are expected to shape a dynamic retail landscape. Adopting the metaverse is essential for retailers to meet changing consumer expectations and maintain their competitiveness, making it the undisputed future of retail.

REFERENCES

Abumalloh, R. A., Nilashi, M., Ooi, K., Wei-Han, G., Cham, T., Dwivedi, Y. K., & Hughes, L. (2023). Adopting a metaverse in the retail industry and its impact on sustainable competitive advantage: Moderating impact of sustainability commitment. *Annals of Operations Research*. doi:10.1007/s10479-023-05608-8

Abumalloh, R. A., Nilashi, M., Ooi, K., Wei-Han, G., Cham, T., Dwivedi, Y. K., & Hughes, L. (2023). The adoption of metaverse in the retail industry and its impact on sustainable competitive advantage: The moderating impact of sustainability commitment. *Annals of Operations Research*. doi:10.1007/s10479-023-05608-8

Alfaisal, R., Hashim, H., & Azizan, U. H. (2022). Metaverse system adoption in education: A systematic literature review. *Journal of Computers n. Education*. doi:10.10 7/s40692-022-00256-6

Alkhudary, R., Belvaux, B., & Guibert, N. (2022). Understanding non-fungible tokens (NFTs): Insights on consumption practices and a research agenda. *Marketing Letters, 34*(2), 321–336. https://doi.org/ doi:10.10 7/s11002-022-09655-2

Bibri, S. E., & Allam, Z. (2022). The Metaverse as a virtual form of data-driven smart cities: The ethics of the hyper-connectivity, datafication, algorithmization, and platformization of urban society. *Computational Urban Science, 2*(1), 22. doi:10.1007/s43762-022-00050-1 PMID:35915731

Buhalis, D., Lin, M., & Leung, D. (2022). Metaverse as a driver for customer experience and value co-creation: Implications for hospitality and tourism management and marketing. *International Journal of Contemporary Hospitality Management, 35*(2), 701–716. doi:10.1108/IJCHM-05-2022-0631

Cheng, X., Zhang, S., Fu, S., Liu, W., Guan, C., Mou, J., Ye, Q., & Huang, C. (2022). Exploring the metaverse in the digital economy: An overview and research framework. *Journal of Electronic Business & Digital Economics, 1*(1/2), 206–224. doi:10.1108/JEBDE-09-2022-0036

Cho, J., Dieck, M. C. T., & Jung, T. (2023). What is the metaverse? Challenges, opportunities, definition, and future research directions. In Springer Proceedins in Business and Economics (pp. 3–26). Springer. doi:10.1007/978-3-031-25390-4_1

De Giovanni, P. (2023). Sustainability of the metaverse: A transition to industry 5.0. *Sustainability (Basel), 15*(7), 6079. doi:10.3390/su15076079

Gerea, C., Gonzalez-Lopez, F., & Herskovic, V. (2021). Omnichannel customer experience and management: An integrative review and research agenda. *Sustainability (Basel), 13*(5), 2824. doi:10.3390/su13052824

Hennig-Thurau, T., Aliman, D. N., Herting, A. M., Cziehso, G., Linder, M., & Kübler, R. V. (2022). Social interactions in the metaverse: Framework, initial evidence, and research roadmap. *Journal of the Academy of Marketing Science, 51*(4), 889–913. doi:10.1007/s11747-022-00908-0

Hurst, W., Spyrou, O., Tekinerdoğan, B., & Krampe, C. (2023). Digital art and the metaverse: Benefits and challenges. *Future Internet, 15*(6), 188. doi:10.3390/fi15060188

Hwang, R., & Lee, M. (2022). The influence of music content marketing on user satisfaction and intention to use in the Metaverse: A focus on the SPICE model. *Businesses, 2*(2), 141 155. https://doi.org/ doi:10.33 0/businesses2020010

Jauhiainen, J. S., Krohn, C., & Junnila, J. (2022). Metaverse and sustainability: Systematic review of scientific publications until 2022 and beyond. *Sustainability (Basel), 15*(1), 346. doi:10.3390/su15010346

Lee, H. J., & Gu, H. H. (2022). Empirical research on the metaverse user experience of digital natives. *Sustainability, 14*(22), 14747. https://doi.org/ doi:10.33 0/su142214747

Li, M., & Yu, Z. (2023). A systematic review on the metaverse-based blended English learning. *Frontiers in Psycholo y, 13*. https://doi.org/ doi:10.33 9/fpsyg.2022.1087508

Lu, S., & Mintz, O. (2023). Marketing on the metaverse: Research opportunities and challenges. *AMS Review, 13*(1–2), 51–166. doi:10.1007/s13162-023-00255-5

Nobile, T. H., & Kalbaska, N. (2020). An exploration of personalization in digital communication. Insights in fashion. *Lecture Notes in Computer Science, 12204*, 456–473. doi:10.1007/978-3-030-50341-3_35

Park, S. M., & Kim, Y. (2022). A metaverse: Taxonomy, components, applications, and open challenges. *IEEE Access, 10*, 4209 4251. https://doi.org/ doi:10.11 9/access.2021.3140175

Pyae, A., Ravyse, W., Luimula, M., Pizarro-Lucas, E., Sánchez, P. L., Dorado-Díaz, P. I., & Thaw, A. K. (2023). Exploring user experience and usability in a metaverse learning environment for students: A Usability Study of Artificial Intelligence, Innovation, and Society (AIIS). *Electronics (Basel), 12*(20), 283. doi:10.3390/electronics12204283

Schumacher, P. (2022). The Metaverse as an opportunity for architecture and society: Design drivers, core competencies. *Architectural Intelligence, 1*(1), 11. doi:10.1007/s44223-022-00010-z PMID:35993030

Schweidel, D. A., Bart, Y., Inman, J. J., Stephen, A. T., Libai, B., Andrews, M., Rosario, A. B., Chae, I., Chen, Z., Kupor, D., Longoni, C., & Thomaz, F. (2022). How consumer digital signals are reshaping the customer journey. *Journal of the Academy of Marketing Science, 50*(6), 1257–1276. doi:10.1007/s11747-022-00839-w PMID:35221393

Shalender, K., Singla, B., & Sharma, S. (2023). Blockchain Adoption in the financial sector: Challenges, solutions, and implementation framework. In K. Mehta, R. Sharma, & P. Yu (Eds.), *Revolutionizing Financial Services and Markets Through FinTech and Blockchain* (pp. 269–277). IGI Global. doi:10.4018/978-1-6684-8624-5.ch017

Shen, B., Wei-Ming, T., Guo, J., Zhao, L., & Qin, P. (2021). How do we promote user purchases in Metaverse? A systematic literature review on consumer behaviour research and virtual commerce application design. *Applied Sciences (Basel, Switzerland), 11*(3), 11087. doi:10.3390/app112311087

Valenti, F., Bikakis, A., Terras, M., Speed, C., Hudson-Smith, A., & Chalkias, K. (2021). Crypto collectibles, museum funding and OpenGLAM: Challenges, opportunities and the potential of non-fungible tokens (NFTs). *Applied Sciences (Basel, Switzerland), 11*(1), 9931. doi:10.3390/app11219931

Waqas, M., Hamzah, Z. L., & Salleh, N. a. M. (2020). Customer experience: A systematic literature review and consumer culture theory-based conceptualization. *Management Review Qua truly, 71*(1), 135–176. https://doi.org/ doi:10.107/s11301-020-00182-w

Yang, X., Cheng, P., Liu, X., & Shih, S. (2023). The impact of immersive virtual reality on art education: A study of flow state, cognitive load, brain state, and motivation. *Education and Information Technologies*. doi:10.1007/s10639-023-12041-8

Ylilehto, M., Komulainen, H., & Ulkuniemi, P. (2021). The critical factors are shaping customer shopping experiences with innovative technologies. *Baltic Journal of Management, 16*(5), 661–680. doi:10.1108/BJM-02-2021-0049

Zhang, X., Chen, Y., Hu, L., & Wang, Y. (2022). The Metaverse in education: Definition, framework, features, potential applications, challenges, and future research topics. *Frontiers in Psycholo y, 13*. https://doi.org/ doi:10.33 9/fpsyg.2022.1016300

Zimmermann, D., Wehler, A., & Kaspar, K. (2022). Self-representation through avatars in digital environments. *Current Psychology (New Brunswick, N.J.), 4*(25), 21775–21789. doi:10.1007/s12144-022-03232-6

Zuo, M., & Shen, Y. (2023). How do features and affordances of a metaverse portal engage users? Evidence from exergames. *Internet Research*. doi:10.11 8/intr-08-2022-0618

KEY TERMS AND DEFINITIONS

Augmented Reality: Augmented Reality (AR) is a technology that superimposes digital information onto the real-world environment. It enhances user experiences by seamlessly integrating digital aspects with the actual world using devices such as smartphones or AR glasses.

Customer Engagement: Customer engagement encompasses the interactions and connections between organizations and consumers, focusing on establishing relationships, delivering tailored experiences, and cultivating loyalty through several channels.

Digital Merchandise: Digital merchandise includes intangible commodities or things accessible in digital formats, typically obtained and utilized within virtual worlds, gaming platforms, or the broader digital realm.

Future Trends in Retail: Upcoming developments in the retail industry involve the growing implementation of digital tactics, the use of augmented reality applications to create immersive shopping experiences, and the incorporation of NFTs to redefine ownership and value in the retail sector.

Metaverse: The Metaverse is a digital realm that surpasses conventional online encounters, allowing individuals to engage in a collective, immersive, and computer-generated setting.

NFTs (Non-Fungible Tokens): Non-Fungible Tokens (NFTs) are distinct digital assets authenticated using blockchain technology. They serve to establish ownership and ensure the genuineness of the asset. NFTs have gained significant popularity in art, gaming, and collectables.

Retail Sector: The retail sector comprises enterprises providing consumer goods and services, encompassing brick-and-mortar storefronts and online commerce platforms and expanding into digital domains.

Chapter 6
The Role of Metaverse for Enhanced Employee Retention:
Retail Leadership Training, Approaches, and Challenges

M. Vaishali
SRM Institute of Science and Technology, Chennai, India

V. Kiruthiga
SRM Institute of Science and Technology, Chennai, India

ABSTRACT

In the ever-evolving retail industry landscape of digital transformation and virtualization, practical leadership training has emerged as a pivotal factor in enhancing employee retention. This study delves into the role of metaverse in retail leadership training for enhanced employee retention to illuminate the symbiotic relationship between metaverse technologies and the cultivation of solid retail leaders. The research seeks to understand how metaverse-based leadership training programs shape leadership competencies within the retail sector and, in turn, influence employee satisfaction and loyalty. This study uncovers a dynamic shift in leadership development by exploring the methods, technologies, and strategies employed in these innovative programs. The findings suggest that metaverse-based training holds the potential to redefine leadership excellence in the retail metaverse, where employees are increasingly operating in virtual spaces. As the digital sphere and physical reality continue to converge, organizations harness the metaverse's power for leadership development.

DOI: 10.4018/979-8-3693-3358-7.ch006

INTRODUCTION

In the ever-evolving retail industry landscape of digital transformation and virtualization, practical leadership training has emerged as a pivotal factor in enhancing employee retention. This study delves into "The Role of Metaverse in Retail Leadership Training for Enhanced Employee Retention" to illuminate the symbiotic relationship between metaverse technologies and the cultivation of solid retail leaders.

The research seeks to understand how metaverse-based leadership training programs shape leadership competencies within the retail sector and, in turn, influence employee satisfaction and loyalty. This study uncovers a dynamic shift in leadership development by exploring the methods, technologies, and strategies employed in these innovative programs.

The findings suggest that metaverse-based training holds the potential to redefine leadership excellence in the retail metaverse, where employees are increasingly operating in virtual spaces. As the digital sphere and physical reality continue to converge, organizations harness the metaverse's power for leadership development. They are better framed to foster employee engagement, drive action, and ultimately retain their talent in this digitally transformed retail landscape.

INTRODUCTION

The retail industry has faced various challenges in recent years, including high employee turnover rates that can impact customer service quality and increase costs related to recruiting and training. However, new immersive technologies like the metaverse present exciting opportunities to transform retail leadership training in ways that could potentially improve employee retention.

In the ever-evolving landscape of the retail industry, talent retention is a perpetual challenge. High employee turnover rates have long been a characteristic concern for retailers, leading to increased recruitment and training costs, as well as a potential decline in customer satisfaction.

This meta-analysis reviews the evidence for VR effectiveness in retail training contexts Ma, J., Sheng, W., & Pahlevansharif, S. (2022). Finds VR outperforms traditional methods.

Effective leadership is a linchpin in addressing this issue, as it can empower employees, improve their job satisfaction, and consequently enhance retention. An empirical study found that retail employees trained using VR simulations showed improvements in sales performance and engagement Cao, Z., Leng, J., Liu, T., & Yin, C. (2022). However, the traditional methods of leadership training in the retail sector often need to provide the immersive, interactive, and adaptable experiences needed to groom exceptional leaders.

In a parallel universe, the metaverse is emerging as a transformative technology with the potential to reshape numerous facets of our lives. It offers an immersive, interconnected digital environment where individuals can interact, learn, and create. The technical paper discusses metaverse opportunities and projections of growth, including use cases in corporate training. Acton, T., Gao, J., Jamshidi, L., & Meng, Y. (2022). This paper delves into the intersection of these two domains, exploring the role of the metaverse in retail leadership training and its implications for employee retention.

The metaverse refers to persistent 3D virtual environments where users can interact through digital avatars. Major companies like Meta are investing billions into developing metaverse platforms, with potential applications across industries including retail. Within the metaverse, realistic simulations can be created to provide engaging, gamified environments for corporate training and skill-building.

For retail managers, metaverse-based training programs could provide highly immersive leadership development experiences. By taking on avatars within simulated retail settings, managers can practice and enhance skills like conflict resolution, performance management, and team-building in lifelike scenarios. This experiential learning can lead to greater confidence and preparedness in real-world management roles.

A Study demonstrating connections between managerial coaching skills and employee engagement/retention. Metaverse could enhance coaching skills. Wang, X., Yang, B., & McLean, G. N. (2020). As retail competes for talent, innovative training programs via metaverse simulations may provide a key competitive advantage. Retailers that utilize this technology early could see significant gains in manager readiness and employee retention. In summary, the metaverse presents a promising new training medium that can prepare retail leaders to nurture talent and sustain a thriving workforce.

In turn, more effective and empathetic retail leaders could improve store culture and employee satisfaction. With better training methods through the metaverse, managers may be better equipped to support employee growth, provide feedback, and foster morale. This people-first mentality can increase employee retention across retail outlets.

The retail industry's challenges are multifaceted, with employees facing a dynamic mix of customer interactions, technological advancements, and diverse team management. Leadership in this context requires unique skills that are not easily cultivated through traditional training methods. The metaverse offers a promising solution to address this gap.

This research embarks on a journey to assess the current state of retail leadership training, unravel the metaverse's potential applications in this field, and analyze the benefits it may offer regarding employee retention. Through a comprehensive exploration of this intersection, we aim to shed light on how the metaverse can revolutionize leadership development in retail, creating leaders better equipped to navigate the industry's complex challenges and, in turn, fostering enhanced employee retention.

STATEMENT OF THE PROBLEM

The retail industry often grapples with high turnover rates, with turnover exceeding 60% annually for many large retailers, as per the Bureau of Labor Statistics (2022). The costs associated with replacing and training new retail employees can be exorbitant, estimated to range between $1000-$2000 per hire, as per Botha et al. (2011). High turnover not only imposes financial costs but also negatively affects customer service quality and brand reputation, as per Hur and Oh (2022). Recent research indicates that inadequate or ineffective leadership training for retail managers is a significant contributor to low morale, lack of engagement, and high attrition among retail sales associates. For instance, Wang, Yang, and McLean (2020) found that deficiencies in managerial coaching behaviors result in lower employee retention. Therefore, identifying and implementing advanced, immersive training methods for developing retail leaders' "soft skills" could serve as a means to improve employee retention through enhanced manager-employee relations.

Retention rates are nearly 70% higher for employees who rate their managers as exhibiting supportive leadership behaviors, compared to those with less supportive managers (Corporate Leadership Council, 2020). Corporate Leadership Council. (2020). Building leadership capability to boost employee retention. Washington, DC: Corporate Executive Board.

Nearly 50% of employees cite poor management as one of the primary reasons for leaving their jobs (Reina, Rogers, Peterson, Byron, & Hom, 2018). These studies demonstrate the substantial impact manager quality and supportiveness have on employee retention rates. Enhanced leadership training through methods like metaverse simulations could potentially help improve retention by equipping retail managers with better skills.

Objectives

This research aims to:

a) There is a need for more experiential and immersive training to prepare leaders for the fast-paced and challenging retail environment.

b) The metaverse can offer immersive simulations that replicate real-world retail challenges—Understanding of retail leadership principles.

c) Metaverse training can improve retail employee retention by equipping leaders with adaptable skills, leading to job satisfaction and reduced turnover rates.

Retail Leadership Training

Current perspectives on retail leadership training involve a shift towards more technology-driven and adaptive approaches, such as e-learning and microlearning, which can cater to the diverse and fast-paced nature of the retail industry. These approaches aim to develop not only traditional leadership skills but also digital literacy and the ability to navigate evolving customer expectations and technology. Additionally, there is a growing emphasis on soft skills, like empathy and communication, in retail leadership training, as these are critical for managing diverse teams and addressing the unique challenges faced in the retail sector.

Challenges in Retail Leadership

Challenges in retail leadership include high employee turnover rates, the need to manage complex and dynamic customer interactions, staying updated with rapidly evolving technology, and effectively leading diverse teams in a competitive and demanding environment. High Turnover Rates: The retail industry presents leaders with a constant opportunity to develop and empower their employees, creating a culture of growth and success.

Complex Customer Interactions: Retail leadership requires navigating a diverse range of customer personalities, preferences, and issues, often within a fast-paced and high-pressure environment. As a result, retail leaders must develop the necessary skills and strategies to manage these challenges effectively while maintaining a professional and respectful demeanor toward customers and team members alike.

Evolving Technology: Retail leadership constantly demands to stay informed and up-to-date with the latest technology trends while also successfully incorporating them into the business's operations. This can be a challenging task, requiring a combination of technical expertise, strategic planning, and effective communication to ensure smooth and efficient implementation. Diverse Team Management: Managing a retail team can be a complex task due to the diversity of age, culture, and experience within the group. Retail leaders must develop strategies to effectively manage this diversity and foster a positive and inclusive work environment that allows all team members to contribute their unique skills and perspectives.

Traditional Training Approaches

Classroom-based Training: Leaders learn through lectures, presentations, and discussions in physical classroom settings during instructor-led sessions.

E-learning: Instructor-led sessions provide an unparalleled opportunity for leaders to learn and grow in a physical classroom setting. Through engaging lectures, informative presentations, and thought-provoking discussions, attendees will gain valuable skills and insights to help them thrive professionally and personally.

Role-playing and Simulations: Instructor-led sessions occur in a physical classroom where leaders gain knowledge and expertise through powerful lectures, comprehensive presentations, and dynamic discussions.

On-the-Job Training: During instructor-led sessions, leaders can learn professionally through lectures, presentations, and discussions. These sessions occur in a physical classroom environment and provide a valuable opportunity for attendees to acquire knowledge and skills that can help them advance in their careers.

Proposed Managerial Model

Figure 1. Proposed managerial model

| New Worker | VR Training | Assessment & Evaluation | Equipment Operation |

Managerial Implications

Implementing immersive metaverse training can significantly impact retail managers and require changes in learning strategies. A key priority is providing adequate time and resources for managers to participate in simulations (Ma et al., 2022). Scheduling coverage for regular training sessions and outfitting sites with needed VR equipment enables adoption. For many retailers, this will necessitate updates to training budgets, facilities, and administration protocols. Ongoing technical support is also crucial, as managers may need guidance in navigating new metaverse environments and controls (Carpenter & Green, 2017).

Retail organizations should take a strategic approach to metaverse content development. Training designers must collaborate with subject matter experts to identify priority skills and realistic scenarios that align with company values and objectives (Wang et al., 2020). Iterative pilot testing and feedback integration can help refine simulations to maximize relevance before the full launch. Companies may also consider gamifying metaverse experiences using points, levels, or competitions to drive engagement.

To complement metaverse learning, social media, and online community integration provide further development opportunities (Macià & García, 2016). Platforms like LinkedIn and Twitter enable curating relevant leadership articles or hosting webinars at scale. Internal online groups can facilitate idea exchange and peer coaching. Ongoing social content creation and interaction creates a more dynamic, digitally enriched training ecosystem.

Finally, retail firms will need to regularly evaluate program impacts through surveys, retention data analysis, and other employee feedback channels. This informs continuous metaverse experience improvements and ensures training initiatives achieve desired workforce outcomes (Dehler et al., 2021). Adjustments may be required over time as technology and skill demands evolve.

Metaverse Applications in Retail Leadership Training

Immersive Decision-Making Simulations: Retail leaders can benefit from participating in realistic, immersive simulations that closely replicate challenging retail scenarios. These simulations are specifically designed to provide participants with an opportunity to practice and improve their decision-making skills in a safe and risk-free environment. By immersing in these simulations, retail leaders can gain a deeper understanding of the complexities of retail operations and learn how to handle difficult situations more effectively. They can also test new strategies and approaches to see how they would fare in real-world scenarios without any potential negative consequences. Overall, immersive simulations provide a valuable and practical tool for retail leaders to enhance their decision-making skills and stay ahead of the curve in this dynamic industry.

Virtual Role-Playing Exercises: Retail leaders can significantly benefit from participating in realistic and immersive simulations that replicate challenging retail scenarios. These simulations provide participants with unique opportunities to practice and enhance their decision-making skills in a safe and risk-free environment. By engaging in these simulations, leaders can gain a deeper understanding of the complexities inherent in retail operations and develop effective strategies to handle difficult situations.

The value of immersive simulations lies in their ability to provide practical, hands-on experience without the potential negative consequences that can arise from real-world scenarios. Leaders can test out new approaches and strategies and receive feedback on their decision-making abilities, all while gaining valuable insights into the retail industry.

Interactive and Collaborative Training Environments: The metaverse provides virtual spaces for retail leaders to collaborate, share insights, and work on projects, fostering a deeper understanding of leadership principles.

Real-Time Performance Analysis and Feedback: The metaverse is an inspiring realm where retail leaders collaborate, share insights, and work on projects, encouraging a deeper understanding of leadership principles.

Building a Learning Culture: To create an environment that fosters growth and success, it's essential to establish a learning culture that encourages continuous improvement and development. This can be achieved by offering opportunities for training, mentorship, and ongoing feedback. By investing in the growth and development of your team members, you'll not only attract but also retain top talent.

However, building a learning culture has its challenges. One of the biggest obstacles is overcoming resistance to change. Some employees may feel uncomfortable trying new things or hesitate to take risks. As a leader, it's essential to provide support and encouragement to help your team members overcome these fears and embrace new opportunities. Another challenge is ensuring that your learning initiatives are effective and impactful. To do this, it's crucial to measure the success of your programs and make adjustments as needed. Additionally, you must ensure that your learning initiatives align with your organization's goals and values. Despite these challenges, building a learning culture is an essential component of creating a successful organization. By investing in the growth and development of your team members, you'll not only attract and retain top talent but create a culture of continuous improvement and success.

The retail industry faces ongoing challenges with high turnover, which can be detrimental to customer service and brand reputation. Research shows ineffective leadership contributes to low employee retention, with the quality of frontline managers directly impacting morale and engagement (Wang et al., 2020). As retail competes for talent, innovative approaches to leadership development are essential. Emerging immersive technologies like the metaverse integrated with social media engagement strategies present potential training solutions.

Figure 2. Scenario 1 (Create)

Figure 3. Scenario 2: (Monitor)

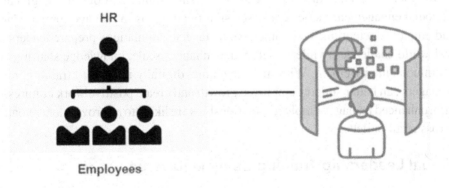

The metaverse, persistent 3D virtual spaces where users interact through avatars, allows highly realistic simulations for corporate training. Retail managers can practice leadership skills like conflict resolution and performance management through lifelike scenarios in a metaverse environment (Ma et al., 2022). Combining

Figure 4. Scenario 3: (Assessment)

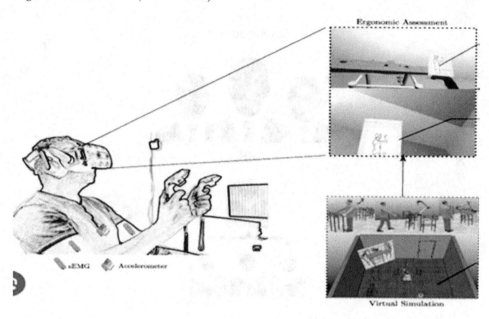

this with social learning on platforms like Facebook, LinkedIn, and YouTube can enhance development. Social channels facilitate collaboration between managers, provide on-demand content, and collect feedback for improving training (Carpenter & Green, 2017).

Retailers implementing metaverse leadership training programs augmented by social engagement tactics could see significant gains in manager preparedness and employee retention. The immersive metaverse simulations prepare leaders for real-world challenges, while social media enhances scale, knowledge sharing, and continuous improvement. With more dynamic, digitally integrated training, retail managers can better support employee growth and create positive work cultures. In turn, enhanced manager-employee relationships are likely to improve talent retention across retail outlets.

Virtual Leadership Training Using Metaverse

- Immersion, The metaverse creates an immersive simulated environment that feels real and allows for realistic practice of leadership skills. This level of immersion can increase engagement and motivation to learn compared to passive training methods.

- Active learning, Retail leaders become active participants in metaverse training through avatars, speech/movement tracking, and interactions. Active learning boosts knowledge retention and transfers better to the job.
- Safe space, The metaverse provides a safe, low-risk environment to try out different leadership approaches without real-world consequences. This encourages experimentation, risk-taking, and skill mastery.
- Feedback, Embedded assessment tools, and data analytics in metaverse training give retail leaders measurable feedback on their learning progress. This supports reflection and helps identify personal growth areas.
- Accessibility, Metaverse training can be accessed remotely on demand which provides flexibility. This facilitates more frequent and convenient development opportunities.
- Scenario variety, A wide range of leadership scenarios can be simulated, giving exposure to diverse situations retail managers may encounter. This builds agility and confidence.
- Socialization and multi-user metaverse environments enable collaborative learning and networking with peer leaders during training. This helps build relationships and support.

The retailers can craft more positive, engaging, and transformative leadership development experiences. Employees are likely to be more receptive to training that is immersive, social, flexible, and data-driven.

Figure 5. Metaverse

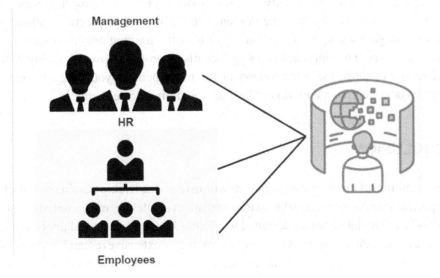

Metaverse: Meet the Alternate Reality

The term "metaverse" refers to a collective virtual shared space that integrates elements of augmented reality (AR), virtual reality (VR), and the internet. It is a digital universe where individuals can interact with each other, digital objects, and the environment. The metaverse is often envisioned as an expansive, immersive, and interconnected digital realm where people can socialize, work, play, learn, and conduct various activities, blurring the lines between the physical and digital worlds. It is a concept that has gained prominence as technology has advanced, and it holds the potential to revolutionize how we interact with and navigate the digital landscape. Companies like Meta Platforms (formerly Facebook) and other tech giants heavily invest in developing metaverse-related technologies and experiences.

Metaverse Evolution and Adoption is a significant phenomenon that describes the continuous progress and popularity of interconnected virtual environments. As technology advances and more companies, businesses, and users show interest, the metaverse is becoming a vast and dynamic world where individuals can interact, create, and engage in various activities. This can include anything from gaming, socializing, shopping, learning, and even working. The metaverse offers limitless possibilities and has the potential to transform the way we live and interact with each other in both virtual and physical spaces.

Training Content Quality

To ensure that metaverse content is aligned with the needs of the retail industry, it is crucial to incorporate real-world applications of metaverse-based retail leadership training. Utilizing case studies and examples provides a practical approach to achieving this goal. By illustrating how the content can be applied in practical situations, learners can gain a deeper understanding of how the training relates to their work and the industry. This approach can significantly improve the overall quality of the content and enhance the effectiveness of the movement. If you have any further inquiries or concerns, please do not hesitate to communicate them.

CONCLUSION

The integration of metaverse applications within retail leadership training constitutes a significant advancement in addressing the distinct challenges encountered by retail leaders. This model has been designed to address key challenges and opportunities specific to the Indian scenario. Our team has conducted extensive research and analysis to develop a comprehensive solution that is grounded in sound methodology and best practices. We believe that this model has the potential to significantly improve outcomes for businesses and organizations operating in India. We are excited to share our findings and look forward to discussing the potential impact of this new model with our colleagues and partners in the business and academic communities. The metaverse's immersive simulations, virtual role-playing, interactive environments, and real-time feedback capabilities possess the potential to revolutionize leadership development. By furnishing retail leaders with adaptable and functional skills and enabling them to navigate the intricate dynamics of the retail industry, the metaverse holds the promise of not only enhancing the efficacy of leadership training but also contributing to improved employee retention. As the metaverse continues to evolve and gain traction, the retail industry must embrace this innovative approach to ensure its leadership is well-prepared to tackle its changing demands.

REFERENCES

Acton, T., Gao, J., Jamshidi, L., & Meng, Y. (2022). Metaverse: Opportunities, growth factors, and the future. *Journal of Management Analytics*, 1-18. https://doi.org/ doi:10.1080/23270012.2022.2024724

Botha, A., Bussin, M., & De Swardt, L. (2011). An employer brand predictive model for talent attraction and retention. *SA Journal of Human Resource Management*, 9(1), 1–12. doi:10.4102/sajhrm.v9i1.388

Bureau of Labor Statistics. (2022). *Job openings and labor turnover summary*. BLS. https://www.bls.gov/news.release/jolts.nr0.htm

Cao, Z., Leng, J., Liu, T., & Yin, C. (2022). Effects of VR retail training on retail employees' job performance and work engagement. *Virtual Reality (Waltham Cross)*, 1–15. doi:10.1007/s10055-022-00678-7

Carpenter, J. P., & Green, M. C. (2017). Working with social media influencers to promote physical activity. *Journal of Sport Management*, 31(5), 477–483.

Dehler, J. (2021). Crowdsourcing technology foresight: A structured literature review. *Technological Forecasting and Social Change*, 170, 120852.

Hur, W. M., & Oh, J. (2022). When employees no longer want to stay: Turnover intention and retail employees' perception of employer brand. *Journal of Retailing and Consumer Services*, 63, 102821.

Ma, J., Sheng, W., & Pahlevansharif, S. (2022). Virtual reality applications in retail: A systematic review and meta-analysis. *International Journal of Information Management, 63*, 102465. doi:10.1016/j.ijinfomgt.2021.102465

Macià, M., & García, I. (2016). Informal online communities and networks as a source of teacher professional development: A review. *Teaching and Teacher Education, 55*, 291–307. doi:10.1016/j.tate.2016.01.021

Reina, C. S., Rogers, K. M., Peterson, S. J., Byron, K., & Hom, P. W. (2018). Quitting the boss? The role of manager influence tactics and employee emotional engagement in voluntary turnover. *Journal of Leadership & Organizational Studies, 25*(1), 5–18. doi:10.1177/1548051817709007

Chapter 7
Building Capabilities and Workforce for Metaverse–Driven Retail Formats

Ranjit Singha

iD https://orcid.org/0000-0002-3541-8752
Christ University (Deemed), India

Surjit Singha

iD https://orcid.org/0000-0002-5730-8677
Kristu Jayanti College (Autonomous), India

ABSTRACT

The metaverse, a breakthrough virtual reality environment, offers boundless retail potential. Metaverse-driven retail needs a good strategy to succeed in a time of changing consumer expectations and the digital revolution. This chapter covers metaverse-driven retail preparation tactics. The metaverse allows retail innovation and adaptation during e-commerce and COVID-19 pandemic upheavals. Understanding metaverse dynamics and developing the abilities is crucial. Determine metaverse applicability to retail, define requisite capabilities, analyze staff competencies, and establish practical training and development programs. Examples include understanding metaverse technology, immersive shopping, data-driven personalization, and strong cybersecurity. Digital fluency, collaboration, design, and cybersecurity awareness are workforce competencies. This chapter stresses metaverse readiness through training, growth, and strategic alignment. It emphasizes that the metaverse transforms reality and opens up new possibilities.

DOI: 10.4018/979-8-3693-3358-7.ch007

INTRODUCTION

The approach in which individuals engage with digital surroundings and commercial activities has undergone a profound transformation in the 21st century. The metaverse is a virtual reality environment where the boundaries between the physical and digital realms become indistinct, playing a crucial role in this shift. Within the metaverse, people can communicate, collaborate, and explore in ways previously only seen in science fiction. The captivating virtual realm has engrossed the minds of technology enthusiasts and visionaries while garnering the interest of diverse enterprises and industries. The retail industry is eager to embrace the metaverse (Abumalloh et al., 2023; Shen et al., 2021). The metaverse represents a significant paradigm shift in our perception and interaction with technology rather than being a passing trend or a specialized term. It has surpassed the limitations of video games and science fiction to evolve into a revolutionary platform that can disrupt and propel numerous industries forward. The metaverse is more than just a technological progression; it signifies a fundamental change in how we engage in labour, social interactions, and consumption of goods and services (Talarico & Leija, 2023; Jauhiainen et al., 2022). Retailers possess a strong understanding of the necessity to uphold flexibility and creativity in an unpredictable setting. The retail landscape has seen a rapid upheaval because of the increase in e-commerce, changes in customer expectations, and unexpected obstacles caused by the COVID-19 epidemic. The advent of the digital era has compelled a reconfiguration of the retail encounter, demanding more immersive, tailored, and captivating approaches to engage consumers. The metaverse is recognized as a viable option that can directly address these requirements (Abumalloh et al., 2023; Giovanni, 2023). This chapter explores the fascinating intersection between the metaverse and the retail industry. With the metaverse gaining prominence in conversations around the future of business and technology, retailers must grasp the potential and the strategic measures to use its capabilities. As merchants adjust to the metaverse, it explores their most urgent concerns and prospects. The focus is on developing a flexible and accomplished staff in this retail environment powered by the metaverse (Lu & Mintz, 2023).

It explores the fundamental principles of the metaverse concerning the retail industry, the essential talents merchants need to thrive in this ever-changing environment, the crucial skills and expertise that employees must have, and practical approaches for training and growth. The objective is to provide retailers with a thorough plan for effectively manoeuvring through the metaverse, guaranteeing their ability to collaboratively generate outstanding consumer experiences and maintain a leading position in retail advancement. The retail industry has consistently demonstrated a dynamic and developing nature, but in recent years, a combination of factors has significantly expedited the pace of transformation. It elucidates the notable transformations in the retail industry and creates a distinctive potential for retailers in the metaverse. Over the past twenty years, e-commerce has profoundly revolutionized the retail sector. Owing to technical improvements and enhanced internet infrastructure, the prevalence of online purchase platforms has surged among customers. E-commerce has revolutionized the old brick-and-mortar retail model by enabling customers to conveniently explore, compare, and purchase products from their homes. Consumers in the twenty-first century had elevated expectations regarding their purchasing experiences. Consumers expect brands to provide comfort, personalization, and a strong emotional bond. Retailers are expected to deliver seamless and consistent experiences across online and offline channels. Merchants have been compelled to allocate technology resources to address these unpredictable requirements and adapt their business practices.

In 2020, the worldwide COVID-19 pandemic accelerated the digital transformation of retail. Due to physical store closures and restrictions, online shopping has increased. Retailers had to adjust rapidly to maintain business continuity and meet the growing demand for digital purchasing experiences. As a result of these alterations, the metaverse emerged as a transformative idea. The metaverse combines mixed, augmented, virtual, and other immersive technologies. It offers a digital universe where users can interact with each other and digital entities in real-time. The metaverse surpasses conventional e-commerce and online purchasing by providing users with an immersive, 3D, and interactive environment to explore, connect, and engage. Due to these seismic changes in the retail landscape, retailers actively seek innovative and adaptable strategies. The metaverse presents a unique and compelling opportunity for retail businesses. It enables the creation of more immersive, personalized, and engaging customer experiences following the expectations of contemporary consumers (Lopes & Reis, 2021).

Retailers must embrace the metaverse and acquire the skills and personnel to exploit this opportunity. The metaverse is quickly becoming an integral component of the digital era, and retailers who can successfully navigate this complex digital environment will thrive in the future retail landscape (Abumalloh et al., 2023). It investigates the essential elements of developing the capabilities and personnel for retailers to adapt to and excel in this metaverse-driven retail environment. It is a strategic necessity, given the current condition of the industry and the trajectory of technology and consumer expectations. It offers readers a comprehensive grasp of the metaverse's role in retail and how to prepare for its integration effectively. To do this, the chapter has been organized with specific aims. It explores the metaverse notion within the retail industry. This inquiry probes into the essence, chronicles, and fundamental technology that facilitate the operation of the metaverse. The reader will comprehend the metaverse's distinctive characteristics compared to other digital environments and its significance in the retail industry. This section will establish the foundation for the following goals.

The competency retailers must develop to be successful in the metaverse. The metaverse requires unique skills and resources, including proficiency in virtual reality technologies, 3D design, and the incorporation of augmented reality. These capabilities allow retailers to create compelling, immersive, and interactive retail experiences. This objective aims to provide retailers with a road map for comprehending and acquiring the skills to succeed in this dynamic environment. The metaverse poses both technological and human challenges. Retailers must equip their employees with skills and competencies to thrive in a metaverse-dominated retail landscape. This section will examine the skills required for employees to navigate the metaverse effectively, including digital literacy, virtual collaboration, inventive design, and data privacy awareness. By analyzing these skills and competencies, readers will understand the essential characteristics a workforce outfitted for the metaverse must have (Tella et al., 2023). This chapter concludes with recommendations on how retailers can effectively train and develop their employees in preparation for the metaverse. Training and development strategies will consist of employee training programs, partnerships with metaverse technology experts, opportunities for continuous learning, and methods for evaluating the effectiveness of training initiatives. Retailers can prepare their teams for success in a retail environment driven by the metaverse by providing insight into these strategies and employing pragmatic approaches.

These key objectives will paint a complete picture of the metaverse's function in retail, outline the capabilities and skills required for success, and provide actionable insights for developing a metaverse-ready workforce. This structured approach aims to equip retailers with the knowledge and strategies to successfully navigate the metaverse's transformational journey while delivering exceptional customer experiences and remaining at the vanguard of retail innovation.

CAPABILITIES FOR METAVERSE-DRIVEN RETAIL

In the context of retail that is driven by the metaverse, a thorough understanding of metaverse technologies and platforms is essential. Retailers must comprehend a spectrum of immersive technologies, including Virtual Reality (VR), Augmented Reality (AR), and Mixed Reality (MR). Understanding the differences between these technologies and their metaverse applications is crucial. Mixed reality combines the two to differing degrees, whereas virtual reality provides an entirely immersive experience. Retailers must know each technology's potential applications and advantages (Liberatore & Wagner, 2021; Goel et al., 2022; Alcaz et al., 2019).

Metaverse platforms' capabilities, user base, and objectives can vary significantly. Retailers should become conversant with Decentraland, Second Life, Roblox, and other emerging blockchain-based metaverses. This information is required for making well-informed decisions about where to establish a physical presence or launch virtual storefronts. Metaverse environments are typically 3D and interactive. Retailers must be able to navigate, create, and manage virtual spaces within these contexts. It includes the capacity to build and customize virtual storefronts, create convincing avatars for brand representatives, and populate virtual spaces with interactive digital objects (Alcaz et al., 2019).

Creation and integration of digital content are required for the metaverse. For virtual storefronts, retailers must understand how to create 3D models, textures, and other assets. They must understand the integration options for product displays, interactive elements, and immersive experiences. In the metaverse, it is essential to design an exceptional user experience. Retailers should understand the principles of user experience (UX) and user interface (UI) design within the metaverse to ensure that virtual stores are user-friendly, simple to navigate, and aesthetically attractive (Shen et al., 2021). The metaverse is capable of real-time collaboration and interaction. Retailers should investigate how to integrate interactive and social elements into their metaverse spaces, such as live events, social gatherings, and consumer engagement opportunities. Understanding metaverse technologies and platforms is essential for retail success propelled by the metaverse. It enables retailers to make informed judgments regarding technology adoption, platform selection, and creative content development, allowing them to offer immersive and engaging metaverse customer experiences. The key to retail success in the metaverse is the capacity to create immersive and highly interactive purchasing environments. This capability is essential for supplying consumers with memorable and engaging experiences in the metaverse (HennigThurau et al., 2022; Shen et al., 2021). Retailers should learn to design and construct 3D virtual storefronts in the metaverse. It involves simulating a physical store's environment while utilizing the digital realm's distinct capabilities. Elements like store layout, product displays, and item placement should be meticulously designed to optimize aesthetic appeal and usability. The metaverse enables retailers to showcase their products in novel and interactive ways. Customers should be able to wear clothing virtually, test-drive digital vehicles, and perform thorough 3D product inspections. It is possible for interactive product presentations to include functions such as the ability to rotate, magnify, and examine products from different angles (Shen et al., 2021).

The capacity to facilitate real-time interactions and social engagement is one of the defining characteristics of the metaverse. Retailers should foster consumer engagement by facilitating interactions between customers and brand representatives. Live events, product launches, and community-building activities can enhance the purchasing experience within the metaverse. Beyond conventional advertising, the metaverse enables retailers to create immersive narratives and narrative experiences. Brands can construct captivating narratives surrounding their products or services, eliciting consumers' more profound emotional responses. This narrative must align with the values and messaging of the brand. Individualization is a fundamental principle of metaverse retail. Retailers should be able to provide highly personalized purchasing experiences catered to each consumer's preferences. It may involve personalized product recommendations, customized avatars, and guided purchasing experiences based on past preferences and behaviour (HennigThurau et al., 2022; Shen et al., 2022).

Using gamification elements can make purchasing in the metaverse more enjoyable and rewarding. Retailers can incorporate gamified elements such as competitions, rewards, and challenges to encourage consumer engagement and loyalty. Retailers can utilize multiple senses to enhance metaverse immersion. For instance, incorporating spatial audio and haptic feedback can enrich and improve the purchasing experience. The transition between the actual and virtual worlds ought to be seamless. It could involve integrating metaverse experiences with physical stores, allowing consumers to transition between online and offline purchasing seamlessly (Abumalloh et al., 2023; Cho et al., 2023). Creativity, technology, and customer-centricity are required to develop immersive and interactive purchasing experiences. In addition to replicating the physical purchasing experience, engaging consumers in novel and exciting ways by leveraging the metaverse's distinctive capabilities. By mastering this capability, retailers can differentiate themselves and offer customers authentic and memorable retail experiences. Personalization is a crucial metaverse capability that enables retailers to tailor customer experiences to their preferences, creating a more engaging and relevant purchasing environment. Data analytics and artificial intelligence (AI) are required to achieve this level of personalization (Shen et al., 2021).

Within the metaverse, retailers should establish comprehensive data acquisition mechanisms. It includes the collection of users' behaviour, interactions, and other relevant data elements. Analyzing these data to gain insight into consumer preferences and habits is crucial. By gathering data, retailers can create comprehensive user profiles for metaverse shoppers. This information should range from previous purchases and product preferences to virtual interactions and in-game behaviours. Real-time data processing is for providing immediate and highly personalized experiences. It allows for modifications to be made in real-time based on customer preferences and behaviour while they are actively engaged in the metaverse (Shen et al., 2021). Retailers should utilize AI for data interpretation and processing. By analyzing user profiles and actions, algorithms powered by artificial intelligence can generate personalized product recommendations, offers, and content. AI-powered chatbots and virtual assistants can provide consumers with individualized assistance and direction. These AI-powered interfaces can respond to questions, make suggestions, and aid based on a user's needs and preferences. Implementing recommendation engines enabled by AI is essential for personalization. These engines can suggest products, services, and experiences corresponding to a customer's past actions, preferences, and metaverse interaction context (Zheng et al., 2022).

In addition to product recommendations, personalized metaverse content should include virtual advertisements and marketing campaigns. AI can facilitate content customization to an individual's preferences and behaviour. Using AI, retailers can create personalized metaverse consumer experiences based on their preferences and behaviours. For example, customers who frequently participate in virtual social events could be directed to similar experiences. Based on real-time consumer data and behaviour, AI can assist retailers in optimizing prices and offers. Dynamic pricing can assure relevant and competitive pricing for customers. Retailers should implement feedback mechanisms to refine and enhance their personalization strategies continuously. Ongoing AI-driven personalization initiatives require customer feedback and metaverse interactions. Using data analytics and AI for personalization is about providing more relevant product suggestions and creating a metaverse purchasing experience that feels uniquely tailored to each individual. With the correct data, analytics, and AI capabilities, retailers can strengthen customer relationships, increase customer loyalty, and enhance the overall metaverse purchasing experience. In a retail environment driven by the metaverse, this capability is essential for establishing a competitive advantage and ensuring consumer engagement and satisfaction.

Security and trust are paramount in the metaverse, where users engage in immersive and interactive experiences. Retailers must establish a secure and trustworthy presence to maintain consumer confidence and protect their assets and customers' personal information. Implement stringent data protection and privacy measures within the metaverse. It includes adhering to data protection regulations, securing customer data, and handling it with utmost care and openness. Implement secure payment and transaction systems to instil confidence in consumers who conduct business in the metaverse. It could entail using encrypted payment gateways and stringent anti-fraud measures (Cheng et al., 2023). Investigate the use of blockchain and cryptography to improve metaverse security. The blockchain can provide transparent, tamper-resistant transaction records, while cryptography can safeguard sensitive data. Implement identity verification measures to guarantee that users are who they claim to be. It could include multifactor authentication, biometric verification, or other secure methods for confirming user identity. Retailers should acquire cybersecurity expertise to safeguard consumer and business assets in the metaverse. Cyber risks are not immune to the metaverse, and robust cybersecurity practices are necessary (Rejeb et al., 2023; Pooyandeh et al., 2022).

Encrypt sensitive information, such as user credentials and payment details, to guarantee confidentiality and security. Use end-to-end encryption to protect communications and transactions and implement content moderation policies and technologies to prevent inappropriate or harmful content from appearing in the metaverse. It is crucial for maintaining a reliable and secure environment. Maintain knowledge of metaverse-specific regulations, develop standards, and adhere to them. The metaverse may have laws governing user privacy, data management, and ownership of virtual assets. Inform consumers of the most effective security measures. It includes creating secure passwords, recognizing phishing attempts, and understanding the importance of safeguarding personal data (Pooyandeh et al., 2022; Cheng et al., 2022). Seek third-party verification and trust certifications to demonstrate your commitment to security and reliability. These endorsements can enhance a business's credibility with customers. Creating and regularly updating incident response plans is to address security vulnerabilities or data leaks. With an established technique, security incidents can be mitigated. Develop a culture of responsibility and openness regarding security practices. Customers should be informed of how their data is managed and that the retailer is concerned with their security (Gupta et al., 2023; Trunfio & Rossi, 2022). In addition to protecting consumer data, establishing a secure and trustworthy metaverse presence entails providing a pleasant and safe environment for metaverse users. The foundation of successful metaverse-driven retail is trust, and retailers must prioritize the security and privacy of their consumers. By mastering this skill, retailers can cultivate confidence, protect their reputation, and increase consumer loyalty in the metaverse.

WORKFORCE SKILLS AND COMPETENCIES

Digital literacy and fluency are foundational skills in a retail environment dominated by the metaverse. In addition to fundamental computer skills, this ability encompasses a comprehensive understanding of metaverse technologies and digital navigation. Employees should have a complete comprehension of the technologies underlying the metaverse, such as virtual reality (VR), augmented reality (AR), and mixed reality (MR), as well as the retailer's specific platforms and tools. This understanding enables employees to appreciate these technologies' unique capabilities and opportunities. The ability to traverse 3D virtual environments is essential. It includes manipulating, transporting, and interacting with metaverse objects. The metaverse's unique navigational tools and interfaces, including gestures, spatial tracking, and voice commands, must be familiar to employees (Cho et al., 2023; Abumalloh et al., 2023). Due to the rapid evolution of digital technologies, employees must be open to learning new tools and platforms and adapting to them. The metaverse is a dynamic environment, so adaptability is essential. This adaptability extends to keeping up with emergent technologies and best practices in the metaverse. Digital literacy must incorporate the capacity for effective communication in digital environments. Employees should be proficient at communicating ideas and information in the metaverse via text, voice, and visual means. It includes utilizing virtual communication tools, understanding the nuances of social presence, and communicating through avatars and virtual gestures (Cheng et al., 2022).

Moreover, digital literacy encompasses troubleshooting common technical issues that may arise in the metaverse. Employees should be able to resolve minor technical problems independently and seek help when necessary. Digital literacy requires understanding user experience (UX) within the metaverse. It includes knowing how users interact with virtual environments, avatars, and digital objects. For the development of user-friendly metaverse experiences, a thorough understanding of UX principles is indispensable. A fundamental component of digital literacy should be understanding data security best practices in the metaverse. It includes recognizing potential security hazards, adhering to company policies, and sharing sensitive information cautiously in digital spaces. Respect for the digital privacy of others, intellectual property rights, and a commitment to responsible digital citizenship are essential components of an ethical understanding of technology use. Digital literacy and fluency are fundamental skills that enable the workforce to navigate the metaverse, interact with customers and coworkers, and contribute to the retailer's success in the digital age. By equipping their teams with these skills, retailers can ensure that they can capitalize on the opportunities presented by the metaverse and deliver exceptional customer experiences. Developing and maintaining meaningful relationships with clients and coworkers in the metaverse requires virtual collaboration and communication skills (Tella et al., 2023). Teams frequently work remotely in a retail environment dominated by the metaverse, and the ability to collaborate effectively in virtual spaces is crucial. Employees should be proficient at collaborating with geographically and temporally dispersed colleagues, partners, and constituents. Practical communication abilities are indispensable in the metaverse. Orally or in writing, employees should be able to communicate ideas, information, and messages clearly and persuasively. They must be able to maximize the use of virtual communication instruments. In virtual spaces, it is essential to establish relationships and rapport with customers and coworkers. Employees must possess interpersonal communication skills, such as active listening, empathy, and the ability to recognize and respond to the emotional and social cues of others.

Employees should be familiar with the norms and etiquette peculiar to virtual environments. It includes the ability to greet others with respect, partake in virtual meetings, use avatars appropriately, and participate in virtual events and social interactions. In a global metaverse, employees must exhibit cultural sensitivity. They should be aware of and respectful of cultural differences when interacting with clients or coworkers from diverse backgrounds. Like any other workspace, the metaverse is susceptible to disagreements and conflict. Employees should be able to address conflicts and resolve disputes constructively in virtual environments (Benjamins et al., 2023). In virtual environments, employees may be required to adapt to new communication tools and platforms. Successful virtual collaboration necessitates a willingness to adjust and proficiency with these tools. Facilitating interactions, conversations, and events is to engage consumers in virtual spaces. (Violante et al., 2019) Employees should be able to design interactive virtual experiences that increase consumer satisfaction and brand loyalty. Employees may be required to deliver virtual presentations or training sessions. Strong presentation skills, including the capacity to engage and captivate a virtual audience, are advantageous. Virtual work often necessitates efficient time management, especially when coordinating multiple virtual meetings and interactions. Employees need time management skills to fulfil their work and customer engagement obligations. Building customer relationships, encouraging teamwork, and ensuring metaverse-driven retail's smooth operation rely on virtual collaboration and communication abilities. Employees who excel in these competencies can cultivate a sense of community, interact meaningfully with customers, and collaborate effectively with coworkers, thereby contributing to the retailer's metaverse success (Abumalloh et al., 2023).

Inventive design and content creation skills are indispensable for generating immersive and engaging consumer experiences in the metaverse. These skills are essential for developing virtual environments, product displays, and marketing content that capture the attention and imagination of metaverse users. As Metaverse environments are typically 3D, employees should be proficient in 3D design, including constructing and manipulating 3D assets. 3D modelling, texturing, and visualization skills are required for designing virtual stores, personas, and digital objects. Employees with creative design skills should be able to develop a range of digital assets, including 3D models, textures, animations, and interactive elements. These assets improve the aesthetics and interactivity of virtual stores and experiences. In the metaverse, it is essential to comprehend user experience (UX) and user interface (UI) design principles. These skills enable employees to design visually appealing and user-friendly virtual environments. It includes the development of virtual storefronts with user-friendly interfaces and aesthetically pleasing components. Creative design skills are required to create immersive virtual environments, replicating or enhancing the physical purchasing experience. It includes the creation of attractive product displays, virtual storefront layouts, and interactive purchasing environments.

Content is a crucial aspect of the metaverse, and employees must be able to produce original and engaging content. It may include consistent virtual advertisements, marketing campaigns, product descriptions, and interactive content. Creative employees should excel at visual narrative. Emotionally captivating narratives and story-driven content can significantly affect the success of metaverse-based retail. This competency involves integrating brand narratives into the metaverse experience. Videos and animations are prevalent throughout the metaverse. Employees with video production skills can create marketing videos, product demonstrations, and virtual excursions that enhance the customer experience (Alcantara & Michalack, 2022). Creating avatars that signify brand representatives or virtual store assistants is essential in metaverse-driven retail. Creative employees are capable of designing compelling visual personas that are consistent with the brand's identity. The presentation of products in the metaverse incorporates creativity. Employees can develop inventive ways to showcase products, allowing customers to try on apparel virtually, test-drive digital vehicles, or participate in interactive demonstrations.

Beyond technical expertise, employees with artistic expression can infuse metaverse content and designs with creativity and artistry, thereby augmenting the visual and emotional appeal of the retail experience. To differentiate themselves and stand out in the competitive landscape of the metaverse, retailers must be capable of designing and producing original content. They permit the creation of visually stunning and emotionally engaging experiences that captivate and resonate with consumers, transforming the metaverse into an exciting and memorable purchasing destination (Chowdhury et al., 2023). Given the substantial potential risks associated with virtual interactions, cybersecurity awareness and a solid commitment to data privacy are non-negotiable in the metaverse. Employees should receive cybersecurity training focusing on the metaverse's unique threats and challenges. It includes recognizing and responding to threats in virtual environments, such as phishing attempts and intrusions (Tank et al., 2019).

Data privacy training ensures that sensitive consumer data is managed securely and follows applicable data protection laws. Employees must understand the importance of protecting consumer data and the consequences of data breaches (Pietro & Cresci, 2021). Employees must be familiar with the most effective methods for administering customer data in the metaverse. It includes storage, transmission, and encryption techniques for sensitive data. Both employee and customer metaverse accounts require secure password management. Employees should generate robust, unique passwords and utilize secure password administration tools (Parlar, 2023). Employees must be trained to respond to security incidents, and retailers must have well-defined incident response plans. It includes reporting security incidents, mitigating associated risks, and working with the incident response team. Employees should adhere to security best practices, such as updating software and applications regularly, utilizing firewalls, and keeping antivirus software up-to-date. They should also be aware of common cybersecurity threats and take precautions against them. Phishing is one of the most widespread cyber threats throughout the metaverse.

Employees should be trained to recognize phishing attempts and understand how to respond, such as avoiding suspicious connections and not disclosing sensitive data. In insecure virtual environments, employees should avoid sharing sensitive data, financial information, and login credentials. They should exercise prudence regarding the information they share and the individuals with whom they share it. Retailers conducting business in the metaverse must be aware of and adhere to metaverse-specific regulations regarding user privacy, data administration, and virtual asset ownership. Employees must be informed of these regulations and the retailer's commitment to complying with them. Employees should be aware of the ethical use of data, which includes adhering to the principles of responsible digital citizenship and respecting consumers' digital privacy and intellectual property rights.

Knowledge of encryption methods and their implementation within the metaverse can facilitate transmitting and storing sensitive information. Cybersecurity awareness and a solid commitment to data privacy are necessary for establishing consumer trust and safeguarding sensitive data. To maintain a trustworthy presence in the metaverse, where customers engage in immersive and interactive experiences, protecting their data and ensuring their security is essential.

TRAINING AND DEVELOPMENT STRATEGIES

Developing comprehensive and effective employee training initiatives and programs is essential to prepare the retail workforce for success in the metaverse. Introduce all employees to the metaverse environment by implementing orientation programs for the metaverse. These programs should cover the basics of metaverse technologies, the retailer's metaverse platforms, and the significance of these technologies in the retail industry. Customize training programs for various positions within the organization. Instruct them in consumer interactions in the metaverse, virtual communication with empathy, and conflict resolution. To facilitate the creation of immersive virtual stores and experiences, provide training in 3D design, content creation, and avatar creation. Create a comprehensive induction process for new employees, including training specific to the metaverse. Provide employees with hands-on experience in metaverse retail settings by combining this with on-the-job training. Skills-building seminars should be held frequently to ensure employees are up-to-date on the latest metaverse technologies and best practices. These workshops may be conducted both in-person and online. Utilize virtual environments and simulated scenarios to provide experiential training. Employees can exercise their abilities, decision-making, and consumer interactions in a controlled, risk-free setting. Create a repository of training materials accessible to employees, including video tutorials, manuals, and documentation. This collection of resources should cover a broad range of metaverse-related topics. Implement assessment mechanisms, exams, and practical examinations to assess employees' acquired knowledge and abilities. In addition, certification programs can be used to recognize and reward employees who excel in training related to the metaverse. Encourage employees to provide feedback on the training program. Utilize this feedback to improve and modify the training materials and methods continuously.

Consider incorporating virtual reality (VR) technology into the training procedure to enhance the immersion. Using VR simulations, employees can familiarize themselves with the metaverse environment. Gamify elements of a training program to make learning more engaging. Gamification can incorporate challenges, leaderboards, and rewards to motivate employees to partake in training actively. Encourage cross-training so that employees can acquire expertise in multiple metaverse-related fields. It improves their adaptability and collaboration capabilities. Establish mentoring programs in which more experienced employees serve as mentors for less skilled employees. Mentoring can facilitate the rapid adaptation of employees to the metaverse environment and industry. By implementing these training programs and initiatives, retailers can ensure their employees are outfitted to navigate the metaverse and provide superior customer service. Continuous learning and skill development will be essential for the long-term viability of metaverse-powered retail. Strategically preparing your retail staff to navigate the metaverse requires collaboration with purveyors and specialists of metaverse technology. The following elements and strategies are essential for effective collaboration:

Develop strategic alliances with purveyors of metaverse technology, such as platform developers and virtual reality experts. These partnerships can provide access to specialized training resources, early access to technological advancements, and insightful industry knowledge. Collaborate with metaverse technology purveyors to develop individualized training programs. It may involve extensive training on their platforms, tools, and APIs to ensure that employees thoroughly understand the technologies they will be utilizing. Collaborate with technology suppliers to gain early access to beta programs and new features. Consult with experts and specialists in metaverse technology to receive expert advice on technology adoption and best practices. It may include individualized training and guidance for employees. Technology companies conduct webinars and update sessions frequently. Encourage employees to learn about the latest metaverse technology developments at these events. Establish a knowledge-sharing relationship with technology providers. Share insights regarding your organization's distinctive requirements and objectives, and collaborate to develop innovative solutions.

Invest in training internal specialists with a thorough understanding of metaverse technologies. Other employees can rely on these specialists for invaluable training, troubleshooting, and direction. Maintain a feedback mechanism with technology providers. Share your experiences, obstacles, and ideas with them to improve their services and tailor their offerings to your retail specifications. Seek endorsements or certifications from technology providers. It can help demonstrate the retailer's commitment to excellence in the metaverse and strengthen the credibility of your training programs. Engage in collaborative research initiatives with technology providers to investigate new use cases, test innovative features, and identify additional retail applications for metaverse technologies. Schedule regular check-ins with technology providers to ensure your workforce's training and support needs are met. Address any issues or concerns immediately—budget for technology provider collaboration and training. Invest in your employees' continuous education to keep up with the ever-changing metaverse landscape (Said, 2023). Collaboration with metaverse technology providers and experts promotes a prosperous, mutually beneficial partnership. Equipping your personnel with in-depth knowledge ensures that your retail operations are at the vanguard of metaverse innovation. These partnerships are essential to your retail organization's success in the metaverse. To keep up with the rapidly changing metaverse landscape, it is crucial to encourage continuous learning and skill enhancements among your retail staff. Create a culture of constant learning within your organization. Encourage employees to view learning as an ongoing process rather than a one-time event.

Invest in or collaborate with online learning platforms offering metaverse courses and certifications. Provide employees with access to a variety of educational resources. Dedicate a portion of your budget to employee training and development. It demonstrates your commitment to the progress and development of their metaverse. Implement periodic skill evaluations to identify employee development opportunities. These evaluations can assist in tailoring upskilling initiatives to satisfy specific needs (Onu et al., 2023; Ribeiro, 2022). Create customized employee learning plans based on their abilities, roles, and goals. These programs may include both short- and long-term objectives for skill development. Focus on specific metaverse-related skills and organize skill augmentation sprints or training programs. These can be intensive, short-term programs designed to improve specific competencies rapidly. Incorporate virtual reality simulations into training programs. These simulations offer personnel realistic metaverse environments to hone their skills (Xie et al., 2021). Identify and cultivate internal metaverse experts who can serve as mentors and teachers for other employees. Motivate these experts to share their knowledge and experiences. Encourage cross-training, wherein employees acquire skills from other departments. It not only increases their skill set but also enhances their collaborative skills. Encourage employees to join retail-focused online communities and metaverse technologies. These forums facilitate networking and the exchange of information. Regularly conduct "lunch-and-learn" sessions where employees can learn about particular metaverse topics during lunch. These unstructured gatherings promote social learning.

Assist employees in attending external courses and conferences related to the metaverse. These events expose participants to the latest industry insights and trends. Consider rewarding employees who actively pursue metaverse-related skill development with benefits or promotions. Maintain channels for employee feedback regarding training and skill development opportunities. Use this feedback to improve your learning programs continuously. Provide development programs addressing leadership's distinctive challenges and responsibilities in a metaverse-dominated retail environment. Develop mentoring programs in which experienced employees serve as mentors for metaverse newcomers. Individualized instruction speeds up the learning process. Opportunities for continuing education and skill development not only maintain the competitiveness of your staff but also contribute to their job satisfaction and professional growth. A well-trained and continuously educated workforce is better equipped to provide exceptional consumer experiences in the metaverse. Implementing effective measurement and evaluation mechanisms ensures your metaverse training programs succeed and produce the desired results. Here are some evaluation techniques for your training programs: Define specific and measurable learning objectives for each training program. These objectives must align with the competencies and skills you want your employees to acquire. Perform pre-training assessments to evaluate the employees' knowledge and abilities before training. Conduct post-training evaluations to assess the participants' development. Monitor the impact of training on organizational outcomes by establishing KPIs. It can include consumer satisfaction, employee engagement, conversion rates, and sales from trained staff. Collect the feedback of employees who have completed training programs. Determine their perspectives on the training's content, delivery, and relevance to their positions. Use practical skill evaluations to evaluate the metaverse-related skills and competencies of employees. It may involve simulations or practical exercises (Hajjami & Park, 2023; Pyae et al., 2023).

Offer certifications or accreditation to employees who effectively complete training programs. These certificates can serve as tangible proof of their proficiency. Encourage managers and mentors to evaluate employee performance in real-world metaverse scenarios based on their observations. Utilize quantitative data (numbers, scores) and qualitative data (comments, feedback) to comprehend the training program's effectiveness comprehensively. Compare the results and performance of employees who received training with those who did not. This comparative analysis can illustrate how activity impacts productivity and customer satisfaction. After a specified period, conduct follow-up surveys to determine if employees utilize the newly acquired skills in their daily work. Observe the retention rates of employees who have received training. Higher retention rates among employees who have received training indicate they are more engaged and content with their responsibilities. Compare the cost of training to its benefits, such as increased sales or improved customer service, to calculate the return on investment (ROI) of training programs. Encourage peer evaluations in which employees evaluate the performance of their peers. It is beneficial for assessing interpersonal and customer-facing abilities. Review the training evaluation data and feedback collected frequently. Utilize this data to improve the training's content, delivery methods, and effectiveness. Evaluate the training's long-term impact on employee performance and customer satisfaction. Continuous monitoring is to ensure that skills remain relevant as technology evolves. Conduct interviews with employees to determine how training has affected their self-assurance, job satisfaction, and organizational advancement opportunities. Measuring the effectiveness of training programs is an ongoing process that allows you to fine-tune your approach, align training with organizational goals, and ensure that employees are well-prepared to excel in metaverse-driven retail. Additionally, it demonstrates a commitment to employee development and the provision of exceptional customer experiences.

CASE STUDIES AND BEST PRACTICES

A prominent automaker adopted the metaverse to enhance the consumer experience. They created a virtual showroom in a 3D virtual environment where consumers could examine and configure vehicles. The company invested in its design team's training so that they could excel at 3D modelling and visualization. It enabled the creation of highly realistic virtual automobile models that consumers could customize. Customers could virtually test-drive vehicles and experience their appearance and feel using VR devices. This immersive experience significantly increased customer engagement. The organization utilized data analytics to perceive customer preferences and virtual showroom conduct. This data was used to personalize the virtual showroom by displaying the most relevant car models and features to consumers. Implementing stringent cybersecurity measures ensures the confidentiality of consumer information and the safety of transactions. Developing consumer trust was a top priority. To thrive in the metaverse, a large retail chain recognized the importance of enhancing its workforce's skills. They implemented a comprehensive talent development program. The retailer tailored training programs to different positions. Store associates were instructed in virtual customer service, while marketing teams were introduced in creating content tailored to the metaverse. The company embraced a culture of continuous learning, encouraging employees to actively seek out online courses, seminars, and industry conferences. Employees were encouraged to acquire skills outside of their job descriptions and cross-train.

It promoted a versatile workforce. The training program's feedback mechanisms were consistent. Feedback from employees was used to adapt and improve training content and methodologies.

A boutique clothes business has ventured into the metaverse to offer clients a virtual shopping experience. The top priority was to ensure the safety and reliability of their existence in the metaverse. Every employee underwent comprehensive cybersecurity training, emphasizing those who engage with virtual clientele. The individuals received guidance on the potential dangers of phishing and were educated on the methods to recognize and address such threats. Stringent data privacy policies were implemented to safeguard consumer data. This involved managing sensitive data, implementing encryption measures, and adhering to data protection standards. Systematic security audits and penetration testing were performed to detect weaknesses in the metaverse. All identified problems were promptly remedied. The retailer educated clients about the metaverse's data protection and privacy measures. The honesty exhibited by the company instilled confidence and trust in their clientele. These case studies and best practices exemplify the pragmatic implementation of the ideas outlined in this chapter, showcasing how businesses may successfully embrace the metaverse while ensuring active consumer participation, enhancing employee skills, and maintaining strong cybersecurity and data privacy measures.

CONCLUSION

The metaverse has emerged as a transformative platform for the retail industry. As retailers seek innovative ways to utilize this technology, developing the skills and personnel required to navigate the metaverse becomes essential. This chapter examined the critical aspects of preparing for a retail environment driven by the metaverse and the strategies needed to prosper in this dynamic setting. In recent years, the retail industry has encountered significant changes, accelerated by the rise of e-commerce, consumer expectations, and the effects of the COVID-19 pandemic. The metaverse presents a unique opportunity for retailers to adapt, innovate, and thrive in the digital age. To harness the metaverse, it is essential to comprehend and cultivate the skills and labour force. It examined the concept of the metaverse in the context of the retail industry, discussed the capabilities required for retailers to excel in the metaverse, analyzed the skills and competencies required for a workforce to succeed in metaverse-driven retail, and offered insights on practical training and development strategies for developing a workforce that is metaverse-ready.

We have examined the capabilities for metaverse-driven retail, such as understanding metaverse technologies and platforms, developing immersive and interactive shopping experiences, applying data analytics and artificial intelligence for personalization, and establishing a trustworthy and secure metaverse presence. These skills are crucial for the success of retailers in the metaverse. In addition, we examined the essential retail workforce skills and competencies, such as digital literacy and fluency, virtual collaboration and communication skills, creative design and content creation abilities, and cybersecurity awareness and data privacy. To deliver exceptional customer experiences, it is essential to equip employees with these skills. The focus was on employee training programs and initiatives, collaboration with metaverse technology providers and experts, continuous learning and upskilling opportunities, and measuring training effectiveness. These strategies are essential for nurturing a metaverse-ready workforce. The metaverse is an exciting frontier for the retail industry, where immersive, personalized, and engaging consumer experiences are conceivable. Focusing on developing essential capabilities, upskilling the workforce, and implementing practical training can position retailers at the vanguard of metaverse-driven retail. The metaverse is not merely a theory; it is a reality, and its limitless virtual universes contain the future of retail.

REFERENCES

Abumalloh, R. A., Nilashi, M., Ooi, K., Wei-Han, G., Cham, T., Dwivedi, Y. K., & Hughes, L. (2023). Adopting a metaverse in the retail industry and its impact on sustainable competitive advantage: The moderating impact of sustainability commitment. *Annals of Operations Research*. doi:10.1007/s10479-023-05608-8

Alcañíz, M., Bigné, E., & Guixeres, J. (2019). Virtual Reality in Marketing: A Framework, review, and Research agenda. *Frontiers in Psychology*, *10*, 1530. doi:10.3389/fpsyg.2019.01530 PMID:31333548

Alcantara, A. C., & Michalack, D. L. (2022). The Metaverse Narrative in the Matrix Resurrections: A Semiotic analysis through costumes. In Springer series in design and innovation (pp. 260–268). Springer. doi:10.1007/978-3-031-09659-4_20

Benjamins, R., Viñuela, Y. R., & Alonso, C. (2023). Social and ethical challenges of the metaverse. *AI and Ethics*, *3*(3), 689–697. doi:10.1007/s43681-023-00278-5

Cheng, R., Chen, S., & Han, B. (2023). Towards zero-trust security for the metaverse. *IEEE Communications Magazine*, 1–7. doi:10.1109/MCOM.018.2300095

Cho, J., Dieck, M. C. T., & Jung, T. (2023). What is the Metaverse? Challenges, Opportunities, Definition, and Future Research Directions. In Springer proceedings in business and economics (pp. 3–26). Springer. doi:10.1007/978-3-031-25390-4_1

Chowdhury, S., Schnabel, M. A., & Lo, T. (2023). Editorial: Metaverse in co-virtual city design. *Frontiers in Virtual Reality, 4*, 1166107. doi:10.3389/frvir.2023.1166107

De Giovanni, P. (2023). Sustainability of the Metaverse: A Transition to Industry 5.0. *Sustainability (Basel), 15*(7), 6079. doi:10.3390/su15076079

Di Pietro, R., & Cresci, S. (2021). *Metaverse: Security and Privacy Issues.* IEEE Xplore., doi:10.1109/TPSISA52974.2021.00032

Goel, P., Mahadevan, K., & Punjani, K. K. (2022). Augmented and virtual reality in the apparel industry: A bibliometric review and future research agenda. *Foresight, 25*(2), 167–184. doi:10.1108/FS-10-2021-0202

Gupta, A., Khan, H. U., Nazir, S., Shafiq, M., & Shabaz, M. (2023). Metaverse Security: Issues, challenges and a viable ZTA model. *Electronics (Basel), 12*(2), 391. doi:10.3390/electronics12020391

Hajjami, O., & Park, S. (2023). Using the metaverse in training: Lessons from real cases. *European Journal of Training and Development.* doi:10.1108/EJTD-12-2022-0144

Hennig-Thurau, T., Aliman, D. N., Herting, A. M., Cziehso, G., Linder, M., & Kübler, R. V. (2022b). Social interactions in the metaverse: Framework, initial evidence, and research roadmap. *Journal of the Academy of Marketing Science, 51*(4), 889–913. doi:10.1007/s11747-022-00908-0

Jauhiainen, J. S., Krohn, C., & Junnila, J. (2022). Metaverse and Sustainability: Systematic Review of Scientific Publications until 2022 and Beyond. *Sustainability (Basel), 15*(1), 346. doi:10.3390/su15010346

Liberatore, M. J., & Wagner, W. P. (2021). Virtual, mixed, and augmented reality: A systematic review for immersive systems research. *Virtual Reality (Waltham Cross), 25*(3), 773–799. doi:10.1007/s10055-020-00492-0

Lopes, M., & Reis, J. (2021). *Impacts of COVID-19 in Retail: A Case Study Research.* IEEE Xplore., doi:10.23919/CISTI52073.2021.9476594

Onu, P., Pradhan, A., & Mbohwa, C. (2023). Potential to use metaverse for future teaching and learning. *Education and Information Technologies.* Advance online publication. doi:10.1007/s10639-023-12167-9

Parlar, T. (2023). Data privacy and security in the metaverse. In Studies in big data (pp. 123–133). Springer. doi:10.1007/978-981-99-4641-9_8

Pooyandeh, M., Han, K. J., & Sohn, I. (2022). Cybersecurity in the AI-Based Metaverse: A survey. *Applied Sciences (Basel, Switzerland)*, *12*(24), 12993. doi:10.3390/app122412993

Pyae, A., Ravyse, W., Luimula, M., Pizarro-Lucas, E., Sánchez, P. L., Dorado-Díaz, P. I., & Thaw, A. K. (2023). Exploring user experience and usability in a metaverse learning environment for students: A Usability Study of Artificial Intelligence, Innovation, and Society (AIIS). *Electronics (Basel)*, *12*(20), 4283. doi:10.3390/electronics12204283

Rejeb, A., Rejeb, K., & Treiblmaier, H. (2023). Mapping Metaverse research: Identifying future research areas based on bibliometric and topic modeling techniques. *Information (Basel)*, *14*(7), 356. doi:10.3390/info14070356

Ribeiro, R. (2022). *"Metaverse" and the educational potential*. Cambridge University Press. https://www.cambridge.org/elt/blog/2021/11/15/metaverse-educational-potential

Said, G. R. E. (2023). Metaverse-Based Learning Opportunities and Challenges: A Phenomenological Metaverse Human–Computer Interaction Study. *Electronics (Basel)*, *12*(6), 1379. doi:10.3390/electronics12061379

Shen, B., Wei-Ming, T., Guo, J., Zhao, L., & Qin, P. (2021). How to promote user purchase in metaverse? A systematic literature review on consumer behaviour research and virtual commerce application design. *Applied Sciences (Basel, Switzerland)*, *11*(23), 11087. doi:10.3390/app112311087

Talarico, C., & Leija, E. (2023). The impact of the scientific metaverse on the biotech industry: How virtual reality helped researchers fight back against COVID-19. Springer eBooks. doi:10.1007/978-3-031-30691-4_5

Tank, D., Aggarwal, A., & Chaubey, N. (2019). Virtualization vulnerabilities, security issues, and solutions: A critical study and comparison. *International Journal of Information Technology : an Official Journal of Bharati Vidyapeeth's Institute of Computer Applications and Management*, *14*(2), 847–862. doi:10.1007/s41870-019-00294-x

Tella, A., Ajani, Y. A., & Ailaku, U. V. (2023). Libraries in the metaverse: The need for meta literacy for digital librarians and digital age library users. *Library Hi Tech News*, *40*(8), 14–18. doi:10.1108/LHTN-06-2023-0094

Trunfio, M., & Rossi, S. (2022). Advances in Metaverse Investigation: Streams of research and future agenda. *Virtual Worlds*, *1*(2), 103–129. doi:10.3390/virtualworlds1020007

Violante, M. G., Vezzetti, E., & Piazzolla, P. (2019). How to design a virtual reality experience that impacts consumer engagement: The case of the virtual supermarket. [IJIDeM]. *International Journal on Interactive Design and Manufacturing*, *13*(1), 243–262. doi:10.1007/s12008-018-00528-5

Xie, B., Liu, H., Alghofaili, R., Zhang, Y., Jiang, Y., Lobo, F. D., Li, C., Li, W., Huang, H., Akdere, M., Mousas, C., & Yu, L. (2021). A review of virtual Reality skill training applications. *Frontiers in Virtual Reality*, *2*, 645153. doi:10.3389/frvir.2021.645153

Zheng, Z., Li, T., Li, B., Chai, X., Song, W., Chen, N., Zhou, Y., Lin, Y., & Li, R. (2022). Industrial metaverse: connotation, features, technologies, applications and challenges. In Communications in computer and information science (pp. 239–263). Springer. doi:10.1007/978-981-19-9198-1_19

KEY TERMS AND DEFINITIONS

Capabilities: The knowledge, assets, and expertise that empower an organization to accomplish its goals and operate with efficiency.

Customer Experience: An environment generated by a computer that offers a three-dimensional, immersive experience.

Innovation: Propagation and advancement in diverse domains through the introduction of novel concepts, processes, or products.

Metaverse: An immersive shared experience virtual collective space that merges the physical and digital domains.

Retail: Frequently involving physical or online establishments, retail is the sale of products or services to consumers.

Training: Refers to the systematic acquisition of competencies, skills, and knowledge via experiential or educational methods.

Virtual Reality (VR): An environment generated by a computer that offers a three-dimensional, immersive experience.

Workforce: The combined labour force or workforce comprising the members of an organization or economy.

Chapter 8
Industry Experts and Business Consultants' Takes on India's Readiness for Metaverse:
A Review of the Retail Industry

Gautam Shandilya
(iD) https://orcid.org/0000-0002-9510-3787
Birla Institute of Technology, Mesra, India

Praveen Srivastava
(iD) https://orcid.org/0000-0001-5310-694X
Birla Institute of Technology, Mesra, India

Abhisek Jana
(iD) https://orcid.org/0000-0003-4495-5151
Birla Institute of Technology, Mesra, India

ABSTRACT

Metaverse is a 21st-century, cutting edge technology that evolved as a science fiction in the early 90's in the western world, which captured the imagination of people across the globe. India, with its 1.4 billion population, the fifth largest economy in the world, and exalted position in software and information technology augurs well for embracing metaverse in future businesses. The present chapter aims to find the acceptance and readiness of Indian retail industry for the use of metaverse in its operation. Authors tried to do qualitative analysis of industry experts' and business consultants' opinion on metaverse in retail sector to find the opportunities and likely trends. This chapter also takes Google trend on metaverse searches into account. A systematic general review of published articles and cases from secondary sources forms the basis of this chapter. Findings suggest that the changing dynamics of social interactions in the Metaverse are on the brink of a revolution, promising transformative impacts on the retail industry and consumer behaviors.

DOI: 10.4018/979-8-3693-3358-7.ch008

INTRODUCTION

Metaverse, a combination of words 'meta' and 'verse' is a computer generated superior universe in which multiuser digital avatars may communicate seamlessly in real time with the help of augmented reality (AR) and virtual reality (VR) (Mystakidis, 2022; Y. Wang et al., 2023) defining it as second life (Hazan, 2008). Metaverse allowed digital transformation of human beings in a shared realm of intertwined (spatial dimensions) space (Bourlakis et al., 2009) by augmenting cloud computing, artificial intelligence, simulation, deep learning, machine learning, extended reality, virtual reality, augmented reality, blockchain technology, non-fungible tokens, chatbots, robotics, crypto currency, 5G, and what nots of IoT and mobile applications (Lee et al., 2021; Park & Kim, 2022).

It gives people an opportunity to have open, interactive, and immersive communication on a virtual three-dimensional social world without bothering about space and time by converging above technological developments breaking the distinction of real world and virtual world (H. Wang et al., 2023) and bring the concept of *Vasudhaiva Kutumbakam* on surface in true sense (Manivannan, 2023). Blockchain technology for metaverse builds confidence of the user about their data security which has become a concern for every user (Gadekallu et al., 2022) necessitating different level of service quality (Gadalla et al., 2013).

Gaming, education, product demonstration, reviews of co purchasers, experts' opinion and reviews, post purchase dissonance can all be done on metaverse (Hazan, 2008; Kye et al., 2021) articulating personalized shopping experience (Adams, 2022).

It is here to stay as an ecosystem to break the social divide of haves and have nots and rich and poor, bringing everyone together on the virtual platform (Duan et al., 2021). A retail theater experience is provided to the consumers to share a

Table 1. Present Metaverse ecosystem

Embedded Technology Convergence	Sociality	Hyper-spatio-temporality action	Transaction mode	Domain
Cloud computing, Artificial intelligence, Simulation, Deep learning, Data analytics, Digital twin, Machine learning, Extended reality, Virtual Reality, Augmented reality, IoT, Blockchain technology, Chatbot, Robotics, 5G, Mobile applications	Virtual social world	Open, Immersive, Interactive	Cryptocurrency, Non-fungible tokens	Gaming, Entertainment, Social networking, Remote working, Education, Space technology, Architecture, Geo-science, Life science, Tourism, Retail business

Source: Authors compilation 2023

unique shopping experience (Papagiannidis & Bourlakis, 2010). The presence of this ecosystem is on traction and so robust that Facebook rebranded its company as Meta (Kim, 2021). A whole new set of virtual economy is a possible reality by metaverse with a projected market of $800 billion by 2024 (Yoo et al., 2023).

The present metaverse ecosystem is depicted in table 1.

PROBLEM STATEMENT

Metaverse retailing maintains the convenience factor for both the customers and retailers by putting back the context and enriching the environment. In this context, human-computer interface and interaction is required to review the best practices at the metaverse-point of sale and benchmark the web-based commerce systems. All the more, despite of India's leading position in software product development, it lacks the robust metaverse ecosystem due to its own fallacy, especially in retail sector. Further research is required to make customers understand the advantages of metaverse technology augmentation in retailing experience. Hence, the present study attempts to fill the gap by analyzing the opinion of experts and business consultants regarding the India's readiness for metaverse in retail sector. In this backdrop, the following objectives are framed for present study:

- To study the present scenario of metaverse presence in Indian market.
- To study the metaverse challenges upfront Indian retail sector.
- To analyze the acceptance and readiness for metaverse in Indian retail market.

METHODOLOGY

This review paper adopts a comprehensive methodology that integrates systematic general review techniques. The approach involves an extensive examination of published articles and case studies from secondary sources, while also incorporating excerpts from a diverse range of interviews for qualitative content analysis. To provide a well-rounded and nuanced understanding of the research, the review process is segmented into three distinct parts, each focusing on soliciting different perspectives from key stakeholders: industry experts and consultants, retailers, and consumers, as well as freelancers who are increasingly shaping the Metaverse landscape. Furthermore, this review encompasses an exploration of Google Trends and Statista data, specifically targeting searches related to the intersection of the Metaverse and the retail industry in the Indian context. This multifaceted approach ensures a thorough examination of the subject matter and provides a robust foundation for our study.

The current paper tries to examine the impact of metaverse on Indian retail sector and whether Indian retail sector is ready for it through the bird's eye view of industry experts and business consultants. Excerpts of these opinion makers are taken from various interviews, views, and blogs at different forums to highlight the foundation of this research. Their opinion tends to be authoritative as they are here to shape the moods, tones, trends, and directions of any business. At the same time searches on Google and other search engines give some indications of readiness trends for metaverse.

To examine the objectives framed for the present study, qualitative analysis was used where authors methodically studied the narratives of the metaverse retail experts, consultants, retailers, and customers towards the scope, challenges, and metaverse retail readiness in India. The qualitative analysis permits for profound studies which yield a treasure of comprehensive information, notwithstanding at the cost of simplification (Patton, 1990), does not seek out to prove any statistical implication or relationship (Denzin & Lincoln, 1994; Patton, 1990; Stake, 1995) and aims to enable the in-depth discovery of observation and to give deep understanding of certain perspectives (Eisenhardt, 1989). Multiple observations and statements from different stakeholders can establish the expansion of the profound analytically founded philosophy of the explored experiences (Miles & Huberman, 1994; Yin, 1984). Pursuing the above, qualitative analysis was considered suitable for this study.

REVIEW OF LITERATURE

Many companies forayed into the concept of 'Second Life' originally a software application 'Linden World' in the early years of 2000 just to leverage of being the first movers (Ondrejka, 2004) but soon had to consider the overall characteristics of the environment to have tangible business gains (Rose, 2007). But researchers like Gibson (1984), had criticized it by owing more to the real world than the second life in its abstract form and found it only suitable for rating and safety. To bridge this gap Harris et al. (2001) and Harris et al. (2003) proposed a concept of retail theater wherein retailers provide a unique and special service allowing customers to enjoy the overall experience while interacting and participating. This led to the advent of metaverse.

Metaverse evolved in the retail space from traditional approach of product-customer orientation of satisfying customer's needs (Kotler, 2000) to customer orientation through electronic retailing (Feinberg & Kadam, 2002) and finally to experience orientation through metaverse retailing (Eroglu et al., 2001; Papagiannidis & Bourlakis, 2010). It overcomes the limitations of two-dimensional online channels by immersing customers in the retailing experience on the internet based virtual platform (Papagiannidis & Bourlakis, 2010) without being isolated from 'two spaces' i.e., virtual world and the real world (Castronova, 2005). Vodafone's 'InsideOut service' has the features to make it possible to call and send SMS both in real world and the second life when the users are offline and online respectively (Papagiannidis & Bourlakis, 2010). Avatars of the customers can easily participate, get engaged and even share the experience among fellow avatars in the metaverse space (K. Harris et al., 2001; R. Harris et al., 2003).

Avatars or the humanoid forms of customers painting a car with his preferred color before purchasing the car or for example checking out the Reebok shoes' size and color, or clothes or wall paints, tiles, and furniture in their houses allow customers to modify, co-design and fit to match their personal requirements are a testament to contemporary customers' focus to satisfy their needs (Namasivayam, 2003). A bride could invite her friends in metaverse space to share her joy while trying out the ceremonial dress and obtain their chaste remarks (Trollop, 2007).

It is found that metaverse is quite used in gaming, social networking, remote working, city planning and architecture, education especially engineering and health education, space technology, entertainment, cinematic visual effects, museums and pilgrim shrines, tourism, electoral campaigns, trade, and businesses and many more such fields. Government of India is also emphasizing on metaverse to utilize it in E-governance (Wasnik & Bhasin, 2022).

To gauge the general and specific objectives of the present study, authors have systematically compiled the opinions of the retail industry experts, business consultants, freelancers, and consumers to understand the overall readiness of Indian retail sector for metaverse in India.

Industry Experts' and Business Consultants' Opinion in Indian Context

Paras Lohani, Founder and CEO, B2B Sales Arrow referred Gartner's prediction of 25% of global population to spend at least one hour every day on metaverse (Paras Lohani, 2022), assuming its growth inevitable. Some of the top entertainment leaders like Nitin Mittal, President at Zee Entertainment Enterprises; Ranga Jagannath, Senior Director at Agora; Sreeram Ananthasayanam, Partner at Deloitte India; Rajat Ojha, CEO and Founder at PartyNite; Ashish Pherwani EY India Leader; Zoe Cocker, Head Yahoo Creative Studios, ANZ; Kamal Gianchandani, CEO of PVR Picture have all seen and gone through the difficulty of making metaverse a reality, are very optimistic about it, go gung-ho over it and at the same time caution the industry to tread the path carefully (Singal, 2022).

Ashootosh Chand and Sudipta Ghosh of PWC, India, sees the enormous opportunity and exponential growth of metaverse as companies are ready to embed metaverse plans (BL Bengaluru Bureau, 2023) by engaging customers, employees and the metaverse ecosystem meaningfully (HT News Desk, 2023) however, finds data breach, cybersecurity, and technological limitations as a challenge.

PWC in its report found that non-fungible tokens through blockchain applications in gaming, fashion and art are building customers' trust and soon can be seen replicated in retail industry (Ghosh et al., 2023).

Deloitte in its report submitted that service led economy with the 55% of gross value added (GVA) of the $2.5 trillion economy in 2020 in India, retail sector accounts for 11.3% of GVA only to be preceded by agriculture with 18.4% GVA and manufacturing 14.7% GVA respectively potentially making it $79-148 billion metaverse business per year (Deloitte, 2023).

Arthur D. Little, a strategy and management consulting company in its report on "Web3 & Metaverse – The Rise of the New Internet & the India Opportunity" predicts $200 billion potential of metaverse business in India by 2035 (Jose, 2023).

A leading market research company IMARC Group in its report titled "India Metaverse Market: Industry Trends, Share, Size, Growth, Opportunity and Forecast 2023-2028" projects India's metaverse market growth at 43% by 2023-2028 (Thapar, 2023).

However, some arguments have the opinion that only virtual assets like Ethereum can be used to purchase goods at e-commerce marketplace platforms like Nikeland in Roblox and cryptocurrencies used to buy physical goods, services and products are out of scope (Statista, 2023). Seemingly, Michael Donnelly, Head of interactive marketing at Coca-Cola and David Stern, Commissioner of National Basketball Association (NBA) have a very negative notion about second life, retail theater and metaverse and find them complete wastage of time citing examples of Reebok, Scion, Aloft Hotel, NBA YouTube with negligible presence on their metaverse space and finding no one else to interact with (Rose, 2007).

Retailers' Opinion

Retail businesses no more remain untouched by the metaverse in India as well. Tanishq's wedding collection 'Romance of Polki', Ceat Tyre's Ceat Shoppe, Mahindra & Mahindra's Thar-themed NFTs and MakeMy Trip's virtual vacation NFTs ventures are already creating a buzz in Indian metaverse retail market (Bhardwaj, 2022).

Tejpal Singh Shekhawat, Founder and CEO of Kalyanam Furniture considers Metaverse as a social platform which blurs the line between online and offline shopping where customers may have immersive shopping experience and estimates $99 billion e-commerce business this year (Shekhawat, 2023) however, sees product authenticity and quality control as major concerns for retail business on metaverse.

Vishal Shah, GM at Lenovo Intelligent Devices Group believes that extended reality (XR) solutions are already thriving at the enterprise level whereas, Kunal Purohit, Chief Digital Services Officer at Tech Mahindra opines that metaverse practices are going to transform the customer's experience and more business outcomes would be delivered very soon (Bagchi, 2023).

Companies like Flipkart, Tanishq, Mahindra & Mahindra, Maruti, and Make My Trip etc. have all forayed into metaverse and expects huge budgetary from the union budget of Government of India to boost and thrust the robust 'Make in India' campaign (Anand, 2023).

Consumers' and Freelancers' Opinion

Metaverse has the potential to create new avenues for e-commerce by driving innovation and certainly creating new job opportunities in the market (ZeeBiz WebDesk, 2023) and a tickling fascination for consumers (Sharma, 2022). With its tech-ready workforce, India as an information technology (IT) hub can usher into metaverse (Priyadarshi, 2023).

Evolving regulatory landscape in India like bringing cryptocurrencies and non-fungible tokens while transferring virtual digital assets (VDA) under tax ambit is surely doing good to metaverse and achieving the target of $1 trillion digital economy by 2030 (Darbari & Hall, 2022).

COVID19 pandemic has also become a blessing in disguise for metaverse business in India as it is surging to reach market value of $337.76 billion by 2029 (Alliance News, 2023). Tata Consultancy Services, Infosys, HCL Technologies, Wipro, LTI Mindtree, and Tech Mahindra are the top metaverse service provider companies in India (Sinha, 2023).

Wajire (2022), is more concerned about the potential challenges associated with the utility of metaverse technology and considers it to be unregulated and unsupervised; control of economy in the hands of few mighty tech companies like Meta, Google, Microsoft, Amazon, Apple etc.; missing accountability due to

Table 2. Key figure values

- 25% of the global population to spend 1 hour every day on metaverse by 2026.
- Retail sector accounted for 11.3% GVA of $2.5 trillion in 2020
- $200 billion potential of metaverse business in India by 2035
- India's metaverse market will grow at 43% CAGR in 2023-28
- India's E-commerce business is at $99 billion in 2023
- India is striving to achieve $1trillion digital economy by 2030
- Metaverse market value to reach $337.76 billion by 2029

Source: Authors compilation 2023

transcend boundaries; data security rising to national security; and cyber-syndrome like use of high computation, consumption of electricity rising to environmental issues. The key figure values are capsuled in Table 2.

The above table shows key economy indicators which Indian Government, industry people, financial experts, business consultants, investors, startup companies, innovators, freelancers, consumers, and other stakeholders are looking forward to.

Data From Internet Showing Trends for Metaverse in Indian Retail Sector

Authors have captured the data showing trends on Google trend and Statista with keywords like metaverse, retail and India. The same has been put in figures to understand the trends for metaverse in Indian retail sector. Figure 1. depicts the day wise number of internet search for metaverse in India over past three months (source: Google trend, data from July to Oct'23). Figure 2. depicts region wise interest shown toward search for metaverse in India over past three months (source: Google trend). Figure 3. depicts different reasons for which Indian companies adopted metaverse in the year 2023 (source: Statista), whereas Figure 4. shows worldwide investment %age in metaverse by leading business sectors as of March 2022 (source: Statista).

From the above figure it can be inferred that metaverse search on Google trend reached its peak with 100 searches in the month of August and since then there is a down surge in the interest.

From the above figure it can be inferred that Chandigarh tops among the Indian subregions in terms of metaverse search on Google trend in past three months.

Figure 1. Interest over time
Source: Google trend, 25th October 2023

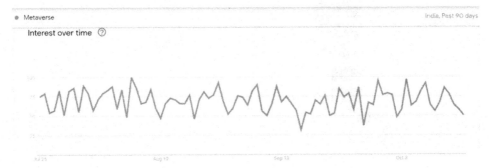

Figure 2. Interest by subregion
Source: Google trend, 25th October 2023

Figure 3. Reasons for metaverse adoption among companies in India in 2023
Source: Statista, 25th October 2023

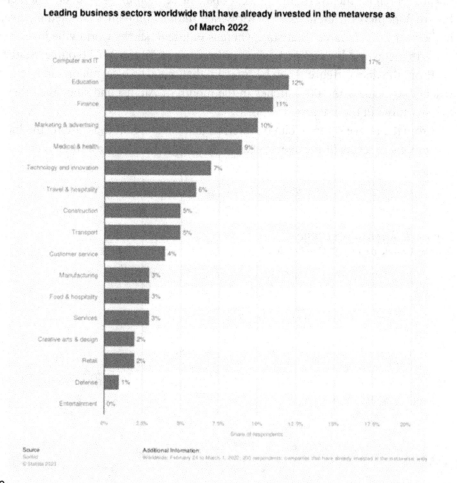

Figure 4. Metaverse investment %age by leading business sectors worldwide
Source: Statista, 25ᵗʰ October 2023

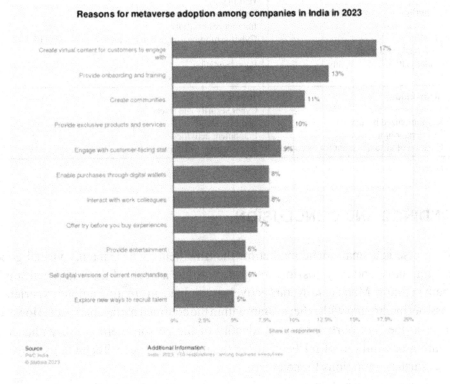

The above figure shows the reasons why Indian companies are adopting metaverse, where virtual content creation tops the list and recruitment is the least important reason.

The above figure shows that out of total investment in metaverse worldwide by March 2022, Computer and IT companies had the maximum investment with 17% and Entertainment had 0% investment. Retail industry had a meagre 2% investment and ranks among the bottom three sectors.

It may be deciphered from the above reviews and searches that potential for metaverse in retail sector in India is quite enormous, but it is still lagging behind in readiness.

SWOT Analysis: Table 3. Depicts SWOT analysis of metaverse in India to better understand the prospects and challenges for metaverse in retail sector.

Table 3. SWOT analysis of metaverse in India

Strengths Robust economy IT hub Tech ready workforce Social platform of company	Weaknesses Technological limitations Internet connectivity Cyber-syndrome – high computation, consumption of electricity Poor regulation Accountability fixation
Opportunities Young population Revolutionized business Next avatar of internet Creation of virtual content for customers	Threats Cyber security and safety Interoperability Fraudulent activities Data security and privacy

Source: Authors compilation 2023

FINDINGS AND CONCLUSION

Metaverse is a small niche market for the time being where mainly virtual goods are purchased and may possibly integrate with the aspects of the traditional supply chain in future. Metaverse avatars actively participate in creating unique experiences possibly integrating with other avatars within the confined metaverse space. However, since it does not portray the real identity of the person there is every chance of creating possibilities of misbehavior in the metaverse space. Technology may also pose further limitations to metaverse.

Metaverse ecosystem in India is still at a nascent and infancy stage. There are umpteen challenges posed in front of metaverse ecosystems. Despite these challenges it provides significant opportunities for growth and innovation. The advancement of technologies and rise of metaverse ecosystems, increasing popularity of e-merchandising and innovative startups shall bring forth the continued growth in metaverse space. The way people are interacting on social platforms, metaverse is going to revolutionize the retail business and consumers alike.

Managerial Implications

The finding of the current study is of importance to the retail business who are eyeing to increase their revenue by adopting the latest technology in the field of metaverse. The opinion of experts and business consultants provides valuable insights for retail managers and executives.

Metaverse is more than just a futuristic concept; it's a reality that is knocking on the doors of the Indian retail sector. Though at nascent stage, the metaverse has already showed its potential in various related fields. With the ever-increasing growth of technology, customers are becoming more demanding and retail businesses cannot afford to close their eyes to this technology-driven demand of customers.

To flourish in this evolving digital landscape, retail managers and executives should not only embrace this change but actively drive it. Still, for metaverse retail concept to be functional in full, retailers need to go at imposing distances to give finer experiences by engaging further with the consumers. By investing in Metaverse technology, redefining customer engagement, safeguarding data, adapting to local nuances, and staying agile in response to industry trends, Indian retailers can carve out a competitive advantage and secure their position as pioneers in this transformative journey.

REFERENCES

Adams, D. (2022). Virtual Retail in the Metaverse: Customer Behavior Analytics, Extended Reality Technologies, and Immersive Visualization Systems. *Linguistic and Philosophical Investigations*, *21*(0), 73–88. doi:10.22381/lpi2120225

Alliance News. (2023). *India Metaverse Market 2023 Industry Overview, Key Technology, Segments, SWOT Analysis, and Forecast Research 2031*. Report Ocean. https://www.barchart.com/story/news/19089545/india-metaverse-market-2023-industry-overview-key-technology-segments-swot-analysis-and-forecast-research-2031

Anand, J. (2023, January). Budget 2023 expectations: What does the Indian metaverse space seek from the policymakers? *India Today*. https://www.indiatoday.in/cryptocurrency/story/budget-2023-expectations-what-does-the-indian-metaverse-space-seek-from-the-policymakers-2327111-2023-01-27

Bagchi, S. (2023, October 9). Enterprise use cases set to drive metaverse momentum. *Mint*. https://www.livemint.com/companies/news/enterprise-use-cases-set-to-drive-metaverse-momentum-11696867750783.html

Bhardwaj, S. (2022). Indian companies storm the metaverse and NFT space. *Forbes India*. https://www.forbesindia.com/article/crypto-made-easy/indian-companies-storm-the-metaverse-and-nft-space/75281/1

BL Bengaluru Bureau. (2023, April 26). Indian business executives keen to integrate the metaverse in organisational activities: PwC report. *The Hindu Business Line*. https://www.thehindubusinessline.com/companies/indian-business-executives-keen-to-integrate-the-metaverse-in-organisational-activities-pwc-report/article66781335.ece

Bourlakis, M., Papagiannidis, S., & Li, F. (2009). Retail spatial evolution: Paving the way from traditional to metaverse retailing. *Electronic Commerce Research*, *9*(1-2), 135–148. doi:10.1007/s10660-009-9030-8

Castronova, E. (2005). *Synthetic Worlds: The Business and Culture of Online Games*. University of Chicago Press.

Darbari, R., & Hall, S. B. (2022). *India could have a key role to play in building the metaverse. Here's why*. WeForum. https://www.weforum.org/agenda/2022/03/india-could-build-metaverse/

Deloitte. (2023). *The Metaverse in India Strategies for Accelerating Economic Impact*. Deloitte. https://www2.deloitte.com/in/en/pages/technology-media-and-telecommunications/articles/the-metaverse-in-asia.html

Denzin, N., & Lincoln, Y. (1994). *Handbook of Qualitative Research*. Sage.

Duan, H., Li, J., Fan, S., Lin, Z., Wu, X., & Cai, W. (2021). Metaverse for Social Good: A University Campus Prototype. *29th ACM International Conference on Multimedia*, 153–161. 10.1145/3474085.3479238

Eisenhardt, K. M. (1989). Building theories from case study research. *Academy of Management Review*, *14*(4), 532–550. doi:10.2307/258557

Eroglu, S. A., Machleit, K. A., & Davis, L. M. (2001). Atmospheric qualities of online retailing A conceptual model and implications. *Journal of Business Research*, *54*(2), 177–184. doi:10.1016/S0148-2963(99)00087-9

Feinberg, R., & Kadam, R. (2002). E-CRM Web service attributes as determinants of customer satisfaction with retail Web sites. *International Journal of Service Industry Management*, *13*(2), 432–451. doi:10.1108/09564230210447922

Gadalla, E., Keeling, K., & Abosag, I. (2013). Metaverse-retail service quality: A future framework for retail service quality in the 3D internet. *Journal of Marketing Management*, *29*(13–14), 1493–1517. doi:10.1080/0267257X.2013.835742

Gadekallu, T. R., Huynh-The, T., Wang, W., Yenduri, G., Ranaweera, P., Pham, Q.-V., da Costa, D. B., & Liyanage, M. (2022). *Blockchain for the Metaverse: A Review*. 17. https://doi.org//arXiv.2203.09738 doi:10.48550

Ghosh, S., Chand, A., Sengupta, V., & Pandit, Y. (2023). *Embracing the metaverse*. PWC. https://www.pwc.in/research-and-insights-hub/embracing-the-metaverse.html

Gibson, W. (1984). *Neuromancer*. Ace Books.

Harris, K., Harris, R., & Baron, S. (2001). Customer participation in retail service: Lessons from Brecht. *International Journal of Retail & Distribution Management*, *29*(8), 359–369. doi:10.1108/09590550110396845

Harris, R., Harris, K., & Baron, S. (2003). Theatrical service experiences. *International Journal of Service Industry Management*, *14*(2), 184–199. doi:10.1108/09564230310474156

Hazan, S. (2008). Musing the Metaverse. *2008 Annual Conference of CIDOC*. http:// digital-heritage.org.il

HT News Desk. (2023, April 26). Is India ready for metaverse? 70% businesses plan integration, says survey. *Hindustan Times*. https://www.hindustantimes. com/technology/technology-news-indian-businesses-metaverse-pwc-india-survey-101682505719797.html

Jose, B. (2023, June 3). Metaverse & Web3 to present India with $200 billion opportunity, driven by retail and financial services: Report. *The Indian Express*. https://indianexpress.com/article/technology/tech-news-technology/metaverse-web3-to-present-india-with-200-billion-opportunity-8640975/

Kim, J. (2021). Advertising in the Metaverse: Research Agenda. *Journal of Interactive Advertising*, *21*(3), 141–144. doi:10.1080/15252019.2021.2001273

Kotler, P. (2000). Marketing Management (Millennium). Prentice-Hall, Inc. Pearson Custom Publishing.

Kye, B., Han, N., Kim, E., Park, Y., & Jo, S. (2021). Educational applications of metaverse: Possibilities and limitations. *Journal of Educational Evaluation for Health Professions*, *18*(32), 1–13. doi:10.3352/jeehp.2021.18.32 PMID:34897242

Lee, L.-H., Braud, T., Zhou, P., Wang, L., Xu, D., Lin, Z., Kumar, A., Bermejo, C., & Hui, P. (2021). All One Needs to Know about Metaverse: A Complete Survey on Technological Singularity, Virtual Ecosystem, and Research Agenda. *Journal of Latex Class Files*, *14*(8), 1–66. doi:10.48550/arXiv.2110.05352

Manivannan, M. (2023, September 14). India has a huge potential to lead the world in metaverse technologies towards Vasudhaiva Kutumbakam. *Financial Express*. https:// www.financialexpress.com/policy/economy-india-has-a-huge-potential-to-lead-the-world-in-metaverse-technologies-towards-vasudhaiva-kutumbakam-3243198/

Miles, M. B., & Huberman, A. M. (1994). Qualitative Data Analysis: An Expanded Sourcebook. *Sage (Atlanta, Ga.)*.

Mystakidis, S. (2022). Metaverse. In *Encyclopedia* (pp. 486–497). MDPI. doi:10.3390/encyclopedia2010031

Namasivayam, K. (2003). The consumer as a "transient employee": Consumer satisfaction through the lens of job-performance models. *International Journal of Service Industry Management, 14*(4), 420–435. doi:10.1108/09564230310489259

Ondrejka, C. R. (2004). A Piece of Place: Modeling the Digital on the Real in Second Life. SSRN *Electronic Journal.* doi:10.2139/ssrn.555883

Papagiannidis, S., & Bourlakis, M. (2010). Staging the New Retail Drama: At a Metaverse Near You! *Journal of Virtual Worlds Research, 2*(5), 225–246. doi:10.4101/jvwr.v2i5.808

Paras Lohani. (2022). *How Metaverse is taking shape in the Indian IT and Event Industry.* Express Computer. https://www.expresscomputer.in/guest-blogs/how-metaverse-is-taking-shape-in-the-indian-it-and-event-industry/89204/

Park, S.-M., & Kim, Y.-G. (2022). A Metaverse: Taxonomy, Components, Applications, and Open Challenges. *IEEE Access : Practical Innovations, Open Solutions, 10*, 4209–4251. doi:10.1109/ACCESS.2021.3140175

Patton, M. (1990). Qualitative Data Analysis. *Sage (Atlanta, Ga.).*

Priyadarshi, P. (2023). *Into The Metaverse: How India Can Leverage The Multi-Billion Dollar Opportunity.* Inc 42. https://inc42.com/resources/into-the-metaverse-how-india-can-leverage-the-multi-billion-dollar-opportunity/

Rose, F. (2007, July). How Madison Avenue is Wasting Millions on a Deserted Second Life. *Wired.* https://www.wired.com/2007/07/ff-sheep/

Sharma, P. (2022, October 16). India and the industrial metaverse. *Business Standard.* https://www.business-standard.com/article/opinion/india-and-the-industrial-metaverse-122101600591_1.html

Shekhawat, T. S. (2023, June 21). The metaverse and the future of retail opportunities and challenges. *The Times of India.* https://timesofindia.indiatimes.com/blogs/voices/the-metaverse-and-the-future-of-retail-opportunities-and-challenges/

Singal, N. (2022, August). How the Metaverse Will Drive Innovation in Entertainment. *Business Today.* https://www.businesstoday.in/magazine/technology/story/how-the-metaverse-will-drive-innovation-in-entertainment-343328-2022-08-01

Sinha, H. (2023). *Top Metaverse Stocks in India to Invest.* Groww. https://groww.in/blog/best-metaverse-stocks-in-india

Stake, R. (1995). The Art of Case Study Research. *Sage (Atlanta, Ga.)*.

Statista. (2023). *Metaverse*. Statista. https://www.statista.com/outlook/amo/metaverse/india

Thapar, A. (2023). *India Metaverse Market 2023 | Industry Size, Trends and Forecast 2028*. Linkedin. https://www.linkedin.com/pulse/india-metaverse-market-2023-industry-size-trends-forecast-thapar

Trollop, C. (2007). *Wearable Second Life*. Second Style. https://blog.secondstyle.com/2007/08/wearable-second-life.html

Wajire, P. (2022). *Exploring the Metaverse: Challenges and Opportunities for India in the 'Next Internet.'* ORF Online. https://www.orfonline.org/research/exploring-the-metaverse/

Wang, H., Ning, H., Lin, Y., Wang, W., Dhelim, S., Farha, F., Ding, J., & Daneshmand, M. (2023). A Survey on the Metaverse: The State-of-the-Art, Technologies, Applications, and Challenges. *IEEE Internet of Things Journal*, *10*(16), 14671–14688. doi:10.1109/JIOT.2023.3278329

Wang, Y., Su, Z., Zhang, N., Xing, R., Liu, D., Luan, T. H., & Shen, X. (2023). A Survey on Metaverse: Fundamentals, Security, and Privacy. *IEEE Communications Surveys and Tutorials*, *25*(1), 319–352. doi:10.1109/COMST.2022.3202047

Wasnik, A., & Bhasin, A. (2022). *Meta-governance: Role of metaverse in India's E-governance*. NITI Aayog. https://www.niti.gov.in/meta-governance-role-metaverse-indias-e-governance

Yin, R. K. (1984). *Case Study Research: Design and Methods*. Sage Publications.

Yoo, K., Welden, R., Hewett, K., & Haenlein, M. (2023). The merchants of meta: A research agenda to understand the future of retailing in the metaverse. *Journal of Retailing*, *99*(2), 173–192. doi:10.1016/j.jretai.2023.02.002

ZeeBiz WebDesk. (2023). *India's Journey into the Metaverse: The Rise of Virtual Reality Technology*. Zee Business. https://www.zeebiz.com/agencies/indias-journey-into-the-metaverse-the-rise-of-virtual-reality-technology-222331

Chapter 9
Omnichannel Approach to Meet Retail Customers' Expectations

Manish Bansal
Malout Institute of Management and Information Technology, India

Sukhbir Kaur
Malout Institute of Management and Information Technology, India

ABSTRACT

Customer expectations are a set of ideas about a product, service, or brand that a customer holds in their mind. Customer expectations can be influenced by a customers' perception of the product or service and can be created or modified by previous experience, advertising, word of mouth, awareness of competitors, and brand image. Rising expectations and changing customers' needs are shaping the face of modern retail. Whenever customers visit an organized retail store, they expect convenience and a better experience. Omnichannel approach encompasses a business strategy that is intended to offer a magnificent shopping experience across all channels i.e. in-store, mobile, and online. An effective omnichannel retail strategy covers the major areas of contact across all possible communication channels to facilitate seamless, customized customer interaction. An omnichannel experience assures a better customer experience and helps in sustaining customer loyalty in the long run.

DOI: 10.4018/979-8-3693-3358-7.ch009

CUSTOMER EXPECTATIONS

Customer expectation can be influenced by a customer's perception of the product or service and can be created or modified by previous experience, advertising, word of mouth, awareness of competitors, and brand image. Rising expectations and changing customers' needs are shaping the face of modern retail. Whenever customers visit an organized retail store, they expect convenience and better store experience. Customers nowadays are more aware and price sensitive. Their expectations are growing day by day and they seek more value for their money. They want variety, good quality products, enhanced shopping experience, quick response to their problems and better services. Retailers should make a commitment for understanding the customer's perspective. Meaningful customer experience can be provided by offering:

- Increased Personalization
- Convenience
- Omnichannel

Reasons Behind Changing Customer Expectations

Consumer nowadays has become multifaceted and more comprehensive due to interaction with large number of economic, social, political and global factors and hence they are becoming increasingly demanding and challenging. Here are some factors causing rapid changes in consumer behaviour:

- **Volatile markets and alarming inflation:** Factors like unpredictable markets and alarming rate of inflation have huge impact on customers' expectations. Customers feel that they have less disposable income. They are looking for ways to carry on smarter purchases, even they are purchasing less.
- **The hybrid method of buying:** Digital revolution has changed the ways of shopping especially after COVID. Now lot more products and services are available online. People have shifted to hybrid lifestyle where they are buying both online and in-store. According to a study by Prosper Insights & Analytics, 33% of adults are shopping less in stores.

Omnichannel Retail

Omnichannel retail is a strategy that facilitates customers to interact with and make purchases, without much effort, across various channels, from wherever they are and in any way. Omnichannel approach encompasses a business strategy that is intended to offer a magnificent shopping experience across all channels i.e. in-store, mobile or online. An effective omnichannel retail strategy covers the major areas of contact across all possible communication channels to facilitate seamless, customized customer interaction. An omnichannel experience assures a better customer experience and helps in sustaining customer loyalty in the long run (Azhari & Benett, 2015).

With the digital transformation, customer expectations are also rising. Customers want a shopping experience where they have a rapport with the organisation, get excellent customer service and all their queries/problems must be handled immediately. Retailers must devise suitable policies to meet expectation of their customers. First, they need to recognize the channels where their customers are present and then create what is required by customers in that particular space. Retailers must deliver integrated experience and once an expectation is created, it must be met. This might be achieved by:

- Ensuring presence on various social media platforms for exposure and better communication with the customer
- Maintaining a help center with well talented staff for addressing email and phone queries
- Allowing customers to make easy returns in the stores.

Features of Omnichannel Retailing

An omnichannel retail experience is beneficial for both customers as well as retailers. Omnichannel retail strategy ensures a seamless experience and reinforces sales channels to increase returns through customer engagement. It works towards an integrated platform for successful retail operations with the use of technological advancements. Some additional factors required for this approach are:

1. Data collection to enhance customer experience

Retailers require to constantly collect information about their customers who are available on various channels. They can compile and analyse this data by suitable technologies and use it for future sales. Further, retailers can use customer reviews and feedback for getting additional knowledge about them. This information can help retailers for monitoring channel-wise traffic, identifying channels in which investments can be made, resource allocation, creating customer database, developing self-service channels, training staff for providing better service to the customers, etc.

2.   Employ techniques to improve efficiency and effectiveness

Omnichannel retail depends on data collection and that data can be used to improve customer experience and enhance internal efficiency. This can help retailers to reap the benefits of achieving greater customer satisfaction. Shoppers usually prefers self-service portals and omnichannel retail can offer services like self-checkout stores and online tools to help customers locate any product, further buy and track without any assistance from sales representative or customer service personnel. Techniques or methods engaged to enhance customer experience can lead to improved efficiency and effectiveness (Hilken et al., 2018).

3.   **Ensure to serve the customers where they are**

Retailers should not try to fetch customers towards their place or location rather they need meet the customers where they are present. At the present time, customers value convenience above all and they expect a meaningful experience every time when they make purchase. Retailers are offering various options or platforms to buy like online stores, brick & mortar stores (Chatterjee, 2016). Even customers have option to buy directly from an Instagram or any social media account. Availability of this omnichannel strategy helps in increasing sales and yielding more profits (Brynjolfsson et al., 2013). According to a report by McKinsey, omnichannel customers shop 1.7 times more and further whenever they shop, they usually end in spending more (Bell et al., 2014).

Prerequisites to Formulate an Omnichannel Retail Strategy

Retailers need to formulate omnichannel retail strategy and following are the tasks involved in it (Banerjee, 2019):

1.   Recognise or identify your customers

First, retailers need to identify their customers and prepare a database. Accurate and timely knowledge about customers behaviour is required for proper market segmentation. Further customer understanding is necessary to offer customised products or services. Some of the factors for which information is required include:

- Customer Demographics
- Behavioural patterns
- Various Income levels
- Perceptions or interests

2.   Choose your channels/platforms

After segmentation, next step is to decide about the suitable channels. Choosing the appropriate channel is challenging task for organisations because a channel right for one company may not suitable to other. As there are large number of channel options available, it may not be possible to select all. Best channels are the ones through customer interactions can be done properly. An effective channel helps to attain customer loyalty and bring new customers. Sales channels can be modified or updated on the basis of customer behaviour, their motivation levels and influences. Following are the main types of channels that an organisation can consider:

- Company website
- Conventional or physical stores
- Various social media platforms
- Messaging and chat platforms
- Email and phone support

3.   Design the channel offerings for better customer experience

The success of omnichannel retail lies in its capability to realize customer preferences and develop suitable strategies that can match those preferences (Juaneda et al., 2016). For providing an appropriate experience (Izogo & Chanaka, 2018), an organisation can offer their services to the customers in following zones:

- **Awareness:** Here the organisation needs to educate their customers about the offerings using social media, live chats, sales representatives etc.
- **Consideration:** In this stage, customers evaluate available options by taking into consideration their pros and cons. It may involve price comparisons, delivery timings, easy returns and useful features. During consideration, the main objective is to create differentiation and ensure customers that your products or services are different from the competitor.
- **Purchase:** During this phase, excellent shopping experience can be delivered.
- **Retention:** It is challenging to retain an existing customer than bringing a new one. Here the goal is to retain the customer by inculcating faith in them. Record customers' shopping history, enable fast deliveries, easy returns etc. are few strategies that can be adopted (Boehm, 2008).
- **Loyalty:** Customer loyalty can be attained by various loyalty programs, offering freebies, special discounts on birthdays etc.

4. Systemize all the processes

Automation of processes is an important requirement as it is not possible to manage large amounts of data. Continuous interaction across the channels, integrated database, avoid duplication of work, timely reply to customers queries and data sorting are few points that require automation of processes.

5. Evaluate

When new retail strategy is launched, it is essential to evaluate ongoing processes. Continuous assessment of customer behaviour patterns and matching your strategies to cope up with the same is required. Further, evaluation ensures that right strategies are incorporated.

Problems Faced by Omnichannel Retail

Omnichannel retail implements a comprehensive and integrated approach for business. Effective strategies lead to successful operations and high returns but it is difficult to carry on all the processes effectively. Some of the challenges faced by omnichannel retail are as follows:

- **Lack of Synchronization of various purchase orders made by the customers:** It is difficult to manage data related to various purchase orders made by customers across different channels. Data from multiple channels is tough to analyse accurately and errors may occur. Poor data synchronization may interfere with effectiveness of omnichannel system.
- **Ineffective logistics:** Logistics and reverse logistics are very important for successful retail operations. It is very difficult to manage customer orders, returns and refunds with ineffective logistics operations. Third party logistics are engaged for smooth processes.
- **Conflicts between various channels:** It is very difficult to achieve consistency across channels. Offline and online interactions become very complicated. Channel that adds more into revenues often get special attention while other channels lag behind. Also, there is disagreement between workforce across channels because of separate sales targets and goals for each channel (Verhoef et al., 2015).
- **Poor visibility:** It is very challenging for organisations to ensure proper visibility. For increasing sales across channels, it is important to ensure easy availability of product. Lack of visibility can result in loss of sales to competitors.

- **Poor customer engagement:** Due to increased scope, number of customers also increases so understanding customer behaviour patterns becomes difficult.

- **Technological challenges:** It is difficult to engage and timely update new methods, equipment and software as technological advancements are taking place at very fast pace. Organisation need well educated and trained staff to manage all the operations.

- **Consumer privacy and frauds:** Ensuring privacy of customer data is quite challenging. Cyber attacks or frauds may lead to failure of business operations.

- **High cost:** High cost is involved in proper data management, use of latest technology and maintaining inventory across channels.

- **Difficult to manage inventory across channels:** Customer expectations are rising due to changes in awareness levels and availability of large variety of product and services across channels. To ensure optimum level of stock of each and every product is very difficult.

- **Data management and analysis:** In omnichannel retail, data management and analysis are very challenging because data from different sources is required to be integrated. Retailers need to collect and analyse data related to customers' needs, interests, preferences, expectations etc.

The Future of Omnichannel Retail

Retail purchases are not limited to Point of Sale only. Retailers are exploring new methods and technologies to serve their customers. Successful retailers will formulate strategies and design operations that will ensure seamless shopping experience for customers. Integrated AI based systems are being incorporated to drive sales across channels. Automated systems with improved analytics, optimum speed of delivery, timely assistance will bring changes in omnichannel retail (JLL Report, 2017).

CONCLUSION

The world is changing fast and adaptation of technology is happening at a quick pace. The retailers have to move fast forward in this competitive otherwise they will be out of retail world in very little time frame. The failures to meet customers' expectations always cost dearly to the retailers. The retailers have to adopt the latest methods like omnichannel approach to retail marketing to sustain in the market. Omnichannel retail strategies require careful planning, implementation, and maintenance. A comprehensive, integrated approach will help the retailer to manage his inventory, understanding the customers, improving the customer service, and ensuring customer loyalty for longer period of time. In the adaptation of Omnichannel retail, the cost involved and stakes for failure are very high. Therefore, it is better for the retailer to pursue Omnichannel retail strategy with a professional approach after considering all aspects to minimise the failures.

REFERENCES

Agates, N.A.H., M. Fleischmann, & J.J.A.E.E. Van Nunen. (2008)/ E-fulfillment and multi- channel distribution—a review. *European Journal of Operational Research,* *187*(2), 339–356.

Azhari, J. E., & Benett, D. (2015). Omni-channel customer experience: An investigation into the use of digital technology in physical stores and its impact on consumers' decision-making process. *XXIV AEDEM International Conference.* IEEE.

Banerjee, M. (2019). Development of Omni channel in India: Retail Landscape, Drivers and Challenges. In W. Piotrowicz & R. Cuthbertson (Eds.), *Exploring Omni channel Retailing.* Springer. doi:10.1007/978-3-319-98273-1_6

Bell, B. D. R., Gallino, S., & Moreno, A. (2014). How to Win in an Omni-channel World. MIT Sloan Management Review, 56(1), 45–54.

Boehm, M. (2008). Determining the impact of Internet channel use on a customer's lifetime. *Journal of Interactive Marketing, 22*(3).

Brynjolfsson, E., Hu, Y. J., & Rahman, M. S. (2013). Competing in the Age of Omni-channel Retailing. MIT Sloan Management Review, 54(4), 23–29.

Chatterjee, N. (2016). *Indian consumers moving towards the Omni channel way of shopping: PwC.*

Emeka, I. E., & Jayawardhena, C. (2018). Online shopping experience in an emerging e-retailing market. *Journal of Research in Interactive Marketing, 12*(2), 193–214. doi:10.1108/JRIM-02-2017-0015

Gioia, D. A., Corley, K. G., & Hamilton, A. L. (2013). Seeking qualitative rigor in inductive research notes on the Gioia Methodology. Organizational Research Methods 16(1), 15–31.

JLL. (2017). *The Future of retail in India is omni-channel.* JLL.

Juaneda-Ayensa, E., Mosquera, A., & Sierra Murillo, Y. (2016). Omni-channel Customer Behavior: Key Drivers of Technology Acceptance and Use and Their Effects on Purchase Intention. *Frontiers in Psychology*, *7*. doi:10.3389/fpsyg.2016.01117 PMID:27516749

Klaus, P. (2013). Exploring online channel management strategies and the use of social media as a market research tool. *International Journal of Market Research*.

Tim, H., Heller, J., Chylinski, M., Keeling, D. I., Mahr, D., & de Ruyter, K. (2018). Making Omni Channel an augmented reality: The current and future state of the art. *Journal of Research in Interactive Marketing*, *12*(4), 509–523. doi:10.1108/JRIM-01-2018-0023

Verhoef, P. C., Kannan, P. K., & Inman, J. J. (2015). From multi-channel retailing to omni-channel retailing: Introduction to the special issue on multi-channel retailing. *Journal of Retailing*, *91*(2), 174–181. doi:10.1016/j.jretai.2015.02.005

Chapter 10
Optimizing Omnichannel Strategies for Electronic Goods in the 21st Century:
Incorporating Metaverse Concepts

Ravishankar Krishnan

(iD) https://orcid.org/0009-0004-6609-6452

Vel Tech Rangarajan Dr. Sagunthala R&D Institute of Science and Technology, India

Elantheraiyan Perumal

VelTech Rangarajan Dr. Sagunthala R&D Institute of Science and Technology, India

Logasakthi Kandasamy

(iD) https://orcid.org/0000-0003-1024-8459

Universal Business School, Universal AI University, India

G. Manoj

Vel Tech Rangarajan Dr. Sagunthala R&D Institute of Science and Technology, India

ABSTRACT

Companies selling electronic items face the challenge of adapting to the rapidly shifting landscape of customer expectations in the digital era. This chapter, presented by the authors, delves deeply into the integration of pioneering metaverse concepts within omnichannel strategies specific to the electronics domain. As a transformative force, the metaverse redefines the traditional paradigms of promotion, sale, and customer experience, answering the burgeoning demand for immersive and personalized shopping journeys. The authors extensively explore the potential and application of groundbreaking technologies such as virtual reality (VR) and augmented reality (AR). Emphasis is given to how the metaverse can seamlessly enhance online shopping platforms, in-store interactions, and proactive customer service initiatives. Furthermore, the chapter illuminates the broad-ranging impact of the metaverse on the retail sector, shedding light on intricate facets such as data-driven insights, requisite infrastructure evolution, and paramount privacy considerations.

DOI: 10.4018/979-8-3693-3358-7.ch010

INTRODUCTION

The retail industry, for products has experienced changes in the 21st century. This transformation has been driven by advancements and changing consumer expectations in the era. Businesses aiming to thrive in this environment have recognized the importance of integrating channels with traditional brick and mortar stores, known as omnichannel retailing (Piotrowicz & Cuthbertson, 2014). Additionally the emergence of the metaverse as a framework and technological frontier has added complexity and opportunities to electronic goods retail.

In this chapter we will thoroughly explore the landscape of optimizing omnichannel strategies for goods in the 21st century with a specific focus, on incorporating metaverse concepts. As we delve into this subject we find ourselves at an intersection of innovation where digital and physical realms merge creating a way for consumers to engage discover products and interact with brands (Liepold, 2023).

accelerating consumer demands, and shifts in purchasing behaviors. The digital era, with its exponential growth in connectivity and accessibility, has led consumers to expect more seamless, instantaneous, and personalized shopping experiences. While once, brick and mortar stores stood as the pinnacle of retail, the contemporary retail paradigm sees these physical outlets as just one facet of a multifaceted retail ecosystem.

Central to this evolution is the concept of omnichannel retailing. As Piotrowicz & Cuthbertson (2014) elucidate, omnichannel retailing is not just about having a presence across multiple channels, but about ensuring consistency, fluidity, and integration across these touchpoints. It's about transcending the limitations of individual channels to offer consumers a unified shopping experience, irrespective of whether they're shopping online from a desktop or mobile device, phoning through a catalog, or visiting in-store. It's the harmonization of these channels which becomes the retailer's strength, offering consumers flexibility and choice.

Yet, as groundbreaking as omnichannel strategies have been for the retail sector, a new frontier has begun to emerge, promising to further redefine the rules of retail: the metaverse. Often described as the next iteration of the internet, the metaverse offers a collective virtual shared space, created by converging virtually enhanced physical reality with interactive digital spaces (Liepold, 2023). In simpler terms, it is a convergence of our physical and digital lives, powered by real-time 3D technology.

For the electronic goods sector, the metaverse provides avenues previously deemed as science fiction. Imagine trying out a new electronic gadget in a virtual store, getting real-time feedback from global user communities, or even customizing products in virtual collaborative spaces. This is not the distant future but the impending reality of retail.

As we venture deeper into this chapter, we aim to unravel the myriad possibilities the metaverse holds for electronic goods retail, and how businesses can effectively weave in these concepts into their omnichannel strategies (Liepold, 2023; Misra et al., 2023). The horizon of retail is expanding, and with the metaverse in the equation, it promises to be a vista of endless opportunities.

The Evolution of Electronic Goods Retail

Recognizing the development of electronic products retail is crucial to grasping the relevance of improving omnichannel strategies (Iglesias-Pradas & Acquila-Natale, 2023). In the last several decades, electronics have gone from being just functional items to being indispensable necessities. Technological developments have accelerated this shift by making electronic items more powerful and more widely available to consumers worldwide. Electronic products, encompassing smartwatches, home automation systems, smartphones, and laptops, have evolved into essential instruments that enhance our personal and professional spheres (Basker, 2016).

Not only are items changing, but so too are the channels through which they are sold and experienced by customers. Because of the rise of e-commerce, consumers can now buy electronics whenever and wherever they choose because to the widespread availability of cellphones and lightning-fast internet connections. Brick and mortar establishments have to change or face going out of style (Chua et al., 2005). Therefore, stores selling electronics have started a digital transformation project with the goal of creating a unified shopping environment for customers using both digital and traditional methods.

The Omnichannel Imperative

The idea of omnichannel commerce is a calculated reaction to the shifting customer behavior patterns. Retailers who use an omnichannel strategy seek to provide customers with a cohesive and consistent brand experience across all platforms, including social media, mobile apps, websites, and physical stores (Lazaris & Vrechopoulos, 2014). The objective is to dismantle the divisions between various channels so that customers can seamlessly connect with the business regardless of their chosen engagement method.

Omnichannel strategies are especially relevant for electronics, where shoppers often do extensive research before buying; reading reviews, comparing specs, getting advice, and checking out products in-store. The challenge for retailers is facilitating that research process and ensuring the transition from online browsing to in-store purchase is smooth and satisfying (Harrisson-Boudreau et al., 2023).

Optimizing omnichannel for electronics is about aligning digital and physical experiences to serve customers' complex needs. It means utilizing technology to enable a seamless journey where shoppers can fluidly switch between channels, find the information they want, and make informed decisions (Asare et al., 2022). The ideal is creating synergies between online and offline channels that allow consumers to self-educate, view options, and buy with total confidence and clarity.

In short, omnichannel is about bridging digitally-empowered consumers with product experiences in a unified retail ecosystem. When done well, it cements brand loyalty by enabling shoppers to engage on their own terms through aligned online and in-person touchpoints (De Giovanni, 2023).

The Metaverse Paradigm

While omnichannel retail has evolved and transformed shopping, the emergence of the metaverse introduces a whole new dimension. The metaverse converges physical and virtual worlds, with digital environments becoming integral to daily life. It is a space where peoples can interact, socialize, work, play, and consume in immersive digital realms (Wang et al., 2022).

Core metaverse technologies like Virtual and augmented reality (VR and AR) can redefine how consumers experience electronics. Imagine virtually trying on clothes, arranging home decor digitally, or testing gadgets in a simulation before buying. These are just some of the examples the metaverse potential.

Integrating metaverse concepts into electronics retailing opens up exciting new avenues for customer engagement, product visualization, and interactive experiences. But, it also raises a lot of questions around the data privacy, infrastructure needs, and businesses adapting to new technologies and consumer expectations (Sergeyeva et al., 2022).

On the other hand, the metaverse presents opportunities to engage shoppers in new immersive environments and enhance product experiences digitally. Then again, retailers will need to navigate uncharted territory, reinventing business models and strategies to align with metaverse-empowered consumers (Koohang et al., 2023).

Ultimately, the metaverse represents a new frontier poised to merge digital life with physical retail in innovative ways. It allows retailers to reimagine electronics shopping if they can keep pace with emerging technologies and practices. The potential exists to engage customers in novel, interactive environments that become an extension of real-world stores (Babu & Mohan, 2022).

Objectives of This Chapter

This chapter explores the convergence of omnichannel strategies and metaverse innovations in electronic goods retail. The key objectives are:

- To provide an extensive examination of the retail electronic products industry current state, emphasizing opportunities and challenges.
- To explore ways companies can improve their strategies to ensur a smooth shopping experience through omnichannel approaches.
- To investigate at how to sell electronic products while including metaverse ideas like virtual and augmented reality, emphasizing creative uses and possible advantages.
- To discuss critical challenges including consumer acceptance, technical infrastructure, and privacy concerns related to metaverse integration.
- To offer insights into how the metaverse may reshape electronic product sales and impact evolving customer expectations.

BACKGROUND

In the twenty first century, the retail environment for electronic goods has experienced significant changes due to the advancement of technology and shifting customer habits. Modern living is no longer possible without electronic products such as computers, cellphones, and smart home appliances, which provide more connectivity and usefulness. As a result, companies' marketing and sales tactics for these goods have also changed (Harrisson-Boudreau[1] et al., 2023). In this context, electronic products sellers must now optimize their omnichannel strategy in order to thrive in a fiercely competitive market. Brand experiences are smooth when physical and digital channels are integrated omnichannel (Kourouthanassis & Giaglis, 2005).

Meanwhile, a disruptive factor that has the potential to change how customers interact with and experience electronic devices is the rise of metaverse concepts based on virtual and augmented reality. Electronics merchants are under pressure to rethink purchasing in both the virtual and physical worlds by fusing omnichannel strategies with metaverse technologies, as customer expectations change in the digital era. The goal of this research is to shed light on this intricate and quickly changing environment (Betancourt, 2016).

Constant technological progress and altering customer behavior have ushered in dramatic changes to the electronic products retail scene in the 21st century. Electronic items have become more important components of modern living style and everyday use, computers and smartphones to wearable technology and smart home appliances. As the goods' features and connection have improved through time, so have the methods used by companies to promote and sell them (Son et al., 2023).

In light of this, firms hoping to thrive in an increasingly competitive market are finding that maximizing omnichannel strategies for electronic products is a critical strategic requirement. Concurrently, the metaverse a theoretical construct grounded in augmented and virtual reality technologies, began to take shape. Simultaneously, a disruptive force that has the ability to change the way customers are approached, sold to, and use technological goods (Fortin & Uncles, 2011).

The Evolution of Electronic Goods Retail

The evolution of devices, from being niche technology to becoming a part of our daily lives has been truly impressive. With advancements in miniaturization, processing power and connectivity electronic devices have not become more powerful but more accessible to people worldwide. As a result these devices have gone beyond their purpose. Now serve as symbols of status, tools for productivity and facilitators of connectivity (Kim & Jung, 2022).

However, this transformation goes beyond innovation, in products; it also encompasses how these electronic goods are introduced to the market and how consumers engage with them. Traditional physical stores have been disrupted by shopping platforms leading us into an era of e-commerce (Hassouneh & Brengman, 2015). To keep up with the needs of today's tech-savvy shoppers, brick and mortar stores have had to embrace digital channels and create unified online and in store shopping environments (Bradley et al., 2012).

The Imperative of Omnichannel Retailing

The idea of omnichannel retailing emerged as a way to adapt to the evolving consumer behavior, in the era. Nowadays shoppers anticipate an cohesive shopping experience that enables them to interact with a brand or product through channels. Whether they start their journey in a brick and mortar store proceed on an app. Complete a purchase, on a website consumers desire uniformity in terms of branding, communication and product availability (Gasparin et al., 2022).

Key Elements of Omnichannel Retailing Include

Channel Integration: The aim of omnichannel strategies is to remove barriers, across sales channels ensuring a cohesive brand experience for customers.

Inventory Management: Successful omnichannel retailers closely monitor their inventory in time allowing customers to access information about product availability across all channels.

Data Utilization: To enable marketing campaigns, it is crucial to leverage data analytics in order to understand customer behavior and preferences effectively.

Customer Engagement: A key focus of omnichannel retail is to prioritize consumer interaction, aiming to provide an engaging purchasing experience.

Challenges and Controversies: The advantages of omnichannel commerce are undeniable, but the practice is not without its share of problems and debates.

Data Privacy: Concerns regarding data privacy and the ethical use of consumer information have been raised as a result of the gathering and use of customer data to allow customization.

Technology Investments: Large expenditures in technology and infrastructure are necessary to achieve seamless integration across several channels, which can be prohibitive for smaller merchants.

Customer Expectations: It can be challenging to satisfy customers' ever-increasing demands for personalized and seamless experiences, and failing to do so can lead to a decline in customer satisfaction and lost revenue.

The Metaverse Emergence

The rise of the metaverse brings a set of challenges and prospects, to the world of electronic goods retail. The metaverse, based on reality (VR) and augmented reality (AR) presents captivating realms where users can interact, collaborate, have fun and shop. This digital landscape provides possibilities, for connecting with customers and revolutionizing product encounters (Chen et al., 2020).

Potential Metaverse Applications in Electronic Goods Retail

1. Virtual Product Experiences: Before making a purchase, customers can virtually test out electrical devices in a simulated setting or try on virtual wearable technology.
2. Interactive Brand Engagement: To connect with customers more deeply, brands may build immersive metaverse experiences. These experiences include virtual showrooms, product debuts, and metaverse customer service.
3. Data Driven Insights: By giving merchants access to helpful information about customer behavior and preferences, the metaverse may help them better customize their product offers and marketing plans.

Challenges and Considerations

The incorporation of concepts, in the industry presents its own set of challenges and considerations;

1. Privacy and Security; When customers engage in experiences it becomes crucial to address concerns regarding privacy and data security by implementing strong protective measures.
2. Technology Adoption; The widespread adoption of technologies may take time and necessitate significant investments in hardware, software and infrastructure.
3. Consumer Acceptance; The level of acceptance among consumers regarding the integration of the metaverse, into their shopping experiences remains uncertain which calls for efforts to overcome skepticism and ensure that user friendly experiences are provided.

In summary, in todays changing market businesses need to prioritize optimizing their omnichannel strategies, for goods if they want to stay competitive. The emergence of concepts brings in a new set of opportunities and challenges offering innovative ways to connect with consumers and redefine the retail experience. In the chapters we will explore the strategies, technologies and important factors that drive this fusion of omnichannel retailing and the metaverse, within the electronic goods industry (Kaddoura & Al Husseiny, 2023; Mathivanan et al., 2021; Xi et al., 2023).

Issues, Controversies, and Problems

Omnichannel approaches and metaverse ideas are converging to create a bright future for the electronic products retail industry. There are, nevertheless, a great deal of complications, debates, and challenges that it raises (Gupta et al., 2023).

1. Data Privacy and Security Concerns:

Data privacy and security are two major issues that have been raised as a result of adopting metaverse principles into omnichannel strategy for electronic products. Data breaches and abuse are a growing concern for retailers as they increasingly rely on the acquisition and analysis of customer data to provide customized experiences.

2. Technology Adoption and Accessibility:

The adoption of metaverse technologies, such as virtual reality (VR) and augmented reality (AR), can be challenging due to hardware price, issues related to accessibility, and the digital divide.

3.   User Experience and Acceptance:

In omnichannel metaverse retail, achieving consumer acceptance and seamless user experiences is the most difficult and complex challenge. Consumers may uninterested immersive experiences, and creating a balance between the actual world and digital one can be challenging.

4.   Ethical and Societal Implications:

Because of the immersive nature of the metaverse, there are raises ethical concerns related to addiction, false information or misleading ideas, and the blurring of fact and fiction.

Retailers of electronic products have a bright future ahead of them thanks to the incorporation of metaverse principles into omnichannel strategy. But as this debate has shown, it is crucial to recognize and deal with the related concerns, disputes, and challenges. To fully utilize the possibilities offered by the metaverse in todays industry businesses must address key concerns. These include safeguarding data embracing technologies enhancing user experience developing infrastructure and considering ethical implications. The retail electronic products business may embrace the revolutionary power of the metaverse while protecting consumer interests and social well-being by being aware of these problems and actively working toward answers .

Future Trends of Metaverse

In times the retail industry, the electronic goods sector has undergone notable changes. The emergence of the metaverse and evolving consumer preferences have brought forth challenges, for retailers. This article explores these concerns. Provides suggestions and advice to succeed in the age of digitalization (Damar, 2021).

The metaverse, a collective virtual space that encompasses augmented reality (AR), virtual reality (VR), and the internet, promises to redefine how we interact with technology and with each other. As we look ahead, several anticipated trends suggest the metaverse's transformative potential in the coming years.

1.   Integration Across Platforms and Devices

In the near future, the metaverse will be characterized by a high degree of integration. It will no longer be confined to high-end VR headsets. Instead, users will seamlessly switch between devices, be it smartphones, computers, or AR glasses, to access different layers of the metaverse (Xu et al., 2022). This integration will make the metaverse more accessible and pervasive, blurring the lines between our digital and physical realities.

2.   Proliferation of Virtual Economies

As the metaverse expands, it will host numerous virtual economies. Digital real estate, virtual goods, and services will have real-world value (Pagoropoulos et al., 2017). Companies will emerge to provide financial services in this space, from banking to insurance, catering to the needs of virtual residents and businesses.

3.   Enhanced Social Interactions

While current virtual worlds offer rudimentary social experiences, the future metaverse promises richer, more immersive interactions. Users will have life-like avatars that can display emotions, engage in meaningful activities, and develop relationships in a manner that mirrors real-world interactions but without physical constraints (Lee et al., 2022).

4.   Expansion in Education and Work

The metaverse will reshape the domains of education and work. Virtual classrooms will offer immersive learning experiences, transporting students to historical events or distant galaxies (De Felice et al., 2023). Meanwhile, companies might shift from physical offices to virtual workspaces, where employees collaborate in innovative and dynamic environments.

5.   Ethical and Regulatory Challenges

With the growth of the metaverse, there will inevitably be a rise in ethical and regulatory challenges. Issues related to digital identity, privacy, data ownership, and even the psychological impacts of prolonged immersion will come to the forefront. Governments and institutions will grapple with how to regulate this new frontier to ensure user safety and rights (DE ASÚA et al., 2022).

6.   Evolving Entertainment Landscapes

The entertainment industry will be revolutionized by the metaverse. Instead of passively watching movies or playing video games on screens, users will step into stories, becoming part of narratives or shaping outcomes with their actions. Concerts, theater performances, and sporting events might have both a physical and virtual audience, with experiences tailored for each (Niu & Feng, 2022).

The metaverse, in essence, will be a melding of many current digital experiences into a more cohesive, expansive, and interactive whole. It promises to reshape industries, redefine social interactions, and challenge our notions of reality and identity.

FUTURE RESEARCH OPPORTUNITIES

Metaverse User Behavior Analysis: Future studies could further explore the behavior of users in the metaverse investigating their motivations and ways in which retailers can enhance their offerings to align with these behaviors. It is important to conduct research that explores ways to make shopping and the metaverse environmentally friendly. This research should consider factors like energy consumption and resource usage aiming to find solutions. To ensure inclusivity in shopping environments it is crucial to invest in research that focuses on making the metaverse more accessible for people with disabilities. This will enable a range of individuals to participate and engage in these experiences. With the growth of the metaverse it becomes essential to address security risks. Future research should concentrate on developing security measures and effective strategies for preventing fraud within these realms (Cho et al., 2022; Dwivedi et al., 2023; Gursoy et al., 2022).

Metaverse-Based Market Research: The metaverse presents an opportunity for conducting market research. Researchers can explore methodologies for gathering consumer insights within environments allowing businesses to better understand their target audiences preferences and behaviors. It is worth investigating the tools and techniques for crafting immersive content within the metaverse. This includes exploring areas such, as 3D modeling, hosting events and storytelling techniques that can enhance user engagement within these spaces.

Integrating principles of metaverse into omnichannel tactics for selling products is an emerging area, with great potential. Staying ahead of these trends is crucial for retailers to remain competitive as the metaverse continues to evolve. Moreover this field presents research prospects that could shape the future of retail in the metaverse. Both retailers and researchers should seize the opportunities offered by this frontier to provide customers with an engaging and captivating shopping experience (Koohang et al., 2023).

CONCLUSION

In the rapidly evolving landscape of the 21st century's retail environment, optimizing omnichannel strategies for electronic goods has never been more crucial. As delineated throughout our discussion, the integration of digital and physical retail platforms, characterized as omnichannel retailing, has become a significant driver of consumer engagement and sales. The rise of the metaverse, with its intricate fusion of virtual and real-world experiences, offers unprecedented opportunities for brands to innovate and deepen their customer relationships. Embracing the metaverse allows electronic goods retailers to provide immersive product experiences, tailor-made customer journeys, and cultivate a sense of community and belonging among consumers. As we move forward, businesses that adeptly intertwine traditional retail practices with metaverse concepts will not only remain competitive but also set new industry standards. The fusion of the digital and physical, enhanced by the metaverse's vast potential, signifies the future of electronic goods retail—a future where consumer engagement, brand loyalty, and innovation reach unparalleled heights.

REFERENCES

Asare, C., Majeed, M., & Cole, N. A. (2022). Omnichannel Integration Quality, Perceived Value, and Brand Loyalty in the Consumer Electronics Market: The Mediating Effect of Consumer Personality. In *Advances in Information Communication Technology and Computing* [Springer.]. *Proceedings of AICTC, 2021,* 29–45.

Babu, M. U. A., & Mohan, P. (2022). Impact of the metaverse on the digital future: people's perspective. *2022 7th International Conference on Communication and Electronics Systems (ICCES),* (pp. 1576–1581). IEEE.

Basker, E. (2016). The evolution of technology in the retail sector. *Handbook on the Economics of Retailing and Distribution,* (pp. 38–53). Springer.

Betancourt, R. R. (2016). *Distribution services, technological change and the evolution of retailing and distribution in the twenty-first century. Handbook on the Economics of Retailing and Distribution.* Edward Elgar Publishing.

Bradley, S., Kim, C., Kim, J., & Lee, I. (2012). Toward an evolution strategy for the digital goods business. *Management Decision, 50*(2), 234–252. doi:10.1108/00251741211203542

Chen, L., Chen, P., & Lin, Z. (2020). Artificial Intelligence in Education: A Review. *IEEE Access: Practical Innovations, Open Solutions, 8,* 75264–75278. doi:10.1109/ACCESS.2020.2988510

Cho, J., tom Dieck, M. C., & Jung, T. (2022). What is the Metaverse? Challenges, Opportunities, Definition, and Future Research Directions. *International XR Conference*, (pp. 3–26). Research Gate.

Chua, C. E. H., Straub, D. W., Khoo, H. M., & Kadiyala, S. (2005). The evolution of e-commerce research: A stakeholder perspective. *Journal of Electronic Commerce Research*, *6*(4).

Damar, M. (2021). Metaverse shape of your life for future: A bibliometric snapshot. *Journal of Metaverse*, *1*(1), 1–8.

De Felice, F., Petrillo, A., Iovine, G., Salzano, C., & Baffo, I. (2023). How Does the Metaverse Shape Education? A Systematic Literature Review. *Applied Sciences (Basel, Switzerland)*, *13*(9), 5682. doi:10.3390/app13095682

De Giovanni, P. (2023). Sustainability of the Metaverse: A transition to Industry 5.0. *Sustainability (Basel)*, *15*(7), 6079. doi:10.3390/su15076079

Dwivedi, Y. K., Hughes, L., Wang, Y., Alalwan, A. A., Ahn, S. J., Balakrishnan, J., Barta, S., Belk, R., Buhalis, D., Dutot, V., Felix, R., Filieri, R., Flavián, C., Gustafsson, A., Hinsch, C., Hollensen, S., Jain, V., Kim, J., Krishen, A. S., & Wirtz, J. (2023). Metaverse marketing: How the metaverse will shape the future of consumer research and practice. *Psychology and Marketing*, *40*(4), 750–776. doi:10.1002/mar.21767

Fortin, D., & Uncles, M. (2011). The first decade: Emerging issues of the twenty-first century in consumer marketing. *Journal of Consumer Marketing*, *28*(7), 472–475. doi:10.1108/07363761111194767

Gasparin, I., Panina, E., Becker, L., Yrjölä, M., Jaakkola, E., & Pizzutti, C. (2022). Challenging the" integration imperative": A customer perspective on omnichannel journeys. *Journal of Retailing and Consumer Services*, *64*, 102829. doi:10.1016/j.jretconser.2021.102829

Gupta, A., Khan, H. U., Nazir, S., Shafiq, M., & Shabaz, M. (2023). Metaverse Security: Issues, Challenges and a Viable ZTA Model. *Electronics (Basel)*, *12*(2), 391. doi:10.3390/electronics12020391

Gursoy, D., Malodia, S., & Dhir, A. (2022). The metaverse in the hospitality and tourism industry: An overview of current trends and future research directions. *Journal of Hospitality Marketing & Management*, *31*(5), 527–534. doi:10.1080/19368623.2022.2072504

Harrisson-Boudreau, J.-P., Bellemare, J., Bacher, N., & Bartosiak, M. (2023). *Check for updates Adoption Potentials of Metaverse Omnichannel Retailing and Its Impact on Mass Customization Approaches*. Production Processes and Product Evolution in the Age of Disruption: Proceedings of the 9th Changeable, Agile, Reconfigurable and Virtual Production Conference (CARV2023) and the 11th World Mass Customization & Personalization Conference (MCPC2023), Bologna, Italy.

Harrisson-Boudreau, J.-P., Bellemare, J., Bacher, N., & Bartosiak, M. (2023). Adoption Potentials of Metaverse Omnichannel Retailing and Its Impact on Mass Customization Approaches. *Proceedings of the Changeable, Agile, Reconfigurable and Virtual Production Conference and the World Mass Customization & Personalization Conference*, (pp. 110–119). Springer. 10.1007/978-3-031-34821-1_13

Hassouneh, D., & Brengman, M. (2015). *Retailing in social virtual worlds: developing a typology of virtual store atmospherics*.

Iglesias-Pradas, S., & Acquila-Natale, E. (2023). The Future of E-Commerce: Overview and Prospects of Multichannel and Omnichannel Retail. *Journal of Theoretical and Applied Electronic Commerce Research*, *18*(1), 656–667. doi:10.3390/jtaer18010033

Kaddoura, S., & Al Husseiny, F. (2023). The rising trend of Metaverse in education: Challenges, opportunities, and ethical considerations. *PeerJ. Computer Science*, *9*, e1252. doi:10.7717/peerj-cs.1252 PMID:37346578

Kim, Y., & Jung, H. (2022). Beauty Industry's Strategic Response to Metaverse Evolution: Focused on Generation MZ. *2022 IEEE/ACIS 7th International Conference on Big Data, Cloud Computing, and Data Science (BCD)*, (pp. 259–264). IEEE.

Koohang, A., Nord, J., Ooi, K., Tan, G., Al-Emran, M., Aw, E., Baabdullah, A., Buhalis, D., Cham, T., & Dennis, C. (2023). Shaping the metaverse into reality: Multidisciplinary perspectives on opportunities, challenges, and future research. *Journal of Computer Information Systems*. doi:10.1080/08874417.2023.2165197

Kourouthanassis, P. E., & Giaglis, G. M. (2005). Shopping in the 21st century: Embedding technology in the retail arena. In Consumer Driven Electronic Transformation: Applying New Technologies to Enthuse Consumers and Transform the Supply Chain (pp. 227–239). Springer.

Lazaris, C., & Vrechopoulos, A. (2014). From multichannel to "omnichannel" retailing: review of the literature and calls for research. *2nd International Conference on Contemporary Marketing Issues,(ICCMI)*, *6*, (pp. 1–6). Research Gate.

Lee, J., Lee, T. S., Lee, S., Jang, J., Yoo, S., Choi, Y., & Park, Y. R. (2022). Development and application of a metaverse-based social skills training program for children with autism spectrum disorder to improve social interaction: Protocol for a randomized controlled trial. *JMIR Research Protocols, 11*(6), e35960. doi:10.2196/35960 PMID:35675112

Mathivanan, S. K., Jayagopal, P., Ahmed, S., Manivannan, S. S., Kumar, P. J., Raja, K. T., Dharinya, S. S., & Prasad, R. G. (2021). Adoption of e-learning during lockdown in India. *International Journal of System Assurance Engineering and Management*, 1–10.

Niu, X., & Feng, W. (2022). Immersive Entertainment Environments-from theme parks to Metaverse. *International Conference on Human-Computer Interaction*, (pp. 392–403). Research Gate.

Pagoropoulos, A., Pigosso, D. C. A., & McAloone, T. C. (2017). The Emergent Role of Digital Technologies in the Circular Economy: A Review. *Procedia CIRP, 64*, 19–24. doi:10.1016/j.procir.2017.02.047

Piotrowicz, W., & Cuthbertson, R. (2014). Introduction to the special issue information technology in retail: Toward omnichannel retailing. *International Journal of Electronic Commerce, 18*(4), 5–16. doi:10.2753/JEC1086-4415180400

Sergeyeva, T., Bronin, S., Turlakova, N., & Iamnytskyi, S. (2022). Integrating Educational Components into the Metaverse. *The Learning Ideas Conference*, 412–425.

Son, S.-C., Bae, J., & Kim, K. H. (2023). An exploratory study on the perceived agility by consumers in luxury brand omni-channel. *Journal of Global Scholars of Marketing Science, 33*(1), 154–166. doi:10.1080/21639159.2022.2153261

Wang, Y., Su, Z., Zhang, N., Xing, R., Liu, D., Luan, T. H., & Shen, X. (2022). A survey on metaverse: Fundamentals, security, and privacy. *IEEE Communications Surveys and Tutorials*.

Xi, N., Chen, J., Gama, F., Riar, M., & Hamari, J. (2023). The challenges of entering the metaverse: An experiment on the effect of extended reality on workload. *Information Systems Frontiers, 25*(2), 659–680. PMID:35194390

Xu, M., Ng, W. C., Lim, W. Y. B., Kang, J., Xiong, Z., Niyato, D., Yang, Q., Shen, X. S., & Miao, C. (2022). A full dive into realizing the edge-enabled metaverse: Visions, enabling technologies, and challenges. *IEEE Communications Surveys and Tutorials*.

Chapter 11
Metaverse Platforms and Entrepreneurs' Emotional Intelligence and Co-Creation Towards Quality Delivery in the Service Industry:
New Normal

Marirajan Murugan
 https://orcid.org/0000-0002-0622-2179
SRM Institute of Science and Technology, Chennai, India

M. N. Prabadevi
SRM Institute of Science and Technology, Chennai, India

ABSTRACT

The industrial revolution is facilitated by metaverse platforms, which encompass and integrates artificial intelligence (AI), machine learning methodologies (ML), augmented and virtual reality (AVR), industrial internet of things (IIoT), digital business transformation, and cloud computing services in the oil and gas service industries. The researchers conducted a literature analysis, analyzing case studies and concept studies from original equipment manufacturers (OEMs) and oil and gas operational service businesses. This research investigates the correlation between metaverse platforms, emotional intelligence, co-creation, and autonomous systems in relation to project quality and delivery throughout the Industrial Revolution. Scientists undertook an empirical investigation to comprehend the effects of metaverse platforms and entrepreneurs' emotional intelligence in the oil and gas industry during the Industrial Revolution.

DOI: 10.4018/979-8-3693-3358-7.ch011

INTRODUCTION

The transition from Industry 5.0 to Industry 6.0 during the Industrial Revolution marked the beginning of the oil and gas services sector's adoption of a metaverse platforms and autonomous system that incorporates 3D system, robots and drones. Industry 6.0 will witness a transition in robotics from Industry 5.0 and subsequent iterations (Chourasia et al., 2022). The co-creation and emotional intelligence (EQ) among MSME entrepreneurs aims to enable the development of adaptable business strategies to address organizational challenges (Prahalad & Ramaswamy, 2004). An autonomous system operates independently to fulfill its assigned responsibilities, ensuring the efficient operation of the facility and meeting client requirements, without the need for human intervention. The metaverse platforms and autonomous system improves plant efficiency, safety, operational reliability, and delivery of high-quality products. Metaverse platforms utilize digital twin technologies, including cloud computing, augmented reality (AR), Virtual reality (VR), blockchain, virtual reality, augmented reality, artificial intelligence, machine learning, and Industry Internet of Things (IIoT). Metaverse platforms and Autonomous systems have been implemented by operational organizations in certain parts of the oil and gas service sector, as discovered by researchers. An entrepreneur's emotional intelligence plays a significant role in comprehending the client's wants and the organization's capital expenditure requirements. The primary idea is to integrate the digital and physical domains with the aim of eliminating human dependence in the oil and gas services industry. Researchers focus on predicting the current progress of metaverse platforms and autonomous systems in Original Equipment Manufacturers (OEMs) and oil and gas service operating companies by analyzing existing literature, case studies, and conceptual studies. Given the present circumstances, researchers recommend that the government and MSME enterprises address the existing disparities and provide opportunities for further investigation.

DEFINITION, LITERATURE REVIEW AND METHODOLOGY

Oil and Gas Service Industry

The upstream, midstream, and downstream sectors are the three main divisions of the oil and gas services industry. Oil prices dropped from $147 to $69 as a result of international business and political factors. The operating company's main goal is to maximize its projected CAPEX and use the newest digital technologies to optimize operations and save costs. Fig. 1 shows energy consumption from 1965 up to 2035.Robots and drone applications in the Oil and gas industry (Onshore and Offshore) are shown in Fig-2.

Figure 1. Shows primary consumption by fuel from 1965 to 2035

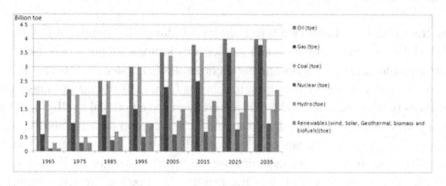

Figure 2. Shows oil and gas plant operations with a metaverse platform and autonomous system (robots and drones)

Metaverse Platforms and Autonomous System

Due to the potential of metaverse platforms in today's industry, operations managements, supply chain, production, operations research and logistics industry should consider in their agenda (Yogesh, 2022). Industry revolutions occur as the oil and gas service sector embraces the latest technological advancements and operational businesses incorporate them. Automated remote operations and 3D digital space have been extensively employed in the oil and gas industry, minimizing the requirement for human involvement. Operating companies utilize a range of advanced technologies such as artificial intelligence, autonomous robots, quantum computing, the Internet of Things, augmented and virtual reality, digital twin and digital transformation, human factor ergonomics and biomechanics, system integration, sensor-based applications, intelligent factories, extensive data analysis, cyber-physical systems, Li-fi, and hybrid technology to ensure compliance of autonomous systems (Das & Pan, 2022). Researchers have identified three types of digital twins and digital transformation: I. Digital Model, II. Digital Shadow and III. Digital Twin (Kritzinger et al., 2018). In the absence of human involvement, autonomous systems and Industry 6.0 achieve success in carrying out given organizational sustainability tasks (Chourasia et al., 2022). Figure 3 depicts autonomous plants that incorporate digital technologies into their operations without the need for human intervention. Figure 3 illustrates the integration of digital technology in autonomous factories, where human involvement is not required for operation.

Drone applications in the Oil and gas service industry are shown in Fig.4.

Figure 3. Shows the Metaverse platforms and autonomous plant without human intervention

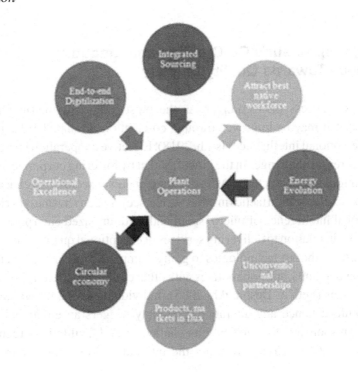

Figure 4. Shows drone applications in the oil and gas industry

MSME Entrepreneur's Co-Creation and Emotional Intelligence Towards Quality Delivery

The business success of a company is the most important metric for MSME entrepreneurs. It may be improved through co-creation (Prahalad & Ramaswamy, 2004) and emotional intelligence (Issah, 2018). Effective cooperation is necessary to address the present challenges in the global market by fostering corporate innovation and enhancing global competence. MSME entrepreneurs are constantly endeavoring to apply various collaboration tactics in order to enhance company business performance. The emotional intelligence of micro, small and medium-sized enterprise (MSME) entrepreneurs in relation to delivering services of exceptional quality: The Company employs state-of-the-art technologies to gain a competitive advantage, gathers data on consumer demands, and collaborates with other companies to enhance the quality of their services (Seth & Deshmukh, 2005). Individuals have a natural inclination to seek comfort; hence any alteration inevitably triggers an emotional reaction. Leaders are responsible for surmounting challenges and facilitating organizational change (Issah, 2018). Comprehending the internal and exterior requirements of the firm is important for entrepreneurs to surmount the challenges of creating an autonomous system and metaverse platforms that will deliver top-notch service. This is where the concept of emotional intelligence becomes relevant. An organization that attains excellence in delivering services in the oil and gas industry is established by entrepreneurs who utilize their emotional intelligence, market and customer orientation, a comprehensive comprehension of service quality concepts and its influencing factors, a proficient measurement and feedback mechanism, an efficient implementation process, and an effective customer support system.

Research Methodology

Researchers have gathered numerous case studies and idea studies from Original Equipment manufacturers and Oil and gas operating firms to thoroughly analyze the metaverse platforms and autonomous system and its efficient delivery. The research methodology employed for this study primarily involves doing a literature review with a specific focus on the oil and gas service industries. The primary

Figure 5. Model for Industrial Revolution (Al-Walaie et al., 2021): Metaverse platforms, autonomous systems, and entrepreneur's emotional intelligence towards quality delivery in the oil and gas industry

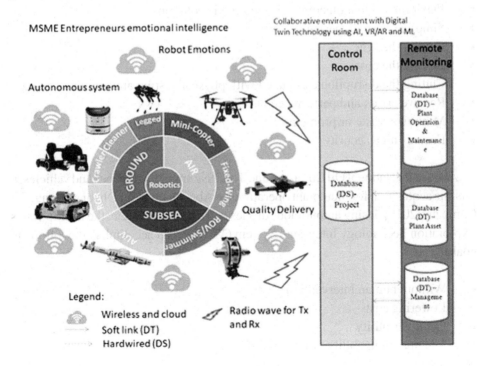

objective of this article is to classify the many contributions to the transformation of metaverse platforms and autonomous systems during the industrial revolution, the achievement of quality delivery resulting from this revolution, and the impact of emotional intelligence of MSME entrepreneurs on their performance in the Oil and gas service industry. Figure 5 depicts the suggested concept for an independent system that achieves high-quality delivery by utilizing the emotional intelligence of the entrepreneur in the oil and gas service. industry.

Metaverse Platform and Autonomous Industrial System

Asea Brown Boveri Robot Studio, an autonomous system, uses the cloud to facilitate real-time communication (Asea Brown Boveri, 2022). Metaverse can help plant owners improve efficiency by using virtual engineering and co-simulation environments. Robot programming and simulation software with cloud-based technology are available from ABB to accomplish the following goals:

- Virtual Collaboration
- Increase productivity
- Increase transparency across the teams
- Overcome business challenges
- A new level of agility
- Flexibility to manufacturers for automatic solutions
- Simplified user experience
- Cutting the time
- Cutting the cost
- Cutting the disruption associated with physical testing and commissioning
- Resolve errors and performance issues
- Minimize waste or problems
- Ensures high security

Abu Dhabi National Oil Company and Total use unmanned drones and vehicles in seismic acquisition for their plant operations in Abu Dhabi (Abu Dhabi National Oil Company, 2019). Using autonomous drones and a ground vehicle, the Multiphysics Exploration Technology Integrated System (METIS) can accomplish the following goals:

- Without human intervention
- Lowering costs
- Good versatility
- The upscaling ability of the system

- Minimize the surface impact of petroleum activities
- Improve the quality of subsurface images
- Overall operational efficiency
- Safer
- Faster
- More efficient
- Cost-effective acquisition system to acquire 3D and 4D high-resolution seismic images of the subsurface
- Real-time image processing
- Lowering geosciences and drilling uncertainties
- Optimizing the field production

Boston Dynamics provides British Petroleum (BP) with an autonomous system, and BP uses SPOT, the agile mobile robot, to enhance safety and efficiency offshore (Boston Dynamics, 2020). Offering SPOT, British Petroleum and Boston Dynamics hope to accomplish the following:

- Boosting employee safety and efficiency
- New ways to engage with customers
- Create efficiencies
- Support new businesses
- Inspection of its remote facilities
- Scanning for abnormalities
- Tracking corrosion
- Checking gauges
- Keeping people away from potentially hazardous work environments
- Improving Safety in Operations
- Improving operational efficiency
- Make technical specialists make an intelligent decision
- Reliable in an industrial environment
- Gather data from remote locations

British Petroleum and Aker BP investigate the use of robots in the offshore oil and gas industry for their oil and gas projects (British Petroleum, 2020). British Petroleum and Aker use robots to accomplish the following:

- More sustainable
- High-quality data capture
- Automatic report generation
- Underwater inspections

- Responding to leaks
- Access difficult places
- Deliver low cost
- Deliver low emission
- Enhance quality
- Reduce risk to humans
- Value for the energy industry
- Enabling better analytic operations
- Data-driven decisions
- Boost productivity
- Improve Safety and efficiency

DiFacto Robotics and Automation demonstrates robot saw jet automation and end-of-line automation (DiFacto Robotics and Automation, 2022). DiFacto offers the robots the following features:

- Suitable design with better quality
- Suitable design with better productivity
- To achieve within the schedule and on time
- Without hindering the production
- Reliable automation
- Improve the profitability
- Enhance the health and Safety of workers
- High quality
- To cover a wide range of manufacturing sectors

Egypt Oil & Gas planned to utilize the autonomous system and demonstrate the Prospects of Robotics in Egypt's Hydrocarbon Industry (Egypt Oil & Gas., 2017). Egypt Oil & Gas planned to utilize robotics to achieve the following:

- Increase human and environmental Safety.
- Cost efficiency
- Increase production
- Access harsh and remote locations
- Pipe handling
- Daily drilling operations
- Pipe inspections
- Tank inspections
- Weather Monitoring
- Pressure and flow measurements

- Remote-controlled underwater vehicles (ROVs)
- Pressure drilling
- Speedup the drilling processes
- Equipment needs repair
- Economically feasible
- Higher efficiency
- Reducing unplanned downtime
- Maximizing well and asset integrity
- Increasing field recovery
- Improving oil throughput
- Saves rig floor space
- Support decision making
- Reducing the size of the drilling crew by at least 40%
- Reduce facility turnaround requirements

Emerson showcases its solutions for autonomous oil and gas production (Emerson, 2021). Emerson provides cloud and edge technologies for their autonomous operations in order to:

- Cost reduction in digital technologies
- Improve competitive advantage
- Increase profits and efficiency
- Improve and accelerate decision-making
- Reduce risks
- Operational analysis and decision-making
- Remote monitoring of data and visual information
- Smart alarming
- Machine health indicators
- Predict leaks and operational issues in pipeline monitoring
- Predictive maintenance
- Automatic analysis and control of well
- Increase production uptime
- Reduce OPEX
- Lower workforce requirements
- Automate disjointed manual processes and integrated third-party systems
- Route optimization

Exxon Mobil uses drones and robots, bringing the future of digital manufacturing in Energy Factor (Exxon Mobil, 2023). Drones and robots are used by Exxon Mobile to accomplish the following tasks:

- To scan the outside of pipes to measure their thickness
- To inspect sky-high towers
- Dashboards tailored specifically to site workers
- For better and speedy decision-making
- Enabling faster and better insights
- Making complex operations more efficient
- Being able to access remote and confined plant areas
- Ensuring safer operations
- Seamless communication
- Lighter emissions footprint and smaller carbon footprint
- Scanning pipeline's insides to measure their linings
- Fly inside holding tanks and take videos
- Efficiently perform tasks

Fanuc provides robots, and their robots are used in the recycling industry (Fanuc, 2022). Fanuc provides robots, and their robots are used in the recycling industry to achieve the following:

- Sort and pick materials at a rate of 55 picks per minute compared to humans at a rate of 40 to 45 picks.
- High-level and actionable insights to the client
- Negative sorting
- Ready to use more quickly (plugged in without retrofitting)
- Working consistently to increase throughput
- Reduce the cost of recycling
- The most effective automated solution
- Train and learn new object detection
- Enabling the robotic waste picking system to adapt to changing material stream composition without any need for upgrades

General Electric's drones and robots provide a revolutionary and unique viewpoint on inspections in the oil and gas industry (General Electric, 2021). General Electric provides robotics, artificial intelligence, and sophisticated analytics in order to accomplish the following objectives:

- To inspect remote offshore platforms
- To inspect thousands of meters below sea level and deep underground areas
- To inspect the middle of scorching deserts
- To achieve a 25% decrease in facility inspection costs
- To achieve a 15% decrease in machine downtime

- To achieve a 25% increase in turnaround intervals
- To alert operators of possible issues regarding the health of equipment
- To have customized dashboards
- To have customized inspection reports
- Smarter maintenance decisions

Gridbots offers Gridbots Robopack for Automated Robotic Case Packers (Gridbots, 2022). Robots from Gridbots can accomplish the following:

- Utilizes single or multiple robots depending on line speed and packaging matrix
- To pick and pack any objects
- To ensure minimum box drops
- To ensure minimum alerts for low taping and low boxes
- 100% picking efficiency
- Highly compact system to use less footprint
- Keeping agility
- Precision in consideration
- High speed and reliability
- Remote surveillance
- Demining
- Real-time tactical information
- To monitor potential threats underground
- To track more than 20 simultaneous targets and lock on to any target within a second for firing
- Direction finding system with an accuracy of +/- 5 degrees (Elevation and Azimuth) and distance of +/- 4% FS up to a range of 1500 meters.
- Surface inspection, including remote locations and confined areas
- Weld inspection, including remote locations and confined areas
- To inspect blasting, including remote locations and confined areas
- To inspect painting, including remote locations and confined areas
- To inspect coating, including remote locations and confined areas
- To inspect grinding, including remote locations and confined areas
- To inspect lapping, including remote locations and confined areas

Hexagon maximizes its empowerment and autonomous system for its sustainable future (Hexagon, 2023). This includes surface inspection, weld inspection, blasting, painting, coating, grinding, lapping, and remote and confined areas. By leveraging intelligent digital reality, Hexagon is able to achieve autonomous operation without the need for human intervention to achieve the following:

- Autonomous mobility
- Autonomous building ecosystem with lower environmental impact
- Autonomous cities safe, resilient, agile and sustainable
- Autonomous defence ecosystems transform complex data and ensure security
- Assure accurate positioning for precision farming and autonomous capabilities
- Autonomous solutions to enable industries to lean, safe and efficient operations
- Autonomous intelligent infrastructure solutions to provide safe heavy lifting, more profitability and low environmental impact
- Autonomous 3D modelling that enables simulation, predictability, and maintenance while reducing waste and increasing productivity.
- Autonomous mines solution provides 100% of a potential value safely.

In the oil and gas sector, Hitachi robots are used for quality checking (Hitachi, 2021). In order to accomplish the following, Hitachi provides a TXplore transformer inspection robot:

- To inspect the internal components of abnormal operation
- To inspect a confined space, a power transformer with an oil spill
- Significant cost savings are accomplished by avoiding oil handling and spillage
- No increased downtime
- Inspection can begin immediately after taking an outage
- Eliminates the need for a confined space rescue team
- Real-time images available to energy transformer experts
- To improve reliability

Honeywell illustrates the transition of the oil and gas industry to an autonomous system, with well heads and pipelines being largely unmanned (Honeywell, 2021). In order to improve safety, dependability, and efficiency—as well as to deliver more situational awareness and respond more quickly—Honeywell provides automation and autonomous operation to achieve the following:

- Delivering more situational awareness
- Faster response time
- Ability to operate closer to limits
- Improved Safety, reliability and efficiency
- Top-tier throughput and quality
- Digital twin performance comparing the current performance and expected performance.
- It is accurately predicting decoking cycles.

- To oversee multiple remote operations such as wellheads, pipelines and offshore platforms
- Asset performance monitoring

Kawasaki offers efficient pelletizing with Kawasaki robots to manage various distant tasks, including wellheads, pipelines, and offshore platforms (Kawasaki, 2021). Kawasaki provides robots that can be used to accomplish the following goals:

- Sustainable improvement in the efficiency and productivity of existing processes
- High quality and flexibility
- Reliability and local proximity
- Long-term investment security
- Working range
- High-speed pelletizing
- Improve production line efficiency
- Will reduce downtime to a minimum
- Significantly reduce the workload of employees

Mitsubishi Electric showcases the new automation future that will be made possible by next-generation intelligent robots (Mitsubishi Electric, 2022). Mitsubishi Electric provides collaborative Robots that can be used to accomplish the following goals:

- Easy control
- Easy programming
- Easy connecting
- Provides high grip force
- Lowering the total cost of ownership
- Enhancing competitiveness
- Improving optimum performance
- Real-time diagnostics
- Predictive maintenance
- Continuous tuning to compensate for mechanical degradation and anomalies
- Design the system in less time with higher reliability and repeatability
- Quick and accurate problem resolution

Multiway's intelligent material handling, palletizing, and intelligent warehousing assistance are just a few of the benefits Mitsubishi Electric's collaborative robot offers (Multiway, 2023). Multiway provides robots for the following purposes:

- Comprehensive control and real-time
- Multi-vehicle collaboration
- High precision storage
- Vehicle road collaboration
- Ensures operational Safety through a triple protection mechanism (Safety sensor protection, control system protection and horizon system protection)
- Automated handling
- Low-cost deployment
- Uncrewed operations
- Machine management to avoid losses
- Automatic control for increased efficiency

Mushiny offers Intelligent Warehousing Automated Storage & Retrieval System (Mushiny, 2021). Mushiny provides robots for the following purposes:

- Logistics robot warehousing solutions
- Dynamic heat algorithms to realize real-time optimized solutions
- Logistics operation efficiency
- More complex orders with minimum cost
- Complex sorting
- High turnover
- Reduces the labour costs
- Significantly increases the level of safety stock
- Improves the accuracy of delivery
- Sampling inspection
- Realizes thorough penetration of intelligent logistics from production to shipment

OGV energy demonstrates the importance of robotics in the oil and gas industry (Robot as a Service-RaaS) (OGV Energy, 2021). OGV Energy utilizes Robot renting as Robot as a Service that can be used to accomplish the following goals:

- To save costs associated with purchasing robotic systems
- Monitored, managed and controlled remotely
- Automated drilling
- Conducting seismic surveys
- Inspection and maintenance
- Design, construction and remote monitoring
- Automated fuelling
- Material Handling

- High reliability and efficiency
- Improving operational Safety

Petronas serves as an example of the New Age of Oil and Gas, demonstrating how to use technology to make businesses viable while cutting expenses, raising efficiency, and boosting output (Petronas, 2019). Robots and drones are used by Petronas to accomplish the following:

- Methodically assesses the structural integrity of a pipeline
- Remotely operated
- Transmit the data instantaneously
- Reduced cost, increased efficiency and fewer safety concerns
- Lower labour costs
- Speedup resource recovery
- Substituting humans to address Brownfield assets
- No emotion
- Consistent in repeatability
- Eliminating scaffolding costs
- Executing metal thickness inspection at height
- Thermal images captured through autonomous surveillance
- Inspect underwater equipment on the seabed

Saudi Aramco exemplifies digitalization and future energy (Saudi Aramco, 2023). Saudi Aramco utilizes Artificial intelligence (AI), Machine learning, big data and analytics, uncrewed vehicles (UVs), blockchain and Internet of Things (IoT) to achieve the following.

- Minimize the carbon footprint
- Operational efficiency and workplace safety
- Reducing CO_2 emissions
- Enhancing fuel efficiency
- Conserving water
- Make consumer products lighter and stronger
- Increase productivity while enhancing reliability
- Inspect pipelines and machinery
- Predictive Modeling

Schneider Electric's efficient and sustainable solutions for energies and chemicals (Schneider Electric, 2022). Industrial metaverse as a way to get closer to reality.

Schneider Electric uses AVEVA's integrated platform in conjunction with artificial intelligence, big data, and cutting-edge industrial software to achieve the following.

- Sustainable business performance
- Minimize risk and increase profitability
- Drive efficient
- Boost collaboration and optimize CAPEX and OPEX
- Increase asset reliability
- Drive engineering efficiency
- Reduce material waste
- Promote circularity, resiliency
- Agility throughout the value chain
- Greater operational insight for safer, secure and safe production
- Secure solutions for remote operations
- Become carbon neutral
- Real-time data visualization

Schlumberger offers neuro-autonomous technologies that provide autonomous directional drilling capabilities that build wells as efficiently and consistently as possible (Schlumberger, 2022). The following goals are attained by Schlumberger through the use of autonomous systems and operations:

- Autonomous directional drilling
- Improved well economics
- Intelligent planning
- Surface automation
- Downhole automation
- Intelligent execution
- Most efficient and consistent
- Real-time reservoir characterization
- Reducing carbon footprints
- Eliminates the need for engineers to travel to well sites
- Diminish HSE risks and environmental risks significantly
- Predictable autonomous solutions

Shell demonstrates robotics in the energy industry, facilitating lead detection and emission control (Shell, 2022). Shell uses robots to help them accomplish the following goals:

- Meet strict environmental targets.
- Increase process efficiency
- Reduce costs
- Minimize the risk exposure for personnel
- Welding car windshields
- Fitting car windshields
- Proactive leak detection
- Proactive corrosion detection
- Emission control
- Control fugitive emissions
- Autonomous gas detection
- Excessive vibration
- Detect changes and predictive emerging issues such as natural phenomena (sand, snow, vegetation, animals)
- Efficient replication
- Remotely operated vehicles (ROVs) and Autonomous underwater vehicles (AUVs) operate 3 kilometres underwater.
- Surveillance inspection of the seabed
- Underwater valve operation
- Underwater coupling of equipment
- Collect more data with a higher frequency
- Reduce costs of subsea and deep water inspection and data collection
- Producing dimensionally accurate 3D modeling
- Unmanned aerial surveillance solutions
- Deep dive into earthquake detection

Pave the way for autonomous energy systems with robots and drones from Siemens (Siemens, 2022). Industrial metaverse provide the virtual environment for persistent simulation, live interaction and can even serve as a kind of cross roads between real and virtual scenarios. Siemens provides ANYbotics and ANYmal robots and drones to accomplish the following:

- Ensuring the operation and Safety of a power plant
- Inspect high-voltage overhead lines
- Time-consuming outages
- Decisive role and ensuring autonomous operation of gas-fired power plants
- Easy to integrate
- Work together seamlessly
- Photo realistic, physics based digital twin
- Make decisions in real time

SNC Lavalin offers an example of how to build on the "New Normal" by speeding autonomous operations in the oil and gas industry (SNC Lavalin, 2022). SNC Lavalin uses autonomous operations to accomplish the following:

- Removing levelised cost of electricity (LCOE)
- To achieve low carbon and net zero footprint
- Emission monitoring across construction
- Energy storage capability into overall grid stability
- Support planning, design, engineering and construction phases
- Whole life cycle costing (WLCC) techniques in design solutions for cost savings

TAL Manufacturing Solutions offers Made in India products. The TAL Brabo Robot is ready to be deployed across industries (TAL Manufacturing Solutions, 2018). The TAL BRABO robots, which are available from TAL Manufacturing Solutions, can be used for the following tasks:

- To pick and place materials
- MIG welding
- Vision inspection
- Perform high-volume tasks
- Perform repetitive tasks
- Perform dangerous or time-consuming tasks
- Increase productivity by 15-30%, with a payback period of 15-18 months
- Raw material handling
- Packaging of finished products
- The high degree of flexibility
- Perform complex functions cost-effectively
- Assembly of parts
- Machine and press tending
- As a sealing application
- Camera and vision-based jobs
- Taking over dull, dangerous and monotonous jobs from human
- To ensure lower cost of capital acquisition by minimizing imports

Total Energies (Energies, 2021) uses the Autonomous Robot for Gas and Oil Sites (ARGOS Project) Challenge in collaboration with the French National Research Agency (The autonomous robots ARGONAUTS, ARGOS, and ORGIP are used by Total Energies to accomplish the following goals:

- To mitigate tough environments
- Optimally efficient operations
- To detect anomalies
- To alert operators
- To monitor process parameters
- To generate 3D maps
- Routine surveillance rounds
- Make situational awareness
- Capability of operating in potentially explosive atmospheres
- To optimize and strengthen the Safety of operations
- Navigate and perform inspections autonomously
- Deliver reliable information and analyses
- Manage internal and external events correctly
- Operate in a degraded situation (loss of wife connection, unknown obstacle detection and navigation)
- Monitor the environment by analyzing the sounds coming from pumps.

Fully autonomous mobile robots from Vistan Nextgen are revolutionizing factory logistics (Vistan Nextgen, 2022). In order to do the following, Vistan Nextgen provides flunkey, AMR, AGV-Tavio, and robot teachers:

- Reduce human interventions in tedious and hectic manual tasks
- Smoother, more innovative and safer
- More efficient and productive
- Supply medicines and foods
- Sanitizing the area
- Temperature check
- Increase throughput
- Eliminate errors
- Improve material traceability
- Quickly deployed in standalone warehouse applications
- Assistant for teachers

Robots and gantries are used by Wipro PARI to deliver packing and palletizing solutions (Wipro PARI, 2021). Wipro PAR provides robotic solutions to accomplish the following:

- Assembly solutions such as engine assembly, transmission assembly and ancillary machines
- Assembly processes such as fastening and vision-based inspection

- Automotive components such as conveyance, assembly pallets and automatic station
- Automated machining
- Automated welding, such as metal inert gas welding (MIG), spot welding and tungsten inert gas welding (TIG)
- Automated warehousing and in-plant logistics solutions
- Automated car parking systems
- Reliable and traceable
- Go and no-go checks
- Measurement and testing
- Precision handling and positioning

Yokogawa demonstrates a journey towards autonomous operations and offers its services for deploying robots and drones in process plants and facilities (Yokogawa, 2020). Yokogawa provides drones and robots for the following tasks:

- Inspect inside and outside pipelines.
- Inspect chimney and infrastructure.
- Inspect inside tanks and vessels.
- Monitor and patrol
- Transport supplies and product
- Operate and manipulate
- Inspect outside vessel
- Improving productivity and operational efficiency, especially in hazardous environments
- Deep water oil exploration
- Subsea inspection
- Less expensive, smaller, more innovative and lighter
- To turn valves, paint structures, push buttons and replace electronic boards.

DISCUSSION

According to this research, the oil and gas services sector is moving toward a metaverse platforms and autonomous system as part of the industrial revolution. In order to satisfy client needs, quality delivery and compliance are crucial. The findings show that most oil and gas sector service areas are still in the conceptual stages of developing metaverse platforms and autonomous systems and their quality delivery. The metaverse platforms and autonomous system provides accurate quality delivery, and customers reciprocate by receiving the right delivery. In certain places, operating businesses have already implemented metaverse platforms and autonomous systems, but the oil and gas industry will need several decades to finish implementing these technologies. Three innovations were discovered by researchers in the data. First, it outlines the existence, future directions, present situation, and feelings of 3D digital space and robots at Original Equipment Manufacturers (OEMs). The second point emphasizes how the metaverse platforms and autonomous system meets client criteria for quality delivery. The third point emphasizes the emotional intelligence of the entrepreneur in recognizing customer needs (Issah, 2018) and meeting them with a self-sufficient system that produces high-quality work. Theoretical definition of the industrial revolution through metaverse platforms and autonomous system, quality delivery, and emotional intelligence of MSME entrepreneurs through industry experiences and interviews are covered in this section.

Categorical Literature Review

To comprehend the current state of affairs, a thorough examination of the metaverse platforms and autonomous system obtained through digital twin technologies from OEMs and operational firms is conducted. Digital twins were divided into three subgroups by researchers (Kritzinger et al., 2018). Drilling wells, offshore platform operations, surveys, quality inspections, logistics, plant operations, and maintenance are areas of focus in the oil and gas industry. The independent system that exists in every nation is depicted in Graph 1.

Figure 6. A categorical literature review of Countries contributing to metaverse platforms and autonomous systems in the Oil and gas service Industry.

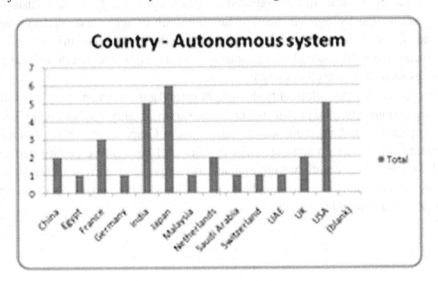

Figure 7. Categorical literature review of drilling, well operations, offshore platform operations, survey, quality inspection, logistics, plant operation, and maintenance in the oil and gas service industry towards quality delivery

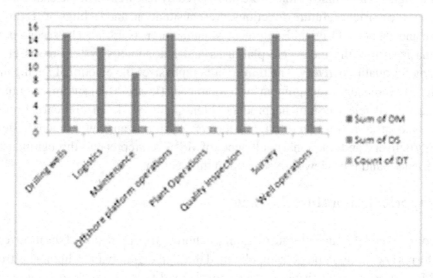

A comprehensive literature assessment of the nations developing metaverse platforms and autonomous systems for the oil and gas services sector is displayed in Graph 1. The metaverse platforms and autonomous system began producing good results in quality inspection, logistics, survey, well operations, and some plant activities in the oil and gas industry through the use of digital twin technologies and quality delivery. Metaverse platforms and Automation system implementation and operation are skills that operational companies possess. To achieve customer expectations, the factory will need to function with its metaverse platforms and autonomous system for a few more decades without the need for human intervention. The metaverse platforms and autonomous system in each segment of the oil and gas services sector is depicted in Graph 2.

In order to provide high-quality service, the oil and gas service industry's drilling, well operations, offshore platform operations, survey, quality inspection, logistics, plant operation, and maintenance are all shown in Graph 2. In certain domains, entrepreneurs can attain self-sufficient systems and human-free quality delivery by leveraging their emotional intelligence to comprehend current technological advancements, market expertise, plant upgrade needs, investment opportunities, and customer demands.

Table 1. Categorical literature review of digital transformation, metaverse platforms and autonomous systems, robot emotions, entrepreneur's emotional intelligence and quality delivery in the oil and gas service industry

Type	Level of integration	Metaverse platforms and Autonomous system	Robot emotions	Quality Delivery	Entrepreneurs emotional intelligence and Co-creation
Case study	DT	Yes	Yes	CMCF, CCSQ, EMFS, EIS, ECCS.	EM, TR, EN, CO, SM, RM
Concept	DT	Yes	No	CMCF, CCSQ, EMFS, EIS, ECCS.	EM, TR, EN, CO, SM, RM
Case study	DT	Yes	Yes	CMCF, CCSQ, EMFS, EIS, ECCS.	EM, TR, EN, CO, SM, RM
Concept	DT	Yes	No	CMCF, CCSQ, EMFS, EIS, ECCS.	EM, TR, EN, CO, SM, RM
Case study	DT	Yes	No	CMCF, CCSQ, EMFS, EIS, ECCS.	EM, TR, EN, SM, RM
Concept	DT	Yes	No	CMCF, CCSQ, EMFS, EIS, ECCS.	EM, TR, EN, CO, SM, RM
Case study	DT	Yes	No	CMCF, CCSQ, EMFS, EIS, ECCS.	EM, TR, EN, CO, SM, RM
Concept	DT	Yes	No	CMCF, CCSQ, EMFS, EIS, ECCS.	EM, TR, EN, CO, SM, RM
Case study	DT	Yes	No	CMCF, CCSQ, EMFS, EIS, ECCS.	EM, TR, EN, CO, SM, RM
Case study	DT	Yes	No	CMCF, CCSQ, EMFS, EIS, ECCS.	EM, TR, EN, CO, SM, RM
Case study	DT	Yes	No	CMCF, CCSQ, EMFS, EIS, ECCS.	EM, TR, EN, CO, SM, RM
Case study	DT	Yes	No	CMCF, CCSQ, EMFS, EIS, ECCS.	EM, TR, EN, CO, SM, RM
Case study	DT	Yes	No	CMCF, CCSQ, EMFS, EIS, ECCS.	EM, TR, EN, CO, SM, RM
Case study	DT	Yes	No	CMCF, CCSQ, EMFS, EIS, ECCS.	EM, TR, EN, CO, SM, RM
Case study	DT	Yes	No	CMCF, CCSQ, EMFS, EIS, ECCS.	EM, TR, EN, CO, SM, RM
Case study	DT	Yes	Yes	CMCF, CCSQ, EMFS, EIS, ECCS.	EM, TR, EN, CO, SM, RM

Table 1. Continued

Type	Level of integration	Metaverse platforms and Autonomous system	Robot emotions	Quality Delivery	Entrepreneurs emotional intelligence and Co-creation
Case study	DT	Yes	No	CMCF, CCSQ, EMFS, EIS, ECCS.	EM, TR, EN, SM, RM
Case study	DT	Yes	No	CMCF, CCSQ, EMFS, EIS, ECCS.	EM, TR, EN, SM, RM
Concept	DT	Yes	No	CMCF, CCSQ, EMFS, EIS, ECCS.	EM, TR, EN, CO, SM, RM
Concept	DT	Yes	No	CMCF, CCSQ, EMFS, EIS, ECCS.	EM, TR, EN, CO, SM, RM
Concept	DT	Yes	Yes	CMCF, CCSQ, EMFS, EIS, ECCS.	EM, TR, EN, CO, SM, RM
Case study	DT	Yes	No	CMCF, CCSQ, EMFS, EIS, ECCS.	EM, TR, EN, CO, SM, RM
Case study	DT	Yes	No	CMCF, CCSQ, EMFS, EIS, ECCS.	EM, TR, EN, SM, RM
Concept	DT	Yes	No	CMCF, CCSQ, EMFS, EIS, ECCS.	EM, TR, EN, CO, SM, RM
Case study	DT	Yes	No	CMCF, CCSQ, EMFS, EIS, ECCS.	EM, TR, EN, CO, SM, RM
Case study	DT	Yes	No	CMCF, CCSQ, EMFS, EIS, ECCS.	EM, TR, EN, SM, RM
Case study	DT	Yes	Yes	CMCF, CCSQ, EMFS, EIS, ECCS.	EM, TR, EN, SM, RM
Concept	DT	Yes	No	CMCF, CCSQ, EMFS, EIS, ECCS.	EM, TR, EN, CO, SM, RM
Case study	DT	Yes	No	CMCF, CCSQ, EMFS, EIS, ECCS.	EM, TR, EN, CO, SM, RM
Case study	DT	Yes	Yes	CMCF, CCSQ, EMFS, EIS, ECCS.	EM, TR, EN, CO, SM, RM
Case study	DT	Yes	No	CMCF, CCSQ, EMFS, EIS, ECCS.	EM, TR, EN, CO, SM, RM

Legend: DT-Digital Twin; DS-Digital Shadow, EI – Emotional Intelligence, Clear market and customer focus(CMCF), Clear understanding of concepts of service quality and factors affecting the same(CCSQ), Effective measurement and feedback system(EMFS), Effective implementation system(EIS), Efficient customer care system(ECCS), EM-Empathy, TR-Trust, EN-Enthusiasm, CO-Collaboration, SM-Self Management; RM-Relationship Management.

OUTLOOK AND CONCLUSION

The study concludes that meeting customer needs for plant operations requires the development of metaverse platforms and autonomous systems that can function without human intervention and deliver high-quality outputs. However, such systems are still in the conceptual stage of the industrial revolution. In order to satisfy client demands, only a limited number of sectors in the oil and gas service industry have started using metaverse platforms and autonomous systems under human supervision. The objective of this study is to provide a model for implementing metaverse platforms and autonomous systems that meets the customer requirements of original equipment manufacturers (OEMs) and operating firms. In order to maximize profitability, owners of micro, small, and medium enterprises (MSMEs) need to develop and implement a strategic plan outlining their company's capital expenditures (CAPEX), potential risks, and corporate goals for the implementation of metaverse platforms and autonomous systems. Entrepreneurs must cultivate their co-creation and emotional intelligence to effectively manage the latest technology for metaverse platforms and autonomous system deployment and achieve exceptional outcomes. Twenty percent of personnel will be engaged in the tasks of implementation, remote monitoring, and research and development until these tasks are completed. However, a staggering 80% of individuals would find themselves without a job and would need to seek different career opportunities. The current activities of the metaverse platforms and autonomous system exhibit outstanding profitability, high accuracy, prompt delivery, and cost-effectiveness. Entrepreneurs face the significant upfront expenses of setting up an independent system. Consequently, an entrepreneur's strategy choices are centered on implementing metaverse platforms and autonomous systems in the oil and gas service sector. Within the oil and gas services industry, it is necessary for the entrepreneur to develop and enforce both internal and external protocols for the integration of metaverse platforms and autonomous systems.

RECOMMENDATIONS, LIMITATIONS, AND FUTURE RESEARCH

The study suggests that the metaverse platforms and autonomous systems used by oil and gas companies are still in the early stages of development and have not been fully implemented yet. There are multiple crucial plant operations in the oil and gas service business. Entrepreneurs in the oil and gas business need to be ready for the implementation of metaverse platforms and autonomous systems in plant operations. Only a limited subset of the supporting sectors in the oil and gas service business have started utilizing the metaverse platforms and autonomous system and providing delivery of superior quality. Establishing formal policies, agreements, and procedures is crucial for the oil and gas service industry, both within the organization and with external entities. In order to oversee and approve the implementation of these activities in the oil and gas service industry, original equipment manufacturers and oil and gas operating firms need to get a set of regulations, instructions, and compliance guidelines from the government and MSME. The deployment of a self-governing system with exceptional delivery is constrained by several limits. 1. Metaverse platforms and autonomous system will be constructed to encompass all onshore and offshore activities related to upstream, midstream, and downstream oil and gas operations. 2. To achieve complete operation of an oil and gas plant, it is necessary to develop a metaverse platforms and autonomous system that operates without any human involvement. 3. It is imperative to ensure the delivery of high-quality services for all elements of oil and gas plant operations without the need for human intervention. 4. The original equipment manufacturer (OEM) must understand the requirements of gas and oil companies to ensure compliance with rules for autonomous systems. The government and MSMEs need to develop policies and rules for OEMs and operational enterprises. 6. Enhancing the co-creation and emotional intelligence of entrepreneurs is crucial for the implementation of a metaverse platforms and autonomous system. Subsequent research will address the limitations that have been highlighted as hindrances by focusing on the self-governing system inside the oil and gas service sector's balancing regions.

REFERENCES

Abu Dhabi National Oil Company. (2019). ADNOC and Total to Use Unmanned Drones and Vehicles in Seismic Acquisition. Abu Dhabi National Oil Company.

Al-Walaie, S. A., Bahwal, O. B., & Alduayj, S. S. (2021). Emerging Robotic Technologies for Oil and Gas Operations. *Journal of Petroleum Technology*, 1944–978X.

Asea Brown Boveri. (2022). *ABB Robot Studio takes to the cloud, enabling real-time collaboration*. Asea Brown Boveri.

Boston Dynamics. (2020). *British Petroleum uses SPOT to improve Safety and efficiency offshore*. Boston Dynamics.

British Petroleum. (2020). *Aker BP explores the use of robots in the offshore oil and gas industry*. British Petroleum.

Chourasia, S., Tyagi, A., Pandey, S., Walia, R. & Murtaza, Q. (2022). Sustainability of Industry 6.0 in Global Perspective: Benefits and Challenges. *MAPAN, 37.* . doi:10.1007/s12647-022-00541-w

DasS.PanT. (2022). A Strategic Outline of Industry 6.0: Exploring the Future. SSRN: https://ssrn.com/abstract=4104696 or doi:10.2139/ssrn.4104696

DiFacto Robotics and Automation. (2022). *Robot saw jet automation and End of line automation*. DiFacto Robotics and Automation.

Duggal, A. S., Malik, P. K., Gehlot, A., Singh, R., Gaba, G. S., Masud, M., & Al-Amri, J. (2022). A sequential roadmap to industry 6.0: Exploring future manufacturing trends. *IET Communications, 16*(5), 521–531. doi:10.1049/cmu2.12284

Egypt Oil & Gas. (2017). *The Prospects of Robotics in Egypt's Hydrocarbon Industry*. Egypt Oil and Gas.

Emerson. (2021). *Technologies for Autonomous Oil and Gas Production*. Emerson.

Energies, T. (2021). *Autonomous Robot for Gas and Oil Sites (ARGOS Project) Challenge, in partnership with the French National Research Agency*. ANR.

Exxon Mobil. (2023). *Drones and robots bring the future to digital manufacturing - Energy Factor*. Exxon Mobil.

Fanuc. (2022). *Fanuc robots put to use in the recycling industry*. Fanuc.

General Electric. (2021). *Drones and Robots Offer Radical New Perspective on Oil and Gas Inspections*. General Electric.

Gridbots. (2022). *GridbotsRobopack, Automated Robotic Case Packers*. Gridbots.

Hexagon. (2023). *Empowering an autonomous, sustainable future*. Hexagon.

Hitachi. (2021). *Robots for quality inspection*. Hitachi.

Honeywell. (2021). *In the journey to autonomous systems in the oil and gas industry, wellheads and pipelines are largely unmanned*. Honeywell.

Issah, M. (2018). Change Leadership: The Role of Emotional Intelligence. *SAGE Open, 8*(3). doi:10.1177/2158244018800910

Kawasaki. (2021). *Effective pelletizing with Kawasaki robots*. Kawasaki.

Kritzinger, W., Karner, M., Traar, G., Henjes, J., & Sihn, W. (2018). Digital Twin in manufacturing: A categorical literature review and classification. *IFAC-PapersOnLine, 51*(11). doi:10.1016/j.ifacol.2018.08.474

Mitsubishi Electric. (2022). *The new future of automation made by next-generation intelligent robots*. Mitsubishi Electric.

Multiway. (2023). *Intelligent Material handling and palletizing and Intelligent warehousing assistant*. Multiway.

Mushiny. (2021). In*telligent Warehousing· Automated Storage & Retrieval System*. Mushiny.

OGV Energy. (2021). *Robotics essential to the oil and gas industry (Robot as a Service-RaaS)*. OGV Energy.

Petronas. (2019). *The New Age of Oil and Gas: Translating technology into business viability: reducing costs, improving productivity, and increasing efficiency*. Petronas.

Prahalad, C. K., & Ramaswamy, V. (2004). Co-creating unique value with customers. *Strategy and Leadership, 32*(3), 3–9. doi:10.1108/10878570410699249

Saudi Aramco. (2023). *Digitalization and Future Energy*. Saudi Aramco.

Schlumberger. (2022). *Neuroautonomous solutions enable autonomous directional drilling capabilities that build wells most efficiently and consistently possible, regardless of the rig, field, or trajectory*. Research Gate.

Schneider Electric. (2022). *Efficient and sustainable solutions for energy and chemicals*. Schneider Electric.

Seth, N. & Deshmukh, S. (2005). Service quality models: a review. *International Journal of Quality & Reliability Management, 22*(9), 913-949. doi:10.1108/02656710510625211

Shell. (2022). *Robotics in the energy industry – Facilitating lead detection and emission control*. Shell.

Siemens. (2022). *Robots and drones pave the way for autonomous energy systems*. Siemens.

SNC Lavalin. (2022). *Accelerating Autonomous Operations in Oil & Gas: Building on the "New Normal."* SNC Lavalin.

TAL Manufacturing Solutions. (2018). *Made in India, the TAL Brabo Robot is ready to be deployed across industries*. TAL Manufacturing Solutions.

Vistan Nextgen. (2022). *Fully autonomous mobile robots transforming manufacturing and logistics*. Vistan Nextgen.

Wipro PARI. (2021). *Packing and palletizing Solutions with Robots and Gantries*. Author.

Yogesh, K. (2022). Metaverse beyond the hype: Multidisciplinary perspectives on emerging challenges, opportunities, and agenda for research, practice and policy. *International Journal of Information Management, 66*. doi:10.1016/j. ijinfomgt.2022.102542

Yokogawa. (2020). *A journey towards autonomous operations – Deploying robots and drones in process plants and facilities*. Yokogawa.

Chapter 12
The Metaverse Economy:
Transforming Money With Digital Currency

S. Catherine
iD https://orcid.org/0009-0007-2403-0879
SRM Institute of Science and Technology, Chennai, India

Meena N. Rani
SRM Institute of Science and Technology, Chennai, India

N. V. Suresh
iD https://orcid.org/0000-0002-0393-6037
ASET College of Science and Technology, India

ABSTRACT

The Metaverse economy represents a paradigm shift in the realm of finance, poised to redefine the concept of money through the utilization of digital currency within virtual environments. Within the metaverse, digital currency facilitates transactions for shopping, gaming, and a diverse array of goods and services. To traverse the virtual realm using a virtual reality headset and controllers purely for recreational purposes, without any predefined objectives. The Metaverse offers unprecedented opportunities for businesses and individuals to engage the exchange, and accumulation. Through immersive experiences, luxury brands and retailers are already capitalizing to cater to evolving consumer preferences, with cutting-edge technologies such as augmented reality and artificial intelligence. The brand Gucci has initiated the sale of their products within the Metaverse, utilizing digital currency for transactions. As the metaverse continues to evolve through advancements in digital currency and technology, it promises to revolutionize the future of money and commerce.

DOI: 10.4018/979-8-3693-3358-7.ch012

INTRODUCTION

The Metaverse Economy defines as the economic system that will exist within the Metaverse. It is a virtual universe, where individuals can interact, create, and trade digital assets. Digital currency is an electronic currency that is used, stored, and exchanged largely on digital platforms. Cryptocurrency, Central Bank Digital Currency (CBDC), and virtual currency are all examples of digital currencies. It is a new emerging concept that has paved the way to use currency. This article explores about the digital currency impact using metaverse platform among online consumers in order to develop a framework.

The Metaverse economy is swiftly evolving as an uncharted territory that holds the potential to revolutionize the landscape of currency. This virtual realm has introduced fresh avenues for both enterprises and individuals to innovate, exchange, and accrue value through unconventional means. As blockchain technology gains traction, the Metaverse emerges as a pivotal arena for financial experimentation and advancement, further amplifying its significance in the realm of finance.

The currency can only be accessed using an electronic device or mobile and is only available digitally. "Digital currencies also enable instant transactions that can be seamlessly executed across borders". Indian retailers are already investigating the metaverse to give customers virtual experiences. Targeting high net worth individuals (HNIs) with tailored and immersive VR/AR shopping experiences is a priority for luxury brands in particular. Gucci Beauty was the first company to provide the beauty mode of Drest, the digital fashion app, which lets users try out 29 of its virtual beauty goods. Gucci Beauty entered the virtual world with this app.

Businesses may successfully analyse consumers' purchasing behaviours by utilising big data analytics, predictive analytics, and algorithms. This allows them to provide highly customised and enjoyable brand experiences. India's retail industry has seen significant shifts in the new millennium, with technology improvements being a major factor. The idea of "phygital," which combines physical and digital retail experiences, is increasingly gaining traction as a substitute for traditional retail chains. Consequently, retailers are dedicating resources to pioneering technologies like augmented reality (AR), virtual reality (VR), mixed reality (MR), and AI-driven tools such as chatbots. Presently, discerning consumers, notably millennials and Gen Z, are in pursuit of personalized services and immersive experiences that go beyond conventional retail practices.

The Metaverse Economy has the power to completely change the world economy since it reduces the need for middlemen like governments and banks and enables people and organisations to deal on a global scale. New economic activities like social experiences, gaming, and virtual real estate development will be made possible by the Metaverse. As a result, there will be more chances for people and companies to add value and for users to be involved in the economy in a more open and decentralised manner.

It has the potential to provide an immersive experience for users and the potential to create new business opportunities. Using Metaverse platform, the business by investing digital currency and trading different types of coins are the new trend of transaction happening around the globe. Metaverse in the online medium for the people willing to buy most items virtually. Buying assets like houses, lands, and other items will also be a part of the metaverse economy. These will be governed by the same ownership laws that apply to the real world. As a result, Metaverse will make online buying easier by enabling digital currency trading. The metaverse will be a simulated setting that replicates the dynamics of online commerce found in contemporary social media.

Cheng et.al. (2022), The person in the virtual living environment is identified specifically by the identity authentication system, many technologies evolved like blockchain, digital twins, brain-computer interfaces, extended reality, and other technologies are among the metaverse's fundamental technologies.

Benefits of Metaverse in Online Shopping

Metaverse platforms can create immersive 3D virtual stores where users can walk around, interact with products, and experience shopping in a lifelike environment. This immersive experience can enhance the engagement and make shopping more enjoyable. In the metaverse, customers can use avatars to try on virtual versions of clothes, accessories, or even makeup. Augmented reality technology can allow users to see how products look on them in real-time, enhancing the online shopping experience and reducing the need for physical stores. In online shopping websites branded companies tried different social features, allowing users to shop with friends or interact with other shoppers. This social aspect can mimic the experience of shopping in a physical store with friends, providing recommendations and feedback in real-time. Retailers can use this data to offer highly personalized shopping experiences, recommending products based on individual tastes and preferences. In the metaverse, products can be showcased in interactive and dynamic ways. For example, a user could see a 3D model of a product, disassemble it to see its components, or see how it works in real-time. This level of interaction can provide a deeper understanding of the product before making a purchase decision. "The Emergence of the Metaverse Economy: Implications for Transaction Costs and Digital Currency" (Smith, 2023) explores the burgeoning Metaverse economy and its implications for transaction costs associated with digital currency. The study examines how the decentralization and borderless nature of the Metaverse impact the traditional transaction costs of money, shedding light on potential efficiencies and challenges.

Chen and Lee conduct a comparative analysis of transaction costs within various digital currency platforms operating in the Metaverse. The research delves into factors such as network fees, processing times, and platform-specific regulations to assess the overall cost-effectiveness of virtual transactions in different Metaverse environments.

"The Role of Blockchain Technology in Reducing Transaction Costs in the Metaverse Economy" (Gupta et al., 2021) mitigating transaction costs within the Metaverse economy. The paper discusses how decentralized ledger systems enhance transparency, security, and efficiency in digital transactions, ultimately reducing the overall costs associated with monetary exchanges in virtual environments. (Wang & Li, 2020) to investigate consumer perceptions of transaction costs and trust in digital currency payment systems within the Metaverse. It assesses factors influencing consumer adoption behaviour, shedding light on the role of perceived transaction costs in shaping payment preferences. Jones and Patel (2023) analyze the impact of regulatory frameworks on transaction costs within the Metaverse, drawing comparisons across different legal jurisdictions. The research examines how varying regulatory environments influence the cost dynamics of digital currency transactions, providing insights into policy implications for policymakers and industry stakeholders.

In some metaverse platforms, users can buy, sell, and trade virtual items and assets using digital currencies or cryptocurrencies. This concept could extend to real-world products, creating a virtual economy where users can own, trade, and sell digital representations of physical goods. Metaverse platforms are accessible globally, allowing businesses to reach a broader international audience without the need for physical stores in every location. This can lead to increased sales and market reach. Virtual try-ons and interactive product experiences can help customers make more informed purchasing decisions, potentially reducing the number of returns due to dissatisfaction with the product's appearance or fit.

Continuous experimentation happening in the form of advertising using the Metaverse is still in the infancy stage. (G Mileva.,2022). Opens to new brands to experiment the strategies in the Metaverse. It offers exciting opportunities for the future of online shopping, there are challenges and considerations such as data privacy, security, and the digital divide that need to be addressed as this technology continues to develop and become more widespread.

Metaverse and Opportunities for Digital Payments

According to McKinsey, the Metaverse provides exciting prospects for digital payments, and it could be worth $5 trillion by the year 2030 when calculating its potential financial value. The diverse use cases demonstrate that the Metaverse represents a significant growth opportunity for several businesses and brands in this decade.

Snider and B Molina (2022) Transforming the retail sector- E-commerce stores can make use of this emerging market to its fullest. Furthermore, the Metaverse can also considered as the right platform in order to introduce new products and market them in a unique manner. Many brands in the retail sector such as Alibaba, Burberry, Nike, and Dyson have already started experimenting with the Metaverse.

It will be interesting to note that business-to-business (B2B) and business-to-consumer (B2C) services allow you to transform your digital products into the Metaverse. Businesses and retailers may interact with their consumers in more fascinating and individualized ways thanks to the immersive experiences and economic opportunities offered by Metaverse.

Effective payment methods are required for these digital services to provide a seamless user experience. In the present scenario and ecosystem, the more commonly used payment method is blockchain-based digital currencies like Bitcoin and Ethereum. However, the Think in-game credits, tokens, and real-world currency also gets converted into a particular metaverse's personalized currencies.

In the long run, Metaverse will see an upsurge in new currencies and payment methods with the advent of Web 3.0. However, the development of new payment methods in this ecosystem will depend on the rate of adoption by its users. In coming years, many new channels and ways of interacting, like ordering goods via Alexa or video live shopping solutions. Metaverse will offer many opportunities for digital payments, virtual world creation, and the development of digital assets. It has the potential to provide an immersive experience for users and the potential to create new business opportunities. (Andrea Sestino, et, al., 2022) revolutionize the way the digital content and it will create new opportunities for digital payments and the buying and selling of Non-Fungible Tokens (NFTs).

Metaverse Use Cases

The metaverse offers users a unique experience that is not possible in real life. Here, users can make digital payments, buy and sell digital assets, and even create their virtual worlds. The metaverse also provides users with the opportunity to meet new people from different countries, gain access to global markets, and participate in activities that cannot be done in the physical world.

The metaverse is also decentralized, meaning that it does not rely on any central authority or government. As such, it is open for anyone to participate and offers users the freedom to explore, create, and engage in digital activities. Customers can utilize digital currencies created by cryptocurrency and blockchain technology for inexpensive financial and other asset transactions.

Governments are embracing the metaverse, which is fueled by new opportunities to increase departmental efficiency. The Metaverse promotes greater large-scale interaction between citizens and government authorities. It also generates a scenario in which distinct regulation and governance norms are required. Payment transactions in the metaverse will aid in the abolition of corruption in public offices. A good example is the establishment of Dubai government offices in the metaverse. The Dubai government has announced a five-year Metaverse strategy that will generate $4 billion in virtual opportunities. This metaverse city might employ up to 40,000 people. Furthermore, the utilities of virtual assets will profit from optimised services in a faster, safer, and more transparent manner. The metaverse's general induction will have an impact.

Also, gaming on the virtual battlefield of the metaverse has already been getting massive traction and funding, despite bear markets. Web2 gaming companies are getting into the metaverse without a second thought, and use cases of this newest technology are now expanding like wildfire. The primary use case of the metaverse is gaming, and there is no doubt about it. Here are a few features that will enable the next million metaverse users:

- Easy onboarding of web 2.0 gamers by offering free education
- Removing barriers to interact with the blockchain-powered gaming
- Offering immutable reward distribution
- Direct and indirect earnings by in-game digital payments.

Figure 1. Metaverse economy

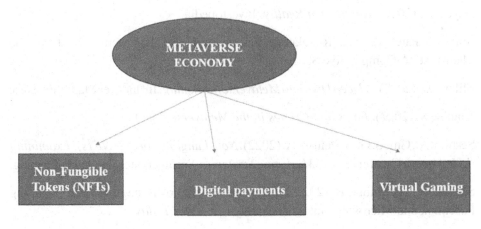

CONCLUSION

The metaverse is already gaining traction, as it offers a wide range of opportunities for users. These include digital payments, Non-Fungible Tokens (NFTs), virtual gaming, and more. It is also becoming increasingly popular with businesses as they can use the metaverse to create virtual stores, host virtual events, and promote their products and services. Users will experience new horizons of digital payments in metaverses.

REFERENCES

Business Insider. (2022). How marketing and advertising is shaping the Metaverse. *Business Insider*.

Cheng, X., Zhang, S., Fu, S., Liu, W., Guan, C., Mou, J., Ye, Q., & Huang, C. (2022). Exploring the metaverse in the digital economy: An overview and research framework. *Journal of Electronic Business & Digital Economics*, *1*(1/2), 206–224. doi:10.1108/JEBDE-09-2022-0036

Davies, M. (2021). *Pros and Cons of the Metaverse*. Konsyse.

Dechalert. (2022). Metaverse jobs are on the rise, but what exactly are they? *Medium*.

Dilella, C., & Dey, A. (2022). *Investors are paying millions for virtual land in the Metaverse*. CNBC.

Faridini, A. (2021). Why The Metaverse Is Marketing's Next Big Thing. *Forbes*.

Hayes, A. (2020). *Augmented Reality*. Investopedia.

Jones & Patel. (2023). Regulatory Frameworks and Transaction Costs in the Metaverse: A Comparative Study.

Mileva, G. (2022). *A Deep Dive into Metaverse Marketing*. Influencer Marketing Hub.

Pandey, S. (2022). *Laws and Crimes in the Metaverse*. Digit.

Sestino, A., Guido, G., & Peluso, A. (2022). *Non-Fungible Tokens (NFTs): Examining the Impact on Consumers and Marketing Strategies*. Springer International Publishing.

Snider, M., & Molina, B. (2022). Everyone wants to own the metaverse including Facebook and Microsoft. But what exactly is it? *USA Today*.

Stapleton, L. (2019). *AR vs. VR: What's the Difference? Marketers Put Augmented and Virtual Reality to Work*. Treasure Data.

Teamwork Commerce. (2022). *5 Retail Metaverse Examples that Create Immersive Experiences and Excited Customers.* Teamwork Commerce.

Waterworth. (2022). 3 Benefits to Becoming a Landlord in the Metaverse. *The Motley Fool.*

Chapter 13
Revolutionary Role of Bioinformatics and Data Analytics in the Healthcare Sector

Piyali Sarkar

iD https://orcid.org/0000-0002-5762-7432
Lovely Professional University, India

Sonia Sharma

iD https://orcid.org/0000-0002-8358-7737
Lovely Professional University, India

ABSTRACT

Big data is a rapidly expanding and applied field that offers the potential to transform the healthcare industry. It enables efficient data modification for patient physiological analysis in bioinformatics. This assessment highlights the current status of big data and analytical techniques in all five healthcare subdisciplines. Stakeholders, including government agencies, healthcare professionals, hardware manufacturers, pharmaceutical companies, individuals, data scientists, scholars, and vendors, are responsible for developing and evaluating big data policies to improve patient outcomes.

INTRODUCTION

The velocity of technology advancement has brought enormous potential to make

DOI: 10.4018/979-8-3693-3358-7.ch013

an extraordinary influence on our everyday lives in several disciplines, particularly in the healthcare industry, because of the sheer magnitude and availability of multidimensional information. Big data is a new, enormous word that will be introduced by the quickly expanding and applied data. Finding information in such complex data is frequently a difficult task. The creation and examination of instruments and techniques for examining such vast amounts of data presents us with a chance to facilitate the shift into a new age. Executing the organization's plans may be greatly aided by having analytics provide data-driven, real-time insights that the organization can access. The greatest advantage of big data analytics is its potential and the necessity of developing novel approaches to deliver the services we require. In contrast to other domains, big data analytics has great promise for the healthcare industry and has garnered more attention in recent years. Decisions made by clinicians are becoming increasingly evidence-based, which means they are depending less on their training and professional judgement and more on vast amounts of studies and clinical data. Larger and more complex electronic health datasets that are difficult or almost impossible to handle using standard, conventional techniques, tools, or software are referred to as "big data" in the context of healthcare. Big data in healthcare is produced by medical records (such as patient records, illness surveillance, hospital records, prescription drug records, health management records, physician records, clinical decision support, or patient feedback). and clinical data (such as electronic medical records, genetic and pharmacological data, financial records, personal images, etc.). Because the creation and administration of these massive health records are thought to be extremely complicated, big data analytics is presented. Big data analytics has the ability to significantly affect our lives by assisting in the prediction, prevention, management, treatment, and cure of disease. This is especially true with the growth of personalised medicine and technological innovation. It also aids in resource management, the advancement of medical research, the development of preventative measures, and the management of epidemics for government organizations, legislators, and hospitals. Due to advancements in information and communication technologies, hard-copy medical data is shifting to cloud-based health records and electronic medical records systems. Data from these systems grew exponentially.

In addition to clinical records, telemonitoring, and medical testing, a growing variety of healthcare applications are now used to collect healthcare data. There are a tonne of subscriptions for these apps. As more and more individuals subscribe to fresh and useful data about health and well-being every day, there were 7.9 billion mobile subscriptions worldwide as of the end of the quarter, referring to the Ericsson Mobility Report of 2019. During that time, 49 million additional subscriptions were added. Because of the world of social media, many applications include large amounts of data. The internet is used by almost 4 billion individuals for a variety of purposes, including email, downloading, browsing, blogging, and entertainment. Additionally, these volumes of data tend to converge on the idea of big data.

Modern methods like cloud computing, data management advancements, visualisation, etc., are vital to healthcare systems for the efficient collection, administration, and manipulation of data. The amount of biomedical informatics databases, such as Proteomics DB, which has 5.17 TB of data and explains 92% of human gene information, is growing quickly. Large volumes are generated from medical photos, such as the 39 GB female datasets included in the Visible Human Project. By 2020, big data in healthcare is expected to reach 35 zeta-bytes in volume. A vast number of healthcare records exist in organised, unstructured, or semi-structured formats, as revealed by the variety in healthcare.

Every day, a multitude of unstructured healthcare records are created, including patient data, physician notes, prescriptions, clinical or formal medical records, radiological film, CT, and MRI pictures, and more. Additionally, actuarial data, automated databases and electronic apps containing information such as patient names, addresses, treatment reimbursement codes, hospital names, physician names, and other details, information from electronic billing and accounting, and some observations of reading clinical and laboratory instruments are included in the structured and semi-structured variety of data related to EMS and EHS. Processing natural language in health fidelity is one of the tools that data analytics offers for converting unorganised data into structured information. Velocity, which might be at rest or moving at a fast speed, is another crucial quality. Healthcare records at rest velocity include notes from physicians or nurses, scripts, videos from documentaries, renderings, X-rays, etc. Additionally, blood pressure readings, insulin pump measurements of daily diabetes glucose, ECG/EKG, and other data are included in medium velocity healthcare data. But occasionally, rapid speed is necessary since it might mean the difference between life and death. This kind of data focuses on real-time information like as heart monitoring, blood pressure monitoring under anaesthesia and trauma, room operations, early detection of infections or illnesses like cancer, etc. Value indicates the extent to which data are advantageous to the healthcare system. For instance, the value of diagnostic records, medication records, and laboratory instrument reading records is higher than that of raw data such as paper prescriptions, official records, or patient information. Veracity refers to the accuracy or comprehensibility of a medical record, which clarifies the documentation of diagnoses, procedures, treatments, and other details, as well as the process of confirming patient, hospital, and reimbursement code information. The literature put forward many healthcare and medical care sectors.

The human body is composed of several intricate, self-regulating mechanisms that ensure every cell, organ, gene, protein, and defence system is functioning properly at all times. Even though it does occur occasionally, some of these facts are difficult to understand, such as how cells can divide on their own when given instructions, maintain growth, recognise foreign invaders and trigger self-defence mechanisms, and function flawlessly every single second of their lives. Even if it may take some time to properly comprehend these ideas, analytics and visualisation may be quite helpful since they can be used to illustrate any complex idea or series of events, even if they happen once a second. This makes the next advantages possible. In the first place, intricate biological simulations may depict minute aspects of what occurs or has occurred every second; in the second place, they can simplify explanations. Learners are able to redo analytics and simulations if something is still unclear. Teachers are also able to clarify any questions students may have. This can offer a two-way procedure to raise the standard and enrich the learning process. Most importantly, though, is that if patients are facing health risks like cancer, any progress in understanding the origins of malignant tumours, locating the tumours' weak points, examining any cancerous genes present, and ultimately formulating a more precise treatment decision based on all the data that has been obtained thus far is crucial. All of these tasks, though, may be difficult and complicated. The well-being of patients must be determined, health research must advance, and sophisticated work that involves analytics and visualisation for bioinformatics and healthcare must be presented in a way that stakeholders can review, verify, and comprehend. Adoption of analytics and visualisation has been shown to be beneficial and to have favourable effects on medical researchers, students, and healthcare communities.

It requires technological infrastructure which includes the elate technologies that underpin the biological analytics service are described in this section. Furthermore, machine learning and artificial intelligence Sophisticated algorithms will be employed in the background. Databases: Selected techniques, like MapReduce and some deep learning, can be employed in tandem to guarantee that data processing optimisation with analytics is possible. Before the simulations, a significant amount of training data may be put into the databases, where it can all be queried and prepared for data processing. Multimedia Instruments Applications and Mathematical Modelling: All mathematical models with various variables may be combined in an efficient manner to create Application Programme Interfaces (APIs) for computation and computations. Privacy of data: To ensure that there are no problems with data privacy and anonymization, training data that is comparable to actual tumours will be utilised.

REVIEW OF LITERATURE

Sedig and Ola (2014) Big data is a broad term for data related to public health. The degree to which public health stakeholders can adequately address societal health problems as they engage in a range of job activities depends on how well and efficiently they use this data. Stakeholders participate in a variety of cognitive tasks while interacting with data, including problem-solving, interpreting, making decisions, and using analytical thinking. The amount, diversity, pace, and authenticity of the data provide challenges for stakeholders that make it difficult for them to carry out their tasks without assistance. Because of this, computer-based information tools are required to assist stakeholders in public health. Unfortunately, while current computational tools are useful for addressing some work-related tasks, they are insufficient for supporting cognitive tasks that require interacting with big, varied, and complicated data sets. In order to support cognitive tasks involving large data, this study introduces visual analytics (VA) tools, a new class of computational tools that combine data analytics with participatory visualisations. In the past, PH has been slow to adopt new computing technologies compared to other industries. In this study, we explore how VA techniques might help with the problems that large data presents.

Anisetti et al. (2017) depicted a wide range of devices, protocols, and technologies are used in "smart cities" to enhance and assist residents' daily lives. Creative public policies, which take the form of directives, initiatives, and strategies meant to achieve a particular objective of raising the standard of living for society as a whole, are crucial to the creation of smart cities. Big Data's development has the potential to improve policy formation and reach previously unheard-of levels of efficiency in a number of areas, notably economic and social policy. Nonetheless, safeguarding the privacy of its citizens is one facet of living in a smart city. In this study, we offer a unique Huge Data-assisted political decision-making method that aims to reconcile privacy protection with quality of life in smart cities by implementing privacy-by-design. The proposed approach is driven by a Privacy Compliant Analysis derived from the EU's GDPR and is predicated on the use of a Big Data Analysis as a Services strategy that is examined within the context of the healthcare policy-making process.

Chang (2017) presents analytics and visualization-based proofs-of-concept for modelling complicated biological research. The focus is on researching malignant tumours, comprehending their growth, examining them, and identifying any weak points so that therapies may be targeted to increase the likelihood of success. Ten gigabytes of training data apiece were produced as a consequence of earlier research that required the collection of thousands of samples, data reading and updating, and simulation. It has been established that gene inspection outputs verifying the presence of cancer are combined with outputs for weak spot, growth, and malignant tumour inspection. An assessment of performance was conducted.

According to Das et al. (2018), big data is the result of combining numerous, complex data sets. They consist of both organised and unstructured data that change so quickly that neither traditional relational database systems nor modern analytical tools can keep up with them. Big Data analytics cannot grow in a linear fashion. It follows a pre-set schema. Big data is becoming quite useful, but just for data backups. Every time, new data is introduced. It also aids in resolving India's major issues. It aids in closing the data gap as well. The preservation or improvement of health via the prevention, diagnosis, and treatment of disease, malady, and other significant and spiritual decline in humans is known as health care. Health professionals at United Health, including specialists, physician associates, midwives, nurses, chemists, psychologists, and other health professionals, provide healthcare. The material provided in this article is mostly focused on big data analytics and how it is used in the medical field. The introduction, difficult elements and worries, the application of big data analytics, technical specifications, research applications, industry applications, and future applications are also included.

Saeeda, Razzak, and Rehman (2020) found since clinical decisions are more promising and evidence-based than other types of judgements, big data analytics has been recommended for several clinical domains to help clinical decision-making. Large-data analytics has transformed the healthcare business and has immense potential for us, owing to the vast amount and accessibility of data in this domain. It guarantees that we will be able to identify issues early on, anticipate them, steer clear of them, and improve our standard of living. Researchers and health care providers are working to stop big data from enhancing health in the not-too-distant future. Numerous technologies and techniques are being used to analyse, process, collect, integrate, and manage vast volumes of organized and unprocessed health care information. In this paper, we address the need for large-scale data analysis in healthcare, its advantages, and methods to improve quality of life. We address the emerging subject of massive data sets and analytical instruments in the five healthcare divisions of medical data analysis and radiology informatics, bio informatics healthcare information systems, public health information science, and medicinal signal analytics. We provide the numerous structures, advantages, and resources of each sector to help individual patients from several perspectives and to produce a cohesive representation of the different healthcare acts that are carried out in the pipeline. The report's discussion of big data analytics' notable applications and challenges in the healthcare sector comes to a close.

ROLE OF BIG DATA IN HEALTHCARE

Large, complicated, linkable information volumes are referred to as "big data". Big Data encompasses information from the medical, the environment, financial, geographical, and social networking domains in addition to genomics and other "omic" sciences. A decade ago, the majority of this digital material remained unavailable. This data tsunami will only get bigger, driven by forces that are unfathomable right now. Through improved illness prediction and prevention, better medication targets for precision healthcare, and new knowledge into the causes and consequences of disease, big data has the potential to improve health.

Furthermore, a growing number of citizen-scientists will make use of this knowledge to advance their own wellbeing. Big Data can speed up the cycle from information to dissemination and help us understand health behaviours (drinking, smoking, etc.). Healthcare stakeholders can benefit from efficient operations and insights into patients' health through the analysis of large data. Numerous advantages can result from big data analytics. The majority of the sources of medical data include electronic medical records, lab information management infrastructure, pharmacy stores, observation and testing instruments, finance (invoices and insurance claims), and hospital resources. New kinds of knowledge are added to sources of information as analytics and data collection technology advance. One example is genetic data that hospitals capture and integrate into electronic medical records. This enormous range of patient data contains insightful information that, when used wisely, may benefit organisations and patients alike.

Among the possible benefits are improved patient care: standard of care Electronic health records assists in compiling medical data, lab testing results, identification, and clinical conditions, among other demographic and medical data. In order to save lives, provide high-quality care, and save costs, medical personnel can use this data to identify links and patterns. sickness prevention an effective healthcare system is not synonymous with higher health expenditures. In addition to lowering costs, preventive care can improve the efficacy and standard of medical treatment. At a time when financial and resource constraints are severe in many nations, health systems have significant problems in promoting and safeguarding health. Reducing mortality and healthcare expenses is greatly aided by early illness identification and prevention.

Accuracy The diversity and amount of healthcare data makes managing it almost difficult with typical analytical methods. Healthcare stakeholders use large amounts of data as part of their company's intelligence strategy to examine past patient admittance rates and staff efficiency. The capacity to cure illnesses Most medical treatments have been reactive, which means that patients don't usually get prescriptions for treatments that might possibly help them recover until their condition shows symptoms. Nevertheless, no two individuals on the earth are going to have a comparable genetic composition. Furthermore, the exact environmental factors that cause the disease to start are unclear, which helps to explain why some people response favourably to a certain medication while others do poorly.

To save resources and money, it is possible to compare patient groups that have the same condition but are receiving various medication regimens in order to discover which treatment strategies are most effective for the same or a comparable disease.

There are many things to learn from a single genome, and some medications seem to work for some people but not for others when it comes to curing illnesses. It is not possible to watch them all in their entirety. However, by examining enormous data sets, big statistics may assist in revealing previously unidentified relationships, underlying trends, and insights. Through the use of machine learning on large datasets, researchers are able to obtain the necessary information to examine human genomes and determine the best course of action for cancer treatment.

The application of genetic data analytics has significant promise for enhancing healthcare quality, safety, and outcomes while also reducing costs. Prognosis and prevention of diseases: "Taking care of yourself can help you live a longer life." Big data analytics is being used by many hospitals, research facilities, and healthcare organisations to transform the ways in which treatments are delivered. Big data analytics is therefore extremely useful in the healthcare industry for lowering overhead, diagnosing and treating illnesses, forecasting epidemics, and increasing the value of human life by preventing fatalities.

Every day, the healthcare industry generates massive volumes of patient data. The majority of these data were formerly collected by healthcare organisations in hard copy, but thanks to advancements in data capture technologies, data is now being collected electronically. Healthcare data analytics has the power to significantly alter the healthcare sector, streamlining procedures and raising standards of care. Researchers studying data analytics, medical professionals, governmental organisations, and pharmaceutical firms pinpoint a variety of distinct ways that big data approaches might assist us in generating evidence-based judgements and policies that will significantly enhance patient outcomes. The following are the main healthcare sectors where big data analytics is having a significant impact: Methodical organising "Early measurement is the foundation of management; without it, management is impossible." A service that is time-sensitive is healthcare. Hospitals are having trouble with patient flow. In order to forecast patient flow, provide a smooth patient flow, and shorten waiting times, machine learning and data analytics are crucial. Early hospital visit prediction assists management in making decisions and implementing the required actions to shorten patient wait times and provide timely care. Numerous apps, such as Patient Flow Manager and Q-nomy, among others, offer a thorough graphical representation of patient data, including drawings of inpatient, outpatient, emergency, and elective hospital systems. Care managers, for instance, might examine check-up outcomes across patients in various demographic groups to determine what deters patients from seeking treatment.

Every person leaves a digital footprint. This section will cover some of the big data analytics technologies that have been employed in the medical industry in the past and present. Forecast for a Heart Attack: It contributes the standard knowledge on big data analytics for medical applications, including heart attack detection and unforeseen medical research of the specific employing Hadoop and IOT technology. It is a project end-user for an online specialised support service. The purpose of this programme is to enable users to access real-time online assistance on their heart illness via an intelligent system. Prognosis of Brain Disease: Brain disorders are another name for brain disease. Serious mental discomfort can result in brain damage such as blood clots, contusions, concussions, strokes, and cerebral oedema. Vomiting, disgust, trouble speaking, insensibility, memory loss, lack of focus, and paralysis are the symptoms. The condition that reveals Parkinson's disease is identified using data mining methods, and the speech data set is utilised to diagnose illnesses in humans. Predicting the development of the disease: After clustering, it has been found that deleting the wrongly categorised data significantly improves classifier performance. The classification effectiveness, understanding, and particularity acquired by the proposed framework are shown to be equivalent to those obtained by other competing techniques across all eight health datasets in the UCI data on the machine learning repository.

A good description of the diabetes data set was easily achieved with the help of Hive & R Analysing diabetes Treatment. With the information provided throughout the approach, some predicting models might be created. In this instance, the inquiry is the only thing finished, but you may still use the publicly available data to build prediction models that work. Analysis of Coronary Artery Heart Disease: The purpose of this analysis was to assess the recommendations made for people who have chest pain and cardiovascular disease in practical cardiology, as well as the most recent results from specialist research. An explanatory and mentality method to the analysis and authority of CAD and AP is high-resolution HRV analysis. Forecast for the Spread of Infectious Diseases: It focuses on an effective examination of the data kinds, sources, and factors utilised in the prediction of measles and dengue fever outbreaks. According to the analysis, there have been few researches on measles outbreak prediction, and the studies that have been done so far have not used information from a range of sources. Mycobacterium tuberculosis is the cause of tuberculosis, according to the prediction. It covers big data applications and resources, big data administration and storage, big data constraints and opportunities, and big data's potential future uses in relation to tuberculosis prognosis and affordable treatment.

Premature Stage of Heart Attack Detection: A medical biosensor-based early heart attack detection device is suggested. This technique has the ability to identify heart attacks several hours before they occur. Heart Disease Prediction: A lot of nursing homes today employ health information systems to manage patient data [25]. These systems are used to extract hidden information that may be used to prepare creative clinical analyses when they contain large amounts of data. The main goal of this investigation is to develop a novel heart illness prediction system that uses real, heart-related data to analyse heart disease. Clinical factors including sexual orientation, blood pressure, and cholesterol are employed as 13 aid elements to build this method. Smoking and being overweight are two additional factors that are employed since they are considered important risk factors for heart disease and can have additional beneficial effects.

The UCI Machine Learning Repository's available dataset on heart contamination has been pre-processed, analysed, and rendered insolvent in order to make it suitable for use as an arranging mechanism in the Intelligent Heart Disease Prediction System. A robust and dependable method for establishing a nonlinear link and calibrating between the various situations was suggested: coactive neuro-fuzzy designing. It has been shown that GA is a highly useful tool for selecting the ideal set of attributes and auto-tuning the Coactive Neuro-Fuzzy Inference System frameworks. Doctors may learn more about the ideal way to calculate the fields that computerised disclosure includes by comparing the computerised disclosure conclusions with the pathologic findings. The research shows that data processing machines cannot transform humans. Diagnosing Long-Term Kidney Disease: The kidney is a vital organ in the human body. The kidney's primary function is to eliminate waste products from metabolic processes. The kidneys are crucial in the body's elimination of foreign substances like creatinine and urea. Renal failure that is persistent is another name for this illness. The condition is caused by a reduction in the kidney's nephron.

HIV/AIDS Disease Forecast: An organism of a certain kind is the HIV virus. HIV remains in the body of a person infected with it for life. Immune system damage is caused by this virus. The immune system weakens the body's defences against illness. AIDS is caused by the HIV virus. Acquired immune deficiency syndrome, or AIDS for short, is a disease of the compromised immune system. The typical table-and-column representation lacks big data, but relational databases have. This is the distinction between big data and relational databases. Data in traditional relational databases must have a schema.

BIOINFORMATICS IN HEALTHCARE FIELD

Bioinformatics is the investigation of mathematical, computerized, and IT-based approaches, plans, formulas, and software tools for collecting, storing, analysing, assembling, modelling, and simulating biological and life science data. Big data serves the purpose of providing efficient methods for modifying data for patient physiological data to be analysed and researched in the field of bioinformatics. Bioinformatics analytics now makes heavy use of Hadoop and MapReduce. Bioinformatics is essentially the synthesis of computer science and biology. Variations are analysed at the molecular level by the biological analysis system. Bioinformatics encompasses a wide range of data types, including route data, RNA, DNA, proteomics (sequencing of proteins), genomics (sequencing of genes), gene onthology, protein–protein interactions, association networks of disease genes, and networks of human diseases. There is a rising tendency in personalised care with the current developments. Every day, the volume of data in bioinformatics grows tremendously. Given that humans have between 30,000 and 35,000 genes, genome sequencing or genomics data are now being categorised as large data for bioinformatics problems. Gene the sequencing process, DNA sequencing, genotyping, expression of genes and other related data are typically referred to as genomics data. DNA, which makes up genes, is composed of three billion pairs of the four building components, or bases, adenine, thymine, cysteine, and guanine. The single genome is around three gigabytes in size. Using micro-arrays for genome analysis has proven beneficial for studying characteristics in a large population and has played a significant role in the treatment of a number of complex illnesses, including diabetes, rheumatoid arthritis, bipolar disorder, hypertension, muscular degeneration, coronary heart disease, and Crohn's disease. Big data analytics is the direction that this genomics data tends to go. Protein-protein interactions and protein sequencing are complex issues in functional genomics within bioinformatics. This is caused by the high number of features in the feature vector, which not only makes for a difficult and cost-effective analysis, but also lowers accuracy.

They demonstrated improved performance in large data feature selection using fuzzy rough set theory applied to hybrid information systems. Upon extraction and selection of the characteristics, the following stage is clustering or classification. The process of supervised learning called classification involves identifying a model that can distinguish between different classes of data or concepts. Using previously trained instances, the model is used to predict the class label of test instances. Although there are other models accessible in the literature, decision trees, neural networks, support vector machine models, K-nearest Neighbour, non-linear as well as density-based classification algorithms, and Naive Bayes are the methods most often employed in a range of applications.

Giveki et al. (2019) used weighted support vector machines according to pre-gained information and modification to diagnose diabetes automatically. They used characteristics from PCA to conduct experiments on datasets of diabetes. SVM was used by Haller et al. (2019) to classify Parkinson's disease patients. The most differentiated voxels were chosen as features for preliminary processing using DTI partial anisotropy data, and support vector machines were used for classification. Son et al. (2018) used support vector machines to forecast patients with heart failure. Similarly, Bhatia et al. (2021) used support vector machines to categorize cardiac disease. They employed an integer-coded evolutionary algorithm to choose the best feature subset. With the help of sophisticated decision trees, huge data categorization and regression are successfully completed.

Decision tree learning was modified by Hall et al. (2020) by producing rules for a sizable training dataset. One "Applied Information Science" is informatics. It combines the ideas and practises of computer science, information technology, management sciences, and behavioural sciences to provide concepts, instruments, and procedures for integrating information systems into public health. Informatics effectively converts unprocessed data into information based on user requirements.

Informatics assists in identifying potential anthrax exposure cases, tracking the screening process, documenting antibiotic prescriptions, and tracking the distribution of confirmed cases and confirmed fatalities. Additional analytical techniques and important studies on healthcare were described in new and creative data sources have emerged in recent years, allowing for the instantaneous collection of data from people directly through technological devices. Social media transforms society and creates a worldwide community. Every day, an exponential amount of data is generated. Big data may be broadly defined as information generated from public health sources. In order to identify hidden informative patterns, big data analytics techniques are applied to gathered, processed, verified, and accessible public healthcare data. The extent to which social health risks may be identified is decided by the efficient use of public health data, which is further utilised to anticipate, monitor, and diagnose illnesses.

CONCLUSION

This assessment presents the current status of big data and analytical techniques in all five healthcare subdisciplines. We list a few healthcare domains that big data technologies that have profoundly changed people's understanding of healthcare operations and hence played a major role in the modern healthcare revolution. Five sub-disciplines of informatics—bioinformatics, clinical informatics, health care informatics, medical computer graphics and imaging information technology, and medical signal analytics—use large data analytical methodologies. These parts offer a thorough description of how different healthcare tasks are completed sequentially to help specific patients from different perspectives. In several healthcare sub-disciplines, the reviews that were previously in place lacked a thorough explanation. A comprehensive analysis of the study is absent from the existing ratings. Numerous healthcare sources, such as biopharmaceutical farms, medical providers, testing facilities, insurance firms, organizations that are not-for-profit, and web-health portals, have been the subject of previous studies looking at big data in healthcare. Healthcare data is analysed using a variety of big data techniques, including data mining, machine learning, cluster analysis, recognition of patterns neural networks, deep neural networks, and spatial analysis. Most of the study handled patient data using Hadoop and comparable technologies, however, these were batch processing techniques. Recent technologies like as Spark, Storm, GraphLab, and others have been used in several research projects to analyse streaming and real-time data.

The application of big data analytics across multiple healthcare domains, such as support for clinical decisions, personalized medicine, operational optimized performance, and healthcare cost-effectiveness, was a key focus of the research. Studies show that applying statistics to healthcare improves the identification of patients and quality. In view of the rapid development in publications within the biomedical and health industries, we have conducted a comprehensive analysis of analytics for healthcare across five sub-disciplines. This survey finds that computational is one of the primary domains where big data analytics is constantly expanding and being applied scientifically, based on the vast and complex amount of bioinformatics data.

Bioinformatics uses a wide range of tools, methods, and platforms to analyse data related to biology, genomics, proteins, and gene sequencing. However, big data applications hold less promise. in additional domains such as medical imaging information technology, clinical information systems, health care information technology, and medical signal analytics.

Big data analytics has experienced exponential development, which is continually expanding and is essential to the advancement of healthcare practises and research. It involves offering resources for gathering, examining, organising, and preserving a sizable amount of complicated, organised, and unstructured data. Big data has drastically changed the healthcare industry by lowering treatment costs, identifying diseases like cancer earlier, and improving the quality of life. They have been used recently to support patient care, community services, early illness identification, healthcare workers, and disease exploration. The big data analytics approaches, tools, methodologies, and architectures in the healthcare industry have all been covered in this study.

the fast, universal use of big data analytics throughout the medical services sector and the Social Insurance Association. That being said, the minor difficulties need to be attended to. It possesses remarkable potential. Nevertheless, by lowering costs, lowering risks, and boosting personalised treatment, big data's future developments in the broader social healthcare framework have the potential to improve and expedite interactions between physicians, executives, logistic managers, and analysts. All parties involved in the healthcare business have an obligation to implement big data analytics. Developing and evaluating big data policies that will improve patient outcomes is the responsibility of stakeholders. Government agencies, healthcare professionals, hardware manufacturers, pharmaceutical companies, individuals, data scientists, scholars, and vendors are all required to participate in the establishment of the big data architecture, which will dictate the future direction of big data analytics in the healthcare industry.

REFERENCES

Anisetti, M., Ardagna, C., Bellandi, V., Cremonini, M., Frati, F., & Damiani, E. (2018). Privacy-aware Big Data Analytics as a service for public health policies in smart cities. *Sustainable Cities and Society, 39*, 68–77. doi:10.1016/j.scs.2017.12.019

Benke, K., & Benke, G. (2018). Artificial intelligence and big data in public health. *International Journal of Environmental Research and Public Health, 15*(12), 2796. doi:10.3390/ijerph15122796 PMID:30544648

Chang, V. (2018). Data analytics and visualization for inspecting cancers and genes. *Multimedia Tools and Applications, 77*(14), 17693–17707. doi:10.1007/s11042-017-5186-8

Das, N., Das, L., Rautaray, S. S., & Pandey, M. (2018). Big data analytics for medical applications. *International Journal of Modern Education and Computer Science, 12*(2), 35–42. doi:10.5815/ijmecs.2018.02.04

Gharajeh, M. S. (2018). Biological big data analytics. [). Elsevier.]. *Advances in Computers, 109*, 321–355. doi:10.1016/bs.adcom.2017.08.002

Iyengar, A., Kundu, A., Sharma, U., & Zhang, P. (2018, July). A trusted healthcare data analytics cloud platform. In *2018 IEEE 38th International Conference on Distributed Computing Systems (ICDCS)* (pp. 1238-1249). IEEE. 10.1109/ICDCS.2018.00123

Jia, Q., Guo, Y., Wang, G., & Barnes, S. J. (2020). Big data analytics in the fight against major public health incidents (Including COVID-19): A conceptual framework. *International Journal of Environmental Research and Public Health, 17*(17), 6161. doi:10.3390/ijerph17176161 PMID:32854265

Khoury, M. J., & Ioannidis, J. P. (2014). Big data meets public health. *Science, 346*(6213), 1054–1055. doi:10.1126/science.aaa2709 PMID:25430753

Majhi, V., Paul, S., & Jain, R. (2019, February). Bioinformatics for healthcare applications. In 2019 Amity international conference on artificial intelligence (AICAI) (pp. 204-207). IEEE. doi:10.1109/AICAI.2019.8701277

Nagaraj, K., Sharvani, G. S., & Sridhar, A. (2018). Emerging trend of big data analytics in bioinformatics: A literature review. *International Journal of Bioinformatics Research and Applications, 14*(1-2), 144–205. doi:10.1504/IJBRA.2018.089175

Ola, O., & Sedig, K. (2014). The challenge of big data in public health: An opportunity for visual analytics. *Online Journal of Public Health Informatics, 5*(3), 223. PMID:24678376

Parihar, J., Kansal, P., Singh, K., & Dhiman, H. (2019, February). Assessment of bioinformatics and healthcare informatics. In *2019 Amity International Conference on Artificial Intelligence (AICAI)* (pp. 465-467). IEEE. 10.1109/AICAI.2019.8701262

Rehman, A., Naz, S., & Razzak, I. (2022). Leveraging big data analytics in healthcare enhancement: Trends, challenges and opportunities. *Multimedia Systems*, *28*(4), 1339–1371. doi:10.1007/s00530-020-00736-8

Ristevski, B., & Chen, M. (2018). Big data analytics in medicine and healthcare. *Journal of Integrative Bioinformatics*, *15*(3), 20170030. doi:10.1515/jib-2017-0030 PMID:29746254

Sarma, M. K., Ningthoujam, R., Panda, M. K., Babu, P. J., Srivastava, A., Das, M., & Singh, Y. D. (2021). Translational healthcare system through bioinformatics. In *Translational bioinformatics applications in healthcare* (pp. 3–21). CRC Press. doi:10.1201/9781003146988-2

Straton, N., Hansen, K., Mukkamala, R. R., Hussain, A., Gronli, T. M., Langberg, H., & Vatrapu, R. (2016, September). Big social data analytics for public health: Facebook engagement and performance. In *2016 IEEE 18th International Conference on e-Health Networking, Applications and Services (Healthcom)* (pp. 1-6). IEEE.

Straton, N., Mukkamala, R. R., & Vatrapu, R. (2017, June). Big social data analytics for public health: Predicting facebook post performance using artificial neural networks and deep learning. In *2017 IEEE International Congress on Big Data (BigData Congress)* (pp. 89-96). IEEE. 10.1109/BigDataCongress.2017.21

Vayena, E., Salathé, M., Madoff, L. C., & Brownstein, J. S. (2015). Ethical challenges of big data in public health. *PLoS Computational Biology*, *11*(2), e1003904. doi:10.1371/journal.pcbi.1003904 PMID:25664461

Chapter 14

Potential Mental and Physical Health Impacts of Spending Extended Periods in the Metaverse:
An Analysis

V. Suganya

iD https://orcid.org/0000-0001-5301-8317
SRM Institute of Science and Technology, Vadapalani, India

N. V. Suresh

iD https://orcid.org/0000-0002-0393-6037
ASET College of Science and Technology, India

ABSTRACT

The metaverse, a burgeoning digital universe of immersive experiences and interactions, has captured the imagination of individuals and industries alike. As people increasingly gravitate towards extended engagement within these virtual realms, questions arise about the potential consequences for mental and physical health. This analysis provides an in-depth examination of the multifaceted health implications stemming from prolonged immersion in the metaverse. In this exploration, we investigate the psychological effects of extended metaverse use, including issues related to social isolation, addiction, and the potential for disconnection from the physical world. We delve into the emotional aspects, exploring how interactions within the metaverse may impact users' self-esteem, emotional well-being, and social relationships. This research seeks to contribute to the growing body of knowledge surrounding the metaverse by offering insights into the intricate relationship between immersive digital experiences and human health.

DOI: 10.4018/979-8-3693-3358-7.ch014

INTRODUCTION

In recent years, the emergence of the metaverse has transformed the landscape of human interaction, blurring the lines between the physical and digital realms. As individuals increasingly find themselves immersed in virtual environments for extended periods, it becomes imperative to scrutinize the potential mental and physical health impacts associated with this evolving digital paradigm.

The metaverse, a collective virtual shared space that is created by the convergence of physical and virtual reality, offers unprecedented opportunities for connection, collaboration, and exploration. However, beneath the allure of this interconnected digital realm lies a complex interplay of factors that may exert profound effects on mental and physical well-being.

On the mental health front, the metaverse poses the risk of exacerbating issues such as digital addiction, social isolation, and the blurring of reality. Extended periods spent navigating virtual landscapes may lead to a detachment from the physical world, potentially fostering feelings of loneliness and disconnection. Moreover, the constant stimulation and immersive nature of the metaverse could contribute to mental fatigue, anxiety, and even the development of virtual-related stressors.

Simultaneously, the physical health impacts of prolonged metaverse engagement merit attention. Sedentary behaviour, a known precursor to various health problems, may become more prevalent as individuals spend extended periods in virtual environments. The lack of physical activity could contribute to issues such as musculoskeletal problems, obesity, and cardiovascular concerns, forming a nexus between digital engagement and physical well-being.

This analysis aims to delve into the intricate web of potential mental and physical health impacts associated with extended stays in the metaverse. By exploring the psychological and physiological consequences of prolonged digital immersion, we seek to shed light on the challenges and opportunities inherent in this transformative era, fostering a nuanced understanding of the implications for human well-being in the evolving landscape of virtual interconnectedness.

Review of Literature

For the majority of individual users, the Metaverse will merely consist of an ongoing evolution of well-known 3D multiplayer games with social media features added. Predicting a psychological effect requires taking into account the amount of time spent online today. In 2022, the average US user (age 18 and over) spent 33 minutes a day on Facebook, 31 minutes on TikTok and Twitter, 29 minutes on Instagram, and 28 minutes on Snapchat (Statista.com, 2022b). Gaming platforms are very popular with people between the ages of 4 and 18. For instance, Roblox is a gaming and game production platform where users are estimated to spend 180 minutes a day on average (Statistia.com, 2021). Users can design their own virtual homes and play a variety of games in this virtual reality. It is possible to purchase clothing and decorations to help the younger users get used to spending money. Roblox reported 52.2 million daily active users globally in the second quarter of 2022 (Statista.com, 2022a). It is a virtual gaming platform, but for younger users in particular, it also acts as their favourite venue for social gatherings because, unlike traditional social media, groups may remain small and enjoy privacy, even from parents. Roblox is more like hangouts in real life, where there is less pressure to pretend, than there is social media like Facebook and Instagram, with its opportunities and pressures to show your own life as positive as possible. By 2026, 25% of people, according to US research firm Gartner, are expected to spend at least one hour a day in the Metaverse. This entails a partial transition from the real world to the virtual world for employment, education, and recreation (Wiles, 2022). Given that Generation Z primarily uses Roblox, this prediction seems reasonable. Born between 1997 and 2012, Generation Z is starting to enroll in colleges and the workforce. Their constant access to VR platforms has helped them socialize; for instance, the initial Roblox version was launched in September 2006. Growing up in a virtual world has made it difficult to distinguish between real life and virtual reality since decisions made in one can have an impact on the other. Human perception is the result of the interaction between internal factors like interest, motivation, and experience and external stimuli that are perceived by the senses. Consequently, perception is a process rather than a straightforward mapping of the environment (Fischer & Wiswede, 1997). Human senses take in stimuli and automatically interpret them in terms of the individual's body. Shape, proportion, posture, and movement are only a few examples of the physical characteristics that might influence how the environment seems to us and can be drawn from different sensory systems (Harris et al., 2015). The Metaverse allows users to represent their actual bodies, but they can also select entirely different ones, up to fantastical entities. When people act in both the physical and virtual worlds from an early age, they see them as the same reality. The experience of different bodily representations can be used to interpret sensor-derived data, meaning that behaviour in the actual world is influenced by what is learned in virtual reality and vice versa (Henz, 2022). A shift in self-perception may result from the regular use of an avatar that is distinct from the real body and its interaction with the surroundings. For this to be a satisfying experience, it is essential that the Metaverse actively promotes the development of a varied and welcoming virtual world in addition to upholding human rights. This means that operators of the various platforms provide an advanced individualization of the avatar's exterior look and that the same laws that govern the actual world also apply in the Metaverse. Large corporations who invest in Metaverse platforms should anticipate that their goals will be commercial use, with prices for virtual commodities that are comparable to those in the real world. The budget and other factors that raise the possibility of crimes like theft or avatar kidnapping may have an impact on the experience's quality.

Objectives of the study:

- To quantify the occurrence of mental health issues, including stress, anxiety, depression, and social isolation, among individuals who spend extended periods in the metaverse.
- To investigate the correlation between the duration of metaverse engagement and changes in psychological well-being, including mood, emotional stability, and overall mental health.
- To identify and quantify physical health consequences associated with prolonged metaverse use, such as sedentary behaviour, eye strain, and musculoskeletal issues.
- To analyse how social interactions in the metaverse differ from those in the physical world.
- To investigate the impact of metaverse socialization on individuals' sense of community and belonging.
- To examine the coping mechanisms employed by individuals to manage stressors related to extended metaverse engagement.
- To evaluate the effectiveness of various coping strategies in maintaining mental and physical well-being.
- To determine if there are demographic variations in the mental and physical health impacts of spending extended time in the metaverse, considering factors such as age, gender, and prior mental health status.
- To assess user satisfaction and overall experience related to extended metaverse use.
- To explore factors contributing to positive or negative experiences and their potential influence on health outcomes.
- To investigate how specific design elements within the metaverse influence user health, including ergonomic considerations, user interface features, and virtual environment characteristics.
- To identify external factors that may moderate the relationship between metaverse use and mental/physical health outcomes.
- To examine lifestyle, social support, and other contextual variables that may influence the impact of extended metaverse engagement.
- To develop evidence-based recommendations for individuals to engage with the metaverse in a manner that promotes mental and physical well-being.
- To offer guidelines for platform developers to incorporate health-conscious features into metaverse design.

Figure 1. Conceptual framework for the study

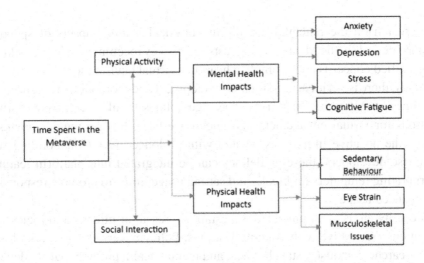

Theoretical Foundations for the topic

Technology Adoption Theories: Explore theories such as the Technology Acceptance Model (TAM) or the Unified Theory of Acceptance and Use of Technology (UTAUT) to understand factors influencing Metaverse adoption.

Psychological Theories: Integrate psychological theories like the Technology-Induced Attention and Cognitive Control theory or the Displacement Hypothesis to explain the cognitive and psychological aspects of extended Metaverse use.

Variables and Constructs:

Independent Variable: Time spent in the Metaverse.

Dependent Variables:

Mental Health Impacts: Anxiety, depression, stress, cognitive fatigue.

Physical Health Impacts: Sedentary behavior, eye strain, musculoskeletal issues.

Mediating and Moderating Factors:

Social Interaction: Explore how the quality and nature of social interactions within the Metaverse mediate or moderate its impact on mental health.

Physical Activity: Investigate the role of physical activities within the Metaverse and their impact on mitigating physical health issues.

Recommendations

The research on the potential mental and physical health impacts of spending extended periods in the Metaverse suggests several key recommendations to address the identified concerns and promote a healthier virtual environment.

Firstly, there is a critical need for the development and promotion of balanced use guidelines for Metaverse platforms. These guidelines should recommend optimal durations for virtual engagement and encourage users to take regular breaks to prevent the negative impacts associated with prolonged use. Collaborating with Metaverse developers, these guidelines can be integrated into platform features, incorporating reminders for breaks and setting usage limits to promote responsible and balanced usage.

Secondly, it is recommended to establish research-informed policies and regulations that evolve with ongoing findings. Policymakers should work closely with researchers, industry stakeholders, and mental health professionals to develop guidelines that prioritize user well-being while allowing for the growth and innovation within the Metaverse space. This collaboration ensures that regulations remain relevant and effective in addressing emerging health concerns.

To address mental health challenges, community support programs tailored for Metaverse users should be established. These programs can include virtual support groups, counseling services, and educational resources focused on mental well-being. Collaboration between mental health organizations and Metaverse platforms is essential in creating effective and accessible support networks within the virtual space.

Integrating physical activities within the Metaverse is another key recommendation. Encouraging developers to create virtual environments that promote movement and exercise can mitigate the physical health risks associated with sedentary behavior. Incentives for platforms prioritizing user health through physical engagement can further drive the adoption of such features.

Finally, user empowerment tools should be developed, allowing users to monitor and manage their virtual activities. Apps or features that enable users to track their Metaverse usage patterns, receive health-related insights, and make informed decisions about their virtual engagements empower individuals to take control of their virtual experiences.

Implementing these recommendations collectively contributes to the creation of a more responsible, user-centric, and health-conscious Metaverse, addressing both mental and physical health impacts associated with extended periods of virtual engagement.

Implications of the Research

The research on the potential mental and physical health impacts of extended periods in the Metaverse holds significant implications for various stakeholders. The findings underscore the critical need for public awareness campaigns to educate users, parents, and educators about the potential risks associated with prolonged Metaverse engagement. Integrating mental health support services within the virtual platforms emerges as a crucial implication, necessitating collaboration between mental health professionals and Metaverse developers. The research highlights the importance of incorporating physical activities within the virtual environment to mitigate sedentary behaviour and associated health issues. Regulatory measures may be warranted to ensure user safety and responsible usage, prompting a dialogue between researchers, policymakers, and industry stakeholders. User interface and experience design must prioritize well-being, influencing user behaviour within the Metaverse. Overall, the implications call for balanced use guidelines, community support programs, and collaborative efforts between the Metaverse industry and health professionals to empower users and create a virtual space that promotes mental and physical health.

CONCLUSION

In conclusion, the research on the potential mental and physical health impacts of spending extended periods in the Metaverse sheds light on a complex intersection between technology, well-being, and human behavior. The implications and recommendations derived from this analysis collectively emphasize the need for a holistic approach to ensure the responsible development and use of Metaverse platforms. The findings underscore the urgency of public awareness campaigns, aiming to educate users, parents, and educators about the potential risks associated with prolonged Metaverse engagement. As technology continues to shape our daily lives, these campaigns become instrumental in fostering informed decision-making and promoting a balanced digital lifestyle. The integration of mental health support services within Metaverse platforms emerges as a pivotal recommendation. Collaborative efforts between mental health professionals and developers can yield innovative solutions, such as virtual counselling services and support groups, addressing the mental health challenges that may arise from extended virtual interactions. Balanced use guidelines are essential in promoting responsible engagement. Recommendations for optimal durations and breaks, when integrated into Metaverse platforms, provide users with the tools to manage their virtual activities responsibly. Moreover, user empowerment through monitoring tools ensures individuals are equipped to make informed decisions about their Metaverse usage, fostering a sense of agency and control. Recognizing the physical health implications, the call for integrating physical activities within the Metaverse becomes crucial. Developers can play a transformative role in creating virtual environments that encourage movement and exercise, mitigating the sedentary behaviour associated with prolonged screen time. As policymakers consider regulatory measures, it is imperative that these measures evolve with ongoing research findings. A dynamic collaboration between researchers, policymakers, and industry stakeholders ensures that regulations remain relevant, balancing the potential of the Metaverse with user well-being. In essence, the research advocates for a conscientious and collaborative approach to the development and use of the Metaverse. By implementing these recommendations, we have the opportunity to shape a virtual space that enhances human well-being, fostering a healthy and sustainable relationship between individuals and emerging technologies.

REFERENCES

Fischer, L., & Wiswede, G. (1997). *Grundlagen der Sozialpsychologie*. Oldenbourg Verlag.

Harris, L. R., Carnevale, M. J., D'Amour, S., Fraser, L. E., Harrar, V., Hoover, A. E. N., Mander, C., & Pritchett, L. M. (2015). *How our body infuences our perception of the world*. Front Psycol. doi:10.3389/fpsyg.2015.00819

Henz, P. (2022). *The societal impact of the Metaverse*. Discov Artif Intell. doi:10.1007/s44163-022-00032-6

Statistia.com. (2021). *Average daily time spent by children in the United States on leading gaming apps from 2019*. Statista. www.stati sta.com/statistics/1249021/us-time-spent-by-children-on-gaming-apps/.

Statista.com. (2022a). *Daily active users (DAU) of Roblox games worldwide from the 4th quarter 2018 to 2nd quarter*. Statista. https://www.statista. com/statistics/1192573/daily-active-users-global-roblox/.

Statista.com. (2022b). *Average daily time spent on selected social networks by adults in the United States*. Statista. https:// www.statista.com/statistics/324267/us-adults-daily-facebook-minutes/.

Wiles, J. (2022). *What is a Metaverse? And should you be buying in?* Gartner. https://www.gartner.com/en/articles/what-is-a-metaverse

Chapter 15
Incorporating the Metaverse Into the Green Banking Revolution:
Spearheading the Implementation of Eco-Friendly Financial Practices

Sonal Devesh

https://orcid.org/0000-0002-2318-8670

School of Business and Management, Christ University, Yeshwanthpur Campus, Bangalore, India

Prasad Mahale

Srinivas University, India

Baranidharan Subburayan

https://orcid.org/0000-0002-7780-4045

School of Business and Management, Christ University, Bangalore, India

ABSTRACT

This study aims to explore the awareness and perceptions of green banking among bankers and customers in rural and semi-urban areas of India. A structured questionnaire was employed to gather information from 807 customers and 200 officials of selected commercial banks, utilizing the snowball sampling method. The study utilized chi-square and factor analysis techniques. The chi-square test results revealed an association between educational status and the customer's opinion regarding green banks. Factor analysis derived three key factors influencing the adoption of green banking: convenience and environmental sustainability, financial and technological advantages, and customer retention and prestige. The findings indicate that green banking services provide more benefits to its customers than traditional banking.

DOI: 10.4018/979-8-3693-3358-7.ch015

INTRODUCTION

The contemporary world places significant emphasis on economic development, but the unsustainable nature of this progress has had detrimental effects on biodiversity, climate, and the environment. The destructive consequences of recent global phenomena such as storms, floods, droughts, and extreme heat compel us to reflect deeply and take decisive action to address the issue of global warming (IDRBT, 2013). Many countries, including India, have pledged commitments to mitigate climate change, with a focus on sustainable development that meets the needs of the present generation without compromising those of future generations

Diverse sectors of the global economy confront a significant obstacle in addressing environmental issues and their ensuing effects on day-to-day operations. Environmental worth is not just recognized by businesses; consumers and the general public are becoming more conscious of these issues. In this setting, green banking—which aims to encourage environmentally friendly practices and lessen the carbon footprint connected with banking activities—emerges as a relatively recent trend in the financial sector. The establishment of a cleaner and more environmentally friendly future is the main goal of green banking, which takes into account the social and environmental consequences. The public's increasing expectations of banks to meet their environmental responsibilities, rising energy prices and consumption, growing consumer interest in eco-friendly goods and services, and the emergence of strict regulatory and compliance requirements are just a few of the reasons why banks are embracing green banking initiatives. Green banking can take many different forms. Some examples include choosing online banking over branch banking, paying bills online rather than via mail, selecting online banks for money market accounts and certificates of deposit, and endorsing local banks who are actively involved in environmental projects. According to a study by Sharma et al. (2022), technology is essential to the advancement of green banking in Indian private sector banks. Green banking refers to procedures and policies that make banks sustainable in terms of the social, environmental, and economic spheres. Its main goal is to improve banking procedures, information technology use, and physical infrastructure while reducing or completely eliminating environmental effect. Customers, bankers, and the economy as a whole are all said to benefit from the idea of green banking.

Materials and Methods

The research is conducted by reviewing literature on various aspects of green banking, including awareness, perception, benefits, strategies, products, services, processes, laws, guidelines, challenges, methods, and initiatives taken by public sector commercial banks. However, there is a notable gap in research focusing on the awareness and perceptions of stakeholders in the context of Green Banking, despite its significance in the economy. The study also observes that various directives and regulatory bodies have not emphasised awareness and perception on this subject. Policies and formal frameworks lack a foundation based on the awareness and perception of stakeholders, and training and development of relevant skills have not been adequately prioritized to enhance understanding. Additionally, there is a lack of relevant awareness programs initiated by authorities or banking institutions, and formal platforms for information sharing and dissemination are not well defined. The study makes recommendations that Reserve Bank of India should think about developing comprehensive and long-lasting policies to acknowledge the importance of green banking in India, after consulting with specialists and scholars. India's banking industry has experienced major changes and difficulties in the twenty-first century, including demonetization, digital banking, online banking, and bank mergers. The banking industry must be able to adjust to change in order to continue existing and expanding. In order to preserve the environment and natural resources, green banking—also known as ethical or sustainable banking—takes social, ecological, and environmental aspects into account. The first Green Bank was established in 2009 in Mount Dora, Florida, USA, which gave rise to the concept. The State Bank of India (SBI) launched its first wind farm project in Coimbatore in 2010 and was a pioneer in creating high sustainability standards in India. Sustainable finance involves incorporating environmental, social, and governance (ESG) factors into investment decisions within the financial sector. The study by Sharma et al. (2022) indicates that over 60 percent of respondents believe that green banking initiatives positively contribute to building customer confidence by enhancing the bank's green brand image. Another study by Parikh et al. (2023) supports the favorable influence of governance factors on equity returns, while environmental factors show an adverse effect. Social factors are deemed inconsequential, suggesting that financial incentives may be necessary to encourage corporations to adopt environmentally and socially responsible practices. Investing in renewable energy, facility upgrades, and adaptable technologies requires substantial financial resources but can lead to a reduction in carbon emissions and a shift away from fossil fuels. Some financial institutions have aligned their loan portfolios with the goals of the Paris Agreement. Stringent regulations in the banking sector prompt central banks and regulatory bodies to introduce collective green banking policies, influencing commercial banks to adopt environmentally friendly practices. This shift can help banks manage risk exposure, contribute to climate-related objectives, and aid economic recovery by channeling investment to climate sensitive sectors. Investing in renewable energy, facility upgrades, and adaptable technologies requires substantial financial resources but can lead to a reduction in carbon emissions and a shift away from fossil fuels. Some financial institutions have aligned their loan portfolios with the goals of the Paris

Agreement Stringent regulations in the banking sector prompt The Reserve Bank of India (IDRBT, 2013) states that the goal of green banking is to minimize the negative environmental effects of internal banking procedures, physical infrastructure, and information technology. Green banking is defined by Neyati Ahuja (2015) as the prudent use of resources, energy conservation, the reduction of carbon footprints, and the endorsement of only ecologically favorable investments. The capacity of banks to anticipate client expectations, particularly with regard to security and convenience is critical to the success of green efforts.

The objectives of this study are

- To examine the relationship between the education status of green banking customers and their perceptions of green banking services, with the aim of determining whether there exists a statistically significant association or if education level plays a negligible role in shaping their perceptions."
- To investigate and establish whether there exists a statistically significant association between individuals' educational status and their perceptions of green banking practices among bankers and customers.
- To ascertain whether there exists statistically significant relationship between the existence and usage of Automated Teller Machines (ATMs) and their impact on motivating customers to embrace green banking initiatives.

The Hypotheses formulated and tested as per the research objectives were the following.

- H1: There is significant association between education status and perception of green banking customers.
- H2: There is significant association between educational status and perception of green banking among bankers.

A structured survey instrument was employed to gather information from the population, which consisted of commercial banks in Uttara Kannada district, Karnataka. The data collection involved both customers and officials of the selected commercial banks. The validity of the questionnaire was ensured through evaluation by three subject-specialized staff members familiar with the topic. The reliability test, conducted using Cronbach's alpha yielded a a satisfactory score of 0.781.

The research adopted a cross-sectional study design with a quantitative approach. The data was collected through primary as well as secondary data. A structured questionnaire was used to collect the information.The population was commercial banks of Uttara Kannada district in Karnataka. The data was collected from customers of the selected commercial banks and the officials in the Bank. There are several public

Table 1. Distribution of the respondents based on banks

Banks	Customer (807)	Bankers (200)
Bank of Baroda	84(10.4%)	41(20.5%)
Bank of India	23(2.9%)	14(7%)
Canara Bank	125(15.5%)	26(13%)
Central Bank of India	13(1.6%)	9(4.5%)
Corporation Bank	54(6.7%)	24(12%)
IDBI	14(1.7%)	3(1.5%)
Indian Oversea Bank	25(3.1%)	9(4.5%)
State Bank of India	248(30.7%)	41(20.5%)
Syndicate Bank	221(27.4%)	33(16.5%)
Total	807(100%)	200(100%)

sector commercial banks in the Uttara Kannada district. The rationale for selecting the Uttara Kannada District is the existence of a well organized and large network of banks. A pilot study was used to find out the reliability of the questionnaire. The validity of the questionnaire was done by three staff members who were familiar and specialized in the subject. Reliability test conducted using Cronbachs alpha was 0.781 and reliability coefficient above 0.7 is considered as sufficient (George D. and Malley P, 2003). Cross sectional study design with a quantitative approach was used for the study. There were several banks in Uttara Kannada district.Out of which, nine important banks were selected in and around Uttara Kannada by purposive sampling method. A total of 807 questionnaires were collected from the customers and 200 officials out of the distributed questionnaires to 1100 customers and 260 officials with a response rate was 80% for customers and 81% of officials. Secondary data was used to collect information regarding the banks.

Table 1 depicts 30.7 percent of the customers were from the State bank of India and 20.5 percent of the bankers from the same bank. 27.4 percent of customers were taken from Syndicate bank and 20.5 percent of the staff from the same bank. Further, 10.4 percent of customers were from Bank of Baroda with 20.5 percent bankers. Bank of India had the least(2.9 percent) of customers and Indian overseas banks had the least bankers

RESULTS

The study employed descriptive statistics, including the calculation of mean and standard deviation, as well as inferential statistics such as the Chi-square test and factor analysis. The Chi-square test was utilized to examine the association between demographic, social, and economic factors and the adoption of green banking. Factor analysis was applied to identify the underlying factors influencing green banking. Likewise, logistic regression was employed to determine the primary factors affecting green banking. Additionally, analysis of variance (ANOVA) was conducted to assess the significance of the means of these factors. The statistical software package SPSS 23.0 was utilized for the data analysis.

Table 2 highlights that among the 200 bankers, 83 percent of them, possessing higher educational qualifications of graduation and postgraduation, showed a preference for green banking. Specifically, 54.3 percent of graduates considered it essential, while 45.7 percent deemed it vital. Similarly, among postgraduates, 51.4 percent perceived it as both vital and essential, with the remaining 48.6 percent finding it desirable. Conversely, among customers with primary and secondary education, nearly 8 percent were uninterested in green banking, along with 6.1 percent of postgraduates. On the other hand, approximately 70 percent of those with higher education believed that green banking should exist. The chi-square test was employed to explore the association between educational status and the opinions of both customers and bankers regarding green banks. The results indicated a discernible difference in the opinions of customers, showing a significant association ($p < 0.001$). In contrast, bankers did not exhibit a substantial difference in their opinions ($p = 0.298$).

Table 2. Perception about adoption of green banking based on education status

		Primary	Secondary	Higher Secondary	Graduate	PostGraduate	Chi Square	p value	Result
Customer	Vital	8(21.1%)	17(22.1%)	57(22.7%)	73(23.5%)	32(24.4%)	39.886	p<0.001	significant
	Essential	27(71.1%)	52(67.5%)	181(72.1%)	216(69.7%)	79(60.3%)			
	Desirable	2(5.3%)	2(2.6%)	12(4.8%)	21(6.7%)	27(15.3%)			
	Not needed	1(2.5%)	6(7.8%)	1(0.4%)	10(3.2%)	8(6.1%)			
Bankers	Vital	1(100%)	8(61.5%)	6(30%)	59(45.7%)	19(51.4%)	4.901	p>0.001	Not Significant
	Essential	0(0%)	5(38.5%)	14(70%)	70(54.3%)	19(51.4%)			
	Desirable	0(0%)	0(0%)	0(0%)	0(0%)	18(48.6%)			
	Not needed	0(0%)	0(0%)	0(0%)	0(0%)	0(0%)			

Source: Author Calculation

Table 3. Perception about adoption of green banking based on education status

		Primary	Secondary	Higher Secondary	Graduate	PostGraduate	Chi Square	p value	Result
Customer	Vital	8(21.1%)	17(22.1%)	57(22.7%)	73(23.5%)	32(24.4%)	39.886	p<0.001	Highly significant
	Essential	27(71.1%)	52(67.5%)	181(72.1%)	216(69.7%)	79(60.3%)			
	Desirable	2(5.3%)	2(2.6%)	12(4.8%)	21(6.7%)	27(15.3%)			
	Not needed	1(2.5%)	6(7.8%)	1(0.4%)	10(3.2%)	8(6.1%)			
Bankers	Vital	1(100%)	8(61.5%)	6(30%)	59(45.7%)	19(51.4%)	4.901	p>0.001	Not Significant
	Essential	0(0%)	5(38.5%)	14(70%)	70(54.3%)	19(51.4%)			
	Desirable	0(0%)	0(0%)	0(0%)	0(0%)	18(48.6%)			
	Not needed	0(0%)	0(0%)	0(0%)	0(0%)	0(0%)			

Source: Author Calculation

Table 3 advocates among the 200 bankers, 83 percent of them having higher educational status of graduation and postgraduation preferred green bank. 54.3 percent of graduates perceived that it is essential and 45.7 percent told its vital. Similarly, among postgraduates, 51.4 percent perceived it is vital and essential and the remaining 48.6 percent were desirable. However, among the Customers with primary and secondary education, nearly 8 percent of people were not interested in green banking along with 6.1 percent of postgraduates also against green banking. Whereas nearly 70 percent of those having higher education felt that green banking should exist. The chi square test was used to find the association between educational status. and the Customer's and banker's opinion regarding green banks. The results showcased there was some difference in the opinion hence it shows significant association(p<0.001). whereas the Bankers does not have much difference in their opinion (p=0.298)

The Table 4 reflects on the relationship between the perception of customers on the usefulness of green banking to save environment based on education status. Nearly

Table 4. Green banking is useful to save the environment from pollution based on education status

		Primary	Secondary	Higher Secondary	Graduate	PostGraduate	Chi Square	p value	Result
Customer	Yes	31(81.1%)	60(77.9%)	214(85.3%)	253(81.6%)	102(77.9%)	4.399	p>0.001	Not Significant
	No	7(18.9%)	17(22.1%)	37(14.7%)	57(18.4%)	29(22.1%)			
Bankers	Yes	1(100%)	13(100%)	20(100%)	122(94.6%)	37(100%)	3.992	p>0.001	Not Significant
	No	0(0%)	0(0%)	0(0%)	7(5.4%)	0(0%)			

Source: Author calculation

Table 5. Services–rotated component matrix

	Component		
	1	**2**	**3**
Green banking services have no time limit since I can use them at any time of the day	.804	.039	.026
Green banking services make the payment easy	.766	.077	.106
It reduces the use of paper and carbon footprint	.738	.173	.057
There is a high degree of convenience in green banking as you can access the banking services from anywhere	.732	.119	-.051
Ease of transferring the funds	.725	.044	.201
Green banking may help in avoiding many risks like robbery in the physical handling of a large amount of cash	.673	.046	-.081
Green banking helps in environmental sustainability	.622	.131	-.295
Green banking services are generally faster than traditional banking which helps customers to avoid long queue in the bank's hall	.433	.302	-.056
Green banking avoids repetitive investment in machinery and equipments	.053	.774	.036
Green banking goes hand in hand with technological advancement	.190	.711	-.157
Green banking services are more profitable than traditional banking service	-.102	.671	.278
Green banking services are generally cheaper than traditional banking	.370	.425	-.012
Adopting green banking helps in retaining more customers	.253	.259	.698
Using green banking services is more prestigious	.266	.440	-.555

Source: Author Calculation Rotation Method: Varimax with Kaiser Normalization.

80% of the customers perceived that green banking was useful to save pollution. Whereas among Bankers most of them(nearly 100%) said that green banking was useful to save pollution. These results prove that education had no impact on their perception. The chi square results indicated that association between education and the perception that green banking saves pollution has no significance.

The factor analysis derived three factors.. The first factor consists of 8 items, the second factor consists of 4 items and the third factor comprised of two items. By using the varimax rotated component matrix, the three factors with all the 14 questions related to the importance to adopt green banking.The first factor was identified as convenience and environmental sustainability, second factor as financial and technological advantages of green banking the third as customer retention and prestige

With the help of the factor analysis, we have taken the some of concerned questions in each factor and its descriptive statistics were given as Mean and Standard deviation. Here we wanted to compare the means of each factor with gender and we could see

Table 6. ANOVA results

	Male		Female		t	p	Result
	Mean	**SD**	**Mean**	**SD**			
Customers							
convenience and environmental sustainability	12.188	5.052	11.707	5.365	1.305	0.192	Insignificant
financial and technological advantages	8.386	2.402	8.061	2.333	1.934	0.053	Insignificant
customer retention and prestige	4.185	1.251	4.089	1.223	1.096	0.274	Insignificant
Bankers							
convenience and environmental sustainability	14.731	3.067	14.691	3.741	0.078	0.938	Insignificant
financial and technological advantages	7.828	2.063	7.727	1.822	0.317	0.752	Insignificant
customer retention and prestige	3.889	1.253	3.746	1.075	0.754	0.452	Insignificant

Source: Author's calculation

that gender-wise there was not much difference in the mean score of these factors. The mean score of convenience and environmental sustainability of males among customers was 12.188 whereas that of females was 11.707, hence the difference was not significant($p > 0.001$).Similarly, there was no significant difference in the mean score of financial and technological advantages and customer retention and prestige among the customers. Among the bankers, most of them were for adopting of green banking inferring gender-wise mean score was somewhat similar in the two groups. In convenience and environmental sustainability, the mean score of males was 14.731, and that of females was 14.691 with no significant difference($p > 0.001$). Further, genderwise mean score of financial and technological advantages and customer retention and prestige was also the same. Thus proving difference between the mean value of the factors across gender was found to be insignificant ($p > 0.05$).

DISCUSSION

Most of the customers use debit card service given by the banks and they are having good knowledge about the same when compared to other services. Banks, in response to the increased demand for digital transactions post-demonetization, may promote and expand their green banking services.

The results of the chi square test indicates that there is a relationship between the education status of customers on adoption of green banking.Therefore accepting

H1. However when it comes to bankers it was found that there is no relationship between education status and adoption of green banking. Thus accepting H2,

The results of the factor analysis derieved three factors influencing the adoption of green banking. Further using an unpaired t-test to make the comparison of these three factors accross gender, it was observed that there was no significant difference between the mean values for males and females both in customers and bankers.

CONCLUSION

In today's society, the topic of green banking is essential and becoming more and more important. The study demonstrates that an individual's educational background has little bearing on whether or not they decide to utilize digital banking. The term "green banking" describes the approach of doing banking business with an emphasis on social responsibility and environmental sustainability. It entails establishing green investments, enacting eco-friendly policies, and lowering the carbon footprint of banking operations. It is evident from the aforementioned analysis that bank clients are not entirely aware of Green Banking's offerings. Nonetheless, the majority of bank staff members are informed about the Green Banking service and its offerings. The study shows that one factor contributing to the poor uptake of green banking services among clients is a lack of knowledge about the process involved in using these products. It is important to remember that the RBI has already published several recommendations on green banking services, including those pertaining to payment methods, project finance, and bank investments that are environmentally beneficial. Even so, not every customer has received the same. Furthermore, the majority of banks do not inform their clientele about the advantages of using green banking.

Furthermore, it is evident from the analysis that consumers' opinions of green banking services are not entirely favorable. Customers continue to be afraid to engage in green banking activities because they believe that doing so is not safe and is readily hackable by anyone. They also feel uneasy because they don't trust e-services and believe that their information could be exploited. However, from the analysis, it is clear that green Banking services provide more benefits to its customers than traditional banking. In conclusion, it may be stated that with green banking, it is certain that the Indian banking industry is all set to unleash its potential to pave the way for transforming India into a modern, digital, paperless, fraud-free, and green India.

The integration of the metaverse in green banking has the potential to revolutionize the way financial institutions operate and interact with customers while promoting sustainability and environmentally responsible practices. An omnichannel approach to co-creating customer experiences through metaverse platforms involves seamlessly integrating various communication and interaction channels within the metaverse to provide a cohesive and immersive experience for customers. This approach leverages the metaverse, a virtual, interconnected, and shared digital universe, to engage customers across multiple touchpoints, both in the virtual and physical worlds. Green banking services are very much useful as it avoids respective investment on machinery and equipment.Banks can establish virtual branches or offices within the metaverse. These branches can provide customers with immersive, interactive, and personalized banking experiences. By reducing the need for physical branches and the associated energy consumption, this approach can help banks reduce their carbon footprint.Banks can create virtual spaces within the metaverse where customers can explore and invest in green and sustainable projects. These portals can provide information on renewable energy, eco-friendly startups, and other sustainable investment opportunities.

The government of India should make sufficient allocation of all funds for green banking activities and thereby motivate the banking industry to implement new green banking initiatives.The Internet of Things (IoT) plays a significant role in the omnichannel strategy by connecting physical devices and sensors. In the metaverse, IoT devices can extend this connectivity to virtual environments. For example, customers' biometric data from wearables might influence their avatars' behavior and health in the metaverse.

This study has presented some important comprehensions on green banking which comprises some limitations that need to be acknowledged. The present study focuses on customers and bankers of 11 talukas of Uttara Kannada districts only. In the coming days, the research can be undertaken considering many districts altogether or there is a scope for making comparative study as well between any districts. Here in this study, the samples taken for the study comprises only selected Public Sector Commercial Bank branches operating in Uttara Kannada district. Hence, other banks such as Rural Banks, Urban Cooperative Banks, District Cooperative Banks, Primary Land Development Bank and Industrial Banks operating in the district can be taken into consideration for further study.

The awareness and perception of bankers and customers of only limited banks are studied in the present research. There is a huge scope to study the bankers and customers of other banks.Since the study is based on the perception of the bank employees there are differences in the views and perception. Hence, future research may concentrate on bank managers, in particular, all over India to get a more comprehensive picture of usage and benefits of green banking service.

Acknowledgments: We would like to thank the banks for permitting us to conduct the study

Conflict of Interests: The authors declare no conflict of interest.

REFERENCES

European Commmission. (n.d.). *Finance*. EC. https://finance.ec.europa.eu/sustainable-finance/overview-sustainable-finance_en

McKinsey. (n.d.). *Banking imperatices for managing climate risk*. McKinsey. https://www.mckinsey.com/capabilities/risk-and-resilience/our-insights/banking-imperatives-for-managing-climate-risk#/

Science Direct. (n.d.). *The Impace of envionrmental, social, and ogverance score on shareholder weatlth*. Science Direct. https://www.sciencedirect.com/science/article/pii/S2666784323000025

Ashis, C. K. (2014). Green Banking Practices In Indian Banks. *Blue Square Publishing House, 1*, 41–54.

Chandra, B. (2010). Green Banking-Towards socially responsible banking in India. *IJBIT, 4*(1).

District Disaster Management Plan – 2019. 1, 01-199.

George, D., & Mallery, P. (2003). *SPSS for Windows step by step: A simple guide and reference. 11.0 update* (4th ed.). Allyn & Bacon.

Goyal, K. A., & Joshi, V. (2011). A Study of Social and Ethical Issues In Banking Industry. *International Journal Of Economics*, 5, 49–57.

Green Bank Academy. (2014). Report on Green Bank in Washington DC. Green Bank Academy.

Gulshan, M. (2015). Green Banking: An Initiative for Sustainable Economic and Environmental Development. *An online interdisciplinary, multidisciplinary & multi-cultural, 4*(3), 36-47.

Herath, H. M. A. K., & Herath, H. M. S. P. (2022). Impact of green banking initiatives on customer satisfaction. *IOSR Journal of Business and Management, 24*(7), 1–19.

IDRBT (2013). Green banking for the Indian banking sector. *Report of RBI, IDRBT Publication*, 1-20. IDRBT.

Iyyanki, Muralikrishna, & Vallimanickam. (2017). Sustainable development. *Science and engineering for industry*, 5-21. Environmental management. doi:10.1016/B978-0-12-811989-1.00002-6

Kanak, T., Saumya, S., & Ritesh, K. (2015). Green Banking For Environmental Management: A Paradigm Shift. *Current World Environment, 10*(3), 1029–1038. doi:10.12944/CWE.10.3.36

Masukujjaman, M., Siwar, C., Mahmud, M. R., & Alam, S. S. (2017). Bankers' perception of green banking: Learning from the experience of Islamic banks in Bangladesh. *Geografa-Malaysian Journal of Society Space, 12*(2).

Meenakshi, S. (2016). Green Computing – A Cloud-Based Architecture for Green Banking. *International Journal of Innovative Research in Computer and Communication Engineering, 4*(5), 8534–8537.

Michael, R. (1994). At what Point can pollution be said to cause damage to the Environment? *The Banker*.

Mir, A. A., & Bhat, A. A. (2022). Green banking and sustainability – a review. *Arab Gulf Journal of Scientific Research, 40*(3), 247–263. doi:10.1108/AGJSR-04-2022-0017

Nanda, S. & Chandra, S. (2012). Profitability in Banks of India: An Impact Study of Implementation of Green Banking. *International Journal of Green Economics, 6*(3), 217-225.

Nath, V., Nayak, N., & Goel, A. (2014). Green Banking Practices- A Review. *International Journal of Research in Business Management, 2*(4), 45–62.

Neyati, A. (2015). Green Banking in India: A Review Of Literature. *International Journal for research in management and pharmacy, 4*, 11-16.

Nigamananda, B. (2011). Sustainable Green Banking: The Need of The Hour. *Busines Spectrum., 1*, 32–38.

Parikh, A., Kumari, D., Johann, M., & Mladenović, D. (2023). ohann,M., Mladenović,D.(2023). The impact of environmental, social and governance score on shareholder wealth: A new dimension in investment philosophy. *Cleaner and Responsible Consumption, 8*, 100101. doi:10.1016/j.clrc.2023.100101

Park, H., & Kim, J. D. (2020). Transition towards green banking: Role of financial regulators and financial institutions. *AJSSR, 5*(1), 5. doi:10.1186/s41180-020-00034-3

Rahman Mahfuzur,, M. S. (2016). The Design and Adoption of Green Banking Framework For Environment Protection: Lessons From Bangladesh. *Australian Journal of Sustainable Business and Society, 2*(1), 1–19.

Rajesh, T., & Dileep, A. S. (2014). Role of Banks in Sustainable Economic development through Green Banking. *International Journal of Current Research and Academic Review, 2*, 136–141.

Rakesh, D, Srinath, V.B., & Karki, R Naveen. (2016). Green Banking: A Conceptual Study on its Issues, Challenges, and Sustainable Growth in India. [IJAIEM]. *International Journal of Application or Innovation in Engineering & Management, 5*(6), 41–46.

Ruchi. (2014). Green banking: a case study of IndusInd bank. *International journal of business and general management (IJBGM), 3*(3), 13-18.

Pravakar, S. & Bibhu, N. (2008). *Green Banking in India.* India Envornmental Portal. http://admin.indiaenvironmentalportal.ord.in/files/green%20b anking.pdf

Sanjoy, P., & Aminul, R. H. (2015). Advancement of green banking layout and trend in Bangladesh. International Journal of Economics. *Commerce and Management, 3*(11), 1160–1182.

Sarita, B. (2012). Green Banking- The New Strategic Imperative. *Journal of Asian Research Consortium, 2*(2), 176–185.

Sharma, M., & Choubey, A. (2022). Green banking initiatives: A qualitative study on Indian banking sector. *Environment, Development and Sustainability, 24*(1), 293–319. doi:10.1007/s10668-021-01426-9 PMID:33967597

Sharma N, Sarika, & Gopal, R. (2014). A Study on Customer's Awareness On Green Banking Initiatives In Selected Public And Private Sector Banks With Special Reference To Mumbai. *IOSR Journal of Economics and Finance, 2,* 28-35.

Shrivastave, P., & Berger, S. (2010). Sustainability principles: A review and directions. *Organizational Management Journal, 7*(4), 246–261. doi:10.1057/omj.2010.35

Shruti, G. (2015). Green Banking: An Overview. *Global Journal of Advanced Research, 2*(8), 1291–1296.

Urvashi, S., Laxmi, L., & Prateek, B. (2014). Sustainability in Indian Banking Industry. *International Journal of Commerce and Business Management, 3*(1), 220–229.

Velan Sakthi Sree, M. (2011). E-Banking Practices In Selected Scheduled Commercial Banks. Department International Business And Commerce Alagappa University.

Yadav, R., & Pathak, G. (2013). Environmental Sustainability through Green Banking: A Study on Private and Public Sector Bank in India. *OIDA International Journal of Sustainable Development, 6*(08), 37–48.

Compilation of References

Abu Dhabi National Oil Company. (2019). ADNOC and Total to Use Unmanned Drones and Vehicles in Seismic Acquisition. Abu Dhabi National Oil Company.

Abumalloh, R. A., Nilashi, M., Ooi, K., Wei-Han, G., Cham, T., Dwivedi, Y. K., & Hughes, L. (2023). Adopting a metaverse in the retail industry and its impact on sustainable competitive advantage: Moderating impact of sustainability commitment. *Annals of Operations Research*. doi:10.1007/s10479-023-05608-8

Aburbeian, A. M., Owda, A. Y., & Owda, M. (2022). A technology acceptance model survey of the metaverse prospects. *AI*, *3*(2), 285–302. doi:10.3390/ai3020018

Acton, T., Gao, J., Jamshidi, L., & Meng, Y. (2022). Metaverse: Opportunities, growth factors, and the future. *Journal of Management Analytics*, 1-18. https://doi.org/ doi:10.1080/23270012 .2022.2024724

Adams, D. (2022). Virtual retail in the metaverse: Customer behavior analytics, extended reality technologies, and immersive visualization systems. *Linguistic and Philosophical Investigations*, (21), 73–88.

Adams, D. (2022). Virtual Retail in the Metaverse: Customer Behavior Analytics, Extended Reality Technologies, and Immersive Visualization Systems. *Linguistic and Philosophical Investigations*, *21*(0), 73–88. doi:10.22381/lpi2120225

Agates, N.A.H., M. Fleischmann, & J.J.A.E.E. Van Nunen. (2008)/ E-fulfillment and multi-channel distribution—a review. *European Journal of Operational Research*, *187*(2), 339–356.

Aggarwal, A., Chand, P. K., Jhamb, D., & Mittal, A. (2020). Leader–Member Exchange, Work Engagement, and Psychological Withdrawal Behavior: The Mediating Role of Psychological Empowerment. *Frontiers in Psychology*, *11*(423), 423. doi:10.3389/fpsyg.2020.00423 PMID:32296361

Agustini, K., Putrama, I. M., Wahyuni, D. S., & Mertayasa, I. N. E. (2023). Applying gamification technique and virtual reality for prehistoric learning toward the metaverse. *International Journal of Information and Education Technology (IJIET)*, *13*(2), 247–256. doi:10.18178/ijiet.2023.13.2.1802

Alcañíz, M., Bigné, E., & Guixeres, J. (2019). Virtual Reality in Marketing: A Framework, review, and Research agenda. *Frontiers in Psychology, 10*, 1530. doi:10.3389/fpsyg.2019.01530 PMID:31333548

Alcantara, A. C., & Michalack, D. L. (2022). The Metaverse Narrative in the Matrix Resurrections: A Semiotic analysis through costumes. In Springer series in design and innovation (pp. 260–268). Springer. doi:10.1007/978-3-031-09659-4_20

Alfaisal, R., Hashim, H., & Azizan, U. H. (2022). Metaverse system adoption in education: A systematic literature review. *Journal of Computers n. Education.* doi:10.107/s40692-022-00256-6

Alkhudary, R., Belvaux, B., & Guibert, N. (2022). Understanding non-fungible tokens (NFTs): Insights on consumption practices and a research agenda. *Marketing Letters, 34*(2), 321–336. https://doi.org/ doi:10.10 7/s11002-022-09655-2

Allal-Chérif, O. (2022). Intelligent cathedrals: Using augmented reality, virtual reality, and artificial intelligence to provide an intense cultural, historical, and religious visitor experience. *Technological Forecasting and Social Change, 178*, 121604. doi:10.1016/j.techfore.2022.121604

Allam, Z., Sharifi, A., Bibri, S. E., Jones, D. S., & Krogstie, J. (2022). The metaverse as a virtual form of smart cities: Opportunities and challenges for environmental, economic, and social sustainability in urban futures. *Smart Cities, 5*(3), 771–801. doi:10.3390/smartcities5030040

Alliance News. (2023). *India Metaverse Market 2023 Industry Overview, Key Technology, Segments, SWOT Analysis, and Forecast Research 2031*. Report Ocean. https://www.barchart. com/story/news/19089545/india-metaverse-market-2023-industry-overview-key-technology-segments-swot-analysis-and-forecast-research-2031

Almusaed, A., Yitmen, I., & Almssad, A. (2023). Reviewing and integrating aec practices into industry 6.0: Strategies for smart and sustainable future-built environments. *Sustainability (Basel), 15*(18), 13464. doi:10.3390/su151813464

Al-Walaie, S. A., Bahwal, O. B., & Alduayj, S. S. (2021). Emerging Robotic Technologies for Oil and Gas Operations. *Journal of Petroleum Technology*, 1944–978X.

Anand, J. (2023, January). Budget 2023 expectations: What does the Indian metaverse space seek from the policymakers? *India Today*. https://www.indiatoday.in/cryptocurrency/ story/budget-2023-expectations-what-does-the-indian-metaverse-space-seek-from-the-policymakers-2327111-2023-01-27

Anisetti, M., Ardagna, C., Bellandi, V., Cremonini, M., Frati, F., & Damiani, E. (2018). Privacy-aware Big Data Analytics as a service for public health policies in smart cities. *Sustainable Cities and Society, 39*, 68–77. doi:10.1016/j.scs.2017.12.019

Anshari, M., Syafrudin, M., Fitriyani, N. L., & Razzaq, A. (2022). Ethical Responsibility and Sustainability (ERS) Development in a Metaverse Business Model. *Sustainability (Basel), 14*(23), 15805. doi:10.3390/su142315805

Ante, L., Wazinski, F. P., & Saggu, A. (2023). Digital real estate in the metaverse: An empirical analysis of retail investor motivations. *Finance Research Letters*, *58*, 104299. doi:10.1016/j.frl.2023.104299

Aritonang, J. (2023, July 21). Deepfakes in the metaverse: Challenges, opportunities, and the road ahead. *Medium*. https://medium.com/@aritonangjoshua95/deepfakes-in-the-metaverse-challenges-opportunities-and-the-road-ahead-e012e83473ed

Arntsen, R. (2023). *The Future People's Sense of Belonging in The City* (Doctoral dissertation, The Savannah College of Art and Design).

Arslan, I. K. (2020). The importance of creating customer loyalty in achieving sustainable competitive advantage. *Eurasian Journal of Business and Management*, *8*(1), 11–20. doi:10.15604/ejbm.2020.08.01.002

Asare, C., Majeed, M., & Cole, N. A. (2022). Omnichannel Integration Quality, Perceived Value, and Brand Loyalty in the Consumer Electronics Market: The Mediating Effect of Consumer Personality. In *Advances in Information Communication Technology and Computing* [Springer.]. *Proceedings of AICTC, 2021*, 29–45.

Asea Brown Boveri. (2022). *ABB Robot Studio takes to the cloud, enabling real-time collaboration.* Asea Brown Boveri.

Ashis, C. K. (2014). Green Banking Practices In Indian Banks. *Blue Square Publishing House*, *1*, 41–54.

Autio, E., & Fu, K. (2015). Economic and political institutions and entry into formal and informal entrepreneurship. *Asia Pacific Journal of Management*, *32*(1), 67–94. doi:10.1007/s10490-014-9381-0

Aydoğan, S. (2023). Connecting Sustainable Development Goals To Airport Sustainability Practices. *The Sdgs And Entrepreneurship*, 282.

Azhari, J. E., & Benett, D. (2015). Omni-channel customer experience: An investigation into the use of digital technology in physical stores and its impact on consumers' decision-making process. *XXIV AEDEM International Conference*. IEEE.

Babu, M. U. A., & Mohan, P. (2022). Impact of the metaverse on the digital future: people's perspective. *2022 7th International Conference on Communication and Electronics Systems (ICCES)*, (pp. 1576–1581). IEEE.

Bagchi, S. (2023, October 9). Enterprise use cases set to drive metaverse momentum. *Mint*. https://www.livemint.com/companies/news/enterprise-use-cases-set-to-drive-metaverse-momentum-11696867750783.html

Bandyopadhyay, A., Sarkar, A., Swain, S., Banik, D., Hassanien, A. E., Mallik, S., Li, A., & Qin, H. (2023). A Game-Theoretic Approach for Rendering Immersive Experiences in the Metaverse. *Mathematics*, *11*(6), 1286. doi:10.3390/math11061286

Banerjee, M. (2019). Development of Omni channel in India: Retail Landscape, Drivers and Challenges. In W. Piotrowicz & R. Cuthbertson (Eds.), *Exploring Omni channel Retailing.* Springer. doi:10.1007/978-3-319-98273-1_6

Basker, E. (2016). The evolution of technology in the retail sector. *Handbook on the Economics of Retailing and Distribution*, (pp. 38–53). Springer.

Basu, T. (2022, February 4). The metaverse has a groping problem already. *MIT Technology Review.* https://www.technologyreview.com/2021/12/16/1042516/the-metaverse-has-a-groping-problem/

Belk, R. (2023). The digital frontier as a liminal space. *Journal of Consumer Psychology.*

Belk, R. W. (2013). Extended self in a digital world. *The Journal of Consumer Research, 40*(3), 477–500. doi:10.1086/671052

Bell, B. D. R., Gallino, S., & Moreno, A. (2014). How to Win in an Omni-channel World. MIT Sloan Management Review, 56(1), 45–54.

Benjamins, R., Viñuela, Y. R., & Alonso, C. (2023). Social and ethical challenges of the metaverse. *AI and Ethics, 3*(3), 689–697. doi:10.1007/s43681-023-00278-5

Benke, K., & Benke, G. (2018). Artificial intelligence and big data in public health. *International Journal of Environmental Research and Public Health, 15*(12), 2796. doi:10.3390/ijerph15122796 PMID:30544648

Betancourt, R. R. (2016). *Distribution services, technological change and the evolution of retailing and distribution in the twenty-first century. Handbook on the Economics of Retailing and Distribution.* Edward Elgar Publishing.

Bhardwaj, S. (2022). Indian companies storm the metaverse and NFT space. *Forbes India.* https://www.forbesindia.com/article/crypto-made-easy/indian-companies-storm-the-metaverse-and-nft-space/75281/1

Bibri, S. E., & Allam, Z. (2022). The Metaverse as a virtual form of data-driven smart cities: The ethics of the hyper-connectivity, datafication, algorithmization, and platformization of urban society. *Computational Urban Science, 2*(1), 22. doi:10.1007/s43762-022-00050-1 PMID:35915731

Biocca, F., & Levy, M. R. (1995). Virtual reality as a communication system. *Communication in the age of virtual reality,* 15-31.

Biocca, F., Harms, C., & Burgoon, J. K. (2003). Toward a more robust theory and measure of social presence: Review and suggested criteria. *Presence (Cambridge, Mass.), 12*(5), 456–480. doi:10.1162/105474603322761270

BL Bengaluru Bureau. (2023, April 26). Indian business executives keen to integrate the metaverse in organisational activities: PwC report. *The Hindu Business Line.* https://www.thehindubusinessline.com/companies/indian-business-executives-keen-to-integrate-the-metaverse-in-organisational-activities-pwc-report/article66781335.ece

Boehm, M. (2008). Determining the impact of Internet channel use on a customer's lifetime. *Journal of Interactive Marketing, 22*(3).

Boston Dynamics. (2020). *British Petroleum uses SPOT to improve Safety and efficiency offshore.* Boston Dynamics.

Botha, A., Bussin, M., & De Swardt, L. (2011). An employer brand predictive model for talent attraction and retention. *SA Journal of Human Resource Management, 9*(1), 1–12. doi:10.4102/sajhrm.v9i1.388

Bourlakis, M., Papagiannidis, S., & Li, F. (2009). Retail spatial evolution: Paving the way from traditional to metaverse retailing. *Electronic Commerce Research, 9*(1-2), 135–148. doi:10.1007/s10660-009-9030-8

Bradley, S., Kim, C., Kim, J., & Lee, I. (2012). Toward an evolution strategy for the digital goods business. *Management Decision, 50*(2), 234–252. doi:10.1108/00251741211203542

British Petroleum. (2020). *Aker BP explores the use of robots in the offshore oil and gas industry.* British Petroleum.

Brooks, R. (2023, August 17). *What is reinforcement learning?* University of York. https://online.york.ac.uk/what-is-reinforcement-learning/

Brooks, T. (2023). Increasing threat of Deepfake Identities. Homeland Security.

Brynjolfsson, E., Hu, Y. J., & Rahman, M. S. (2013). Competing in the Age of Omni-channel Retailing. MIT Sloan Management Review, 54(4), 23–29.

Buana, I. (2023, June 30). *Metaverse: Threat or opportunity for our social world? in understanding metaverse on sociological context.* Journal of Metaverse. https://dergipark.org.tr/en/pub/jmv/issue/72588/1144470

Buhalis, D., Lin, M., & Leung, D. (2022). Metaverse as a driver for customer experience and value co-creation: Implications for hospitality and tourism management and marketing. *International Journal of Contemporary Hospitality Management, 35*(2), 701–716. doi:10.1108/IJCHM-05-2022-0631

Bureau of Labor Statistics. (2022). *Job openings and labor turnover summary.* BLS. https://www.bls.gov/news.release/jolts.nr0.htm

Business Insider. (2022). How marketing and advertising is shaping the Metaverse. *Business Insider.*

Calvo, A. V., Franco, A. D., & Frasquet, M. (2023). The role of artificial intelligence in improving the omnichannel customer experience. *International Journal of Retail & Distribution Management, 51*(9/10), 1174–1194. doi:10.1108/IJRDM-12-2022-0493

Cao, Z., Leng, J., Liu, T., & Yin, C. (2022). Effects of VR retail training on retail employees' job performance and work engagement. *Virtual Reality (Waltham Cross),* 1–15. doi:10.1007/s10055-022-00678-7

Carpenter, J. P., & Green, M. C. (2017). Working with social media influencers to promote physical activity. *Journal of Sport Management, 31*(5), 477–483.

Castronova, E. (2005). *Synthetic Worlds: The Business and Culture of Online Games.* University of Chicago Press.

Chandra, B. (2010). Green Banking-Towards socially responsible banking in India. *IJBIT, 4*(1).

Chang, V. (2018). Data analytics and visualization for inspecting cancers and genes. *Multimedia Tools and Applications, 77*(14), 17693–17707. doi:10.1007/s11042-017-5186-8

Chatterjee, N. (2016). *Indian consumers moving towards the Omni channel way of shopping: PwC.*

Chen, Z., Wu, J., Gan, W., & Qi, Z. (2022, December). Metaverse security and privacy: An overview. In *2022 IEEE International Conference on Big Data (Big Data)* (pp. 2950-2959). IEEE.

Cheng, R., Chen, S., & Han, B. (2023). Towards zero-trust security for the metaverse. *IEEE Communications Magazine,* 1–7. doi:10.1109/MCOM.018.2300095

Cheng, X., Zhang, S., Fu, S., Liu, W., Guan, C., Mou, J., Ye, Q., & Huang, C. (2022). Exploring the metaverse in the digital economy: An overview and research framework. *Journal of Electronic Business & Digital Economics, 1*(1/2), 206–224. doi:10.1108/JEBDE-09-2022-0036

Chen, L., Chen, P., & Lin, Z. (2020). Artificial Intelligence in Education: A Review. *IEEE Access : Practical Innovations, Open Solutions, 8,* 75264–75278. doi:10.1109/ACCESS.2020.2988510

Chen, Y., & Cheng, H. (2022). The economics of the metaverse: A comparison with the real economy. *Metaverse, 3*(1), 19. doi:10.54517/met.v3i1.1802

ChenY.LinW.ZhengY.XueT.ChenC.ChenG. (2022). Application of active learning strategies in metaverse to improve student engagement: An immersive blended pedagogy bridging patient care and scientific inquiry in pandemic. Available at SSRN 4098179. doi:10.2139/ssrn.4098179

Cho, J., Dieck, M. C. T., & Jung, T. (2023). What is the metaverse? Challenges, opportunities, definition, and future research directions. In Springer Proceedins in Business and Economics (pp. 3–26). Springer. doi:10.1007/978-3-031-25390-4_1

Cho, J., tom Dieck, M. C., & Jung, T. (2022). What is the Metaverse? Challenges, Opportunities, Definition, and Future Research Directions. *International XR Conference,* (pp. 3–26). Research Gate.

Chourasia, S., Tyagi, A., Pandey, S., Walia, R. & Murtaza, Q. (2022). Sustainability of Industry 6.0 in Global Perspective: Benefits and Challenges. *MAPAN, 37.* . doi:10.1007/s12647-022-00541-w

Chowdhury, S., Schnabel, M. A., & Lo, T. (2023). Editorial: Metaverse in co-virtual city design. *Frontiers in Virtual Reality, 4,* 1166107. doi:10.3389/frvir.2023.1166107

Chua, C. E. H., Straub, D. W., Khoo, H. M., & Kadiyala, S. (2005). The evolution of e-commerce research: A stakeholder perspective. *Journal of Electronic Commerce Research, 6*(4).

Concept: Subpopulation analysis. (n.d.). Dataiku Knowledge Base. https://knowledge.dataiku.com/latest/ml-analytics/model-results/concept-subpopulation-analysis.html

Csikszentmihalyi, M., and Csikszentmihalyi, M. (2014). Toward a psychology of optimal experience. *Flow and the foundations of positive psychology: The collected works of Mihaly Csikszentmihalyi*, 209-226.

Damar, M. (2021). Metaverse shape of your life for future: A bibliometric snapshot. *Journal of Metaverse, 1*(1), 1–8.

Darbari, R., & Hall, S. B. (2022). *India could have a key role to play in building the metaverse. Here's why*. WeForum. https://www.weforum.org/agenda/2022/03/india-could-build-metaverse/

Das, N., Das, L., Rautaray, S. S., & Pandey, M. (2018). Big data analytics for medical applications. *International Journal of Modern Education and Computer Science, 12*(2), 35–42. doi:10.5815/ijmecs.2018.02.04

DasS.PanT. (2022). A Strategic Outline of Industry 6.0: Exploring the Future. SSRN: https://ssrn.com/abstract=4104696 or doi:10.2139/ssrn.4104696

Davenport, T., & Kalakota, R. (2019). The potential for artificial intelligence in healthcare. *Future Healthcare Journal, 6*(2), 94–98. doi:10.7861/futurehosp.6-2-94 PMID:31363513

Davies, M. (2021). *Pros and Cons of the Metaverse*. Konsyse.

De Felice, F., Petrillo, A., Iovine, G., Salzano, C., & Baffo, I. (2023). How Does the Metaverse Shape Education? A Systematic Literature Review. *Applied Sciences (Basel, Switzerland), 13*(9), 5682. doi:10.3390/app13095682

De Giovanni, P. (2023). Sustainability of the metaverse: A transition to industry 5.0. *Sustainability (Basel), 15*(7), 6079. doi:10.3390/su15076079

DeBrusk, C. (2020, September 3). The risk of machine-learning bias (and how to prevent it). *MIT Sloan Management Review*. https://sloanreview.mit.edu/article/the-risk-of-machine-learning-bias-and-how-to-prevent-it/

Dechalert. (2022). Metaverse jobs are on the rise, but what exactly are they? *Medium*.

Dehler, J. (2021). Crowdsourcing technology foresight: A structured literature review. *Technological Forecasting and Social Change, 170*, 120852.

Deloitte. (2023). *The Metaverse in India Strategies for Accelerating Economic Impact*. Deloitte. https://www2.deloitte.com/in/en/pages/technology-media-and-telecommunications/articles/the-metaverse-in-asia.html

Denzin, N., & Lincoln, Y. (1994). *Handbook of Qualitative Research*. Sage.

Dhiman, R., Chand, P. K., & Gupta, S. (2018). Behavioural Aspects Influencing Decision to Purchase Apparels amongst Young Indian Consumers. *FIIB Business Review, 7*(3), 188–200. doi:10.1177/2319714518790308

Di Pietro, R., & Cresci, S. (2021). *Metaverse: Security and Privacy Issues*. IEEE Xplore., doi:10.1109/TPSISA52974.2021.00032

DiFacto Robotics and Automation. (2022). *Robot saw jet automation and End of line automation*. DiFacto Robotics and Automation.

Dilella, C., & Dey, A. (2022). *Investors are paying millions for virtual land in the Metaverse*. CNBC.

Dinh, T. L. H. (2023). *Customer behaviors toward Metaverse/Metaverse as a stimulus for customer experience: implications for Marketing*. Research Gate.

Dionisio, J. D. N., Iii, W. G. B., & Gilbert, R. (2013). 3D virtual worlds and the metaverse: Current status and future possibilities. *ACM Computing Surveys*, *45*(3), 1–38. doi:10.1145/2480741.2480751

District Disaster Management Plan – 2019. 1, 01-199.

Duan, H., Li, J., Fan, S., Lin, Z., Wu, X., & Cai, W. (2021). Metaverse for Social Good: A University Campus Prototype. *29th ACM International Conference on Multimedia*, 153–161. 10.1145/3474085.3479238

Duggal, A. S., Malik, P. K., Gehlot, A., Singh, R., Gaba, G. S., Masud, M., & Al-Amri, J. (2022). A sequential roadmap to industry 6.0: Exploring future manufacturing trends. *IET Communications*, *16*(5), 521–531. doi:10.1049/cmu2.12284

Dwivedi, Y. K., Hughes, L., Baabdullah, A. M., Ribeiro-Navarrete, S., Giannakis, M., Al-Debei, M. M., & Wamba, S. F. (2022). Metaverse beyond the hype: Multidisciplinary perspectives on emerging challenges, opportunities, and agenda for research, practice and policy. *International Journal of Information Management*, *66*(1), 542–555. https://medium.com/building-the-metaverse/the-metaverse-value-chain-afcf9e09e3a7,2021. doi:10.1016/j.ijinfomgt.2022.102542

Dwivedi, Y. K., Hughes, L., Wang, Y., Alalwan, A. A., Ahn, S. J., Balakrishnan, J., Barta, S., Belk, R., Buhalis, D., Dutot, V., Felix, R., Filieri, R., Flavián, C., Gustafsson, A., Hinsch, C., Hollensen, S., Jain, V., Kim, J., Krishen, A. S., & Wirtz, J. (2023). Metaverse marketing: How the metaverse will shape the future of consumer research and practice. *Psychology and Marketing*, *40*(4), 750–776. doi:10.1002/mar.21767

Egypt Oil & Gas. (2017). *The Prospects of Robotics in Egypt's Hydrocarbon Industry*. Egypt Oil and Gas.

Eisenhardt, K. M. (1989). Building theories from case study research. *Academy of Management Review*, *14*(4), 532–550. doi:10.2307/258557

Emeka, I. E., & Jayawardhena, C. (2018). Online shopping experience in an emerging e-retailing market. *Journal of Research in Interactive Marketing*, *12*(2), 193–214. doi:10.1108/JRIM-02-2017-0015

Emerson. (2021). *Technologies for Autonomous Oil and Gas Production*. Emerson.

Energies, T. (2021). *Autonomous Robot for Gas and Oil Sites (ARGOS Project) Challenge, in partnership with the French National Research Agency.* ANR.

Eroglu, S. A., Machleit, K. A., & Davis, L. M. (2001). Atmospheric qualities of online retailing A conceptual model and implications. *Journal of Business Research, 54*(2), 177–184. doi:10.1016/S0148-2963(99)00087-9

Ertemel, A. V., Civelek, M. E., Eroğlu Pektaş, G. Ö., & Çemberci, M. (2021). The role of customer experience in the effect of online flow state on customer loyalty. *PLoS One, 16*(7), e0254685. doi:10.1371/journal.pone.0254685 PMID:34264997

European Commmission. (n.d.). *Finance.* EC. https://finance.ec.europa.eu/sustainable-finance/overview-sustainable-finance_en

Exxon Mobil. (2023). *Drones and robots bring the future to digital manufacturing - Energy Factor.* Exxon Mobil.

Fadilpašić, S. (2023, September 10). *How do hackers sell and trade your data in the metaverse?* MUO. https://www.makeuseof.com/how-hackers-sell-trade-data-in-metaverse/

Fanuc. (2022). *Fanuc robots put to use in the recycling industry.* Fanuc.

Faridini, A. (2021). Why The Metaverse Is Marketing's Next Big Thing. *Forbes.*

Feinberg, R., & Kadam, R. (2002). E-CRM Web service attributes as determinants of customer satisfaction with retail Web sites. *International Journal of Service Industry Management, 13*(2), 432–451. doi:10.1108/09564230210447922

Filipova, I. A. (2023). Creating the Metaverse: Consequences for Economy, Society, and Law. *Journal of Digital Technologies and Law, 1*(1), 7–32. doi:10.21202/jdtl.2023.1

Fischer, L., & Wiswede, G. (1997). *Grundlagen der Sozialpsychologie.* Oldenbourg Verlag.

Fortin, D., & Uncles, M. (2011). The first decade: Emerging issues of the twenty-first century in consumer marketing. *Journal of Consumer Marketing, 28*(7), 472–475. doi:10.1108/07363761111194767

Gadalla, E., Keeling, K., & Abosag, I. (2013). Metaverse-retail service quality: A future framework for retail service quality in the 3D internet. *Journal of Marketing Management, 29*(13–14), 1493–1517. doi:10.1080/0267257X.2013.835742

Gadekallu, T. R., Huynh-The, T., Wang, W., Yenduri, G., Ranaweera, P., Pham, Q. V., & Liyanage, M. (2022). Blockchain for the metaverse: A review. arXiv preprint arXiv:2203.09738.

Gadekallu, T. R., Huynh-The, T., Wang, W., Yenduri, G., Ranaweera, P., Pham, Q.-V., da Costa, D. B., & Liyanage, M. (2022). *Blockchain for the Metaverse: A Review.* 17. https://doi.org//arXiv.2203.09738 doi:10.48550

Gamma, K., Mai, R., Cometta, C., & Loock, M. (2021). Engaging customers in demand response programs: The role of reward and punishment in customer adoption in Switzerland. *Energy Research & Social Science, 74*, 101927. doi:10.1016/j.erss.2021.101927

Gasparin, I., Panina, E., Becker, L., Yrjölä, M., Jaakkola, E., & Pizzutti, C. (2022). Challenging the" integration imperative": A customer perspective on omnichannel journeys. *Journal of Retailing and Consumer Services, 64*, 102829. doi:10.1016/j.jretconser.2021.102829

GeeksforGeeks. (2023, December 21). *How to detect outliers in machine learning.* GeeksforGeeks. https://www.geeksforgeeks.org/machine-learning-outlier/

General Electric. (2021). *Drones and Robots Offer Radical New Perspective on Oil and Gas Inspections.* General Electric.

George, A. H., Fernando, M., George, A. S., Baskar, T., & Pandey, D. (2021). Metaverse: The next stage of human culture and the internet. [IJARTET]. *International Journal of Advanced Research Trends in Engineering and Technology, 8*(12), 1–10.

George, D., & Mallery, P. (2003). *SPSS for Windows step by step: A simple guide and reference. 11.0 update* (4th ed.). Allyn & Bacon.

Gerea, C., Gonzalez-Lopez, F., & Herskovic, V. (2021). Omnichannel customer experience and management: An integrative review and research agenda. *Sustainability (Basel), 13*(5), 2824. doi:10.3390/su13052824

Gharajeh, M. S. (2018). Biological big data analytics. []. Elsevier.]. *Advances in Computers, 109*, 321–355. doi:10.1016/bs.adcom.2017.08.002

Ghosh, S., Chand, A., Sengupta, V., & Pandit, Y. (2023). *Embracing the metaverse.* PWC. https://www.pwc.in/research-and-insights-hub/embracing-the-metaverse.html

Gibson, W. (1984). *Neuromancer.* Ace Books.

Gioia, D. A., Corley, K. G., & Hamilton, A. L. (2013). Seeking qualitative rigor in inductive research notes on the Gioia Methodology. Organizational Research Methods 16(1), 15–31.

Glimmerveen, L., Ybema, S., & Nies, H. (2020). Engaged yet excluded: The processual, dispersed, and political dynamics of boundary work. *Human Relations, 73*(11), 1504-1536.

Goel, P., Mahadevan, K., & Punjani, K. K. (2022). Augmented and virtual reality in the apparel industry: A bibliometric review and future research agenda. *Foresight, 25*(2), 167–184. doi:10.1108/FS-10-2021-0202

Golf-Papez, M., Heller, J., Hilken, T., Chylinski, M., de Ruyter, K., Keeling, D. I., & Mahr, D. (2022). Embracing falsity through the metaverse: The case of synthetic customer experiences. *Business Horizons, 65*(6), 739–749. doi:10.1016/j.bushor.2022.07.007

Goyal, K. A., & Joshi, V. (2011). A Study of Social and Ethical Issues In Banking Industry. *International Journal Of Economics, 5*, 49–57.

Green Bank Academy. (2014). Report on Green Bank in Washington DC. Green Bank Academy.

Grewal, D., Levy, M., & Kumar, V. (2009). Customer experience management in retailing: An organizing framework. *Journal of Retailing, 85*(1), 1–14. doi:10.1016/j.jretai.2009.01.001

Gridbots. (2022). *GridbotsRobopack, Automated Robotic Case Packers*. Gridbots.

Gulshan, M. (2015). Green Banking: An Initiative for Sustainable Economic and Environmental Development. *An online interdisciplinary, multidisciplinary & multi-cultural, 4*(3), 36-47.

Gunawan, I. (2022). CUSTOMER LOYALTY: The Effect Customer Satisfaction, Experiential Marketing and Product Quality. *KINERJA: Jurnal Manajemen Organisasi dan Industri, 1*(1), 35-50.

Gupta, A., Khan, H. U., Nazir, S., Shafiq, M., & Shabaz, M. (2023). Metaverse Security: Issues, challenges and a viable ZTA model. *Electronics (Basel), 12*(2), 391. doi:10.3390/electronics12020391

Gursoy, D., Malodia, S., & Dhir, A. (2022). The metaverse in the hospitality and tourism industry: An overview of current trends and future research directions. *Journal of Hospitality Marketing & Management, 31*(5), 527–534. doi:10.1080/19368623.2022.2072504

Hahn, R. W., & Stavins, R. N. (1992). Economic incentives for environmental protection: Integrating theory and practice. *The American Economic Review, 82*(2), 464–468.

Hajjami, O., & Park, S. (2023). Using the metaverse in training: Lessons from real cases. *European Journal of Training and Development*. doi:10.1108/EJTD-12-2022-0144

Han, D. I. D., Bergs, Y., & Moorhouse, N. (2022). Virtual reality consumer experience escapes: Preparing for the metaverse. *Virtual Reality (Waltham Cross), 26*(4), 1443–1458. doi:10.1007/s10055-022-00641-7

Harmeling, C. M., Moffett, J. W., Arnold, M. J., & Carlson, B. D. (2017). Toward a theory of customer engagement marketing. *Journal of the Academy of Marketing Science, 45*(3), 312–335. doi:10.1007/s11747-016-0509-2

Harris, K., Harris, R., & Baron, S. (2001). Customer participation in retail service: Lessons from Brecht. *International Journal of Retail & Distribution Management, 29*(8), 359–369. doi:10.1108/09590550110396845

Harris, L. R., Carnevale, M. J., D'Amour, S., Fraser, L. E., Harrar, V., Hoover, A. E. N., Mander, C., & Pritchett, L. M. (2015). *How our body infuences our perception of the world*. Front Psycol. doi:10.3389/fpsyg.2015.00819

Harris, R., Harris, K., & Baron, S. (2003). Theatrical service experiences. *International Journal of Service Industry Management, 14*(2), 184–199. doi:10.1108/09564230310474156

Harrisson-Boudreau, J.-P., Bellemare, J., Bacher, N., & Bartosiak, M. (2023). Adoption Potentials of Metaverse Omnichannel Retailing and Its Impact on Mass Customization Approaches. *Proceedings of the Changeable, Agile, Reconfigurable and Virtual Production Conference and the World Mass Customization & Personalization Conference*, (pp. 110–119). Springer. 10.1007/978-3-031-34821-1_13

Harrisson-Boudreau, J.-P., Bellemare, J., Bacher, N., & Bartosiak, M. (2023). *Check for updates Adoption Potentials of Metaverse Omnichannel Retailing and Its Impact on Mass Customization Approaches.* Production Processes and Product Evolution in the Age of Disruption: Proceedings of the 9th Changeable, Agile, Reconfigurable and Virtual Production Conference (CARV2023) and the 11th World Mass Customization & Personalization Conference (MCPC2023), Bologna, Italy.

Hartson, R., & Pyla, P. S. (2012). *The UX Book: Process and guidelines for ensuring a quality user experience.* Elsevier.

Hassouneh, D., & Brengman, M. (2015). *Retailing in social virtual worlds: developing a typology of virtual store atmospherics.*

Hayes, A. (2020). *Augmented Reality.* Investopedia.

Hazan, S. (2008). Musing the Metaverse. *2008 Annual Conference of CIDOC.* http://digital-heritage.org.il

Hennig-Thurau, T., Aliman, D. N., Herting, A. M., Cziehso, G. P., Linder, M., & Kübler, R. V. (2023). Social interactions in the metaverse: Framework, initial evidence, and research roadmap. *Journal of the Academy of Marketing Science, 51*(4), 889–913. doi:10.1007/s11747-022-00908-0

Henz, P. (2022). *The societal impact of the Metaverse.* Discov Artif Intell. doi:10.1007/s44163-022-00032-6

Herath, H. M. A. K., & Herath, H. M. S. P. (2022). Impact of green banking initiatives on customer satisfaction. *IOSR Journal of Business and Management, 24*(7), 1–19.

Hespanhol, L., & Dalsgaard, P. (2015). Social interaction design patterns for urban media architecture. In Human-Computer Interaction. Springer.

Hexagon. (2023). *Empowering an autonomous, sustainable future.* Hexagon.

Hitachi. (2021). *Robots for quality inspection.* Hitachi.

Honeywell. (2021). *In the journey to autonomous systems in the oil and gas industry, wellheads and pipelines are largely unmanned.* Honeywell.

HT News Desk. (2023, April 26). Is India ready for metaverse? 70% businesses plan integration, says survey. *Hindustan Times.* https://www.hindustantimes.com/technology/technology-news-indian-businesses-metaverse-pwc-india-survey-101682505719797.html

Hudson, J. (2022). Virtual immersive shopping experiences in metaverse environments: Predictive customer analytics, data visualization algorithms, and smart retailing technologies. *Linguistic and Philosophical Investigations*, (21), 236–251.

Hurst, W., Spyrou, O., Tekinerdoğan, B., & Krampe, C. (2023). Digital art and the metaverse: Benefits and challenges. *Future Internet, 15*(6), 188. doi:10.3390/fi15060188

Hur, W. M., & Oh, J. (2022). When employees no longer want to stay: Turnover intention and retail employees' perception of employer brand. *Journal of Retailing and Consumer Services, 63*, 102821.

Hwang, R., & Lee, M. (2022). The influence of music content marketing on user satisfaction and intention to use in the Metaverse: A focus on the SPICE model. *Businesses, 2*(2), 141 155. https://doi.org/ doi:10.33 0/businesses2020010

IDRBT (2013). Green banking for the Indian banking sector. *Report of RBI, IDRBT Publication*, 1-20. IDRBT.

Iglesias-Pradas, S., & Acquila-Natale, E. (2023). The Future of E-Commerce: Overview and Prospects of Multichannel and Omnichannel Retail. *Journal of Theoretical and Applied Electronic Commerce Research, 18*(1), 656–667. doi:10.3390/jtaer18010033

Innis, D. E., & La Londe, B. J. (1994). Customer service: The key to customer satisfaction, customer loyalty, and market share. *Journal of Business Logistics, 15*(1), 1.

Issah, M. (2018). Change Leadership: The Role of Emotional Intelligence. *SAGE Open, 8*(3). doi:10.1177/2158244018800910

Iyengar, A., Kundu, A., Sharma, U., & Zhang, P. (2018, July). A trusted healthcare data analytics cloud platform. In *2018 IEEE 38th International Conference on Distributed Computing Systems (ICDCS)* (pp. 1238-1249). IEEE. 10.1109/ICDCS.2018.00123

Iyyanki, Muralikrishna, & Vallimanickam. (2017). Sustainable development. *Science and engineering for industry*, 5-21. Environmental management. doi:10.1016/B978-0-12-811989-1.00002-6

Jansson, J., Marell, A., & Nordlund, A. (2011). Exploring consumer adoption of a high involvement eco-innovation using value-belief-norm theory. *Journal of Consumer Behaviour, 10*(1), 51–60. doi:10.1002/cb.346

Jauhiainen, J. S., Krohn, C., & Junnila, J. (2022). Metaverse and sustainability: Systematic review of scientific publications until 2022 and beyond. *Sustainability (Basel), 15*(1), 346. doi:10.3390/su15010346

Jia, Q., Guo, Y., Wang, G., & Barnes, S. J. (2020). Big data analytics in the fight against major public health incidents (Including COVID-19): A conceptual framework. *International Journal of Environmental Research and Public Health, 17*(17), 6161. doi:10.3390/ijerph17176161 PMID:32854265

JLL. (2017). *The Future of retail in India is omni-channel.* JLL.

Jo, H. (2023). Tourism in the digital frontier: A study on user continuance intention in the metaverse. *Information Technology & Tourism, 25*(3), 307–330. doi:10.1007/s40558-023-00257-w

Jones & Patel. (2023). Regulatory Frameworks and Transaction Costs in the Metaverse: A Comparative Study.

Jose, B. (2023, June 3). Metaverse & Web3 to present India with $200 billion opportunity, driven by retail and financial services: Report. *The Indian Express.* https://indianexpress.com/article/technology/tech-news-technology/metaverse-web3-to-present-india-with-200-billion-opportunity-8640975/

Juaneda-Ayensa, E., Mosquera, A., & Sierra Murillo, Y. (2016). Omni-channel Customer Behavior: Key Drivers of Technology Acceptance and Use and Their Effects on Purchase Intention. *Frontiers in Psychology, 7.* doi:10.3389/fpsyg.2016.01117 PMID:27516749

Jung, S. H., & Jeon, I. O. (2022). A study on the components of the Metaverse ecosystem. *Journal of Digital Convergence, 20*(2).

Kaddoura, S., & Al Husseiny, F. (2023). The rising trend of Metaverse in education: Challenges, opportunities, and ethical considerations. *PeerJ. Computer Science, 9,* e1252. doi:10.7717/peerj-cs.1252 PMID:37346578

Kanak, T., Saumya, S., & Ritesh, K. (2015). Green Banking For Environmental Management: A Paradigm Shift. *Current World Environment, 10*(3), 1029–1038. doi:10.12944/CWE.10.3.36

Kawasaki. (2021). *Effective pelletizing with Kawasaki robots.* Kawasaki.

Kenney, M., & Zysman, J. (2019). Work and value creation in the platform economy. *Work and labor in the digital age, 33*(1), 13-41.

Khoury, M. J., & Ioannidis, J. P. (2014). Big data meets public health. *Science, 346*(6213), 1054–1055. doi:10.1126/science.aaa2709 PMID:25430753

Kim, Y., & Jung, H. (2022). Beauty Industry's Strategic Response to Metaverse Evolution: Focused on Generation MZ. *2022 IEEE/ACIS 7th International Conference on Big Data, Cloud Computing, and Data Science (BCD),* (pp. 259–264). IEEE.

Kim, J. (2021). Advertising in the Metaverse: Research Agenda. *Journal of Interactive Advertising, 21*(3), 141–144. doi:10.1080/15252019.2021.2001273

Klaus, P. (2013). Exploring online channel management strategies and the use of social media as a market research tool. *International Journal of Market Research.*

Knox, J. (2022). The metaverse, or the serious business of tech frontiers. *Postdigital Science and Education, 4*(2), 207–215. doi:10.1007/s42438-022-00300-9

Kolo, K. (2021). *9 AR Platforms Bring Augmented Reality Content in the Classroom*. The VRARA. https://www.thevrara.com/blog2/2021/10/26/9-desktop-ar-platforms-to-bring-ar-content-in-the-classroom

Koohang, A., Nord, J., Ooi, K., Tan, G., Al-Emran, M., Aw, E., & Wong, L. (2023). Shaping the metaverse into reality: Multidisciplinary perspectives on opportunities, challenges, and future research. *Journal of Computer Information Systems*. doi:10.1080/08874417.2023.2165197

Kop, M. (2022). Abundance and Equality. *Frontiers in Research Metrics and Analytics, 7*, 977684. doi:10.3389/frma.2022.977684 PMID:36531753

Kotler, P. (2000). Marketing Management (Millennium). Prentice-Hall, Inc. Pearson Custom Publishing.

Kourouthanassis, P. E., & Giaglis, G. M. (2005). Shopping in the 21st century: Embedding technology in the retail arena. In Consumer Driven Electronic Transformation: Applying New Technologies to Enthuse Consumers and Transform the Supply Chain (pp. 227–239). Springer.

Kraus, S., Kanbach, D. K., Krysta, P. M., Steinhoff, M. M., & Tomini, N. (2022). Facebook and the creation of the metaverse: Radical business model innovation or incremental transformation? *International Journal of Entrepreneurial Behaviour & Research, 28*(9), 52–77. doi:10.1108/IJEBR-12-2021-0984

Kritzinger, W., Karner, M., Traar, G., Henjes, J., & Sihn, W. (2018). Digital Twin in manufacturing: A categorical literature review and classification. *IFAC-PapersOnLine, 51*(11). doi:10.1016/j.ifacol.2018.08.474

Kulshrestha, D., Tiwari, M. K., Shalender, K., & Sharma, S. (2022). Consumer Acatalepsy Towards Buying Behaviour for Need-Based Goods for Sustainability During the COVID-19 Pandemic. *Indian Journal of Marketing, 52*(10), 50–63. doi:10.17010/ijom/2022/v52/i10/172347

Kye, B., Han, N., Kim, E., Park, Y., & Jo, S. (2021). Educational applications of metaverse: Possibilities and limitations. *Journal of Educational Evaluation for Health Professions, 18*(32), 1–13. doi:10.3352/jeehp.2021.18.32 PMID:34897242

Lacity, M., Mullins, J. K., & Kuai, L. (2022). What type of metaverse will we create. (BCoE Whitepaper) University of Arkansas.

Lamba, S. S., & Malik, R. (2022). Into the metaverse: Marketing to Gen Z consumers. In *Applying Metalytics to Measure Customer Experience in the Metaverse* (pp. 92–98). IGI Global. doi:10.4018/978-1-6684-6133-4.ch008

Lazaris, C., & Vrechopoulos, A. (2014). From multichannel to "omnichannel" retailing: review of the literature and calls for research. *2nd International Conference on Contemporary Marketing Issues,(ICCMI), 6*, (pp. 1–6). Research Gate.

Ledro, C., Nosella, A., & Vinelli, A. (2022). Artificial intelligence in customer relationship management: Literature review and future research directions. *Journal of Business and Industrial Marketing, 37*(13), 48–63. doi:10.1108/JBIM-07-2021-0332

Lee, H. J., & Gu, H. H. (2022). Empirical research on the metaverse user experience of digital natives. *Sustainability, 14*(22), 14747. https://doi.org/ doi:10.33 0/su142214747

Lee, J. Y. (2021). A study on metaverse hype for sustainable growth. *International journal of advanced smart convergence, 10*(3), 72-80.

Lee, C., Kogler, D. F., & Lee, D. (2019). Capturing information on technology convergence, international collaboration, and knowledge flow from patent documents: A case of information and communication technology. *Information Processing & Management, 56*(4), 1576–1591. doi:10.1016/j.ipm.2018.09.007

Lee, H. J., & Gu, H. H. (2022). Empirical Research on the Metaverse User Experience of Digital Natives. *Sustainability (Basel), 14*(22), 14747. doi:10.3390/su142214747

Lee, J., Lee, T. S., Lee, S., Jang, J., Yoo, S., Choi, Y., & Park, Y. R. (2022). Development and application of a metaverse-based social skills training program for children with autism spectrum disorder to improve social interaction: Protocol for a randomized controlled trial. *JMIR Research Protocols, 11*(6), e35960. doi:10.2196/35960 PMID:35675112

Lee, L.-H., Braud, T., Zhou, P., Wang, L., Xu, D., Lin, Z., Kumar, A., Bermejo, C., & Hui, P. (2021). All One Needs to Know about Metaverse: A Complete Survey on Technological Singularity, Virtual Ecosystem, and Research Agenda. *Journal of Latex Class Files, 14*(8), 1–66. doi:10.48550/arXiv.2110.05352

Li, M., & Yu, Z. (2023). A systematic review on the metaverse-based blended English learning. *Frontiers in Psycholo y, 13*. https://doi.org/ doi:10.33 9/fpsyg.2022.1087508

Liberatore, M. J., & Wagner, W. P. (2021). Virtual, mixed, and augmented reality: A systematic review for immersive systems research. *Virtual Reality (Waltham Cross), 25*(3), 773–799. doi:10.1007/s10055-020-00492-0

Lopes, M., & Reis, J. (2021). *Impacts of COVID-19 in Retail: A Case Study Research.* IEEE Xplore., doi:10.23919/CISTI52073.2021.9476594

Lu, S., & Mintz, O. (2023). Marketing on the metaverse: Research opportunities and challenges. *AMS Review, 13*(1–2), 51–166. doi:10.1007/s13162-023-00255-5

Macià, M., & García, I. (2016). Informal online communities and networks as a source of teacher professional development: A review. *Teaching and Teacher Education, 55*, 291–307. doi:10.1016/j.tate.2016.01.021

Ma, J., Sheng, W., & Pahlevansharif, S. (2022). Virtual reality applications in retail: A systematic review and meta-analysis. *International Journal of Information Management, 63*, 102465. doi:10.1016/j.ijinfomgt.2021.102465

Majhi, V., Paul, S., & Jain, R. (2019, February). Bioinformatics for healthcare applications. In 2019 Amity international conference on artificial intelligence (AICAI) (pp. 204-207). IEEE. doi:10.1109/AICAI.2019.8701277

Maksymyuk, T., Gazda, J., Bugár, G., Gazda, V., Liyanage, M., & Dohler, M. (2022). Blockchain-empowered service management for the decentralized metaverse of things. *IEEE Access: Practical Innovations, Open Solutions, 10*, 99025–99037. doi:10.1109/ACCESS.2022.3205739

Maloney, D. (2021). *A youthful metaverse: Towards designing safe, equitable, and emotionally fulfilling social virtual reality spaces for younger users.*

Manivannan, M. (2023, September 14). India has a huge potential to lead the world in metaverse technologies towards Vasudhaiva Kutumbakam. *Financial Express.* https://www.financialexpress.com/policy/economy-india-has-a-huge-potential-to-lead-the-world-in-metaverse-technologies-towards-vasudhaiva-kutumbakam-3243198/

Marr, B. (2024, January 18). The metaverse and its Dark Side: Confronting the reality of virtual rape. *Forbes.* https://www.forbes.com/sites/bernardmarr/2024/01/16/the-metaverse-and-its-dark-side-confronting-the-reality-of-virtual-rape/?sh=77663ef02b66

Martínez-Peláez, R., Ochoa-Brust, A., Rivera, S., Félix, V. G., Ostos, R., Brito, H., Félix, R. A., & Mena, L. J. (2023). Role of digital transformation for achieving sustainability: Mediated role of stakeholders, key capabilities, and technology. *Sustainability (Basel), 15*(14), 11221. doi:10.3390/su151411221

Masukujjaman, M., Siwar, C., Mahmud, M. R., & Alam, S. S. (2017). Bankers' perception of green banking: Learning from the experience of Islamic banks in Bangladesh. *Geografa-Malaysian Journal of Society Space, 12*(2).

Mathivanan, S. K., Jayagopal, P., Ahmed, S., Manivannan, S. S., Kumar, P. J., Raja, K. T., Dharinya, S. S., & Prasad, R. G. (2021). Adoption of e-learning during lockdown in India. *International Journal of System Assurance Engineering and Management*, 1–10.

Ma, Z. (2023). Energy metaverse: The conceptual framework with a review of the state-of-the-art methods and technologies. *Energy Informatics, 6*(1), 42. doi:10.1186/s42162-023-00297-w

McKinsey. (n.d.). *Banking imperatices for managing climate risk.* McKinsey. https://www.mckinsey.com/capabilities/risk-and-resilience/our-insights/banking-imperatives-for-managing-climate-risk#/

Meenakshi, S. (2016). Green Computing – A Cloud-Based Architecture for Green Banking. *International Journal of Innovative Research in Computer and Communication Engineering, 4*(5), 8534–8537.

Meghan, R. (2022). Metaverse Hype to Transition into New Business Models that Extend Digital Business. https://www.gartner.com/en/newsroom/press-releases/gartner-predicts-65--of-b2b-sales-organizations-will-transition.

Michael, R. (1994). At what Point can pollution be said to cause damage to the Environment? *The Banker.*

Miles, M. B., & Huberman, A. M. (1994). Qualitative Data Analysis: An Expanded Sourcebook. *Sage (Atlanta, Ga.).*

Mileva, G. (2022). *A Deep Dive into Metaverse Marketing*. Influencer Marketing Hub.

Mir, A. A., & Bhat, A. A. (2022). Green banking and sustainability – a review. *Arab Gulf Journal of Scientific Research*, *40*(3), 247–263. doi:10.1108/AGJSR-04-2022-0017

Mitsubishi Electric. (2022). *The new future of automation made by next-generation intelligent robots*. Mitsubishi Electric.

Mittal, G., & Bansal, R. (2023). Driving Force Behind Consumer Brand Engagement: The Metaverse. In Cultural Marketing and Metaverse for Consumer Engagement (pp. 164-181). IGI Global.

Mogaji, E., Wirtz, J., Belk, R. W., & Dwivedi, Y. K. (2023). Immersive time (ImT): Conceptualizing time spent in the metaverse. *International Journal of Information Management*, *72*, 102659. doi:10.1016/j.ijinfomgt.2023.102659

Mohanty, M. K., Mohapatra, A. K., Samanta, P. K., Agrawal, G., & Agrawal, G. (2022). Exploring metaverse: A virtual ecosystem from management perspective. *Journal of Commerce*, *43*(4), 1–11. doi:10.54063/ojc.2022.v43i04.01

Multiway. (2023). *Intelligent Material handling and palletizing and Intelligent warehousing assistant*. Multiway.

Mushiny. (2021). In*telligent Warehousing· Automated Storage & Retrieval System*. Mushiny.

Mystakidis, S. (2022). Metaverse. In *Encyclopedia* (pp. 486–497). MDPI. doi:10.3390/encyclopedia2010031

Nagaraj, K., Sharvani, G. S., & Sridhar, A. (2018). Emerging trend of big data analytics in bioinformatics: A literature review. *International Journal of Bioinformatics Research and Applications*, *14*(1-2), 144–205. doi:10.1504/IJBRA.2018.089175

Nagendran, A., Compton, S., Follette, W. C., Golenchenko, A., Compton, A., & Grizou, J. (2022). Avatar led interventions in the Metaverse reveal that interpersonal effectiveness can be measured, predicted, and improved. *Scientific Reports*, *12*(1), 21892. doi:10.1038/s41598-022-26326-4 PMID:36535981

Nair, V., Garrido, G. M., Song, D., & O'Brien, J. F. (2023, December 13). *Exploring the privacy risks of adversarial VR game design*. arXiv.org. https://arxiv.org/abs/2207.13176

Nakamoto, S. (2008). Bitcoin: A peer-to-peer electronic cash system.

Namasivayam, K. (2003). The consumer as a "transient employee": Consumer satisfaction through the lens of job-performance models. *International Journal of Service Industry Management*, *14*(4), 420–435. doi:10.1108/09564230310489259

Nanda, S. & Chandra, S. (2012). Profitability in Banks of India: An Impact Study of Implementation of Green Banking. *International Journal of Green Economics, 6*(3), 217-225.

Nath, V., Nayak, N., & Goel, A. (2014). Green Banking Practices- A Review. *International Journal of Research in Business Management, 2*(4), 45–62.

Neyati, A. (2015). Green Banking in India: A Review Of Literature. *International Journal for research in management and pharmacy, 4*, 11-16.

Nigamananda, B. (2011). Sustainable Green Banking: The Need of The Hour. *Busines Spectrum., 1*, 32–38.

Ning, H., Wang, H., Lin, Y., Wang, W., Dhelim, S., Farha, F., & Daneshmand, M. (2023). A Survey on the Metaverse: The State-of-the-Art, Technologies, Applications, and Challenges. *IEEE Internet of Things Journal.*

Niu, X., & Feng, W. (2022). Immersive Entertainment Environments-from theme parks to Metaverse. *International Conference on Human-Computer Interaction,* (pp. 392–403). Research Gate.

Nix, N. (2023). Meta doesn't want to police the metaverse. kids are paying the price. *Washington Post.* https://www.washingtonpost.com/technology/2023/03/08/metaverse-horizon-worlds-kids-harassment/

Njoku, J. N., Nwakanma, C. I., Amaizu, G. C., & Kim, D. S. (2023). Prospects and challenges of Metaverse application in data-driven intelligent transportation systems. *IET Intelligent Transport Systems, 17*(1), 1–21. doi:10.1049/itr2.12252

Nobile, T. H., & Kalbaska, N. (2020). An exploration of personalization in digital communication. Insights in fashion. *Lecture Notes in Computer Science, 12204*, 456–473. doi:10.1007/978-3-030-50341-3_35

OGV Energy. (2021). *Robotics essential to the oil and gas industry (Robot as a Service-RaaS).* OGV Energy.

Oladele, S. (2023, September 8). *A comprehensive guide on how to monitor your models in production.* neptune.ai. https://neptune.ai/blog/how-to-monitor-your-models-in-production-guide#:~:text=Monitoring%20predictive%20performance%20(with%20evaluation,results%20over%20time)%20from%20there

Ola, O., & Sedig, K. (2014). The challenge of big data in public health: An opportunity for visual analytics. *Online Journal of Public Health Informatics, 5*(3), 223. PMID:24678376

Ondrejka, C. R. (2004). A Piece of Place: Modeling the Digital on the Real in Second Life. SSRN *Electronic Journal.* doi:10.2139/ssrn.555883

Onu, P., Pradhan, A., & Mbohwa, C. (2023). Potential to use metaverse for future teaching and learning. *Education and Information Technologies.* Advance online publication. doi:10.1007/s10639-023-12167-9

Pacifico, A., Giraldi, L., & Cedrola, E. (2023). Student Performance in E-learning Systems: An Empirical Study.

Pagoropoulos, A., Pigosso, D. C. A., & McAloone, T. C. (2017). The Emergent Role of Digital Technologies in the Circular Economy: A Review. *Procedia CIRP, 64*, 19–24. doi:10.1016/j. procir.2017.02.047

Pandey, S. (2022). *Laws and Crimes in the Metaverse*. Digit.

Papa, A. M. (2022). The Metaverse, at the crossroads of creating a new world and ambiguous predictions-analysis of trends, features and impacts on consumers and businesses. [JRISS]. *Journal of Research & Innovation for Sustainable Society, 4*(2).

Papagiannidis, S., & Bourlakis, M. (2010). Staging the New Retail Drama: At a Metaverse Near You! *Journal of Virtual Worlds Research, 2*(5), 225–246. doi:10.4101/jvwr.v2i5.808

Paras Lohani. (2022). *How Metaverse is taking shape in the Indian IT and Event Industry*. Express Computer. https://www.expresscomputer.in/guest-blogs/how-metaverse-is-taking-shape-in-the-indian-it-and-event-industry/89204/

Parihar, J., Kansal, P., Singh, K., & Dhiman, H. (2019, February). Assessment of bioinformatics and healthcare informatics. In *2019 Amity International Conference on Artificial Intelligence (AICAI)* (pp. 465-467). IEEE. 10.1109/AICAI.2019.8701262

Parikh, A., Kumari, D., Johann, M., & Mladenović, D. (2023). ohann,M., Mladenović,D. (2023). The impact of environmental, social and governance score on shareholder wealth: A new dimension in investment philosophy. *Cleaner and Responsible Consumption, 8*, 100101. doi:10.1016/j.clrc.2023.100101

Park, S. M., & Kim, Y. (2022). A metaverse: Taxonomy, components, applications, and open challenges. *IEEE Access, 10*, 4209 4251. https://doi.org/ doi:10.11 9/access.2021.3140175

Park, H., & Kim, J. D. (2020). Transition towards green banking: Role of financial regulators and financial institutions. *AJSSR, 5*(1), 5. doi:10.1186/s41180-020-00034-3

Park, S.-M., & Kim, Y.-G. (2022). A Metaverse: Taxonomy, Components, Applications, and Open Challenges. *IEEE Access : Practical Innovations, Open Solutions, 10*, 4209–4251. doi:10.1109/ACCESS.2021.3140175

Parlar, T. (2023). Data privacy and security in the metaverse. In Studies in big data (pp. 123–133). Springer. doi:10.1007/978-981-99-4641-9_8

Patel, N. (2018). *The benefits and importance of customer satisfaction*. neilpatel. com.

Patton, M. (1990). Qualitative Data Analysis. *Sage (Atlanta, Ga.)*.

Petkov, M. (2023). *Metaverse AI: The Definitive Marketing Guide to Navigating a $150 Trillion Opportunity*. Independent publishing.

Petronas. (2019). *The New Age of Oil and Gas: Translating technology into business viability: reducing costs, improving productivity, and increasing efficiency*. Petronas.

Piotrowicz, W., & Cuthbertson, R. (2014). Introduction to the special issue information technology in retail: Toward omnichannel retailing. *International Journal of Electronic Commerce*, *18*(4), 5–16. doi:10.2753/JEC1086-4415180400

Pooyandeh, M., Han, K. J., & Sohn, I. (2022). Cybersecurity in the AI-Based Metaverse: A survey. *Applied Sciences (Basel, Switzerland)*, *12*(24), 12993. doi:10.3390/app122412993

Prahalad, C. K., & Ramaswamy, V. (2004). Co-creating unique value with customers. *Strategy and Leadership*, *32*(3), 3–9. doi:10.1108/10878570410699249

Pravakar, S. & Bibhu, N. (2008). *Green Banking in India*. India Envornmental Portal. http://admin.indiaenvironmentalportal.ord.in/files/green%20banking.pdf

Priyadarshi, P. (2023). *Into The Metaverse: How India Can Leverage The Multi-Billion Dollar Opportunity*. Inc 42. https://inc42.com/resources/into-the-metaverse-how-india-can-leverage-the-multi-billion-dollar-opportunity/

Pyae, A., Ravyse, W., Luimula, M., Pizarro-Lucas, E., Sánchez, P. L., Dorado-Díaz, P. I., & Thaw, A. K. (2023). Exploring user experience and usability in a metaverse learning environment for students: A Usability Study of Artificial Intelligence, Innovation, and Society (AIIS). *Electronics (Basel)*, *12*(20), 283. doi:10.3390/electronics12204283

Rahman Mahfuzur,, M. S. (2016). The Design and Adoption of Green Banking Framework For Environment Protection: Lessons From Bangladesh. *Australian Journal of Sustainable Business and Society*, *2*(1), 1–19.

Rajesh, T., & Dileep, A. S. (2014). Role of Banks in Sustainable Economic development through Green Banking. *International Journal of Current Research and Academic Review*, *2*, 136–141.

Rakesh, D, Srinath, V.B., & Karki, R Naveen. (2016). Green Banking: A Conceptual Study on its Issues, Challenges, and Sustainable Growth in India. [IJAIEM]. *International Journal of Application or Innovation in Engineering & Management*, *5*(6), 41–46.

Rane, N., Choudhary, S., & Rane, J. (2023). Metaverse for Enhancing Customer Loyalty: Effective Strategies to Improve Customer Relationship, Service, Engagement, Satisfaction, and Experience. *Service, Engagement, Satisfaction, and Experience.*

Rathore, B. (2019). From Trendy to Green: Exploring AI's Role in Sustainable Fashion Marketing. *International Journal of New Media Studies: International Peer Reviewed Scholarly Indexed Journal*, *6*(2), 12–22. doi:10.58972/eiprmj.v6i2y19.120

Rehman, A., Naz, S., & Razzak, I. (2022). Leveraging big data analytics in healthcare enhancement: Trends, challenges and opportunities. *Multimedia Systems*, *28*(4), 1339–1371. doi:10.1007/s00530-020-00736-8

Reina, C. S., Rogers, K. M., Peterson, S. J., Byron, K., & Hom, P. W. (2018). Quitting the boss? The role of manager influence tactics and employee emotional engagement in voluntary turnover. *Journal of Leadership & Organizational Studies*, *25*(1), 5–18. doi:10.1177/1548051817709007

Rejeb, A., Rejeb, K., & Treiblmaier, H. (2023). Mapping Metaverse research: Identifying future research areas based on bibliometric and topic modeling techniques. *Information (Basel), 14*(7), 356. doi:10.3390/info14070356

Ribeiro, R. (2022). *"Metaverse" and the educational potential.* Cambridge University Press. https://www.cambridge.org/elt/blog/2021/11/15/metaverse-educational-potential

Ristevski, B., & Chen, M. (2018). Big data analytics in medicine and healthcare. *Journal of Integrative Bioinformatics, 15*(3), 20170030. doi:10.1515/jib-2017-0030 PMID:29746254

Rose, F. (2007, July). How Madison Avenue is Wasting Millions on a Deserted Second Life. *Wired.* https://www.wired.com/2007/07/ff-sheep/

Ruchi. (2014). Green banking: a case study of IndusInd bank. *International journal of business and general management (IJBGM), 3*(3), 13-18.

Said, G. R. E. (2023). Metaverse-Based Learning Opportunities and Challenges: A Phenomenological Metaverse Human–Computer Interaction Study. *Electronics (Basel), 12*(6), 1379. doi:10.3390/electronics12061379

Salvioni, D. M., & Almici, A. (2020). Transitioning toward a circular economy: The impact of stakeholder engagement on sustainability culture. *Sustainability (Basel), 12*(20), 8641. doi:10.3390/su12208641

Sanjoy, P., & Aminul, R. H. (2015). Advancement of green banking layout and trend in Bangladesh. International Journal of Economics. *Commerce and Management, 3*(11), 1160–1182.

Sarita, B. (2012). Green Banking- The New Strategic Imperative. *Journal of Asian Research Consortium, 2*(2), 176–185.

Sarma, M. K., Ningthoujam, R., Panda, M. K., Babu, P. J., Srivastava, A., Das, M., & Singh, Y. D. (2021). Translational healthcare system through bioinformatics. In *Translational bioinformatics applications in healthcare* (pp. 3–21). CRC Press. doi:10.1201/9781003146988-2

Saudi Aramco. (2023). *Digitalization and Future Energy.* Saudi Aramco.

Saxena, K. (2023). *Future Prospects of Augmented Reality in the Education Industry.* Coding Ninjas. https://www.codingninjas.com/studio/library/augmented-reality-in-education-industry

Schlumberger. (2022). *Neuroautonomous solutions enable autonomous directional drilling capabilities that build wells most efficiently and consistently possible, regardless of the rig, field, or trajectory.* Research Gate.

SchmittM. (2023). Big Data Analytics in the Metaverse: Business Value Creation with Artificial Intelligence and Data-Driven Decision Making. Available at SSRN 4385347. doi:10.2139/ssrn.4385347

Schneider Electric. (2022). *Efficient and sustainable solutions for energy and chemicals.* Schneider Electric.

Schumacher, P. (2022). The Metaverse as an opportunity for architecture and society: Design drivers, core competencies. *Architectural Intelligence*, *1*(1), 11. doi:10.1007/s44223-022-00010-z PMID:35993030

Schweidel, D. A., Bart, Y., Inman, J. J., Stephen, A. T., Libai, B., Andrews, M., Rosario, A. B., Chae, I., Chen, Z., Kupor, D., Longoni, C., & Thomaz, F. (2022). How consumer digital signals are reshaping the customer journey. *Journal of the Academy of Marketing Science*, *50*(6), 1257–1276. doi:10.1007/s11747-022-00839-w PMID:35221393

Science Direct. (n.d.). *The Impace of envionrmental, social, and ogverance score on shareholder weatlth*. Science Direct. https://www.sciencedirect.com/science/article/pii/S2666784323000025

Sergeyeva, T., Bronin, S., Turlakova, N., & Iamnytskyi, S. (2022). Integrating Educational Components into the Metaverse. *The Learning Ideas Conference*, 412–425.

Sestino, A., Guido, G., & Peluso, A. (2022). *Non-Fungible Tokens (NFTs): Examining the Impact on Consumers and Marketing Strategies*. Springer International Publishing.

Seth, N. & Deshmukh, S. (2005). Service quality models: a review. *International Journal of Quality & Reliability Management, 22*(9), 913-949. doi:10.1108/02656710510625211

Shaheen, M. Y. (2021). Applications of Artificial Intelligence (AI) in healthcare. *RE:view*. doi:10.14293/S2199-1006.1.SOR-.PPVRY8K.v1

Shalender, K. (2022). Key variables in team dynamics in small businesses and start-ups. In New teaching resources for management in a globalised world (pp. 141–153). World Scientific. doi:10.1142/9789811239212_0007

Shalender, K., Singla, B., & Sharma, S. (2023). Blockchain Adoption in the financial sector: Challenges, solutions, and implementation framework. In K. Mehta, R. Sharma, & P. Yu (Eds.), *Revolutionizing Financial Services and Markets Through FinTech and Blockchain* (pp. 269–277). IGI Global. doi:10.4018/978-1-6684-8624-5.ch017

Shapiro, C., & Varian, H. R. (1999). *Information rules: A strategic guide to the network economy*. Harvard Business Press.

Sharma N, Sarika, & Gopal, R. (2014). A Study on Customer's Awareness On Green Banking Initiatives In Selected Public And Private Sector Banks With Special Reference To Mumbai. *IOSR Journal of Economics and Finance, 2*, 28-35.

Sharma, P. (2022, October 16). India and the industrial metaverse. *Business Standard*. https://www.business-standard.com/article/opinion/india-and-the-industrial-metaverse-122101600591_1.html

Sharma, M., & Choubey, A. (2022). Green banking initiatives: A qualitative study on Indian banking sector. *Environment, Development and Sustainability*, *24*(1), 293–319. doi:10.1007/s10668-021-01426-9 PMID:33967597

Shekhawat, T. S. (2023, June 21). The metaverse and the future of retail opportunities and challenges. *The Times of India*. https://timesofindia.indiatimes.com/blogs/voices/the-metaverse-and-the-future-of-retail-opportunities-and-challenges/

Shell. (2022). *Robotics in the energy industry – Facilitating lead detection and emission control*. Shell.

Shen, B., Wei-Ming, T., Guo, J., Zhao, L., & Qin, P. (2021). How do we promote user purchases in Metaverse? A systematic literature review on consumer behaviour research and virtual commerce application design. *Applied Sciences (Basel, Switzerland)*, *11*(3), 11087. doi:10.3390/app112311087

Shrivastave, P., & Berger, S. (2010). Sustainability principles: A review and directions. *Organizational Management Journal*, *7*(4), 246–261. doi:10.1057/omj.2010.35

Shruti, G. (2015). Green Banking: An Overview. *Global Journal of Advanced Research*, *2*(8), 1291–1296.

Sia, C. C. (2023). The Role of Legal Governance Framework in the Metaverse World. In *Strategies and Opportunities for Technology in the Metaverse World* (pp. 321–330). IGI Global. doi:10.4018/978-1-6684-5732-0.ch017

Siemens. (2022). *Robots and drones pave the way for autonomous energy systems*. Siemens.

Simonite, T. (2021, May 5). It began as an AI-fueled dungeon game. it got much darker. *Wired*. https://www.wired.com/story/ai-fueled-dungeon-game-got-much-darker/

Singal, N. (2022, August). How the Metaverse Will Drive Innovation in Entertainment. *Business Today*. https://www.businesstoday.in/magazine/technology/story/how-the-metaverse-will-drive-innovation-in-entertainment-343328-2022-08-01

Singh, J. P., Chand, P. K., Mittal, A., & Aggarwal, A. (2020). High-performance work system and organizational citizenship behaviour at the shop floor. *Benchmarking*, *27*(4), 1369–1398. doi:10.1108/BIJ-07-2019-0339

Sinha, H. (2023). *Top Metaverse Stocks in India to Invest*. Groww. https://groww.in/blog/best-metaverse-stocks-in-india

Siririka, P. (2023). *Integrating informal sector can propel financial reach*. Newer Alive. https://neweralive.na/posts/integrating-informal-sector-can-propel-financial-reach

Smith, G. (2020). Mitigating Bias in Artificial Intelligence, Berkeley Haas Center for Equity Google. Google Cloud. https://cloud.google.com/discover/what-is-supervised-learning

SNC Lavalin. (2022). *Accelerating Autonomous Operations in Oil & Gas: Building on the "New Normal."* SNC Lavalin.

Snider, M., & Molina, B. (2022). Everyone wants to own the metaverse including Facebook and Microsoft. But what exactly is it? *USA Today*.

Son, S.-C., Bae, J., & Kim, K. H. (2023). An exploratory study on the perceived agility by consumers in luxury brand omni-channel. *Journal of Global Scholars of Marketing Science*, *33*(1), 154–166. doi:10.1080/21639159.2022.2153261

Sood, D., Tandon, D., & Sood, P. (2022). Social Influence: Decisions of Online Brand Communities and Millennials. In *Applying Metalytics to Measure Customer Experience in the Metaverse* (pp. 161–172). IGI Global. doi:10.4018/978-1-6684-6133-4.ch014

Stake, R. (1995). The Art of Case Study Research. *Sage (Atlanta, Ga.)*.

Stapleton, L. (2019). *AR vs. VR: What's the Difference? Marketers Put Augmented and Virtual Reality to Work*. Treasure Data.

Statista. (2023). *Metaverse*. Statista. https://www.statista.com/outlook/amo/metaverse/india

Statista.com. (2022a). *Daily active users (DAU) of Roblox games worldwide from the 4th quarter 2018 to 2nd quarter*. Statista. https://www.statista. com/statistics/1192573/daily-active-users-global-roblox/.

Statista.com. (2022b). *Average daily time spent on selected social networks by adults in the United States*. Statista. https:// www.statista.com/statistics/324267/us-adults-daily-facebook-minutes/.

Statistia.com. (2021). *Average daily time spent by children in the United States on leading gaming apps from 2019*. Statista. www.stati sta.com/statistics/1249021/us-time-spent-by-children-on-gaming-apps/.

Straton, N., Hansen, K., Mukkamala, R. R., Hussain, A., Gronli, T. M., Langberg, H., & Vatrapu, R. (2016, September). Big social data analytics for public health: Facebook engagement and performance. In *2016 IEEE 18th International Conference on e-Health Networking, Applications and Services (Healthcom)* (pp. 1-6). IEEE.

Straton, N., Mukkamala, R. R., & Vatrapu, R. (2017, June). Big social data analytics for public health: Predicting facebook post performance using artificial neural networks and deep learning. In *2017 IEEE International Congress on Big Data (BigData Congress)* (pp. 89-96). IEEE. 10.1109/BigDataCongress.2017.21

Strutt, D. (2022). A Simple Tool for Remote Real-Time Dance Interaction in Virtual Spaces, Or "Dancing in the Metaverse". *Critical Stages/Scènes critiques, 25*.

Suh, A., Cheung, C. M., & Lin, Y. Q. (2019, July). Revisiting User Engagement: Concepts, Themes, and Opportunities. In PACIS (p. 150).

TAL Manufacturing Solutions. (2018). *Made in India, the TAL Brabo Robot is ready to be deployed across industries*. TAL Manufacturing Solutions.

Talarico, C., & Leija, E. (2023). The impact of the scientific metaverse on the biotech industry: How virtual reality helped researchers fight back against COVID-19. Springer eBooks. doi:10.1007/978-3-031-30691-4_5

Tank, D., Aggarwal, A., & Chaubey, N. (2019). Virtualization vulnerabilities, security issues, and solutions: A critical study and comparison. *International Journal of Information Technology : an Official Journal of Bharati Vidyapeeth's Institute of Computer Applications and Management, 14*(2), 847–862. doi:10.1007/s41870-019-00294-x

Tariq, S., Abuadbba, A., & Moore, K. (2023, September 10). *Deepfake in the metaverse: Security implications for virtual gaming, meetings, and offices.* arXiv.org. https://arxiv.org/abs/2303.14612v2 doi:10.1145/3595353.3595880

Tayal, S., Rajagopal, K., & Mahajan, V. (2022, March). Virtual reality based metaverse of gamification. In *2022 6th International Conference on Computing Methodologies and Communication (ICCMC)* (pp. 1597-1604). IEEE. 10.1109/ICCMC53470.2022.9753727

Teamwork Commerce. (2022). *5 Retail Metaverse Examples that Create Immersive Experiences and Excited Customers.* Teamwork Commerce.

Tella, A., Ajani, Y. A., & Ailaku, U. V. (2023). Libraries in the metaverse: The need for meta literacy for digital librarians and digital age library users. *Library Hi Tech News, 40*(8), 14–18. doi:10.1108/LHTN-06-2023-0094

Teng, Z., Cai, Y., Gao, Y., Zhang, X., & Li, X. (2022). Factors affecting learners' adoption of an educational metaverse platform: An empirical study based on an extended UTAUT model. *Mobile Information Systems, 2022*, 2022. doi:10.1155/2022/5479215

Thaler, R. H., & Sunstein, C. R. (2009). *Nudge: Improving decisions about health, wealth, and happiness.* Penguin.

Thapar, A. (2023). *India Metaverse Market 2023 | Industry Size, Trends and Forecast 2028.* Linkedin. https://www.linkedin.com/pulse/india-metaverse-market-2023-industry-size-trends-forecast-thapar

Tim, H., Heller, J., Chylinski, M., Keeling, D. I., Mahr, D., & de Ruyter, K. (2018). Making Omni Channel an augmented reality: The current and future state of the art. *Journal of Research in Interactive Marketing, 12*(4), 509–523. doi:10.1108/JRIM-01-2018-0023

Tractinsky, N., Katz, A. S., & Ikar, D. (2000). What is beautiful is usable. *Interacting with Computers, 13*(2), 127–145. doi:10.1016/S0953-5438(00)00031-X

Trollop, C. (2007). *Wearable Second Life.* Second Style. https://blog.secondstyle.com/2007/08/wearable-second-life.html

Trunfio, M., & Rossi, S. (2022). Advances in Metaverse Investigation: Streams of research and future agenda. *Virtual Worlds, 1*(2), 103–129. doi:10.3390/virtualworlds1020007

Upadhyay, U., Kumar, A., Sharma, G., Gupta, B. B., Alhalabi, W. A., Arya, V., & Chui, K. T. (2023). Cyberbullying in the Metaverse: A Prescriptive Perception on Global Information Systems for User Protection. [JGIM]. *Journal of Global Information Management, 31*(1), 1–25. doi:10.4018/JGIM.325793

Urvashi, S., Laxmi, L., & Prateek, B. (2014). Sustainability in Indian Banking Industry. *International Journal of Commerce and Business Management, 3*(1), 220–229.

Vadakkepatt, G. G., Winterich, K. P., Mittal, V., Zinn, W., Beitelspacher, L., Aloysius, J., Ginger, J., & Reilman, J. (2021). Sustainable retailing. *Journal of Retailing, 97*(1), 62–80. doi:10.1016/j.jretai.2020.10.008

Valaskova, K., Machova, V., & Lewis, E. (2022). Virtual Marketplace Dynamics Data, Spatial Analytics, and Customer Engagement Tools in a Real-Time Interoperable Decentralized Metaverse. *Linguistic and Philosophical Investigations, 21*(0), 105–120. doi:10.22381/lpi2120227

Valenti, F., Bikakis, A., Terras, M., Speed, C., Hudson-Smith, A., & Chalkias, K. (2021). Crypto collectibles, museum funding and OpenGLAM: Challenges, opportunities and the potential of non-fungible tokens (NFTs). *Applied Sciences (Basel, Switzerland), 11*(1), 9931. doi:10.3390/app11219931

Van Doorn, J., Lemon, K. N., Mittal, V., Nass, S., Pick, D., Pirner, P., & Verhoef, P. C. (2010). Customer engagement behavior: Theoretical foundations and research directions. *Journal of Service Research, 13*(3), 253–266. doi:10.1177/1094670510375599

Vayena, E., Salathé, M., Madoff, L. C., & Brownstein, J. S. (2015). Ethical challenges of big data in public health. *PLoS Computational Biology, 11*(2), e1003904. doi:10.1371/journal.pcbi.1003904 PMID:25664461

Velan Sakthi Sree, M. (2011). E-Banking Practices In Selected Scheduled Commercial Banks. Department International Business And Commerce Alagappa University.

Verhoef, P. C., Broekhuizen, T., Bart, Y., Bhattacharya, A., Dong, J. Q., Fabian, N., & Haenlein, M. (2021). Digital transformation: A multidisciplinary reflection and research agenda. *Journal of Business Research, 122*, 889–901. doi:10.1016/j.jbusres.2019.09.022

Verhoef, P. C., Kannan, P. K., & Inman, J. J. (2015). From multi-channel retailing to omni-channel retailing: Introduction to the special issue on multi-channel retailing. *Journal of Retailing, 91*(2), 174–181. doi:10.1016/j.jretai.2015.02.005

Violante, M. G., Vezzetti, E., & Piazzolla, P. (2019). How to design a virtual reality experience that impacts consumer engagement: The case of the virtual supermarket. [IJIDeM]. *International Journal on Interactive Design and Manufacturing, 13*(1), 243–262. doi:10.1007/s12008-018-00528-5

Visconti, R. M. (2022). From physical reality to the Metaverse: A Multilayer Network Valuation. *Journal of Metaverse, 2*(1), 16–22.

Vistan Nextgen. (2022). *Fully autonomous mobile robots transforming manufacturing and logistics.* Vistan Nextgen.

Wajire, P. (2022). *Exploring the Metaverse: Challenges and Opportunities for India in the 'Next Internet.'* ORF Online. https://www.orfonline.org/research/exploring-the-metaverse/

Wang, D., Fu, H., & Fang, S. (2019). The relationship between relational quality and megaproject success: The moderating role of incentives. *Engineering Management Journal, 31*(4), 257–269. doi:10.1080/10429247.2019.1624099

Wang, H., Ning, H., Lin, Y., Wang, W., Dhelim, S., Farha, F., Ding, J., & Daneshmand, M. (2023). A Survey on the Metaverse: The State-of-the-Art, Technologies, Applications, and Challenges. *IEEE Internet of Things Journal, 10*(16), 14671–14688. doi:10.1109/JIOT.2023.3278329

Wang, Y., Su, Z., Zhang, N., Xing, R., Liu, D., Luan, T. H., & Shen, X. (2022). A survey on metaverse: Fundamentals, security, and privacy. *IEEE Communications Surveys and Tutorials*.

Wang, Y., Su, Z., Zhang, N., Xing, R., Liu, D., Luan, T. H., & Shen, X. (2023). A Survey on Metaverse: Fundamentals, Security, and Privacy. *IEEE Communications Surveys and Tutorials, 25*(1), 319–352. doi:10.1109/COMST.2022.3202047

Waqas, M., Hamzah, Z. L., & Salleh, N. a. M. (2020). Customer experience: A systematic literature review and consumer culture theory-based conceptualization. *Management Review Qua truly, 71*(1), 135–176. https://doi.org/ doi:10.10 7/s11301-020-00182-w

Wasnik, A., & Bhasin, A. (2022). *Meta-governance: Role of metaverse in India's E-governance.* NITI Aayog. https://www.niti.gov.in/meta-governance-role-metaverse-indias-e-governance

Waterworth. (2022). 3 Benefits to Becoming a Landlord in the Metaverse. *The Motley Fool.*

Westcott, K., Loucks, J., & Arbanas, J. (2023). *2023 Digital media trends: Immersed and connected.* Deloitte Insights.

Wigfield, A. (1994). Expectancy-value theory of achievement motivation: A developmental perspective. *Educational Psychology Review, 6*(1), 49–78. doi:10.1007/BF02209024

Wiles, J. (2022). *What is a Metaverse? And should you be buying in?* Gartner. https://www.gartner.com/en/articles/what-is-a-metaverse

Williams, N., & Vorley, T. (2015). Institutional asymmetry: How formal and informal institutions affect entrepreneurship in Bulgaria. *International Small Business Journal, 33*(8), 840–861. doi:10.1177/0266242614534280

Winter, C., Kern, F., Gall, D., Latoschik, M. E., Pauli, P., & Käthner, I. (2021). Immersive virtual reality during gait rehabilitation increases walking speed and motivation: A usability evaluation with healthy participants and patients with multiple sclerosis and stroke. *Journal of Neuroengineering and Rehabilitation, 18*(1), 1–14. doi:10.1186/s12984-021-00848-w PMID:33888148

Wipro PARI. (2021). *Packing and palletizing Solutions with Robots and Gantries.* Author.

Xie, B., Liu, H., Alghofaili, R., Zhang, Y., Jiang, Y., Lobo, F. D., Li, C., Li, W., Huang, H., Akdere, M., Mousas, C., & Yu, L. (2021). A review of virtual Reality skill training applications. *Frontiers in Virtual Reality, 2*, 645153. doi:10.3389/frvir.2021.645153

Xi, N., Chen, J., Gama, F., Riar, M., & Hamari, J. (2023). The challenges of entering the metaverse: An experiment on the effect of extended reality on workload. *Information Systems Frontiers*, *25*(2), 659–680. PMID:35194390

Xu, M., Ng, W. C., Lim, W. Y. B., Kang, J., Xiong, Z., Niyato, D., Yang, Q., Shen, X. S., & Miao, C. (2022). A full dive into realizing the edge-enabled metaverse: Visions, enabling technologies, and challenges. *IEEE Communications Surveys and Tutorials*.

Yadav, R., & Pathak, G. (2013). Environmental Sustainability through Green Banking: A Study on Private and Public Sector Bank in India. *OIDA International Journal of Sustainable Development*, *6*(08), 37–48.

Yang, X., Cheng, P., Liu, X., & Shih, S. (2023). The impact of immersive virtual reality on art education: A study of flow state, cognitive load, brain state, and motivation. *Education and Information Technologies*. doi:10.1007/s10639-023-12041-8

Yawised, K., Apasrawirote, D., & Boonparn, C. (2022). From traditional business shifted towards transformation: The emerging business opportunities and challenges in 'Metaverse'era. *Incbaa*, *2022*, 162–175.

Yin, R. K. (1984). *Case Study Research: Design and Methods*. Sage Publications.

Ylilehto, M., Komulainen, H., & Ulkuniemi, P. (2021). The critical factors are shaping customer shopping experiences with innovative technologies. *Baltic Journal of Management*, *16*(5), 661–680. doi:10.1108/BJM-02-2021-0049

Yokogawa. (2020). *A journey towards autonomous operations – Deploying robots and drones in process plants and facilities*. Yokogawa.

Yoo, K., Welden, R., Hewett, K., & Haenlein, M. (2023). The merchants of meta: A research agenda to understand the future of retailing in the metaverse. *Journal of Retailing*, *99*(2), 173–192. doi:10.1016/j.jretai.2023.02.002

Zallio, M., & Clarkson, P. J. (2022). Designing the metaverse: A study on inclusion, diversity, equity, accessibility and safety for digital immersive environments. *Telematics and Informatics*, *75*, 101909. doi:10.1016/j.tele.2022.101909

ZeeBiz WebDesk. (2023). *India's Journey into the Metaverse: The Rise of Virtual Reality Technology*. Zee Business. https://www.zeebiz.com/agencies/indias-journey-into-the-metaverse-the-rise-of-virtual-reality-technology-222331

Zhang, X., Chen, Y., Hu, L., & Wang, Y. (2022). The Metaverse in education: Definition, framework, features, potential applications, challenges, and future research topics. *Frontiers in Psycholo y, 13*. https://doi.org/ doi:10.33 9/fpsyg.2022.1016300

Zhang, X., Chen, Y., Hu, L., & Wang, Y. (2022). The metaverse in education: Definition, framework, features, potential applications, challenges, and future research topics. *Frontiers in Psychology*, *13*, 6063. doi:10.3389/fpsyg.2022.1016300 PMID:36304866

Zhao, Y., Jiang, J., Chen, Y., Liu, R., Yang, Y., Xue, X., & Chen, S. (2022). Metaverse: Perspectives from graphics, interactions and visualization. *Visual Informatics*, *6*(1), 56–67. doi:10.1016/j.visinf.2022.03.002

Zheng, Z., Li, T., Li, B., Chai, X., Song, W., Chen, N., Zhou, Y., Lin, Y., & Li, R. (2022). Industrial metaverse: connotation, features, technologies, applications and challenges. In Communications in computer and information science (pp. 239–263). Springer. doi:10.1007/978-981-19-9198-1_19

Zimmermann, D., Wehler, A., & Kaspar, K. (2022). Self-representation through avatars in digital environments. *Current Psychology (New Brunswick, N.J.)*, *4*(25), 21775–21789. doi:10.1007/s12144-022-03232-6

Zuo, M., & Shen, Y. (2023). How do features and affordances of a metaverse portal engage users? Evidence from exergames. *Internet Research*. doi:10.11 8/intr-08-2022-0618

About the Contributors

Babita Singla is a professor at Chitkara Business School, Chitkara University, Punjab, India. She has a Ph.D. in management and is UGC-NET qualified. She has over 14 years of experience in teaching, research, and administration. Her areas of expertise are marketing, e-commerce, omnichannel, and retail. In her career, she has been involved in important academic and research assignments such as being the guest editor of a reputed journal, organizing and conducting international and national-level conferences and faculty development programs, and providing guidance for research projects. She has research publications in reputable international and national journals such as Scopus, SCI, etc., and has presented research papers at various national and international conferences. In the short span of 14 years of her career in academia and administration, she has authored and edited several books on retailing, supply chain management, branding, customer relationship management, and product management, covering the course content of various universities nationwide. She has successfully delivered guest sessions at international and national universities.

Kumar Shalender is a Post-Doctoral Fellow of the Global Institute of Flexible Systems Management and a Doctor of Philosophy in Strategic Management. He is currently serving as an Associate Professor at Chitkara Business School, Chitkara University, Punjab, India and has more than 14 years of experience in the domain of Business Policy, Strategic Management, and Business Model Development. He Has a total of 70 Publications in reputed journals including presentations at international/national conferences and book chapters to his credit. His current research areas include the field of Metaverse, Blockchain Technology, and Sustainable Development with a special focus on sustainable cities and mobility ecosystems in India.

Nripendra Singh is a Fulbright Fellow, which is a flagship program of the United States Department of State, Bureau of Educational and Cultural Affairs under the Council for International Exchange of Scholars. He completed research at The Pennsylvania State University. As visiting research scholar, Dr. Singh has been involved with various renowned institutions such as University of California at Berkley and Technology University, Hoboken, New Jersey. He is a post-doc fellow of the Global Institute of Flexible Systems & Technology, under the aegis of Indian Institute of Technology (IIT), Delhi (India). He earned two doctorate degrees, first from University of Lucknow (India) in Business Administration and second from Iowa State University, Ames-Iowa, He has two MBA degrees in Marketing Management and Computer Management from University of Pune (India). As a certified professional, he completed Preparing Future Faculty program from the Center for Excellence in Learning and Teaching at Iowa State University, Ames, IA. He is also a Campus-2-Capitol Fellow of Bard College-New York.

***

Arpan Anand is an accomplished Assistant Professor at Jaipuria Institute of Management, Noida. With a solid background in the corporate sector and a passion for academia, he blends practical expertise with scholarly knowledge. His commitment to research excellence is evident through his publications in journals of repute. Dr. Anand is known for his innovative teaching methods, creating an engaging learning experience for his students.

Sonal Devesh is a Associate Professor in School of Business and Management at Christ University, India. She has a PhD in Statistics with more than twenty four years of experience in teaching and research. She has 15 years of international experience in teaching and research. Having completed Diploma in Research Methodology, Statistical Package of Social Sciences (SPSS) and Epidemiology, she has published papers in various peer reviewed, ABDC and Scopus indexed journals and presented papers in international conferences. She is the co- author of the Book of Business Research: A practical Guide with SPSS. She has also conducted training courses in Statistical Package of Social Sciences (SPSS) and Research Methodology. She received best paper award frim Institute of chartered Accounts of India for one of her research papers in Digital Banking.

Abhisek Jana received his Ph.D. in Management Studies from IIT (ISM), Dhanbad. He also holds a Master's degree in Tourism Management from IGNOU; B.A. in International Hospitality Management from QMUC, Edinburgh, UK along with Diploma in Hotel Management & Catering Technology from IIHM, Kolkata. Prior to joining Birla Institute of Technology, Mesra he worked at The Carlton Hotel, Edinburgh, UK and TajSats Fight Catering, Kolkata.

Priya Jindal is currently working as an Associate Professor at Chitkara Business School, Chitkara University, Punjab, India, and holds a master's degree in commerce and economics. She earned her doctorate in management. She has contributed more than 16 years in teaching. She supervised four Ph.D. research scholars and two M.Phil candidates. There are numerous research papers to her credit in leading journals among them ten research paper has been published in Scopus Indexed Journal. Her areas of research included Banking, Finance, and insurance. She has filed more than 18 patents and one copyright. She is the editor of two books under IGI publications and one of the books gets indexed in Scopus.

Logasakthi Kandasamy has been associated with Universal AI University, Karjat as an Associate Professor. He has received best research contribution award and best faculty award from one of the promising engineering Institution in Tamil Nadu. Logasakthi is Qualified with UGC-NET & TN-SET for Assistant Professor. Published more than 20 papers in reputed journals which includes Scopus and ABDC indexed. Researcher, Teacher and Trainer in HR&OB for las one and half decade.

K.P. Jaheer Mukthar is a dedicated faculty member in the Department of Economics at Kristu Jayanti College, Autonomous. With a passion for economics and a commitment to education, Jaheer brings expertise and enthusiasm to his role. He is known for his engaging teaching style and his ability to inspire students to explore the complexities of economic theory and its practical applications. Jaheer's academic background and professional experience make him a valuable asset to the college community.

M.N. Prabadevi, associate professor in SRM IST, Vadapalani has more than 18 years of teaching, corporate and research experience in Entrepreneurship, Human Resource Management, Leadership & Management, SHRM, Employee Engagement, Learning and Development, Economics and Indian models in Entrepreneurship.Organized an event UNLOCK 2021" Business Plan Competition, Conducted various workshops, My story sessions and conferences and B-Plan competitions for management students, especially to develop their entrepreneurial skills among students fraternity, Heading 'Udyamee' - Acceleration and Innovation cell at Department of Management Studies, SRMIST Chennai, Being a Coordinator for Rural Entrepreneurship Development Cell (REDC) @ SRMIST, vadapalani campus, Organized a workshop Transforming Business Ideas in to Workable Business Model by Mr. Hemachandran, CEO,& Co Founder of Brand Avatar, Portfolios undertaken as a Exam cell coordinator, Timetable coordinator, Academic audit committee coordinator, Year coordinator and Spoc person for Directorate of entrepreneurship and Incubation centre, Associated with University of Nizwa and organized an International Conference on Reinventing Business Practices, Startups & Sustainability at SRMIST in 2021, Guiding PhD Scholars, many Master students, and undergraduate Students and coordinated various Guest lectures, Industrial Visits and workshops.

Prasad Mahale is Assistant Professor Assistant Professor in Institute of management and commerce, Srinivas University, India. He is an accomplished academic professional with a strong background in commerce. He earned his PhD from Mangalore University, showcasing his dedication to education and research with a remarkable teaching journey spanning over a decade, Dr. Mahale has honed his expertise in the field. Notably, he has also assumed the role of a Principal, demonstrating his leadership capabilities. His contributions are impressive, having published extensively. His research has found its way into 26 reputable journals, including those recognized by UGC-CARE and Scopus. Additionally, he has shared his insights in the form of 10 conference proceedings papers. Dr. Prasad Mahale's commitment to academia and research is truly commendable.

Marirajan Murugan, received the B.E degree from Madras university in 1997, the M.B.A degree from Madurai Kamaraj University in 2011, Executive Program in Business Management in IIM, Lucknow in 2022. He is currently pursuing the Ph.D degree in Management at SRM IST. He has published twelve papers in reputed Scopus, ABDC, Springer nature, UGC carelisted journals including few book chapters. He has received a Guinness award for participating as an author for the record title of thickest book in the world. He is working as Project Engineering Manager in an EPC company, a leader, Mentor and a technocrat with determination and self-discipline, a UK certified professional engineer and an all-rounder in the field of Oil & Gas, Refinery, Petrochemicals, Chemicals, Power, Metals & Minerals, Defence and Infrastructure as Engineering services provider and EPC Contractor. Having 26 years' of experience in the diversified industry sectors, he assists as Mentor for E&C Services. and has worked with companies-Petrofac, Tecnimont, Kentz, Litwin, Reliance and Mukand Engineers. During this period, he has handled different roles as Consulting Engineer, Oil & Gas Operator and EPC Contractor. He has strong experience in design and implementation of oil and gas production system and other diversified sectors and was extensively involved in Asset Integrity, Process Safety Management, Life Extension Studies, safety studies and Risk Assessment activities, Multi disciplinary engineering management, Project Management. Mentor responsibilities includes alignment of organisation to market requirements and constantly pursing excellence in the businesses.

Meena Rani N., associate Professor, SRMIST, Vadaplani, who has 20 years of experience in the teaching and published articles in scopus and ABDC B category journals.

Baranidharan S. is currently working as an assistant professor at School of Business and Management, Christ University, Bangalore. He has 7 years of teaching and 5 Years of full time research experience. He has published 61research articles that are indexed in Scopus, WoS, ABDC, etc., and he has published 7 case studies in international and national journals. He has published six patents, and also he has published 22 finance and economics blogs in different newspapers and magazines. He has completed an MBA at Pondicherry University and a PhD in management at Bharathidasan University. He is an expert in financial economics, corporate finance, financial econometrics, and stock market technical analysis.

Catherine.S. working as Assistant Professor in SRMIST, Vadapalani , who has 18 years of teaching and Industry experience in the field of Marketing, Logistics and Supply chain Management, organized an International Conference and Publication in Springer nature series and editor in renowned Journals.

Piyali Sarkar, B.Sc, B.Ed. M.SC (Zoology), M.A. (Education), pursuing PH.D (Education), Computer diploma in teacher training, Assistant Headmistress, Barabisha High School (H.S.), PGT. Ms. Piyali Sarkar completed her studies, B.Sc. in Zoology from Krishnath College, Berhampore under University of Kalyani in the year 2007 and M. Sc. In Zoology from University of Kalyani in the year 2009. She started her career in RICE (Roy's institute of Competitive Exams.) as a teacher trainer later joined Barabisha High School (H.S.) by cracking West Bengal School Service Commission Exam., in the year 2010 till the date. Now she is working in the same institute as Assistant Headmistress. She completed her B.Ed. from NSOU in the year 2015 and M.A. in Education in the year 2017. She joined Lovely Professional University as a part time research scholar in the year 2018. She is pursuing her Ph.D. under Dr. Sonia Sharma, Assistant Professor, LPU which is now in final submission stage. She has total more than 13 years' experience in the field of academic and administration. Her areas of research are as Education. Educational psychology, Higher Education, Educational technology. She has more than 14 published (10 under publications UGC CARE) in her account, her research papers have published in Scopus and various ISBN Books, ISSN National and International journals/peer reviewed journals/ugc approved journals/conferences. She has attended more than 5 workshops sponsored by UGC, HRDC, ICSSR. She has attended more than 15 conferences/seminars including international and national with paper presentations and publications as well as a participants.

Gautam Shandilya is an academician with an experience of more than 20 years in industry and academia. He has several research papers, books, edited books, and book chapters to his credit. His interests lie in Tourism, Fast Food, Relationship Marketing, Entrepreneurship. He is Associate Editor of Journal of Hospitality Application and Research (JOHAR), an ABDC indexed Journal. He has presented research papers at several national and international conferences.

Sonia Sharma B.Sc, B.Ed. M.SC (Zoology), M.ED, PH.D (Education), UGC NET (Education), Computer diploma in teacher training, M. A Sociology (pursuing) Assistant Professor Department of Education /Zoology. Dr (Ms) Sonia Sharma completed her studies, B.Sc, B.Ed, M.Sc M.Ed. Panjab University Chandigargh. G.N.D.U. Amritsar, Bhoj Open University, Madhya Pradesh, and Ph.D from Punjabi University, Patiala campus and two years computer diploma in "Teacher Training" from ISO certified Soft Brain Setting Standard in Education and MA Sociology pursuing. She started her career in Miri Piri Missionary school and later on joined an International school (G.V.I), Ludhiana, where she worked as a senior science teacher, Coordinator, Vice Principal and Principal. During this period she achieved INSPIRE Science participation certificate (as a Guide/Instructor) at state level in Ludhiana, International Olympiad of English language, Inspiring Award (as a Principal), to enhance academic level of students in English language by IOEL, "Gold medal" as an active Principal by Indira Gandhi Vigyan Sanshodhan Sanstha, Pune., She organized various events of Sahodya Sports meet, Diwali Mela, inter and intra school competitions 20082012 along with these she was also nominated for Bharat Vidya Shiromani award, Jan 2012 and for International Gold star award in Dubai, Sept 2013. Later on she joined RIMT University, Mandi Gobindgarh as Lecturer in department of Education where she formed the colleges as well as duties assigned by Punjabi University, Patiala as an "External Instructor/ Supervisor" for skill in "teaching of science" and for B. Ed and MA in Education Classes and After on she joined Shri Ganesh College of Education as a Assistant Professor, Haryana. After that she joined DAV University, Jalandhar, as a Assistant Professor where she framed Course design/syllabus for Four Year Integrated B.Sc B.Ed course. She also organized 7 days FDP workshop as core committee member and she was alsowell active member of many committees. She has total more than 16 years' experience in the field of academic and administration. Her areas of research are as Education. Educational psychology, Higher Education. She has feminist approach in her research. She has more than 42 published (11 under publications UGC CARE) in her account, her research papers have published in Scopus and various ISBN Books, ISSN National and International journals/peer reviewed journals/ugc approved journals/conferences She has attended more than 8 workshops sponsored by UGC, HRDC, ICSSR. She has attended more than 35 conferences/seminars including international and national with paper presentations and publications as well as a participants, Her article has been published in news Paper of "Nava zamana" Jalandhar. Presently, she is guide of two Ph.D students, and two students are completing their dissertation under my supervision. One dissertation already published. She has life time membership of Council of Teacher Educator, sessional membership of Indian Science congress association (ISCA). Research experience: 3 dissertation done and 3 students are pursuing Ph.D Reviewer: • SAGE, ERIC International Journal

Prathmesh Singh is a dual enrollment (undergraduate) student at the Pennsylvania Western University, Clarion, PA, USA. His research interests include information sciences and bio-medical technologies. In his leisure time, he loves to play basketball and robotics.

Ranjit Singha is a Doctorate Research Fellow at Christ (Deemed to be University) and a distinguished American Psychological Association (APA) member. His expertise lies in research and development across various domains, including Mindfulness, Addiction Psychology, Women Empowerment, UN Sustainable Development Goals, and Data Science. He has earned certifications from renowned institutions, including IBM and The University of Oxford Mindfulness Centre, UK, in Mindfulness. Additionally, he holds certifications as a Microsoft Innovative Educator, Licensed Yoga Professional, Certified Mindfulness Teacher, and CBCT Teachers Training from Emory University, USA. Mr Ranjit's educational qualifications include PGDBA (GM), MBA (IB), MSc in Counseling Psychology, and completion of a Senior Diploma in Tabla (Musical Instrumentation). His dedication to continuous learning is evident through his involvement in the SEE Learning® (Social, Emotional, and Ethical) Learning program. As a committed researcher and educator, Mr Ranjit focuses on mindfulness and compassion-based interventions. He has an impressive publication record, having authored twenty-three research papers, ten chapters, four books, and five edited books. His research interests encompass various aspects of mindfulness, such as assessment, benefits of mindfulness-based programs, change mechanisms, professional training, mindfulness ethics, cognitive and neuropsychology, and studies related to high-risk behaviours. Apart from his research endeavours, Mr Ranjit has extensive teaching experience, instructing courses in diverse subjects like Forensic Psychology, Positive Psychology, Organizational Planning, Strategic Management, Psycho Metric Tests, Counseling Skills, Disaster Management, Basic Computer Science, Business Planning, Business Law, and Auditing. He has mentored numerous Postgraduate and undergraduate research projects, demonstrating his commitment to nurturing young minds in psychology. Ad Hoc Reviewer at International Journal of Cyber Behavior, Psychology and Learning (IJCBPL), Reviewer and author at IGI Global, and Editor and Reviewer at TNT

Publication. Furthermore, Mr Ranjit actively provides personal counselling services, showcasing his genuine concern for his students' well-being and academic success. His unwavering dedication to research and education has solidified his position as a valuable contributor to psychology.

Surjit Singha is an academician with a broad spectrum of interests, including UN Sustainable Development Goals, Organizational Climate, Workforce Diversity, Organizational Culture, HRM, Marketing, Finance, IB, Global Business, Business, AI, Women Studies, and Cultural Studies. Currently a faculty member at Kristu Jayanti College, Dr. Surjit also serves as an Editor, reviewer, and author for prominent global publications and journals, including being on the Editorial review board of Information Resources Management Journal and a contributor to IGI Global. With over 13 years of experience in Administration, Teaching, and Research, Dr. Surjit is dedicated to imparting knowledge and guiding students in their research pursuits. As a research mentor, Dr. Surjit has nurtured young minds and fostered academic growth. Dr. Surjit has an impressive track record of over 75 publications, including articles, book chapters, and textbooks, holds two US Copyrights, and has successfully completed and published two fully funded minor research projects from Kristu Jayanti College.

Praveen Srivastava is an experienced academician with a demonstrated history of working in the education management industry for more than 20 years. He is skilled in Mendeley (Recipient of Mendeley Advisor Certification), MOOC Courses, Customer Relationship Management and ICT. Authored and edited three books and several journal articles. He is also recipient of "Award of Excellence" by IIT Mumbai for being amongst the top performer of the FDP on "Use of ICT in Education for Online and Blended learning" in 2016. In 2018, IIT Mumbai awarded him with the Top Performer badge in two weeks Faculty Development Program (FDP 301X) on "Mentoring Educators in Educational Technology". He is also Editor-In-Chief of JOHAR, an ABDC Indexed Journal.

N.V.Suresh, Vice Principal in ASET science and technology, He have been awarded as a Best Teacher Award Winner From Lions International for the year 2023.Published 50 articles in reputed journals.

Arnav Upadhyaya is a student at Monta Vista High School in Cupertino, California. He is passionate about technology and its impact on society.

Vaishali M. is a research scholar from SRM University with 6+ years of corporate HR experience.

Index